Political Spectacle and the Fate of American Schools

The *Critical Social Thought* Series
edited by Michael W. Apple, University of Wisconsin—Madison

Political Spectacle and the Fate of American Schools

Mary Lee Smith

with

Linda Miller-Kahn
Walter Heinecke
Patricia F. Jarvis

ROUTLEDGEFALMER

NEW YORK AND LONDON

Published in 2004 by
RoutledgeFalmer
29 W 35th Street
New York, NY 10001
www.routledge-ny.com

Published in Great Britain by
RoutledgeFalmer
11 New Fetter Lane
London EC4P 4EE
www.routledgefalmer.com

RoutledgeFalmer is an imprint of the Taylor & Francis Group.
Printed in the United States of America on acid-free paper.

10 9 8 7 6 5 4 3 2 1

Library of Congress Cataloging-in-Publication Data for this book is available on file.

ISBN 0–415–93200–9 (hbk.)
ISBN 0–415–93201–7 (pbk.)

Contents

Prologue

MARY LEE SMITH

Sometimes the book writes you. This is what Michael Apple told me during an early conversation about this book-to-be. Looking back two years, I realize that this is one of those books.

I first encountered Murray Edelman's theory of symbolic politics when I supervised the dissertation of Mary Catherine Ellwein. Along with Gene Glass, she was studying the process by which policy makers set cutoff scores on tests that serve as gate keepers. How do policy makers set a criterion on a test to determine which third-graders may be promoted to fourth grade, which high school seniors may graduate, which students get the chance to enroll in elite universities and teacher training programs? To make sense of these processes, she selected organization and conflict theories from the field of sociology. As the data were generated, she found that neither of these frameworks proved useful. She had discovered that negotiation and power brokering—not statistical, technical procedures—were the means by which policy makers determined the cutoff scores. Setting high standards made the policy makers appear tough-minded and serious about achievement, but the standards were undermined by the practice of erecting "safety nets" that preserved discretion over decisions such as whether to promote or retain third-graders, irrespective of whether they passed or failed the test. She also found that once they had a policy in place, policy makers seemed to lose interest in what happened as a result of the policy. If the goals of these policies were to improve efficiency and achievement, policy makers never bothered to study whether the goals had been reached or what the costs were or whether consequences were fair. Taking a long period to ponder such puzzles, she ultimately turned this data over in the light of Edelman's theory of symbolic politics and found a good fit. His theory helped her determine that it was not instrumental effects that mattered so much to policy makers but rather the *appearance* of having done something. When a policy exists primarily for the sake of appearances—that counts as a symbolic policy.

In Edelman's book, *the Symbolic Uses of Politics*, he contrasted the politics that we are taught at school and the politics that we actually experience. Books and popular mythology present images of democratically engaged citizens deliberating freely and rationally over the central issues of their lives. These images no longer characterize modern politics. Instead society is deeply bifurcated, according to Edelman. First, there is the small group that actively contends over real goods behind the scenes and constructs and deploys symbols. Then there is the much larger group, the spectators, that reacts to those symbols and remains passive and disengaged from the secreted, material exchanges. The symbols that most people consume are primarily emotional: anxiety about crises and problems (real or constructed), reassurance (that a strong and competent leader is doing something to address those problems), diffused feelings of patriotism, desire for revenge or "closure." Public policies that grow out of this degenerate form of politics are more apt to induce such feelings rather than to bring about real change. Most education policies have this character, resulting in rather feckless consequences in material terms, but providing for policy makers a public image of "doing something." Interesting ideas, but to me at the time Edelman's theory was little more than an amusing way to explain the events behind policy.

Edelman took his ideas to an even darker place in his 1988 book, *Constructing the Political Spectacle.* In it he showed how words float free of their concrete referents, how it is impossible to trace the consequences and costs of political actions and policies, how we participate in the rituals of politics but not the substance of politics, how journalists and (it pains me to admit it) researchers hide behind a facade of objective, independent inquiry and themselves become actors in the theatrical production. The political spectacle portrays a world of illusions, semblances, magicians' slights of hand. Edelman scoffed at the idea that policy (as our graduate programs often allege) is "the authoritative allocations of values" or that policy researchers "speak truth to power."

Education events eventually caught up with political spectacle theory, as more and more political figures began to tout educational crises and propose sweeping government solutions. George H.W. Bush aspired to be the "education president." Lamar Alexander and Bill Clinton based their political platforms on government imposition of high standards and high stakes tests. These kinds of policy—or so corporate moguls whispered in politicians' ears—would solve the "crises" of public schools. Noisy rhetoric and contradictory research studies surrounded education policies such as those offering vouchers, reducing class size, and equalizing financial resources. Legislative and judicial bodies at local, state, and federal levels mandated policies to solve educational problems. Education researchers such as Lauren Resnick tried speaking truth to power, advocating higher standards and forward-looking tests, only to find out later that the state had turned these progressive ventures on their heads. The former governor of Colorado became the Chief Education Officer of Los Angeles schools. Other school districts appointed corporate leaders and even military officers to be their superintendents. The Illinois legislature took control from Chicago parent councils and gave it to the mayor who appointed his finance minister to command and control the district and solve its problems, by hook or by crook. All these examples spanned the gap between politics and education policy. Wasn't it time for a political and social analysis of education policy?

Edelman's lessons hit close to home in 1994. I had undertaken, along with several graduate students and support from the Center for Research on Educational Standards and Testing (who in retrospect must regret it) to study the consequences of the Arizona Student Assessment Program (ASAP). ASAP was intended (or so it seemed) to make schools accountable to the state's curriculum standards and also to push teachers toward more progressive pedagogy and away from traditional, drill-and-kill teaching. As is true of any big reform, ASAP created upheaval in schools and controversies in political circles. It represented the vision of the person who was state superintendent at the time. Three years of ASAP and three years of research later—intensive case studies as well as extensive surveys—and we were finally ready to present our conclusions (which we hoped might inform policy and improve the program). We concluded that ASAP was slowly having an impact, particularly because many Arizona teachers had increased their instruction of writing and problem solving. However, adaptation was slow and depended on the ability and willingness of individual districts to pour resources into capacity development. There were also problems with the test itself. But, given more time and money to refine the tests and help teachers enhance their abilities to teach in these more progressive ways, ASAP was far from a total failure.

Literally, as the pages of the final report emerged from the printer, a colleague telephoned to tell me that the newly elected state superintendent had just cancelled ASAP (mere days before it was to be administered), declaring it had intractable problems. She announced that a new assessment policy—with her own mark on it—would soon go into production. With no ASAP, there wasn't much point in continued research on its effects, so we shelved our report. I began to wonder how the new superintendent (the second highest elected officer in this state) arrived at her precipitous and unexpected decision. What expert advice had she sought? What research or cost calculations had influenced her? Which, if any, stake holders had she consulted? When the answers to these questions emerged, conventional theories of education policy could not account for what happened. I turned again to Edelman to guide me through the political and historical analysis of an education policy from the gleam in someone's eye through its metamorphoses to its eventual, sometimes chaotic collisions in classrooms, to its consequences, short- and long-term, intended or not. Edelman's theory fit the evidence and changed the way I think about policy.

And like a child with a new hammer, I began to see the whole policy world as something that ought to be nailed down. My students subsequently studied policies of choice, teacher education, and school desegregation from Edelman's framework. Evidence piled up to dizzying levels—stuffing file cabinets and book cases, heaping stacks of transcripts, news clippings, bills from Amazon.com and call slips from the libraries of six universities—until we reached the point of saturation and conviction. Each day's *New York Times* and each hit on the Internet brought more material. The political spectacle had, for me, become personal. The book had begun to write me.

The Oxford English Dictionary defines spectacle this way:

> something exhibited to view as unusual, notable, or entertaining; an eye-catching or dramatic public display; an object of curiosity or contempt, as in "he made a spectacle of himself."

So, this is a book about dramatic public displays that characterize education policy. We mean to explore Edelman's ideas and the cases of education policies that fit them. Who are we to attempt such a thing? First, we are scholars of policy. We are not professionals in the disciplines of political science or other social sciences that insiders might claim necessary for this analysis. We are, however, close readers of those fields. We are parents and teachers and administrators and professors and policy workers, and our experiences with schools reflect those various perspectives. Don't blame our political affiliation. The political spectacle is no respecter of parties. To speed our critics along and save them a few steps, let us state that we are not sworn enemies of tests or standards or accountability or charter schools. We are not radical skeptics or constructivists or postmodern nihilists or hopeless idealists. Nevertheless, we apologize to no one in our pursuit of clarity, our willingness to look behind the curtains of political theater, our valuing of rationality (no matter its limits), and of participatory democracy. We believe that public schools are essential to the health of democracy and that democracy is essential to the continuation of public schools. But, as Edelman and others realized, democracy is poorly served by the political spectacle.

In the interval of time we spent writing this book five events captured political spectacle better than our evidence and analysis ever could.[1] The first was the election and post-election campaign of 2000. We watched Al Gore change his persona between acts—in the time between the first and second debates (of course we all know they weren't real debates, but rehearsed and polished impressions constructed from polling results and public relations experts). We remarked about how the Republican National Convention even cast the delegates as actors in the spectacle, with cameras carefully noting the few non-white faces. We heard the scripted lines, saw the choreographed movements. We read and heard the inflated, bloated language—slogans that make one feel good but still float out in the air unrelated to ordinary life in the real world: new leadership, free market, moral compass, tax relief. Our eyes followed the cameras in helicopters tracking trucks with disputed ballots from Miami to Tallahassee. We watched with embarrassment or cynicism as election judges held up ballots to the light, looking for hanging chads. We heard the hyped-up language of television commentators as they talked about constitutional crises, theft of election, villains and heroes and clowns invented for the crisis du jour.

September 11, 2001 stopped us cold. Like everyone else, we feared, we grieved, we expressed our patriotism and our support for government action and we hoped for the preservation of our nation and our way of life. Yet for all of the genuine disaster and crises that we experienced as a result of the terrorist attacks, we also saw how this event served as political spectacle for all sides. The terrorists acted in ways both instrumental and symbolic: Instrumental in the wasted lives and property and economic effects; symbolic in their choice of targets and methods. Our own leaders engaged deeply in (and then some pulled back from) the inflated language of spectacle as they spoke of war and crusade and blind revenge. Metaphors push us in particular policy directions and have implications far beyond poetic figures of speech and stump rhetoric. What if metaphors different from war had won the day—mass murder, pure evil, crimes against humanity—instead of war? And we watched the front-stage/back-stage bifurcation of political action. Conservative Republicans urged President Bush to use his popularity and the temporary quiescence of the Democratic Senate to push through legislation and policy that had nothing to do with legitimate reactions to the terrorist threat: a strategic missile defense shield, capital gains tax reductions, nominations of right-wing justices, the bail-out of airlines that had already been close to insolvency before September 11, massive compensation to corporations said to suffer as a consequence of terrorist attacks, raids on the previously sacrosanct social security trust, even a national test to make schools accountable.

The collapse of Enron (so soon after September 11 that the President's list of corporations to rescue included Enron) revealed to the public a whole world of backstage action where government and corporations merge and act in the special interests of a select few. We saw for a brief moment that the institutions designed to protect the public—regulatory agencies, accounting and financial analysis—became so entangled with the corporations they were supposed to monitor that they went down with them. The worst aspects of our economic system were revealed as we learned that Enron was not alone. The mess spread vertically—accountants, lawyers, investment bankers, corporate boards—and horizontally—to WorldCom and other corporations that worked quite differently on stage and backstage.

The fourth defining event was the passage and implementation of the No Child Left Behind legislation. This law instituted harsh and far-reaching federal mandates on schools. It is ironic that an administration that professes (onstage) its belief in freedom above other values passed the most standardized and centralized program in the nation's history. To make sure that educators don't slip out of the law's restrictions, a dedicated staff stands ready to impose its penalties on anyone who sees education in other, un-"sanctioned," ways. Whatever readers might think about systematic phonics as the sole, official method of teaching kids how to read and whatever readers might think about the efficacy of high stakes tests to make schools accountable and raise achievement, they ought to be clear about the elements of political spectacle in this program. First, know that this program allocates tangible values backstage and symbols onstage. Schools and students bear the costs. Second, policy makers appropriate the term "scientific research" as the foundation and justification of its provisions. After reading this book, we hope that you see that scientists ought to blush at how the term scientific was used.

For researchers especially, the fifth defining event was the attempt by the Department of Education to censor and suppress any research that fails to support its programs—research, in other words, that demonstrates the fallacies of policies to end social promotion, research that demonstrates the dysfunctional effects of high-stakes testing, research that demonstrates that phonics is not the superior, exclusive method of teaching children how to read—all these studies to be crammed down Orwell's memory hole.

To celebrate its triumphs, the Department of Education even has, heaven help us, a song to celebrate the law. According to a *New York Times* writer (June 23, 2002), two television producers wrote the song. As an aside, the writer noted that this pair had recently received a $4 million grant from the department. In an analysis of the policy process as theater, what could be more apt? The song, performed on a 25-city tour, goes like this:

> We're here to thank our president,
> For signing this great bill.
> That's right! Yeah,
> Research shows we know the way,
> It's time we showed the will!

Political spectacle everywhere. Political spectacle that affects education policy in perverse ways, as this book will show—this book that wrote me.

Construction of the Book

The book emerged as a series of choices about authorship and voice, organization and language. It was important that the book present a unity of voice and perspective. I thus incorporated the research of Linda, Walt, and Patricia, and melded it together to construct a kind of unity and coherence.

I began the book assuming that its readers would comprise scholars with shared vocabulary and concepts. Of course, scholars in the field of education policy differ among themselves in attitudes, values, and interpretations, but they do share argot and background knowledge. For such an audience a book requires a formal and familiar writing style. As my perspective crystallized, however, I began to think of a potential readership much more inclusive and diverse. I decided to make fewer assumptions about how much our potential readers already knew, and attempted a writing style to match more closely the expectations and language of a literate, but not specialized, audience. I decided to expand and vary the modes of representation, adding epigraphs that might stimulate readers' associations and responses. I decided to include vignettes as another way to represent what we had learned.

A vignette is like a scene from a (nonfiction) movie or book. It presents an action and characters and setting, and crafts them to tell a truth beyond literal data. It attempts to display the tangible particularity of people's lives to show truthful, plausible interpretations. The vignettes that introduce the chapters in this book are based on literal data, from interview transcripts and observation write-ups and documents gathered in the contexts of the cases. They are non-literal in other ways, for example, in the point of view of the narrator, or the blending of two characters into one or the con-catenating of two events into one. To illustrate, the vignette in Chapter Two is literal in its facts, its content taken directly from press releases and observation notes that researchers took down, yet the narrator is invented and sections of the literal transcripts are elided. The vignette in Chapter Three is based on real incidents, but we put words in the mouth of a narra-tor. Martha is the pseudonym of a real actor who used many of these words in an interview with Linda. In Chapter Four, a narrator is again invented to portray our point of view, although the incidents at the two high schools are true accounts. For dramatic effect, we shortened by three weeks the time between the incident at South and the incident in Scottsdale. Chapter Five begins with a vignette snatched from notes I took at a real professional meeting. I use my own point of view as a firsthand observer. Chapter Six begins with a vignette constructed from the actual words spoken by the policy makers that the researcher observed first-hand and recorded. That vignette shows that truth is stranger than fiction. You couldn't make that stuff up. The vignettes that open and close the book are crafted as medita-tions based on evidence and my experience.

An explanation is necessary about pronouns and gender. The use of the slash (she/he to indicate that the generalized subject might be either male or female) bothers me a great deal, although people use that convention to show they make no implicit assumptions about whether the gender of a generalized subject is male or female. When syntax was poorly served by choosing the plural forms, I chose one or the other in each context, for ex-ample, sometimes calling a general researcher or practitioner "he" and sometimes "she," and then trying to balance things out in the aggregate. In Chapter Six, however, I deliberately chose to refer to the businessperson as he. We understand perfectly well that many businesses and a few large cor-porations have females at the top of the organization. However the sheer disproportion of males in these roles cannot be overlooked. Besides, isn't there something masculine about the factory, corporate model? That model came originally from military organizational culture and later was imposed on large bureaucracies. What I am saying here is that the gender of pronouns was deliberately chosen.

Like slashes, citations in text break up the text and make the arguments harder to follow and parse. It was decided, therefore, to refer the readers to notes at the end of each chapter to reference other research.

Here is a guide to the organization of the book. In the first chapter we lay out the theory of symbolic politics and the political spectacle, and illus-trate its elements with brief examples. The second chapter presents the case of assessment policy in Arizona. Only political spectacle theory makes sense of these events. Chapter Three presents another case, this one about school choice and how elite parents in a single Colorado school district manipulated public policy for their particular interests. Chapter Four presents a case history of a school in the throes of desegregation and shows how political actors manipulated desegregation policy in such a way that the ultimate outcomes were nothing like the policy intents. In this chapter we pay special attention to the role of mass media in policy and political spectacle and identify the media as actors in the spectacle, not just observers and reporters of it. Researchers—those paragons of science and objectivity—also turn out, under close scrutiny—to be actors in the political spectacle, as Chapter Five details. In the political spectacle, rationality takes a beating. We show how this happened in research on reading, although we could just as well have taken on research in English immersion, or vouchers, or technology, or social promotion and shown similar actions and events. In Chapter Six, we take a critical look at the role that the corporate world plays in education policy played out in political spectacle. Finally, in Chapter Seven, we sum up the evidence and try to find some reason for optimism—about what might be done to ameliorate the damage done by political spectacle to schools. Is it sensible any more even to discuss rational policy making and policy changes? The reader must judge.

Notes

1. Notes are unusual in prefaces, but we could not resist. During the final editing, California raised the ante as 193 candidates (including a pumped-up action hero, two pornographers, a watermelon-smashing comedian, a punk-rock musician, a marijuana activist, and a former child actor, a retired boxer, and a onetime baseball commissioner sought to replace the sitting governor. In reporting this scene, CNN used this crawl line: POLITICAL SPECTACLE. Thanks, CNN. Thanks, California.

Acknowledgments

We wish that both Murray Edelman and Mary Catherine Ellwein were alive to receive our thanks and judge the success of our venture, but there are many others who also deserve recognition and gratitude.

We wish to thank Michael Apple for encouraging and supporting this book. Many colleagues read drafts of chapters and offered helpful suggestions. David Berliner tops this list. A more steadfast, responsive colleague one could not ask for. While he was dean of my college, he also granted me some time with a limited course-load so that I could work on the book. Gene Glass retains a special place in our pantheon of writers and editors, and we thank him for his help with our scholarship and writing style.

Others who helped us by reading and reacting to working drafts were Carole Edelsky, Greg Camilli, Gerald Bracey, Roslyn Mickleson, Lora Monfils, Lorrie Shepard, and Beatriz Arias. Ernie House, in his reactions to our AERA presentation, helped us to see that the illusion of rationality in the political spectacle must be met by more and better rationality, not less. Thanks to Professor Ron Bruner for saving us from utter cynicism and showing that the institutions of American democracy are still, for the most part, in place and offer a potential way out of the degenerate politics we currently experience. So, more democracy, not less.

A special thanks is due to Barbara Gereboff, whose dissertation proved so enlightening about political spectacle in state teacher education and certification policies. Another is due to Audrey Noble, whose dissertation research first shed light on the politics behind Arizona's assessment policy.

We apologize if we missed someone. It goes without saying—although every acknowledgement section repeats this sentiment anyway—that none of these people deserves the blame for mistakes we made but all deserve credit for supplying their ideas.

Cathy Coulter deserves our eternal thanks for helping us craft the writing. Along with Cathy, two other remarkable women, Carol Christine and Leslie Poyner, helped, without stint, as part of my writers group. Without their patient reading of each draft, I would have faltered and the project halted somewhere around Chapter Three. The group also gently but firmly guided me toward a somewhat less pessimistic conclusion to the book.

Collectively we wish to thank our families for not minding too much our various mental absences and lapses, and for asking fairly often, "Is it done yet?" Jeffrey Kahn also provided advice about legal issues from time to time and read most of the chapters to pester us about accuracy.

This manuscript passed through the hands of many editors at Routledge—each one competent and helpful. Thanks to them.

Thanks to CRESST for long-ago funding of the ASAP and AIMS research. Thanks to *Teachers College Record* and *Education Policy Analysis Archives* for letting us have more than one forum for, respectively, the material on assessment policy and choice policy. We also want to express our gratitude for the many people who gave their time and energies as we conducted our studies.

CHAPTER 1

School Policy under
the Spotlights

ALL THE POLICY WORLD'S A STAGE (A VIGNETTE)

Consider two photographs that I cut out of the *New York Times*. One is of Bush. The other is of Gore. Both photographs were taken at political conventions, Bush's at the Republican and Gore's at the Democratic. Each shows the candidate peering out from behind a curtain, presumably at the convention delegates out front.

The photographs were taken from the perspective of the delegates, but with powerful telephoto lenses so that you get the sense both of intimacy and great distance. As an American citizen in the year 2000, from this perspective you know somehow that you are part of the audience—you and millions of television viewers—the spectators of a theatrical production. As a member of the audience you know that you have no role in the play. Well, of course you can vote, but you know that your vote is just a formality, that the winner has already been decided in some small, snowy state far away. All you can do is applaud or hiss, or find a movie of the week to watch instead, or walk out of the room. No matter which of these actions you choose, you remain separate from the action on the stage. Or behind the stage where the gears and trap doors are, and, of course, where "the money" is—that you will never see, although you can guess. So you sit back, resigned, and wait for what will happen. You expect scenery and props—red, white, and blue balloons are a sure thing. You anticipate that music will be played—music that will give you a lift or make you feel like weeping with patriotism or joy. Or, if you are a member of the opposition party, or no party, the music makes you sneer. Either way, you expect to see some fancy footwork and to hear some stirring lines that someone took the trouble to choreograph and author ahead of time. You figure that the candidate and his impresario will read those lines from the teleprompter (invisible, of course to the television audience), and that they will have rehearsed them many times. They will chant words like "democracy," "patriotism," or "compassion"; and phrases like "the new economy," and "the good of the people." You know there will be special effects, some magic performed for your gratification. You understand at some level that not all of what you see will be strictly true, but it will pick you up and carry you away into a different world, one constructed for your entertainment, with soft-focus lenses and violins.

Both men look pensive—waiting in the wings for their cues. Are they thinking about strategic missile defense or strategic image management? About financing schools or financing their campaigns?

If you look again—closer, between the pixels—perhaps you will reflect on the status of American politics, that it is not exactly what we learned about in civics class. And perhaps your mind might stray to the sad state of schools and school policy as it plays out in this political spectacle.

Politics and Education Policy

This book explores the interplay of education policy and contemporary politics. We begin this chapter with simple, conventional definitions involving commonplace notions about what policies are, how they work, and what they do. Then we show how policies flow out of politics and how politics flow out of policies. When stakes are high—and stakes of public education are higher in the year 2002 than ever before—the political processes that underlie policy reveal themselves (or ought to) as particularly salient. Then we introduce the heart of this book: an argument about how American politics have become detached from their democratic foundations and how these conditions of politics distort public policies, especially education policies. Murray Edelman provided a set of ideas to explain this detachment and distortion and named it the political spectacle. We provide concrete examples from education policy to illustrate these ideas. We end the chapter with an argument about historical and cultural circumstances that relate to political spectacle and about why political spectacle seals the fate of American schools.

First things first. What is a policy but a rule (sometimes tacit and informal but more often formal, written, and official) that regulates how a polity must conduct itself. The State (that is, government and its administrative apparatus) allocates values to groups of people by enacting policies. By the term "values" we do not refer to such things as family values or religious values. By values we mean the benefits, opportunities, responsibilities, costs, risks, and burdens that the State confers on groups within its jurisdiction by virtue of the policies it enacts.

School policies allocate values to groups. Consider the following hypothetical case. The legislature of state "A" decides to make a policy to reduce the ratio of pupils to teachers in elementary schools. The putative positive values that such a policy allocates include the following four possibilities. First, elementary students benefit from smaller classes in that they receive more attention from teachers and greater opportunities for a richer and more particularized curriculum. These conditions translate into higher academic achievement, which translates into credentials and opportunities. Second, society as a whole benefits from the intersection of higher academic attainment and better economic growth. Third, the business sector benefits because better-educated students make better employees. Businesses do not have to invest so much on training. Fourth, teachers in the smaller classes benefit from a lighter workload and more opportunities to work with students on a more personal basis.

The hypothetical policy thus allocates values to the groups listed above. But it also allocates negative values, or costs and burdens. The cost of reducing class size falls to taxpayers. Or, if the legislature mandates a reduction in the size of classes but fails to provide additional funds to reduce them, then the districts must redirect existing funds from other programs. The constituencies of these latter programs then bear the costs of the policy. Herein lies the conventional theory of policy processes and their relationship to politics. Most textbooks offer the following description of the policy process. Rational and democratic politics yield policies that respond to real social and educational needs and problems. Policy makers consider a range of solutions to these problems and select the best alternatives that can bring about the best outcomes. They conduct an adequate analysis of the outcomes of the policies so they can make refinements and report to the public (through media without vested interests) so that citizens can subsequently act in the political process in more informed ways. So, according to this idealized view, pluralistic politics spawn rational policy-making in a democratic republic. But outside of textbooks in the policy sciences, is this the way things really work?

Returning to the hypothetical case, suppose that in order to pay for reducing class size in elementary schools, class size at high schools must be increased. Otherwise, high school teachers must forego new computers and equipment for science laboratories. In the latter instance, the already extant group of teachers fractures into two groups that are in competition with each other over their relative shares of benefits and costs.

In an ideal political world, both sets of teachers sit down with each other and with key policy makers to negotiate their competing interests.

They try to persuade one another through the quality of their respective arguments and ultimately agree about trade-offs that balance the scales. Perhaps the high school teachers become persuaded that higher achieving elementary school children eventually become high school students who are more accomplished and ready to learn. Or perhaps the policy makers agree to raise the budget for high schools the following year so that the heavier burden on high schools is temporary. Once the various interests are settled in this public forum, policy makers set out to write the legislation and regulations that accomplish the desired ends of the policy. To ascertain whether the desired ends are later attained and the costs and relative risks conform to what was planned and promised, policy makers commission research and evaluation studies to provide rational and objective information. The information that these studies provide becomes part of subsequent debate and decision-making. Again we ask, is this scenario credible?

Of course, this hypothetical case is ridiculously oversimplified and laden with hidden assumptions, caveats and traps. Do teachers teach differently and better when they face a smaller number of pupils? Does reducing class size raise achievement? How is it possible for the policy makers to know the answers to those questions? Can the research on the topic be trusted?

Further, do the two competing groups—elementary and high school teachers—bring the same degree of power to the negotiating table or the same degree of influence over policy makers? Or instead, are the high school teachers not as articulate as the elementary teachers and therefore less able to argue for their interests? Perhaps the high school teachers possess more cultural capital than the teachers of little children and thus influence policy makers unduly.

The hypothetical case we present also assumes that both groups represent their two interests fairly and completely. But what happens when a policy maker at the table has some third interest group in mind or is herself a member of a fourth interest group? What if the elementary school teachers secretly plan to remove the high school teachers from future negotiations? What if they decide among themselves that their apparent compromise is just an initial, tactical step in a secret long-term plan to diminish the power of the high school teachers to bargain for their interests? What if the policy maker who settles the current dispute has no authority to make promises in the future?

The exceptions and contingencies grow more complex as more details are brought to bear. But an idealized relationship between politics and policy assumes that mutual, good-faith persuasion and tradeoffs between groups having roughly equivalent power will yield good policy outcomes that are fair to both interest groups and have reasonable and obvious expectations for certain benefits and costs—both to those groups and to society as a whole.

Now, how does this version of policy stand up to what we know about contemporary American politics? Not very well, according to political theorists Anne Schneider, Deborah Stone, and Murray Edelman. Schneider used the term "degenerative politics" to describe the relationship that now exists between politics and policy. Stone ridiculed what she called "the rationality project" (that conventional view of policy noted above) and instead called for an analysis of policy that takes account of "the polis," or political community. Edelman characterized twentieth-century American politics as "political spectacle," invoking the metaphor of theater.

What do these ideas about politics suggest for education policy? Returning to the hypothetical case from the perspective of degenerative politics, suppose that a key policy maker is the wife of the CEO of a computer business. What if she hires researchers from an anti-tax, anti-education think thank to produce findings that contradict the relationship of class size and achievement and promote the idea that technology is the magic bullet for improving achievement? What if she appears to negotiate in good faith with the teachers but knows at the outset that her decision will benefit contributors to her next campaign? What if the group with the most to lose by the policy is not even invited to the discussion? What if she expresses platitudes about achievement at the table but out in the hallway makes deals on grounds other than achievement? Or what if she agrees to reduce class size (so she could appear to be a friend of education) but reduces it by such a small amount (say, from 35 to 32) that no tangible benefits and few costs can result from the policy? All of these "what ifs" are possible, and all are, in one form or another, based on fact. All of them suggest—not an idealized relationship of politics and policy—but instead a case of degenerative politics and political spectacle.

In a nutshell, that is the argument of this book: policies that emerge from degenerative politics create perverse consequences in schools, frustration and perplexity among the public. We offer readers the chance to test our argument in the details of case histories, abbreviated in this chapter and elaborated in the chapters to follow.

Conventional Theories of Policy in Politics

The definition of politics that best suits our perspective of the ingrained contradiction in American society comes from Anne Schneider and Helen Ingram:

> The term "politics" is associated in the popular vernacular with the strategic manipulation of power to serve personal or narrow special interests at the expense of more legitimate concerns. This construction has eclipsed the classic understanding of politics as the means through which collectivities make decisions to serve the general (public) interests of the entire society.[1]

We define a policy as "the rules by which society is governed," or the "authoritative allocation of values." These are the conventional definitions that students and scholars encounter in standard texts. Applying these definitions to the class size reduction example above, one sees that the legislature (an "authoritative" body) wrote legislation (the "rules" by which schools would be "governed" and organized) to reduce the ratio of pupils to teachers as a means to improve achievement (one of the "values" to be allocated).

When we think about a policy we encompass more than the *text* of a policy (say, the legislation and accompanying regulations). We include as well the ideals and discourse that underlie that policy. We also consider the *instrument* the State uses to implement the policy and to allocate its values. Instruments are means to an end and include mandates, inducements (incentives and penalties), demonstrations, and "system changes."[2] Assessment policy in Arizona (see Chapter Two) used mandates as its policy instrument. The policy demanded that the performance of certain students be tested and that the results of the tests be publicly posted. An example of an inducement is a policy instrument that offers bonuses to schools that increase achievement. Taking money away from those schools that fail to increase achievement counts as another kind of inducement—a penalty. New Jersey has a policy to increase accountability and achievement by allowing the state to assume control over schools that persistently fail—another kind of inducement. Voucher programs are system changes in that they change the traditional ways that students are assigned to their schools. Parental choice replaces neighborhood assignment. The Tennessee class size reduction policy (known as STAR) is an example of a demonstration. The state conducted an experiment in a sample of schools for the purpose of predicting what would happen if class size were to be reduced across the state.

When a policy lacks an instrument or provides an instrument so weak that it could not reasonably be expected to effect the desired outcome, that policy falls into the category of hortatory or symbolic.

Some policies have multiple instruments. An assessment policy, for example, might function as hortatory (providing signals to teachers that they should raise their content standards and make them coherent with state or national standards as well as sending signals to the business community that it can forthwith trust a diploma to mean something). In addition the policy might include a mandate (requiring a test over those standards to determine students' high school graduation). The state might also provide inducements for raising scores.

Administrative authorities implement policies by translating them into instruments and programs. Educators further translate the policy and its instruments into classroom activities and experiences for pupils. In other words, a policy is far more than a written text, but a trajectory of aims, understandings, actions, and consequences that shift over time.[3]

Consequences of policies are both manifest and hidden, intended and unintended. Policies also yield costs and opportunity costs. In an ideal policy world, all these consequences would be evaluated and reported.

The intense scrutiny that governments now direct at schools has increased markedly over the past forty years or so. Legislation, court rulings, and regulations have proliferated and piled one atop another, creating a kind of geological record of values and programs over recent decades. Each program began with great hope; some passed away with great disappointment. Many policies remain on the books but attract attention no longer, effectively passing without notice. Attempts to reform schools by changing policies have become nonstop.

Although education is by now firmly fixed as a function of Federal government, it was not always so. The U.S. Constitution reserved to the states the right to govern schools. Until recently, states or local entities financed and ran public schools. But two explosions of the 1950s and 1960s—the launch of *Sputnik* and the civil rights revolution—convinced the majority (not everyone then or now) that the Federal government has interests— economic, social justice, and national defense interests—in what happens in public schools.[4] Civil Rights rulings and laws as well as the Elementary and Secondary Education Act of 1965 formalized Federal interests, although most school policies remained under the authority of the separate states. In many states the power to control schools drifted or lurched from local to state government, because people believed that centralizing and consolidating school functions would enhance the values of efficiency and standardization. In the 1980s, policy makers emphasized the need to reform schools as a way of enhancing the economy (see Chapter Six). Once on the government stage, public schools became subject to the shifting political trends that characterized the last half of the 20th century.

By 2002, the Federal government's hold on schools had solidified as a result of the reauthorization of the Elementary and Secondary Education Act (ESEA, also known as the "No Child Left Behind" legislation). Among other things, ESEA placed a federal mandate on states to test every child in grades 3–8 every year on math and reading. The legislation pushed schools to adopt reading programs that emphasize phonics skills. It insisted that it would approve and fund only those programs that had stood up to rigorous experimental tests (the consequences of which we consider in depth in Chapter Five). For the first time, federal policy covered preschool education, but funded only those programs that met the scientific test. The ESEA legislation was the culmination of a half-century of government influence on schools through education policy.

Since governments are political creatures, and because our political system is based on contending political parties and factions, American political trends have influenced education policy-making and the ways schools are governed and defined. As concerns for equality of opportunity waxed and waned in relation to the political climate, so have educational policies regarding equality of educational opportunity. Economic trends (recessions, international economic competitive pressures) have likewise produced consequences in policies meant to affect schools.

Moreover, the influence of Federal, state, and local government, relative to each other, has changed over political eras. The Carter administration increased the authority of the Federal government over school policy by creating a Department of Education administered by a cabinet-level Secretary. The creation of the post of Secretary of Education symbolized the Federal role and also reflected the political will of an important political ally—the teachers' professional associations. The Reagan administration aimed to reverse this course, perhaps in a general project to reduce the size of government and also to reduce the power of labor organizations. Through a system of block grants the Reagan administration increased the authority of the states relative to the federal government. Abolition of the Department of Education remains a topic over which the two parties contend.

This brief history of education policy suggests many points in which politics, as conventionally defined, have intruded. To study policy without studying politics is to miss crucial dynamics and divisions. Education policies reflect the politics of the times and illustrate, at any particular time and place, which groups have more power to influence the state in its allocation of values.

School policy makers and researchers of education policy have long debated whether policies actually affect what goes on behind the closed classroom door. Scholars have used the phrase "loosely coupled system" to characterize the problematic relationship of policy making to classroom action. They have used terms like "systemic reform" to solve the variations and incoherence present in running schools, and tighten the couplings between the levels of authority in the school system. Nevertheless, the skeptic could well point out the lamentable record of policies—systemic or not—to achieve their desired effects. Many policy theorists and researchers ignore the political uses of policies as well as the underlying social conditions that weaken even the best policy reforms. Although the empirical record for the successful implementation of school policies is weak, policies do have effects, if not always the ones the policy makers had in mind. Thus we argue that the political events underlying the policy process condition the fate of American schools.

What kinds of effects do policies have on classrooms and schools? First, some policies have effects consonant with the original intentions and ideals behind them. These are *instrumental policies.* STAR (Student/Teacher Achievement Ratio), the Tennessee program to test the effects of reduced class size on achievement, is an example of an instrumental policy. The state provided adequate means to attain the goals of the policy. There was a clear relationship between means and ends. The state included all the constituent groups, both professionals and policy makers, in a full discussion of potential costs and benefits, advantages, and disadvantages. The state government provided enough resources to insure that the policy could be implemented as it had been defined. The state monitored the implementation of the program and commissioned expert, independent researchers to study the effects of the program. All these elements fit STAR in the category of instrumental policies.

Second, a policy may have no effect at all because it functions primarily as a symbol, without any substantive instrument that logically could be expected to lead to policy goals. In this category we would fit Goals 2000, passed during the Clinton administration. One of these national goals stated that, by the year 2000, all children would begin school "ready to learn." No matter how worthy such a goal might be, the government failed to develop an instrument—that is, any practical means for achieving it. Another example of such a symbolic policy consists of legislation in several states that mandates the posting of the Ten Commandments in all schools. One can infer that the policy embodied a hope to reduce school violence. However, we think that most reasonable people would agree that, had this text been posted outside the Columbine High School library, it would not have deterred Eric Harris and Dylan Klebold from their murderous acts. Policies such as these represent a symbolic move by policy makers in Colorado who wanted to signal the public at large or a particular interest group that they are doing something—anything—to address a problem. These are examples of *symbolic policies.*

Sometimes policies start out instrumental and later become symbolic because the government agency failed to provide the means to the ends. Instruments for carrying out the policy intent are available and may even be implemented. But sufficient funds are not attached to the policy to carry it out successfully. The Arizona Student Assessment Program falls into this category. As we detail in Chapter Two, the state mandated that students take "performance tests," which require them to write out answers to open-ended, problem-solving items (rather than the typical multiple choice items that schools more often use). The state failed to provide enough funds and time to develop adequate test items and scoring systems. It failed to provide training for teachers to modify their approach to instruction. That kind of modification turned out to be far more complex than was originally thought.

A third category consists of effects that are beyond scrutiny. Consider the example of Arizona's charter school policies. In their enthusiasm for a free market model of publicly funded and privately managed schools the legislature and administrative authority produced regulations so loose that it became impossible even to count the number of charter schools in operation or the numbers of students in them on a given day. Nor was there any mechanism available to judge (or even to know) what went on in these schools or how public money was spent. The Milwaukee and Florida experiments with vouchers were even more hidden. The archdiocese in Milwaukee withheld information on the academic progress of students who used vouchers to attend Catholic schools. Florida exempted from state assessment those private schools that enrolled students with vouchers. Without even such basic information, the public cannot possibly know the effects of a policy or participate intelligently in the debate over its values.

Fourth, policy effects may be unintentionally deleterious; the policy produces unanticipated effects or costs, or effects contrary to the policy goals. Unfortunately, there are too many examples of this, and they rarely become public. Falling into this category are the policies of Texas and Chicago intended to raise achievement and increase accountability. Policy makers mandated high-stakes testing to determine which students were eligible to graduate or advance to the next grade. President Clinton praised the Chicago policy, calling it a model of national school reform. During his campaign for the presidency, George W. Bush claimed that a similar policy in Texas had been highly successful. Whether these policies did what they were supposed to do remains unproven. What did happen, and this can hardly be refuted, was that thousands of mostly poor and minority children dropped out of school.[5] Evidence from independent investigations suggests that these policies had unintentional and deleterious side effects.

Whatever the effects of a policy, politics come to bear. In the next section we consider contrasting viewpoints on the role of politics in policy.

Un-Conventional Theories of Politics in Policy

Most scholars define policy as the authoritative and rational allocation of values. They believe that policies arise as sensible responses to public needs. A consensus about the common public good develops out of citizen and political debate; administrative authorities develop regulations, instruments, and programs that are likely to meet those needs. These means are enacted and the public learns about the relationship of means to ends—how well the instruments and programs meet the needs and goals of the policy. The conventional view conceives the policy process as relatively linear and straightforward. Deborah Stone called this conception "the rationality project" and argued that it fails to square with the record of history and experience.

Revisionist views such as Stone's reflect the confluence of politics and policy (two words with common origins). As an alternative to the model of rationality project she offers a model of policy within the "polis," or political community:

> The model for studying policy should account for the possibilities of changing one's objectives, of pursuing contradictory objectives simultaneously, of winning by appearing to lose and turning loss into an appearance of victory, and . . . of attaining objectives by portraying oneself as having attained them.[6]

The rationality project hypothesizes a rational connection between means (the instruments of programs) and ends (policy goals and intentions). It fails to capture "the essence of policy making in political communities: the struggle over ideas. Ideas are a medium of exchange and a mode of influence even more powerful than money and votes and guns." Stone continued:

> Furthermore, each type of policy instrument is a kind of political arena, with its peculiar ground rules, within which political conflicts are continued. Each mode of social regulation draws lines around what people may and may not do and how they may or may not treat each other. But these boundaries are constantly contested, either because they are ambiguous and do not settle conflicts, or because they allocate benefits and burdens to the people on either side, or both. Boundaries become real and acquire their meaning in political struggles.[7]

Murray Edelman's ideas about policy go further, as he defined it this way:

> A "policy," then, is a set of shifting, diverse, and contradictory responses to a spectrum of political interests. . . . The name of the policy provides a ground for ignoring the inconsistencies. . . . The name typically reassures, while a focus upon policy inconsistencies and differences might be disturbing.[8]

Our purpose in this book is to explore the contemporary political climate as it bears on educational policy. Our studies of particular education policies (testing in Arizona, desegregation in the southwest, school choice in Colorado) convince us that the course of these policies can best be explained by a theory of political spectacle. This theory holds that contemporary politics resemble theater, with directors, stages, casts of actors, narrative plots, and (most importantly) a curtain that separates the action onstage—what the audience has access to—from the backstage, where the real "allocation of values" takes place.

Since (as we argue) the dominant trend in American politics is spectacle, we believe that the plotting, casting, posing, and entertaining that characterize theater have affected and continue to affect public schooling in ways that citizens and scholars should heed.

What is spectacle? If we are using the device as a metaphor, what do we imply by it? The word, the OED tells us, comes from the Latin word *spectaculum*, a public show, and is closely related to the words "spectate" or "spectator." Spectacle is defined as "an organized (usually public) display or entertainment," especially "one on a large or splendid scale"; a "display or ceremony"; "a person or thing as an object of public curiosity, contempt, or admiration"; a "theatrical display or pageant."

How are politics like a public theatrical display? What is political spectacle theory? Murray Edelman, its principal theorist, described it this way:

> Basic to the recognition of symbolic forms in the political process is a distinction between politics as a spectator sport and political activity as utilized by organized groups to get quite tangible benefits for themselves. For most men most of the time politics is a series of pictures in the mind, placed there by television news, magazines, and discussions. The pictures create a moving panorama taking place in a world the public never quite touches.[9]

If the political process allocates tangible benefits to the few but only symbolic benefits for the many, we must ask about the consequences of political spectacle on educational policy. Are the taxpayers and patrons of schools mere spectators rather than active participants? Is the public involved only at the level of symbolism? Are the policy makers acting out roles, posing for the cameras, providing entertainment rather than substance? Are there tangible benefits of various policies doled out behind the scenes? If so, are the schools that are being constructed in the climate of political spectacle the kind of schools that we want? Are they the kind of schools that enhance and realize the best in children? In society as a whole?

Elements of Political Spectacle

The primary elements or categories of the political spectacle theory comprise the following: symbolic language; casting political actors as leaders, allies, and enemies; dramaturgy (staging, plotting, and costuming); the illusion of rationality; the illusion of democratic participation, disconnection between means and ends; distinguishing the action on stage from the action backstage.

Symbolic Language

Language is at the heart of political spectacle, and language is always ambiguous. In political campaigns, the use of such words as "patriotism," "democracy," and "compassion" is metaphorical. So is the use of such words as "accountability," "high standards," "freedom of choice," and the like in conversations about school policy. Concrete referents to these abstract words are lacking, so that no tether ties these words and images to the world of experience and intractable, concrete details. Or rather, there are so many different mental pictures that form in the minds of the public when they hear these words that one can scarcely pin down the specific meaning of the person who spoke them. Who could be against "accountability"? Who could argue against "freedom of choice?" But Edelman argued that the meaning of such terms depends on the context in which they were spoken, who spoke them, and to whom they were spoken. "[D]ictionary meanings are operationally close to irrelevant" when words are used for political purposes.[10]

Words and numbers appear precise and rational; yet depend entirely on context and interpretation. An achievement test score epitomizes this contradiction between appearance and reality. To enact policies of high-stakes testing, a state must select a score to separate those students who pass from those who fail. Often the process of setting the passing score follows political, rather than technical, logic. In the Arizona case (Chapter Two), a committee sat around a table trying to choose a cutoff point—a number or percentage of correct items that a student must attain to graduate. The committee's task was to decide on a number that would thereafter separate students who had mastered state standards from those who had not. Their reasoning was more political than statistical. That cutoff score had to be politically credible, whether or not it was technically sound. They settled on 75 percent. In subsequent discussions, the use of the 75 percent statistic, seemed precise, technical, objective, and apolitical. But numbers, like words, perform symbolic functions and cover up underlying actions that turn out to be arbitrary, inconsistent, and subjective.

Political rather than technical rationality dominated standard-setting in many other states and also distorted portrayals of the results of policies. George W. Bush boasted that his accountability policy (Texas Assessment of Academic Skills, or TAAS) had been responsible for a substantial improvement in achievement. The "Texas Miracle," the apparent gain on TAAS, thus became part of his election campaign. A researcher from outside the system found that the content of the test changed from one year to the next; in fact the items on the second test were easier than the items the year before. The average gains on the test, therefore, reflected alterations on the test itself rather than real improvements in academic accomplishment.[11] Thus apparently "precise" numbers, like a cutoff score of 75 percent or a 20 percent improvement in achievement, dissolve into ambiguity if one examines the particulars closely enough.

Such symbolic ambiguity creates a kind of fog. It holds the public in a thrall. The gain in test scores may not be real, but it seems real, and the public lacks the means to see their way through. Politicians use ambiguous language to unite a public and create an impression of consensus that does not exist. For example, "accountability" suggests something quite different to accountants, to educators, and to testing experts. Politicians gloss over real differences in definitions and values in order to pass legislation such as high-stakes testing. Glossing and conflation of disparate aims occur in most policies in the political spectacle.[12]

When we think of the strategic use of ambiguous and symbolic language, we can find no more important example than "English for the Children," an initiative brought before the Arizona voters in 2000. This initiative was designed to eliminate bilingual education for children learning the English language and replace it with a single year of classes in English immersion. Ron Unz, a rich entrepreneur from California, had sponsored a similar referendum in California and then brought the campaign to Arizona. He based his argument on the results of polls that asked Hispanic parents this question: "How important is it for your child to learn to speak English?" This question yielded a predictably high rate of agreement, which Unz then used to claim that most parents preferred English immersion programs. The findings could just as well have meant that Hispanic parents wanted their children to learn both English and Spanish, or that they wanted them to learn English but not to fall behind in their other subjects (a possibility that some research suggests). These were the details that Unz thought best to gloss. In any case, who could argue with a program called "English for the Children"?

Ambiguous, multivalent words create anxiety in the public when politicians use them to evoke a crisis. The paradigm case of using lurid language in education policy is *A Nation at Risk*, a work prepared by the federal government. Its author, Terrell Bell, presented achievement test data that had been portrayed in such a way as to suggest a decline over the years and to show a deficiency of achievement in U.S. students when compared to those of other nations. He fretted that the decline in educational achievement was so severe that, had a foreign power done to our country what our schools have done, it would be considered an act of war:

> [T]he educational foundations of our society are presently being eroded by a rising tide of mediocrity that threatens our very future as a Nation and a people.[13]

This use of graphic, metaphorical language planted a connection in people's minds between academic achievement and national defense, and between achievement and economic competitiveness. It evoked images of a depleted, diseased, and failed public school system, one that endangers U.S. economic health and even its national security. These images have become engrained in the background assumptions the public holds. The metaphors persist long after tangible referents vanish (if they ever existed). Invoking crises serves the political spectacle in two ways. First, it serves as a pretext for radical actions offered by policy makers to correct the alleged conditions, and secondly it arouses emotional rather than analytic, critical responses on the part of the public. First the public is made afraid of the crisis and then is made passive in the face of policies to correct it.

Edelman wrote that the public colludes with the policy maker in defining both problems and solutions. If the problem is as complicated and vast as an act of war, then we as citizens must lack the power or expertise to fix it. So we leave it to the experts. "The terms 'problem' and 'crisis' are inducements to acquiesce in deprivations."[14] The public complies just when it should be asking, "What is the factual link between school achievement and economic productivity?" Or, "What are the ways in which achievement decline is the same as, and different than, economic decline?" Or, "Is there really a decline at all?" Instead the public tends to accept the politicians' construction of problems and solutions. It is now an article of faith that American schools are weak.[15]

When a politician offers up a metaphor, she encourages the public to think of one thing as another—to generalize the traits of one thing to those of another. As an example, certain Arizona policy makers attempted to make high school graduation contingent on passing a test. Passing a graduation test, they reasoned, would assure the business community that students with high school diplomas were competent. To promote this policy they deployed the metaphor of "seat-time" as a way of depicting the existing system for getting a diploma. By using this metaphor, policy makers suggested that, under the current rules, all students had to do was to sit passively for the required number of hours in order to graduate. This metaphor neglects several contradictory details. Under the old system students took a series of courses from a series of teachers, each of whom employed the standards of his or her field to judge whether the student had earned a passing grade. Students graduated after they passed enough of such courses, that number determined by professional accrediting agencies and local school boards. They did not (most of them, anyway) just sit. Under the new policy, a supposedly technical decision rule supplanted the system of accumulated professional judgments, shifting authority and power from professionals to state technocrats.

This story illustrates that metaphorical language obscures the details and quiets the critical responses that might churn up if the public scrutinized the facts and gave the matter some thought. But, who could argue with "competency"? Who would defend "seat-time"? Edelman noted:

> [T]he employment of political speech and writing [functions] as a ritual, dulling the critical faculties rather than awakening them. Chronic repetition of clichés and stale phrases that serve simply to evoke a conditioned uncritical response is a time-honored habit among politicians and a mentally restful one for their audiences.[16]

By now the public recognizes when politicians use hortatory and self-serving language during a campaign, and it grows cynical. Many recognize such language when politicians use it, but probably do not understand its political function. Cynicism is just another form of quiescence. Americans have the sense that, by talking in this way, candidates are creating a form of persuasion, a form of self-presentation, a canned image. We crave instead authentic and spontaneous exchanges—the unscripted moments, but hear few. During the 2000 presidential election campaign, the public was titillated when a reporter with a tape recorder caught candidates Bush and Cheney in such a whispered exchange. "That [reporter] is a real asshole," says one. "Yeah, big time," says the other. Neither the form nor the content of the exchange would have taken place on the stage, if the speakers had known that others might hear it. One can instantly recognize how hortatory language in front of the theater curtain assumes an entirely different form and character from insider language backstage. Edelman argued that hortatory language on stage offers symbolic reassurance while bargaining language backstage offers tangible benefits. There is no ambiguity in the words used backstage because those words have concrete referents—real gains and real losses.

Political language is banal because the public has heard the words so often. Political language is strategic (officials use it to advance a political goal). Political language generates emotional responses rather than critical responses or concrete actions. Political language bemuses, obfuscates, befogs, mystifies, lulls, glosses.

The term "accountability" serves as a key example. The same word evokes quite different associations in different groups. In the corporate world, accountability usually refers to a command and control process, wherein managers at one level tightly control the next level down by setting performance standards and evaluating performance. In contrast to the corporate model of accountability, professionals such as doctors define accountability as practicing in accord with professional norms and values. Rather than to the corporate organization, the doctors orient their actions to the profession and to patients, and adopt voluntarily a code of conduct. Following those codes generally implies that a doctor adapts to the patient and context, which may mean diversifying practice rather than standardizing it. Teachers tend to associate professional norms with the word accountability, although the ubiquity of testing policies may cause them to join most of the public in equating accountability with achievement testing.

What the concept of accountability shows about the political spectacle has to do with two things: 1) that different groups hold various and ambiguous referents about the same word, and 2) that rarely do the different groups recognize the differences or sit down together to resolve them. Instead, the ambiguity persists in a general fog in which politicians and officials do whatever they do, for example, in the name of "accountability."

Casting Political Actors as Leaders, Enemies, and Allies and Plotting Their Actions

Characters are cast to play certain roles. Interest groups construct roles such as leader, ally, and enemy and individuals assume the roles. But the public generally believes that such roles are natural and inevitable and fails to recognize them as social constructions. The public believes that leadership is a trait that people have more or less of, based on their genetic endowment or early upbringing. This is the cult of personality in which social and situational causes are submerged in beliefs about the power of individuals to influence events.

To believe instead that leadership is a role that certain individuals take on and shape themselves to fit—that belief is more consistent with political spectacle theory. According to Edelman, persons who want to be seen as leaders reinforce images of themselves by acting in formal, public settings as leaders are supposed to act. That is, they engage in "a dramaturgical performance emphasizing the traits popularly associated with leadership: forcefulness, responsibility, courage, decency, and so on."[17]

Faced with a series of complex crises (invented and real), the public needs leaders and thus colludes in casting particular individuals in leadership roles. Edelman wrote that for the public,

> [t]he idea of leadership makes a complex and largely unknowable social world understandable even while it assuages personal guilt and anxiety by transferring responsibility to another.[18]

The popular media reinforce the theory that leadership is a natural, psychological trait by publishing more reports about politicians' personality than about substantive issues and more about their individual characters than about their political records. People view media events such as presidential debates to determine whether the candidates have facial ticks or whether they make grammatical errors or fail to act presidential. People, assisted by popular media, fixate on whether the candidates seem sincere or act presidential. Since they recognize that the public concentrates on the superficial, media consultants focus their preparation for these events on image rather than substance. The perspiration and five o'clock shadow on Richard Nixon's face during the 1960 presidential debates changed for good or ill how candidates worry about self-presentation and how the public colludes in this concern.[19]

When people construct themselves as leaders they try to build connections between themselves and innovative policies, emphasizing the apparent differences between their own qualities and programs verses those of their predecessors or competitors. In Chapter Two we describe how the newly elected state superintendent in Arizona undid the assessment program of her predecessor, hyping the apparent differences between the old and new. This action accentuated her image of energy and innovation. The new broom swept clean, or so it seemed.

Part of the process of constructing oneself as leader involves evoking crises as justification for one's policy initiatives. For example a precipitous (though possibly artifactual) test score decline becomes a pretext for changing curriculum to the leader's favorite alternative (or to the favorite of the leader's political supporters). The leader supplies the apparent justification—the dire risk that the decline implies, say, to the state's economic health.

Defining policy actors as leaders insures quiescence and justifies unequal privileges and authority. In the political spectacle leaders identify crises and launch programs they think will produce dramatic outcomes in a short time. The public seldom has the chance to judge a program by its long-range benefits and burdens. Because the leader accentuates the dramatic response, the public stands little chance to trace the real success or failure of the leader's policies. Often, the leaders are long-gone before the public notices the consequences of policies.

Leaders also create enemies and stage battles for dramaturgical effects. Media reinforce the aspects of spectacle rather than substance. According to Edelman:

> Because politics involves conflict about material advantages, status, and moral issues, some people are always pitted against others and see them as adversaries or as enemies. . . . They help give the political spectacle its power to arouse passions, fears, and hopes. . . .
>
> Leaders have much to gain by exaggerating the threat the enemy poses and by distorting the facts of the enemy's record. The leader has much to gain by discounting the arguments of enemies and portraying them as irrational and ideological (while the leader is rational and fair-minded).[20]

Evocation of enemies seems to serve tactical purposes most effectively when they are lumped into a known stereotype. In assessment policy as well as choice policy, educators who oppose government policies are labeled "educrats" or "apologists for the educational establishment." Figure 1 captures a most glaring and perverse example of constructing enemies. The *Tempe Tribune* published this editorial cartoon depicting Professor (and then Dean) David Berliner of Arizona State University as a storm trooper holding a weeping child by a metal leash. The figure holds Berliner's book, the *Manufactured Crisis*. In that book (written with Bruce Biddle), the authors argued that the achievement decline claimed by *A Nation at Risk* amounted to a jeremiad unwarranted by evidence. The *Tribune* had often editorialized about the failures of public schools, turned teachers' associations into villains, and advocated vouchers (thus, the leash image). The editorial cartoonist condensed in a single image a range of negative stereotypes: the inadequacy of teacher education, the silliness of education scholarship, the anti-family perspective of public schools, and the fascistic hold of monopolistic public institutions over a helpless public.

In the political spectacle, persons become actors, take on roles, and polish their image. Cultural critic Daniel Boorstin defined image this way:

Fig. 1 Reprinted with permission by *The East Valley Tribune*, copyright 1999.

An image is "a studiously crafted personality profile of an individual, institution, corporation, product, or service. It is a value, caricature. . . . When we use the word 'image' in this new sense, we plainly confess a distinction between what we see and what is really there. . . . Thus an image is a visible public 'personality' as distinguished from an inward private 'character'. . . we imply that something can be done to it: the image can always be more or less successfully synthesized, doctored, repaired, refurbished, and improved, quite apart from . . . the spontaneous original of which the image is a public portrait." The alteration is "less a change of heart than a change of face." An image must be ambiguous and open-ended . . . "an invitation [to suspend] critical judgement."[21]

M. Kakutani wrote of the post election campaign of 2000 that language had reached "dismaying levels of phoniness, spin, and distortion" approaching the sort of "Manichean language used in the cold war" to depict the opposition, language heretofore used

> only by extremists . . . appealing only to audience's baser emotions of anger and competitiveness—rather than loftier ideals of pluralism and self sacrifice . . . the combatants in this brawl not only make it more difficult for the next occupant of the Oval Office to govern effectively . . . but coarsen the national discourse . . . [which] labels everyone a hero or a villain.[22]

In the political spectacle, characters are cast, and their story lines are plotted. But stories, like metaphors, appeal to intuition, emotion, and tacit assumptions rather than to reason. Deborah Stone wrote about different kinds of plots. Stories of decline depict conditions as worsening and thus requiring a brave leader to step in. *A Nation at Risk* is a prime case of stories of decline. Another type of story is the conspiracy tale. Conspiracy tales "always reveal that harm has been deliberately caused or knowingly tolerated, and so evoke horror and moral condemnation."

Another kind of narrative, "blame-the-victim stories," place the responsibility for declines and crises at the doorstep of teachers, parents, and children, rather than on politicians and policies.[23] Governor Fife Symington openly thwarted a Supreme Court order to equalize school funding among Arizona school districts. Equal funding for schools was not necessary, he said. It was all a matter of choice. Good parents who want better education for their children should choose another school. He declared that housing was a free market, and parents in the low-income parts of town could simply move to Scottsdale, where resources were more ample. Bad parents, by implication, were the ones who failed to exercise their right to choose.

Stone stated that metaphors, synecdoches, and other symbolic devices create intuitive and emotional reactions rather than critical and thoughtful reactions in the audiences that receive them.

> Symbolic devices are especially persuasive and emotionally compelling because their story line is hidden and their sheer poetry is often stunning. . . . The most important feature of all symbols, both in art and politics, is their ambiguity [because a] symbol can mean two (or more) things simultaneously. . . . Ambiguity enables the transformation of individual intentions and actions into collective results and purposes. . . . [A]mbiguity allows leaders to aggregate support from different quarters for a single policy. . . . [A]mbiguity allows leaders of interest groups and political movements to bring together people with wishes for different policies. . . . [A]mbiguity allows leaders of interest groups and political movements to bring together people with wishes for different polices.[24]

In the political spectacle, aspects of theater such as characters, scripts, and plots, work their way into policies. In the production that is the No Child Left Behind legislation one can see all these elements: heroes and villains, oft-repeated slogans, and the narrative, which suggests to the popular mind that this policy can readily correct deeply embedded social problems by making kids pass tests.

Dramaturgy: Political Stages, Props, and Costumes

According to Edelman, political acts take place in contexts that suggest that a few individuals are actors and most are spectators. These formal settings reinforce and justify the social distance between the two groups and legitimize " a series of future acts (whose content is still unknown) and thereby maximizing the chance of acquiescence."[25] Policies announced from in front of the presidential seal, rules handed down from a Federal Court bench or from other formal or evocative settings function this way.

Recall an incident that occurred during the 2000 post election campaign, in which one candidate held a press conference. Two American flags flanked the podium with the official seal. Later, a candidate from the other party gave a press conference with five American flags backing him. Still later a candidate appeared in front of a huge array of flags. This time the candidates went too far, and their posing provided fodder for comedians.

Trucks transporting disputed ballots from Miami to Tallahassee provided another opportunity for dramatic staging—complete with television cameras in helicopters. Media over-report the dramatic and the visual, an issue we take up in Chapter Four.

About such incidents, Frank Rich wrote, "the disconnect lives on between the invented drama and the everyday life of most Americans." He referred to the theatrical quality of the candidates, for example, The "unctuous disingenuousness" of Gore attending the movie *Men of Honor.*

> But as Mr. Gore's touch football photo-op didn't turn him into a Kennedy, neither did Mr. Bush's facial bandage transform him into John McCain.[26]

Political party conventions function as the most obvious stage of political spectacle. Conventions have lead actors and bit-players, costumes and props. The role of the delegates is ambiguous. The Republican convention of 2000 set up the audience to appear more diverse than it was, with television cameras dwelling on the few nonwhite faces in the crowd. The live "audience" responded when the light went on, much as they would at the taping of an episode of *Friends.*[27]

Daniel Boorstin called such theatrical occasions "pseudo-events." He defined a pseudo-event as:

> a happening [that] is "not spontaneous, but comes about because someone has planned, planted, or incited it. . . . It is planned primarily . . . for the immediate purpose of being reported or reproduced. . . . [and] arranged for the . . . media. . . . Its relation to the underlying reality of the situation is ambiguous. . . . In the last half century a larger and larger proportion of our experience . . . has come to consist of pseudo-events. We expect more of them and we are given more of them. They flood our consciousness.[28]

Boorstin's concept of pseudo-event encompasses more than politics, and includes any public entertainment, sports contest or spectacle. In contemporary American culture, all of these—politics with entertainment, entertainment with sport—seem to converge with one another as we reform them into dramatic narratives with characters, settings, and plots.

> Press releases also function this way, as an inaccurate documentation of public, spontaneous events . . . to secure "news coverage" for an event . . . one must issue, in proper form, a "release". . . . The release is news pre-cooked . . . is written in the past tense but usually describes an event that has not yet happened. . . . More and more new events become dramatic performances in which "men in the news" simply act out more or less well their prepared script and seems more authentic than the spontaneous event itself.[29]

Caryn James wrote of the post election campaign, that the ABC program *Nightline* began with Ted Koppel:

> reciting ABC's slogan for the post-election drama: in a solemn cadence suited to imminent nuclear disaster, he declared, "A Nation Waits." Brian William's booming voice carried a hollow echo of Red Scare days. . . . Television viewers were mildly curious or gripped, weary or disengaged. . . . But nowhere (except in the street demonstrations carefully staged for the cameras in Florida) was there a sense of high anxiety. Yet the anchors and commentators maintained a relentlessly hysterical tone, an apocalyptic attitude. . . .[30]

Another theatrical element in the political spectacle is the creation of a narrative to sell a policy or contest it. Deborah Stone wrote about narratives:

> Definitions of policy problems usually have narrative structure; that is, they are stories with a beginning, a middle, and an end, involving some change or transformation. They have heroes and villains and innocent victims, and they pit the forces of evil against the forces of good. The story line in policy writing is often hidden.[31]

There could be no more obvious example than the narratives of the post election campaign of 2000. For members of each party, the story was one of stealing the election from the rightful winner, stories of heroic stands or villainous attacks. The beginning of the story was election night, when most things were going smoothly, then came the complicating actions of Gore's concession and retraction of the concession, various stand-ins and second fiddles taking the stage or conspiring offstage, resolutions sought and thwarted. Heroes and villains were constructed (Katherine Harris as either the Bush groupie or Joan of Arc; Richard Daley as either the spawn of past dirty elections or the brave *consigliere*). The drama continued until the final denouement of the Supreme Court ruling that disputed Florida votes could not be counted. Partway through the events of post-election period, members of the public began demanding that it end, urging that one or the other candidate admit defeat—as if this was a theatrical production gone on too long and needing a climax and resolution, which all stories have. But of course, social and human events have no natural beginnings and endings. Social communities construct them as needs arise.

Neal Gabler equates modern life to movies:

> after decades of public-relations contrivances and media hype, and after decades more of steady pounding by an array of social forces that have alerted each of us personally to the power of performance, life has *become* art [his italics], so that the two are now indistinguishable from each other. . . . The deliberate application of the techniques of theater to politics, religion, education, literature, commerce, warfare, crime, *everything*, has converted them into branches of show business, where the overriding objective is getting and satisfying an audience.[32]

With all these political theatrics, what can reasonably be expected from school policies? Can the winner of an election produce sound education policy when the campaign rhetoric went so far as to declare Gore's request for a recount of votes an "attempted coup d'etat" or likened the Florida Secretary of State to a "Soviet commissar"?

Democratic Participation as Illusion[33]

The conventional model of the policy process conceives that the public, once informed of the objective facts about the details of a policy, is in a better position to participate in the policy process. But Edelman argued that:

> the public is constantly reminded that its role is minor, largely passive, and at most reactive. The intense publicity given to voting and elections is itself a potent signal of the essential powerlessness of political spectators . . . an individual vote is more nearly a form of self-expression and of legitimation than of influence and that the link between elections and value allocations is tenuous.[34]

In the political spectacle, leaders act. Others react. Most people believe they participate in democracy by voting or at most by testifying at hearings where policies are under consideration. According to Edelman, however, in politicized policy making the actions of the public amount to mere rituals—highly formalized and far removed from where the real decisions are made. The broad visions and fine details of policies are worked out backstage.

Realizing that participation is a formality creates a self-fulfilling prophecy. If a person believes she lacks control over government and policy making, she then takes less active interest in it and rarely takes action in relation to it. Passivity, cynicism, and resigned detachment exacerbate political spectacle.

Democracy suffers in the political spectacle. Over the decades of the 1980s and 1990s the balance of power over public schools shifted from the school patrons and professionals to elites in the corporate world and other interest groups. Chicago Public Schools changed from decentralized control by parent councils to a centralized, top-down system. Control over schools in Los Angeles shifted from a superintendent and elected school board to a CEO (former Colorado Governor Roy Romer) and an appointed advisory council. Such policy shifts did not come about by

democratic actions on the part of those affected but came from state legislatures and local business councils, with no discussion by the public.

As we describe in Chapter Three, elite groups of parents often work to
establish control over how their children's schools are organized. They use
their cultural capital to obtain values for their own children, without regard to the general public good. So democracy for the few is still possible in
the political spectacle. Often such parents use ambiguous language to obtain what they feel their children need, such as special programs for the
gifted, homogenous tracks, and the like. Although some individuals benefit, others with less cultural capital lose. For every small seminar there is a
large lecture class; for every high track there exists a low track, often with
impoverished curriculum and less able teachers.

Aside from the elite parents, for most of the public, genuine and democratic participation amounts to illusion. We recall how the Arizona Department of Education stifled democracy first by stacking like-minded people on
committees to write state standards. Then almost as if it were a ritual, the
Department held large, open meetings for educators and the public to respond to drafts of the standards. To get a chance to speak, members of the
audience had to submit their questions in advance so that the department
could screen out questions they might have trouble answering. Those who
passed this screen lined up behind a microphone in the audience. In turn,
each person was allowed only three minutes to speak. No dialogue about any
issue occurred. Officials on the podium did not appear to be paying serious
attention, although one clerk took notes. Nothing was changed as a result of
these meetings. The state superintendent often disparaged meetings like
these as mere opportunities for "grandstanding." Several years later, as the
state standards and assessment policy began to crumble, she convened a
group of elite insiders to advise her about the next steps the department
should take. She justified the lack of wider public input this way: "Unfortunately, these town halls do turn into food fights."[35]

Theatrical metaphors and constraints on democracy could hardly be
more obvious. Staging public meetings creates the impression that democracy has been served. We particularly recall a public forum in which the
Arizona Board took public comments about the cutoff score for the state
graduation test that would determine who would be allowed to graduate.
Although we tried to show evidence of the disproportionate rates of minority students that were likely to fail such a cutoff, members of the state
board on their dais showed no interest in these statistics, talked among
themselves, and then rang a bell to indicate that our three minutes were up.
Later, in a series of closed-door sessions, they decided on a cutoff score of
75 percent because that would be credible to the business community.
Democratic participation is itself part of the spectacle.

Polling

The widespread use of opinion polls has largely displaced authentic participation in policy decisions and the allocation of educational values. Indeed, political actors look to the results of focus groups and polls to formulate a set of symbolic gestures. For example, politicians test the reactions of focus groups to labels and slogans such as "end social promotion," "make schools accountable," and "English for the children." Then pollsters are commissioned to gauge the public's reactions to those labels. Politicians then point to the results of polls that show the majority of the public favors "ending social promotion." The findings of polls thus provide a justification for such policies.

Politicians also use polling results to indicate what kinds of symbols best promote themselves. They then adopt hairstyles, hand gestures, and slogans that the polls show would be popular.[36] Susan Herbst, in her book *Beyond Numbered Voices*, emphasized the hypocritical use of polling results:

> Machiavelli believed that if a ruler was to gain control over the populace, he must seem humane to the masses regardless of his true feelings for them. . . . Superficial appearances matter most of all.[37]

Public opinion polls play key functions in political spectacle. A sense of seeking the common good has given way over time to estimating the sentiment of majorities that polls measure. Herbst wrote (echoing Edelman's category of symbolic vs. instrumental policy): "At times data is . . . instrumental, as when a legislator seeks to understand the mood of his or her district [on a policy issue]. . . . At other times, quantitative public opinion data are used as rhetorical weapons." Interest groups and political parties commission polls and then make public only the data that fit their interests, that is, to sell a particular person or program.

Herbst identified polls with instrumental rationality, a mode of thinking that equates technical procedures with truthful findings. Polls seem credible to people because they seem objective and technical—such is the magical force of numbers. Furthermore, few people, including journalists, question the numerical outcomes of polls, put them into context of larger social issues, or attempt to resolve differences in the findings of alternative polls.[38]

Herbst wrote that:

> By using numbers to describe the public mood, we have begun to alter the form of public expression itself. . . . Now that we can efficiently condense public sentiment into numerical symbols, public opinion has become a commodity: News organizations, politicians, pressure groups, and others with an interest in public opinion purchase data in hopes of gaining power, attention, and profit.[39]

Polls distance the public from authentic political action. Over time, as the extent of polling has increased, public cynicism toward government has also increased, along with general political alienation.

> [R]esponding to polls is a *reactive* form of political expression. . . . Because of its routinized procedures [polling] does not demand the same level of emotional (and physical) intensity as does [*sic*] striking, demonstrating, door-to-door canvassing or attending meetings.[40]

Since people answer the polling questions privately and anonymously, they can answer without fear of being held accountable for consistency over time or among issues. The respondent may speak without having any information or having engaged in thoughtful reflection and conversation about the topic. Since polling takes place privately, citizens lack the chance to discuss issues with others, which might cause them to learn more about the issues and perhaps modify them. Private polling tends to atomize the public, isolating them from one another and therefore disempowering them. It tends to diminish the kinds of grass roots collective action that requires social interaction among people.

Although the public often criticizes polls for reasons of sampling ("No one asked me!"), survey research methodologists have solved most problems of sampling. In that respect, at least, the technology works.[41] The greater problem in polling is the bias that comes from poor rates of response to pollsters. Even worse are problems introduced because polling questions are ambiguous, leading, and otherwise poorly stated. Differences in word choice can create vast differences in the numbers of people who endorse a policy or express their opinions. In an experiment conducted to test the effects of word choice on response patterns, a researcher asked about people's agreement with government programs to help people who were poor. When the question involved the term "welfare recipient," far fewer endorsed such programs. When the term "poor people" was used instead, many more survey respondents agreed with the policy.[42]

Education analyst Richard Rothstein wrote:

> Gallup polls now consistently find dissatisfaction with the nation's schools. But just as consistently, respondents report satisfaction with their own children's schools. . . . The Business Roundtable, an association of corporate officers, claimed that its polling showed the "strength of support" for ending social promotion. "Fully three-quarters supports requiring children to pass a reading and math test for promotion," the association announced. But its poll also found that most people thought grades and teacher evaluations were better guides to promotion than standardized tests. Large majorities were more broadly skeptical of standardized tests. . . . If popular opinion is not based on informed deliberation, the use of it by elites does not truly enhance democracy.[43]

When public opinion polls, whether conducted poorly or well, substitute for genuine democratic participation, you have a recipe for political spectacle. What is more, the illusion of democracy provides a cover for a few people backstage to negotiate real benefits for themselves.

Illusion of Rationality

Deborah Stone wrote that, policy analysts—caught in "the rationality project," would like to think that their concepts are above politics, but this is not possible. Instead, policy analysis is "itself a creature of politics; it is strategically crafted argument, designed to create ambiguities and paradoxes and to resolve them in a particular direction."[44] Edelman added, "any political analysis that encourages belief in a secure, rational, and cooperative world fails the test of conformity to experience and to the record of history."[45]

According to Edelman, "complete rationality in decision-making is never possible . . . because knowledge of consequences of any course of action is always fragmentary, because future values cannot be anticipated perfectly, and because only a few of the possible alternative courses of action ever come to mind."[46] In political acts, actors evoke symbols of rationality. They point to the results of public polls, census statistics, or declining test scores to justify actions they want to take on political grounds.

Actors in the political spectacle often use numbers and the results of polls and research studies to bolster their claims that they are acting rationally. But Stone pointed out that counting something always involves first making decisions about the category and its definition and boundaries. Someone must decide what characteristics can be counted as in or outside the category. We may use numbers (averages) to describe the academic achievement of children in large and small classes, but before we can count, we have to decide what "large" and "small" mean in this instance.

Counting the unemployed, the homeless, or the children who need special education requires first the linkages of particular characteristics of individual persons to the definition of the category. Do we exclude the hyperactive child (as federal rules for educating the handicapped once did but no longer do)? Do hyperactive children and children with attention deficit disorder share enough characteristics in common to justify lumping them together? Does Johnny have enough characteristics to justify including him in the count of learning disabled students?

Numbers are symbols. Counting entities requires prior categorization of them. The validity of arguments based on counting things depends on validity of categorizing them. No matter how perfectly the counting was done, no matter how sophisticated the statistics and measurement, assumptions about categorization rest on shaky foundations.

> Debating the size of a phenomenon is one of the most prominent forms of discourse in public policy. . . . [N]umbers are invoked to give an air of finality to each side's opinions . . . [but] every number is a political claim about "where to draw the line."[47]

George W. Bush believed that high stakes tests, by themselves, are enough to scare teachers and students into working harder. The policy required that all students take the TAAS. As the stakes of TAAS were raised, however, schools found ways to exempt more disabled and non-English-speaking children, thereby blurring the definition of "all children."

Many examples of flexible categories in policy analysis can be raised with respect to research and evaluation of policies. Even the well-respected STAR project failed to mention the status of non English-speaking students in its otherwise carefully crafted experiment. The category of "student," again apparently obvious, had ambiguous boundaries.[48]

However, we should not blame STAR because, as Stone argued about policy research, information is always incomplete and subject to interpretation and never definitive or above politics.

> But in politics, the important thing is what people make of such reports. People act on what they believe to be [true]. . . . Interpretations are more powerful than facts . . . and what we believe . . . depends on who tells us (the source) and how it is presented (the medium, the choice of language, the context [and] . . . the timing. . . . Because politics is driven by how people interpret information, much political activity is an effort to control interpretations.[49]

Nevertheless, numbers and the act of enumerating offer powerful mechanisms, according to Stone:

> [O]nce a phenomenon has been converted into quantifiable units, it can be added, multiplied, divided, or subtracted, even though these operations have little meaning in reality. Numbers provide the comforting illusion that incommensurables can be weighed against each other, because arithmetic always "works": arithmetic yields answers.[50]

And these powerful mechanisms convey power to those who work with them. To gather and maintain power, policy makers are often tempted to use them to serve special interests. Wrote Stone:

> Measures in the polis are not only strategically selected but strategically presented as well. Numbers never stand by themselves in policy debates; they are clothed in words and symbols and carried in narrative stories. . . . Numbers in policy debates cannot be understood without probing how they are produced by people. . . . Numbers are "thus artifacts of political life."[51]

Stone and Edelman cast doubt on the veracity of numbers and the attitude that counting is the highest form of rationality. Although rationality is an illusion, the public must believe in the rational and ethical underpinning of the action or else it will fail the test of credibility and authority. Thus do policy researchers become political actors or pawns of politicians by producing studies and statistics that appear objective and rational, a matter we take up again in Chapter Five.

In the rationality project, people are believed to be rational actors who make reasoned choices. But Stone points out that in the political world, actions come about for emotional reasons. Social reasons may govern who cooperates with and who fights with whom. Building coalitions, taking sides, and negotiating deals replace or stand equal to reason in explaining actions in the political spectacle.

The arguments above do not discount entirely the place of research in policy. Far from it. Properly interpreted, research studies can contribute to policy arguments. Moreover, for politicians and policy makers to ignore the research literature may also constitute irrationality. The attacks on "social promotion" in Texas and Chicago contradicted a substantial body of research that shows grade repeaters make less academic progress than if they had been promoted. Once retained in his grade, a student is far more likely to drop out of school than he would have been had he progressed through the grades in the normal pattern of age-to-grade.[52] Governor Bush also had to ignore that Texas schools already had one of the highest state percentages of grade repetition. So, there was little social promotion to end. Ending social promotion provides the image of tough-mindedness and rigor. Conveying the image overshadows in importance the rational consideration of policy means and ends.

Politicians in the political spectacle often appear irrational if one looks only at policies as means and substantive goals as ends. But adopting a different perspective shows that policy makers do operate rationally toward political goals, or dealing out benefits to cronies behind the scenes, who then reciprocate with campaign donations and the like. What could be more rational than that?

Disconnection of Means and Ends

One can distinguish instrumental from symbolic policies by judging whether their goals have credible relationship to the means provided or suggested to achieve them. Is there a technology or research evidence that connects programs to desired outcomes? Are teachers equipped to deliver the programs? Have enough time and material resources been provided to develop and implement them? Is there any provision for monitoring implementation or assessing effects? If not, one suspects a primarily symbolic policy. Symbolic policies reinforce the leadership image of those that propose them and instill quiescence among others—a dulling of critical response. Calling for a reduction in class size positions the political actor as a friend of education and defender of high achievement standards. The public is lulled into acquiescence: something seems to be done to address the problem that worried them. People in such a state are unlikely to ask about the potential side effects on teacher supply and classroom availability (or what children are most likely to be taught by uncertified teachers as a result).[53] The high costs of the program may make implementation prohibitive. The leader symbolically benefits while material benefits for children will be unequally distributed and largely out of sight—or entirely absent.

Even the notion of means and ends assumes a rationality in politics that is seldom present. Problems and courses of action (policy goals and policy instruments) are themselves social constructions. That is, some political actors view poverty as a problem to be solved, others as an inevitable part of the natural order and thus beyond the means of policy to remedy.

According to Edelman:

> The language that constructs a problem and provides an origin for it is also a rationale for vesting authority in people who claim some kind of competence. Willingness to suspend one's own critical judgment in favor of someone regarded as able to cope creates authority. . . . People with credentials accordingly have a vested interest in specific problems and in specific origins for them.[54]

Some teachers and parents define the presence of especially active and distractible children in elementary schools as a problem to be solved. But whose problem is it and who ought to address it? Attributing the problem to the child's brain chemistry suggests that medical doctors should control its solution. Defining the same problem as arising from the social environment implies that a psychologist or social worker is the right person to rectify it. The winning definition and attribution empowers certain groups and disempowers and silences the voices of others.

As for solutions, policy makers often construct mere gestures and feints. Edelman wrote that:

> The most common course of action is the enactment of a law that promises to solve or ameliorate the problem even if there is little likelihood it will accomplish its purpose. . . . Political maneuver thrives upon publicized actions that mean less than meets the eye.[55]

But even symbolic policies have effects, though they are not necessarily related to the problem they were set to solve. Edelman wrote:

> The construction of problems sometimes carries with it more far reaching perverse effects: it helps perpetuate or intensify the conditions that are defined as the problem, an outcome that typically stems from efforts to cope with a condition by changing the consciousness or the behavior of individuals while preserving the institutions that generate consciousness and behavior. . . . Im-

prisonment may help perpetuate crime by exposing prisoners to knowledge-able criminals who teach them techniques. It also eventually releases most pris-oners into a society from which they have become even more estranged than they were before their imprisonment and in which they lack resources to cope in any way other than renewed resort to crime.[56]

To illustrate, the high-stakes testing policy followed by Chicago Public Schools had the perverse effect of driving large numbers of low-achieving students out of school. This left them with no way to correct their poor liter-acy or improve their ability to get work. It also exposed them more to antiso-cial experiences and alienated them further from society. The policy failed (although it appeared to succeed if one looked narrowly enough) because it was directed at the visible *form* of the problem (low test scores) rather than to the underlying social conditions that gave rise both to the low test scores and to inadequate education in poor communities. A modern person looks back, bemused, at the practice in Victorian London of sending debtors to prison, thus preventing them from working to repay their debts. That policy punished them, yes, but it could not address the palpable problem. It seems irrational to us. Is driving poor students from school any different?

Distinction between Onstage Action and Backstage Action

Who reaps the benefits and who bears the burdens and costs of a policy? Of an education policy one ought to ask how it affects the resources and opportunities of students, educators, and the public as a whole; how it spreads the risks and cushions the blows that sometimes attend to policies and programs.

In the political spectacle there is a sharp distinction between those val-ues allocated to the general public and those values allocated to a favored few. Edelman believes that only a few members of society reap real bene-fits. These benefits include material profits—dollars and cents, contracts and tax abatements. But they also encompass opportunities for political office and administrative posts, such as ambassadorships. In addition, we would include real benefits to the status or public relations image of a per-son or organization (which then can be converted into material benefits). Finally we include benefits to special interest groups with particular ide-ologies and contacts with the politician. Benefits such as these are negoti-ated behind the scenes and out of sight. The concept of these "onstage" and "backstage" machinations originated in the work of Erving Goffman.[57]

Critic Frank Rich captured the distinction between onstage and backstage politics in the 2000 presidential campaign. For public consumption, the two parties engaged in skirmishes in the culture war over objectionable content in movies and music lyrics. Both parties made "phony threats against the en-tertainment industry." Meanwhile, offstage, neither party mentioned the pending merger of America Online and Time-Warner.

> Consumer advocates . . . believe that an unchecked AOL Time Warner may have enough technological and economic clout to dictate how Americans use the coming cable TV–Internet box (and what content they get at what price) . . . But even as Mr. Gore proposes government intervention . . . he offers nothing but dead silence about AOL Time Warner . . . which will have a far more lasting effect on child culture. . . . Media corporations . . . are seeking favors—big regulatory favors that increase their hold on our culture, airwaves and wallets . . . [and are] big contributors to both parties. Everyone is in the tank.[58]

For the spectators—the majority of the public, tangible benefits of a policy are beside the point. Instead, this part of society gets symbolic "benefits." Symbolic benefits are less than they seem. Symbolic language and ritual produce emotions in the general public, but little else.

Backstage, a few actors negotiate for themselves material benefits, using the informal language of barter, in contrast to the stylized, formal, abstract, ambiguous language characteristic of the performance onstage. The public can sometimes gain brief glimpses of insider bargaining.[59] Recall that at the Republican National Convention of 2000, the real negotiations over policy took place not on the convention floor or even in the platform committees, but at private parties. [60] Investigative reporters noted that open meetings consisted largely of pro forma votes based on decisions made earlier and in private. One television camera got as far a hotel room door where a party was going on and deals were being made, but reporters left meekly when party operatives slammed the door. The camera shot recalled the final scene in *The Godfather* in which Michael Corleone's aide closes the door to his wife, who nevertheless gets a glimpse of the lieutenants paying fealty to the new Don.

During the campaign for Republican presidential nomination in 2000 the *Arizona Republic* printed a story about candidate John McCain announcing his education platform. He intended to focus on providing access to the Internet for every school in the country. To compete in the New Economy, he claimed, students need appropriate technology. The need for Internet technology and his intention to meet that need were the symbols offered to the public. The photograph that ran with the news report showed McCain smiling up at a man bending over him, whispering in his ear. The smiling man was James O. Robbins, the CEO of Cox Communications, one of McCain's leading contributors.[61] The newspaper failed to mention that Cox Communications stood to reap substantial profits if McCain won the election and made good on his education policy—the corporation produces just the technology needed to implement it. The *New York Times* reprinted the photo without identifying the contributors.

Tangible benefits of educational policy sometimes accrue to entrepreneurs who identify potential profit centers, a topic we discuss in greater depth in Chapter Six. The tangible benefits contrast with the symbolic benefits available to the public. In January, 2001 William Bennett, the Secretary of Education during the Reagan administration, with several other prominent conservatives (all harsh critics of public schools), launched a new enterprise that offers online achievement tests to subscribers. The child takes the test, the score of the test is compared to the scores of children across the nation who have taken the same test. The company then provides lists of commercially available educational materials and learning games that purport to help the parents improve the child's performance. The owners of this business hope to tap the home school and charter school market as well as individual parents. A *New York Times* business writer called the venture:

> a fresh gusher in the for-profit education market. By some estimates, that market grew to $105 billion last year [2000]. . . . Profits from the education industry are "expected to reach $170 billion by 2005 . . .[62]

Extracting profits from education exemplifies material benefits for the few. Even the small subset of the public that is aware of the education industry probably approves of it as a part of the free market. Yet the industry pursues government policies to increase profits —through tax exemptions and the like—and the pursuit occurs completely out of public sight. Political spectacle is replete with ironies. Few public figures could match Bennett at the game of deploying symbols; for example, the images of the public schools in moral decay, in a slough of low expectations and performance, in constant danger from explosions of violence. On stage, political figures such as Bennett promote to the general public the symbolic benefits of "parent choice," of "core knowledge," and "accountability" through testing. Largely out of sight the same people line up tangible benefits for themselves and their allies.

Tangible benefits also accrue to individuals who seek to advance their careers. Some appointments also enhance the symbolic capital of the nominator. The notion of a token woman or a token minority appointment is well understood by the public and serves as a good example of political symbolism. After President Bush nominated Rodney Paige as his Secretary of Education, the *Houston Press* wrote as follows about the warm reception Paige received from Congress and the media, warmer, perhaps than his record might warrant.

> The Houston Independent School District suddenly became the best urban district in the nation, and the 67-year-old superintendent Paige the premier leader in public education.
>
> The storm over how former football coach Paige was elevated to the superintendency in 1994 has long since passed beyond the local media's memory. . . . But it is helpful to remember that he was an unpaid HISD board member who joined a coalition of white trustees. At the time, Paige . . . was a dean of education at troubled Texas Southern University and the founder of a

new business, the Houston Education Collegium. By accident or design, he then bootstrapped himself, with a little help from his colleagues, into what became a $260,000-a-year job as superintendent.

Paige provided an invaluable minority front for the campaign by the Houston business community to reform and decentralize the district . . . McAdams believes that most public education problems arise "because urban school districts are under direct democratic control." He bragged in his report that he and the other white trustees boosted Paige into the top HISD position as a front man for the business community's effort. . . .[63]

We have shown the components that make up political spectacle in the previous section and have sampled a few instances of how each of these components function. We believe that political spectacle is a condition of political life in a particular time and place and a reflection of the social order at that time and place.

The Place of Political Spectacle in the Social Order

Why is political spectacle so much a part of education policy in this era? How does it both reflect and create the conditions of educational practice? Political spectacle represents the cultural intersection of governance, the economy, and media. As cohesive as this pattern seems, the extent of political spectacle varies over time. Various patterns of relationships among these categories create more or less of the ingredients of political spectacle in different eras. [64] Ingredients that explain the extent of political spectacle involve the strength or weakness of democracy in a particular era, and the degree of economic equality that characterizes the society. John Judis wrote that participation is strong during strong democratic eras (such as the 1930s and 1960s). Citizens vote more often, most citizens participate in organizations—parties, unions, business associations—that compete for policy values (with government acting as referee among competing groups), and when disinterested and learned advisers provide information and guidance to government. There is a powerful sense of the common good. The public has the best chance of influencing policy formation and government generally.[65] Government power is held in check by a constitution and laws. Robert McChesney wrote that eras of strong democracy are those in which citizens enjoy individual rights and freedoms, including the right to vote in elections, but also are those in which public institutions exist that provide checks on the power, say, of capitalism or religion.[66]

In eras when democracy is strong and political participation is active and direct, the language of politics is the language of concrete phenomena. Citizens bid for honest allocation of values and costs, and officials operate more often in the open than backstage. Citizens have more access to information about how values get allocated and more chances to contest unfair or irrational actions by government.

In times of great economic inequality and low political participation, political language becomes more abstract and the allocation of real values occurs more often backstage. Ordinary people are distanced and alienated from government. Political language is more ambiguous and policies more often symbolic. The public cares less about issues than about the personalities and character of leaders and would-be leaders. Politics grow more adversarial, for the sake of the contest itself and to satisfy private individual interests. Rather than focusing on governance, newly elected officials focus on the next election. Their actions are crafted and staged to advance their political fortunes. Symbols dominate substance. Institutions that counterbalance social and political inequalities are themselves weakened or nonexistent. Despite sovereign rights, voting is more a ritual than a lever of democratic participation and power.

In our era, McChesney described corporatism (the control of government by large corporations) in the mass media:

> the rise of *neoliberalism* is a main factor that accounts for the corporate media boom . . . and the collapse of democratic political life. . . . [It] refers to the policies that maximize the role of markets and profit-making and minimize the role of nonmarket institutions. It is the deregulation provided by neoliberalism that has been instrumental in allowing the wealthy media corporations to grow and prosper as they have . . . [N]eoliberalism is a political theory; it posits that society works best when business runs things and there is as little possibility of government "interference" with business as possible . . . where the political sector controls little and debates even less. In such a world political apathy and indifference are quite a rational choice for the bulk of the citizenry.[67]

What explains the political spectacle and its variations across decades? To address causes, we must look beyond a reductionistic model of causality. It is too simple to picture a single arrow from some cause to some effect—something like the force that travels from one's arm to a hammer, and from the hammer to a nail.[68] Instead we draw on a holistic view that cultural theory provides.

Culture is what makes humankind human—that which is transmitted across generations rather than genetically inherited. A culture consists of learned life-ways or patterns that people have constructed out of a history of social interactions. Once constructed, the cultural patterns and relationships become a wellspring for actions that people of that culture take. Elements of culture encompass patterns of language, art, technology, media of communication, religion, familial relationships, labor, governance, social organization, ethnicity, education, economics, medicine, and mobility. These elements are linked together in a complex network or system in that the elements and their relationship to each other move, more or less in concert, over time. Sets of beliefs, knowledge, and ideology hold this structure together.

To ask a cultural question about a particular group at a particular time is to inquire about how, for example, that group has organized itself by social class or how it has organized itself by religion. Furthermore, one asks about the ways in which social divisions and religious groupings coincide, fit together, or operate independently of each other. Do most members of social class A also practice religion 1, while most members of social class B practice religion 2? Does one's language relate to the kind of occupation one can pursue? Can a person with little wealth choose a marital partner who has much wealth, or choose a partner at all? How do the types of occupation fit together with the divisions of people into ethnic groups? How does gender relate to knowledge of calculus? How are social class groupings related to access to media, to kinds of education, to government, to the economy? How does education relate to government (e.g., does the government interfere with education or leave it alone)? To gender (are all teachers male and do only females go to school)? Do people believe that one can harm one's mother by stepping on a crack? Which people have access to concrete sidewalks in the first place?

Yet culture, despite this picture of coherence and stability, changes over time and among social groups that exist within it. The cultural world that human groups create for themselves and transmit to the next generation can be amended, altered, revised, and remade by people acting in concert. Ongoing experiences in a classroom, for example, provide possibilities for such undoing of cultural patterns.

Culture is both reenacted and resisted. Cultural patterns are neither inevitable nor natural nor God-given. Individuals ignore laws; they work together with others to defy regulations, challenge dominant norms and values, and conspire to form competing social worlds with alternative beliefs and norms.

But even assuming the possibilities for variation and change, cultural patterns form a kind of template for actions of people—a matrix that organizes actions that connect, for example, the relationships between governance (hence politics and power distributions) to the economy (hence labor and distributions of wealth). These relationships are held together by a set of beliefs and ideologies. For example, in a culture in which the poor have no chance to influence government there may exist the common idea that "the natural aristocracy" ought to rule.

Ideological beliefs provide justifications for extant and developing structural relationships. The arts provide representations of the relationship. Communications media and schools provide the transmission. The cultural network organizes behavior. Behavior becomes habitual so that eventually no one questions the pattern that links the poorest children to the schools with the least resources provided by the government. People begin to take the pattern for granted, assuming perhaps that it is the natural order or the one that the free market has created, or the best one. Legislators organize their rule making as if the pattern were real. Courts organize their interpretation of rules as if the pattern were real. Police organize their enforcement of rules as if the pattern were real—as if no reasonable alternatives exist.

In contemporary American culture the linkages among governance, economics, and education are strong. To be favored by wealth is also to receive the best education and to exercise the most power over governance and policy; the converse is true as well. Being poor almost always means having the least educational opportunities and the least participation in governance. Communication media give the impression that this pattern is inevitable and impossible to remedy. Furthermore, as both Boorstin and Gabler (quoted earlier in the chapter) noted, media power forms a tight connection with both economic wealth and political power in contemporary America. Ideological justification for existing structural arrangements gets repeated so often that most people accept it and are socialized to it.

The education policies of an era express government actions toward schools. Education policy expresses the relationship of politics, economy, and the schools, wrapped in the ideology and beliefs about schools that are dominant in a particular time and place. In times of robust democracy, education policies are more likely to reflect tangible values for the public because more of the public participates in policy making over the most important issues of their children's lives in schools. In times of political spectacle, policies for the promotion of equalitarian, compensatory, and communitarian values are forsaken. Education policies in the political spectacle serve the special interests of the few (often policies that stratify and segregate) and hide behind a mask of common sense and the common good.

In the political spectacle, the actions of allocating values are hidden behind a curtain. Education policies link the state to the daily life of schools and what students experience directly. The curriculum as students experience it is, as Michael Apple and others have labeled it, the "hidden curriculum."

Hidden curriculum consists of the messages that schools convey to students, apart from reading, writing, and arithmetic—what people understand as the official curriculum. In the current era of standards and testing, the state attempts to prescribe a coherent curriculum, a curriculum that serves the interests of the economy and the state. The official curriculum creates and transmits knowledge; the hidden curriculum distributes it among segments of the school population. The messages of hidden curriculum involve norms such as order, punctuality, efficiency in getting work done and getting from place to place, the dominance of teachers and their agendas over students and students' agendas, as well as the distribution of authority and power in the institution. As well, students learn from such policies and practices that there is a common body of accomplishment that the state prescribes irrespective of individual students' (or teachers') creativity or interest. More problematic parts of hidden curriculum involve messages about students' capabilities and worth, what opportunities they have available to them and are worthy of, i.e., the proper place of students in school life and society generally. As a simple example, consider that when educators identify certain students as handicapped, they signal that individuals differ in their intrinsic capabilities and should be assigned different kinds of education. Different levels of results are therefore both expected and justified by different placements. The differential treatment reflects the social order outside the school, in that students with little wealth and of lower social class are also those sorted out and consigned to the lowest-quality of educational offerings and the least desirable labels. Because they receive the lowest quality schooling, they thereafter have the least chance to develop cultural capital in the form of official school knowledge as well as the implicit skills, values, norms, and the capacities to move successfully through the culture and economy. Sorting students into slots is rationalized both on psychological grounds ("students benefit most when instruction is tied to their particular abilities") and on the grounds of efficiency ("sorting students into groups allows the most efficient coverage of the official curriculum").[69] Ideological beliefs support the social order and convey in ambiguous language and narratives that students themselves are solely responsible for their success and failure and that they (and their parents) should be blamed for their failure or praised for their success. Such messages provide a kind of socialization whereby students internalize the beliefs the hidden curriculum promulgates.

Political spectacle provides a cover for the hidden curriculum. Schools may claim that they adhere to meritocratic principles when in fact they sort children into slots that reflect the place of each in a class system. Hidden curriculum reflects the larger social order but hides from an inattentive and passive audience both its process and effects. It is hidden by artful narrative, metaphors, and ambiguous images that conceal the distribution of real benefits and costs behind a curtain. Political spectacle thrives on apparent but false rationality and ritualistic but false democratic participation. It withers in an atmosphere of authentic democratic participation in politics and policy.

Hidden curriculum does not occur automatically or inevitably as the result of education policy. Educators must enact such ideologies in their practices. People have the agency to practice either inequality or equality.[70] Students have the agency to reject the hidden curriculum in the same ways that they reject the official curriculum. As Apple pointed out, a good deal of resistance goes on in schools, whereby students and teachers contest the messages they might otherwise accept passively. Schools, he emphasized, are places both of reproduction and production—creative opposition, concerted struggles against socialization, and contradictory beliefs that "see through to the heart of the unequal benefits of a society . . ." (p.14). Schools are the places where struggle over these contradictions takes place. Students may, for example, construct knowledge different from the official knowledge and use it in new ways. Teachers may recognize the built-in inequities and practice in ways to mitigate them. Teachers and parents may organize themselves politically to challenge what the hidden curriculum produces. When social inequities grow so massive that the ideology of efficiency reveals its contradictions, political pressure causes the government to step in to correct them.[71]

We have shown in this section that the political spectacle is a description of the state of political life in a particular era, and how political life forms an integrated whole with economics, communication, and language. In the next few chapters, we illustrate how particular cases of education policy can best be understood as instances of political spectacle.

Notes

1. Schneider and Ingram (1997), pp. 2–3.
2. See McDonnell and Elmore (1987); Stone (1997) for taxonomies of policy instruments.
3. Ball (1994).
4. Federal government attention was, however, directed at southern schools during the Reconstruction.
5. Heubert and Hauser (1998); Heubert (2002); McNeil and Valenzuela (1999).
6. Stone (1997), p. 9.
7. Stone (1997), p. 13.
8. Edelman (1988), p. 16.
9. Edelman (1985), p. 5.
10. Edelman (1985), p. 139.
11. Stotsky (1998). The rise in test scores may also have come about because students predicted to test poorly were systematically excluded from testing, and more in subsequent years than in the first year, thus making it seem as if the policy had been effective. Also see Haney (2000).
12. Edelman (1985); Kingdon (1995); Stone (1997).
13. National Commission on Excellence in Education (1983), p. 1.
14. Edelman (1988), p. 31.
15. Critics of public schools present evidence that is far from conclusive. Attempts to counter the picture of schools that "declining test scores" offers have earned Berliner and Biddle (1995) and others the label of "apologist for the educrats."
16. Edelman (1985), p. 124.
17. Edelman (1985), p. 81.
18. Edelman (1988), p. 39.
19. The debate between Nixon and Kennedy is widely understood to be a turning point in political history. Those people who heard the debate on radio were much more likely to tell pollsters that Nixon had won the debate. Those who had watched the debates on television were more likely to say that Kennedy won the debate. See Boorstin (1987).

20. Edelman (1988), p. 73.
21. Boorstin (1987), pp. 183–194.
22. Kakutani, (2000).
23. Stone (1997), pp. 152 ff.
24. Stone (1997), p. 158.
25. Edelman (1985), p. 98.
26. Rich (2000a). "Like a sports competition, the post election is not a fierce partisan civil war so much as a nearly substance-free battle over the single, nonideological issue of who will win. . . . Not a civil rights debate, or a prosecution of a war . . . or even the ascendency of liberalism or conservatism."
27. Ash (2000) added that old, white men dominated the post election campaign.
28. Boorstin (1987), pp. 11–12.
29. Boorstin (1987), p. 19.
30. James (2000).
31. Stone (1997), p. 139.
32. Gabler (1998), pp. 4–5.
33. Edelman refers to democratic participation and rationality as myths. We recognize that in the political spectacle, they are apt to be absent, though they exist as potentialities. Therefore we refer to them as illusions.
34. Edelman (1988), p. 97.
35. Kossan (2000).
36. The movement of both national parties to the political center may then result from both listening to the same polls.
37. Herbst (1993), p. 50.
38. McChesney (1999).
39. Herbst (1993), p. 153.
40. Herbst (1993), p. 156.
41. However some polls commissioned to push a particular interest may not use representative samples and should not be confused with polls conducted by legitimate organizations. Likewise, polls that invite television viewers to call in or Internet users to express their preferences can not be considered representative of the general population.
42. Herbst (1993), p. 123.
43. Rothstein (2000).
44. Stone (1997), p. 7.
45. Edelman (1988), p. 4.
46. Edelman (1988), p. 68.
47. Stone (1997), p. 167.
48. Finn and Achilles (1999); Ritter and Boruch (1999); Nye and Hedges (1999); Hanuschek (1999).
49. Stone (1997), p. 167.
50. Stone (1997), p. 176.
51. Stone (1997), pp. 185–186.
52. Grissom and Shepard (1989); Rumberger (1995); Heubert and Hauser (1998).
53. Fetler (1994).
54. Edelman (1988), pp. 20–21.
55. Edelman (1988), p. 25.
56. Edelman (1988), p. 25.
57. Goffman (1959). Also see Hilgartner (2000) for an analysis of how research studies and scientific advice are framed in such a way as to gain authority while preserving secrecy and privilege.
58. Rich (2000b).
59. McChesney (1999).
60. A *New York Times* editorial on 8/6/00 argued that "there were two parallel conventions in Philadelphia . . . one a televised coronation . . . the other an endless parade of off-camera fund-raising events in hotel suites, private clubs, and restaurants. . . . In these genteel settings . . . corporations and wealthy individuals unloaded millions of dollars in an effort to buy influence with a Bush-Cheney administration. . . . The convention hall was full of talk about political morality . . . but like so much else at this convention, there was a big gap be-

tween words and reality, and while the words promised reform, the reality was the spectacle of huge sums of money changing hands." Soft-Money Conventions (2000).

61. Barker (1999).
62. Steinberg (2001).
63. Fleck (2001). Houston's apparent success was called into question when it was revealed that the district recorded drop-outs as transfers.
64. Judis (2000) Judis identified two other eras besides our own when political spectacle was apparent: the 1880s and the 1920s.
65. Judis (2000).
66. "When I talk about 'democratizing' our society, I mean that we should create mechanisms that make the rule of the many possible [which] means . . . reducing social inequality and establishing a media system that serves the entire population and that promotes democratic rule" (McChesney, 1999), p. 5.
67. "Neoliberalism is associated with the rise of Reagan and Thatcher . . . [but its elements go back much further]. James Madison argued that the goal of government must be 'to protect the minority of the opulent against the majority" (McChesney, 1999), p. 6.
68. A Marxist analysis would find a pattern in which economic class determines language, culture, and educational divisions of society.
69. The book *The Bell Curve* by Herrnstein and Murray (1994) lays out these arguments in the most straightforward ways.
70. "An advanced corporate economy requires the production of high levels of technical knowledge to keep the economic apparatus running effectively . . . what is actually required is not the widespread distribution of this high status knowledge to the populace in general. . . . Thus, certain low levels of achievement on the part of 'minority' group students, children of the poor, and so on can be tolerated. It is less consequential to the economy than is the generation of the knowledge itself" (Apple, 1982), p. 46.
71. Apple (1988).

CHAPTER 2

Testing the Theory
in Testing Policy

God hath numbered thy kingdom;
Thou art weighed in the balance and art found wanting.
The Book of Daniel, V, 26 & 27

And all this writing on the wall
Oh I can read between the lines
Dire Straits, "Hand in Hand," *Making Movies*

TESTING POLITICS (A VIGNETTE)

March 25, 1996—this is the day for the Arizona Board of Education to approve, or not, the Arizona Standards for Reading, Writing, and Math. We are here to witness.

Dignified and formal, the members of the Board emerge from their private chambers, stifle their whispers and chuckles, and seat themselves in their high-back leather chairs. They are arranged behind a polished dark walnut desk, slightly concave around them as if to separate themselves from the spectators, maybe even to protect them from us. Imagine the Supreme Court, minus the robes. The ritual attracts our eyes to them, but their gaze aims for the middle distance, somewhere just above our heads. Occasionally they speak, sotto voce, to each other or to the staff that scurries around, getting them pitchers of water or official-looking papers, or fiddling with the microphones and tape recorders. They assume the anonymous authority of any group of worthies on a raised dais anywhere in the Western World.

You have to know the characters, though, to make sense of the play. Lisa Graham Keegan fills the lead role. It's hard to take our eyes off her. As a legislator she earned the tag "Voucher Queen." Now she occupies the second-highest elected office in Arizona as the Superintendent of Public Instruction.

43

Newspapers and magazines have often portrayed her as the darling of the right wing of the national Republican party. It was Keegan who, immediately after taking office, had dismantled the assessment policy of her predecessor, Diane Bishop, and started the ball rolling toward today's meeting. Make no mistake: This is Keegan's meeting, just as the State Standards and the promised Arizona Instrument to Measure Standards are her productions.

The *Arizona Republic* refers to Keegan as Governor Symington's chief rival to be the Republican nominee in the next gubernatorial election. And it was Keegan who called for the resignation of Symington because of his recent indictments in Federal court for financial misdeeds. (Symington fought back by proposing the elimination of the Department of Education, Keegan's current theater of operations.)

There is Janet Martin, who runs a back-to-the-basics charter school. She is so "hooked on phonics" that she held the Reading Standards hostage for nearly a year until they included systematic phonics instruction all the way to eighth grade. It was Martin who made *ex parte* telephone calls to the test companies who were bidding for contracts to do the assessments, ordering them to include phonics at every grade level. It was Martin who demanded that the state decertify any teacher preparation program that refused to "explicitly" train prospective teachers in "explicit" phonics. The progressive educators sitting around me in the audience believe she is the enemy.

There is Kenneth Bennett, whom businessman Symington had appointed to the Board to represent business interests. It was Bennett who had admitted without apparent shame that, when the appointments were made to the committees to write the standards, no curriculum experts had been included: "We don't want to know what they know."

There is the usually feisty superintendent of a largely Hispanic district, whom many in the audience hope would be the voice for social justice. (But alas, no one assumes that role.) Several other players occupy seats on the Board, but play second fiddle to the central characters.

I should say something about the audience. We sit in hard chairs in the drab boardroom. We include educators (of course, only district administrators rather than classroom teachers can get away from the schools during the weekday), many of the people who worked on writing and refining the standards, a few odd representatives of testing corporations (the ones in expensive suits), and a few policy observers like ourselves. A microphone is set up for spectators to comment on the proceedings.

In the seat next to mine, a teacher, who must have requested personal leave to attend this meeting, seems to be reviewing her talking points, tailoring them to the three minutes maximum that the Board allows each speaker.

The Board's agenda calls for debate over the proposed standards in math, reading, and writing. Then the Board will vote on whether to authorize the standards. Since several of the Board members themselves have participated on the committees (a direct involvement that was unprecedented), everyone expects that the approval will be routine.

But "routine" is not what you would call the last tumultuous year. Keegan had heeded the advice of her corporate partners and consultants from conservative think tanks to kill the performance test of her predecessor and construct new achievement standards and tests. She expected that the task could be completed in a few weeks and could be done by parents, citizens, students, and a few educators—no experts needed. Corporate partners and think tank representatives were assigned to "facilitate" the work of the committees and report back the results. The driving buzz words were almost all straight out of the corporate world: quality standards, accountability for products, performance standards, inducements, standardization of curriculum, frequent testing (quality control). The Department of Education had appointed members of the committee that represented Keegan's political constituency. Her idea was that standards should be something every parent could understand and for which parents could hold schools accountable. Neither the initial composition of the committees nor the instructions provided to them allowed much room for educational progressivism. Progressive philosophy had dominated the discourse (if not always the reality) during the previous assessment policy, under the previous Secretary.

My neighbor is muttering. "Where's the conceptual stuff? Where's the authentic stuff?"

You can't blame her. In the official talk, you can't find much in the Standards that suggests solving novel problems, content integration, authentic reading and writing, or performance assessment. And controversy is all you hear about teaching and testing students whose first language isn't English.

However, a group of progressive educators had managed to resist and had waged a quiet battle to be included in the committees writing and revising the standards. Many of them are sitting around me in today's meeting. The ones I know seem satisfied that many of their concerns had been fought out in the committees, which slowed down the process but resulted in a more eclectic set of documents. Even Keegan, who rejected everything that progressivism stands for, eventually agreed to the more balanced approach.

As I say, we expect the meeting to go smoothly.

Suddenly, we become conscious of somewhat noisy group approaching from the back of the room. It is the Governor's entourage, his policy staff (including Diane Bishop, who recently switched from Democrat to Republican and from state superintendent to governor's advisor), reporters, his assistants passing out copies of a press release with his prepared remarks, and Symington himself in the lead. You can see the shock on the faces of the Board members. They had not expected the governor today.

Symington asks permission to address the Board. He reads from his release as we follow along.

(He would not, as it turns out, abide by the three-minute limit, I should warn you now.)

> I have been following the effort by the board and Lisa Graham Keegan to develop curriculum standards for Arizona's public schools. I support the concept, but I am concerned about the direction the board may be taking. In my travels around the state and discussions with concerned parents, the most pressing question they have is this: What are you teaching my children? This exercise of developing Standards gives us a chance to consider that question.

(Many people probably hadn't realized that Symington had taken the slightest interest in the standard-setting process.) He continues:

> In education, we have been making the same mistake humanity always makes again and again. We have casually cast aside the settled and true in favor of the trendy and allegedly exciting. Most of the social and academic "innovations" the so-called professional educators have brought to our classrooms are wasteful at best and insidious at worst. I stopped by today because some of this reckless drift toward fads and foolishness is evident in the standards currently under consideration. The reading standards, for instance, mention nothing about phonics for primary school students, nor say, great works of literature for those in high school. They do, however, insist that our students learn to "use consumer information for making decisions," and to "interpret visual clues in cartoons." The mathematics standards state that students should be able to "explore, model, and describe patterns and functions involving numbers, shapes, data, and graphs, and use simulations to estimate probabilities." Educational concepts more familiar to most of us, such as multiplication and division, are unmentioned.
>
> These standards ask students to "understand the nature, distribution, and migration of human population on Earth's surface" which causes me to wonder what other planet's surface human populations might be migrating on. The geography standards require nothing by way [of] identifying the nations of the world on a map, their capitals, or their core exports.
>
> There are only so many hours in a school day and so many days in a school year. The claim of government schools on the time of young people is necessarily limited. When that time is spent on "dance styles," or for another example, "participation in multicultural physical activities," it is not spent memorizing rules of grammar, diagramming sentences or learning to use mathematics in a way that teaches reasoning skills. It is not spent learning the geographical history of the world or the development of Western Civilization. It is not spent studying an essential work of literature that adds to a child's understanding of human nature or moral precepts.

(My neighbor shakes her head. Symington has mistakenly thought that the draft standards had neglected facts and grammar. As he continues his calumny, she continues to wince.)

> The central purposes and elements of a quality education are unchanging. We jeopardize our future and that of our children by substituting fads and jargon for bedrock educational concepts. It is parents who always have and always will be most important to children's education. As I read these proposed standards, I wonder how we can keep parents involved in the education of their children. If education is re-defined in a lot of pointy-headed jargon that only an elitist core of "professionals" could ever understand, we will freeze parents out of the process.
>
> The public education system spends over $3.5 billion taxpayer dollars annually, with absolutely no accountability for results.

("No accountability? Arizona students are the most tested in the country," my neighbor whispers to me. And by now, the others in the audience are buzzing, arguing with each other, trying to piece together some sense from his remarks.)

> We have a school report card that is virtually toothless because we have no independent, uniform testing system in place to evaluate our student's progress. We must restore the Iowa Test of Basic Skills of every student, every year in grades 3 through 12 immediately; we cannot wait two or more years for the Department of Education to revise the state testing program. We must set high graduation standards for all students. No, not all students will shine in class, but all should graduate only after demonstrating a grasp of basic things like reading, writing, mathematics, and history.

Having dropped this bomb, Symington leaves the room to address the media in the hall. Before taking a break, Keegan defends her standards and addresses some factual errors in Symington's critique. But shocked as they are, everyone—even Keegan herself—notices that a policy event has been transformed into a political maneuver. The campaign for the governorship has opened right in front of our eyes. The angry and frustrated spectators spill into the hall. The progressives realize that months of work to keep a hold on curriculum and assessment policies have come to nothing. They had envisioned a more-or-less rational and democratic participation. They were wrong.

Assessment Policy and Political Spectacle[1]

Assessment policy epitomizes the political spectacle. The most common reform in American schools since about 1985[2] is the imposition of academic standards and high-stakes tests as a way to make schools "accountable." To most people, accountability means testing.

In the above vignette, one can recognize elements of political spectacle theory that we catalogued in Chapter One: the symbolic and ambiguous language, the casting of leaders, heroes, and villains, and the sheer theatricality that characterized assessment policy in Arizona. And although Arizona's politics are in some ways especially spectacular, the state is far from alone, as we will show later in the chapter. Where policy goes, politics follow.

Accountability is a concept that glosses political and institutional arrangements and exchanges. One person is said to be accountable to another person or entity by virtue of the roles each plays in an institution or polity; accountable for certain actions or accomplishments; accountable as demonstrated by some indicator or measure. The indicator provides information such as a school's test scores or frequency counts of goals attained.

Tests have other functions besides demonstrating accountability. A state may use tests to provide information to show, for example, whether test scores are going up or down with the passage of time. A state may use tests as a lever to reform and improve schools. A state may use tests to enforce a policy—that is the accountability function. Sometimes a state tries to use the same test to serve more than one of these functions.[3] And although the state may pursue multiple functions in its assessment policy, many contradictions threaten the credibility of such a strategy.

Why the contradiction? To choose a test as a lever for accountability or reform, a state dips into two different realms of discourse and practice—the political and the psychometric. Psychometrics (the science of measurement) emphasizes rational and empirical standards for the use of tests.[4] The profession of psychometrics demands that a test must be reliable and valid. For example, if a state uses a test to determine which students can graduate and which cannot, then the state must present research that shows that incompetent students score low on the state test and competent students score high. A cutoff score must accurately divide competent from incompetent students, based on collateral evidence such as alternative tests or employee or college evaluations. Psychometricians practice technical rationality.

How does technical rationality work? Picture some psychometricians gathered around a table to consider whether a state test is reliable and valid. Their conversation is rational, their reasoning based on empirical evidence. Theirs is a world where technical expertise matters, where professional and disciplinary knowledge sway the outcome of deliberation. They calmly discuss whether the pattern of correlation on their computer printouts warrants their endorsement of the test's validity. They refer to professional standards and to peer review of their empirical findings. Such work takes time, and they are willing to proceed with care and deliberation and a concern for fairness. They weigh the possible costs and benefits of their actions.

When the state uses tests to enforce accountability or encourage school reform, issues of accountability clash with issues of validity and policy makers clash with testing experts. In a political arena, policy makers think of experts as just one more interest group. They may select psychometric experts for help with assessments, but they want them to reinforce a policy aim and message, rather than to engage in open-ended inquiry. The very fact of appointing an expert functions as a symbol of rationality, whether or not the state pays attention to the substance of the expert's report. That a policy maker fails to listen to psychometricians should surprise no one. Policy in the political spectacle is quite immune to demands for professional standards and technical rationality.

Those who are most concerned about assessment policy live in the polis or political community.[5] Picture the polis. The actors are engaged in conflict with each other over the distribution of power. They negotiate among interest groups, build alliances, employ tactics, construct and deploy symbols.[6] Their world comprises advocates, adversaries, competition, and rhetoric, shifting goals and backstage deals.

How does this work? Imagine high-stakes testing policy in the polis. In a backroom some people whisper in each other's ears or talk on cell phones to their constituents or passionately bang their fists on the table as they discuss the failure of schools and how those failures hurt the local economy. The mayor hires a Chief Education Officer and charges him to improve the school or else. Over time, power shifts in the district from elected school site councils and the school board to the CEO and his advisory board. Deciding that teachers have too much autonomy and not enough energy or ability, the CEO decides to use a test to get schools under control (any halfway credible test will serve the purpose, provided it does not cost too much). The publisher of the test also happens to sell the texts and work sheets that help teachers prepare their students to pass the test. The CEO hires a public relations consultant who calls a press conference to announce that principals' jobs will forthwith be determined by their schools' average test scores. Students will have to attain a certain score (the cutoff score to be the subject of political negotiations) on the test to graduate from high school. The whole program goes into effect the next month to capitalize on a window of political opportunity. The CEO may call in some testing experts, but might not follow their advice if it conflicts with political goals. As a testing publisher related, "Reliability and validity are just words to policymakers."

To call for accountability is to assert a political right—to demand that a particular individual or institution assume some responsibility and demonstrate it in a certain form.[7] To call for educational accountability is also to express dissatisfaction with the status of public schools or who is believed to control them. *A Nation at Risk*[8] expressed enough discontent with schools to set a plethora of state assessment policies on their trajectories. And despite the debate about whether the discontent was warranted, no one can doubt the influence of this report. Not only did most state governments adopt its recommendations, but the Federal education policy of at least three presidents has promoted national standards and tests. The message of that document (and many that followed) was that public schools were failing to address and meet ambitious academic standards, and such failure threatens American economic competitiveness. The report recommended that governments assume responsibility. State and Federal governments should establish high academic standards and mandate testing programs to make schools accountable.

Although states might have introduced alternative policies to reform schools (e.g., equalization of financial resources across schools, professional development to revitalize the professional workforce, lower class size, or universal preschool), they chose standards and achievement tests as the principal mechanisms to make schools accountable for results. Since they assumed that people respond only to incentives and threats of punishment, they attached consequences to the test scores.[9]

In the polis, tests are useful policy instruments because they are cheaper and quicker than alternative reforms such as reeducating teachers or reducing class size. Tests provide standardization and bureaucratic control over teaching and learning. Furthermore, politicians incline toward tests because opinion polls show that the general public believes schools and students should be accountable for outcomes, as measured by tests and enforced by sanctions.[10]

Low test scores trigger consequences such as the following: A state ties teachers' pay increases to the average of their students' test scores. A district ranks schools and teachers by the average of their students' test scores. A district bases pay raises on the average gains students make between September and May. A state institutes a rating system that will assign "stars" to schools (as is done in restaurant reviews). The state distributes incentive payments based on whether the schools exceeded academic expectations, or whether the schools raised scores from one year to the next. The state assumes control over the personnel and operations of schools that fail to make progress. A district determines students' graduation based on whether they attain a certain score on an achievement test. These and more have been designed to raise academic standards, make schools' curricula coherent and standard, and make schools accountable.

By the year 2000 only one state had failed to enact academic standards and one other still lacked tests to measure its standards. About half the states had attached rewards or penalties to the scores of schools.[11] By 2002, the federal government had enveloped the states' assessment policies in the No Child Left Behind act. But long before that time, Arizona was part of the movement to reform schools through standards and assessments, and at one time was said to lead it. In the early 1990s the state assessment policy was referred to as ASAP, the Arizona Student Assessment Program. ASAP was intended to provide accountability but also to raise achievement and lead teachers toward a new form of pedagogy. By late in the decade, however, ASAP was proclaimed a failure, and Arizona assessment policy went through a radical revision, led by a new state superintendent. Only a political analysis could explain how and why this happened.

Arizona's Assessment Policy as a Case of Political Spectacle

ASAP History

All stories begin at arbitrary points. We picked 1983 because, before *A Nation at Risk*,[12] education policy was more a local than a state or federal concern. True, some politics characterized educational policy before that time. In Arizona, the legislature derived its authority for mandating assessment in 1971 and delegated to the Arizona Board of Education (ABOE) the authority to determine who, what, when and how. The details of who must be tested—on what tests and schedules, and for what purposes the scores would be used—varied somewhat over the years. Prior to ASAP, the ABOE decreed that all Arizona students take a norm-referenced test, the Iowa Test of Basic Skills (ITBS). The Arizona Department of Education (ADE) released data, and the newspapers regularly computed and published the ranking of schools. Many policy makers assumed that publishing schools' results by grade level would make educators work more diligently on the academic curriculum covered by the standardized achievement tests. Besides the ITBS, the state mandated that each district administer tests of basic skills to all students. By 1987, Arizona students experienced one of the highest test burdens in the nation.

Educators chafed over the amount of testing. In 1987, the Board of Education appointed representative groups of educators and content specialists to write content frameworks, hold hearings across the state, and revise the frameworks accordingly. Staff of the Arizona Department of Education guided the work of these committees toward the newly emerging principles of constructivism and progressivism. Almost a decade later, an influential staff member reflected on their work:

> The Language Arts Essential Skills looked at what people were learning about from a constructivist philosophy of education. It looked at what the writing teachers were saying and the writing professors, writing research was saying about writing as a process. It looked at new ways of reading instruction, somewhat whole-language based or literature, and it looked at integrating the language arts so that you didn't teach reading separately from writing.

Standardized testing stood in the way of curricular reform. Said a progressive reformer:

> We had these curriculum frameworks that were representing the latest and the best thinking in the content areas, and those were mirroring what we know about the way people learn. And that the dramatic difference between what we said we wanted and what the tests were measuring, and then the new ideas circulating in the testing circles about "what you test is what you get." You can't test writing as a process with a multiple-choice test.

C. Diane Bishop, an influential member of the ABOE in the late eighties, was elected state Superintendent and head of ADE in 1991. Then a Democrat, she had taught high school mathematics and thus "understood higher-level thinking in mathematics." Bishop's ideas found support among the curriculum specialists at ADE, the Arizona English Teachers Association, the Arizona Education Association, local affiliates of the National Council of Teachers of Mathematics, the Center for Establishing Dialogue in Education, and local university professors. ADE commissioned two research studies to further ADE's agenda. One study found that the ITBS only tested 26 percent of the state's goals. Another survey found that most educators disputed the validity of the state norm-referenced tests, believed that they spent too much time preparing students for tests, and believed that the tests had deleterious effects on students, teachers, and the curriculum. Coalitions formed among educators and some state reformers to try to eliminate the ITBS and institute more student- and teacher-centered assessment. These progressive educators believed that reforms were impossible given the stakes attached to a multiple-choice test. Many also believed that the ITBS discriminated against children just learning English.

The building momentum for reform of assessment policy masked differences between two groups: the progressives camp and the high-stakes accountability camp. The legislature reflected the latter. One legislator said of ASAP:

> This assessment is an accountability measure, because we want those Essential Skills taught. And the only way we know that it's going to be done is if you drop in and take an assessment of that. . . because there really have been no accountability measures up until now. . . . It was a matter of "here we have the Essential Skills" and I think there was ample evidence that many school districts weren't focusing on those Essential Skills. I think that was a driving force to put this all under a legislative piece and put a little teeth into this thing.

Few legislators involved in the birth of ASAP had concern for, or understanding of, those principles of schooling that so motivated the policy actors at ADE and in the professional associations. Nevertheless, the actors (legislators, ADE, Superintendent, and Board of Education) came together in the Goals for Educational Excellence project to develop new assessment policy and write enabling legislation. The report concentrated on accountability principles more than reform ideals. For example, "The keys to the future were . . . a combination of basic skills—communication and computation—education must emphasize measurement of results to be accountable for accomplishing its goals."

ADE discourse, which is all most educators had access to, soft-pedaled accountability and emphasized progressive reform through assessment. Three reform-minded officials at ADE set the tone. They envisioned classrooms where instruction could be more holistic, thematic than it was and where teachers could encourage students to be actively engaged and able to make connections, solve complex problems, and communicate their thoughts. They believed that assessment must be authentic and integrated with instruction, subjects integrated with each other around interesting, real-life problems, that teachers should be co-learners, coaches, collaborators, facilitators of learning, and actors rather than targets of curricular reform, that instruction should follow new research on cognition, multiple intelligence, constructivist learning theory and the like. Against this reform coalition, however, was a legislature more interested in holding teachers' "feet to the fire" than in changing the way they taught. As the makeup of the legislature grew more conservative and Republican, legislators complained more often about the "subjective" scoring of the performance tests and about the "anti-business and environmental activist attitudes" that had crept into the content of the tests.

About three years into ASAP, the three key reformers left the department, each pursuing different career opportunities. The staff which remained proved to be less thoroughly grounded in progressive education, more committed to traditional teaching and testing, and hence less effective in maintaining that course. While the ASAP Unit changed faces and voices, the Assessment Unit stayed the same. The accountability forces within the department had begun to dominate the discourse.

To get the bill passed, the Goals for Educational Excellence panel had promised the legislature that the new program would cost no more than the previous testing program. Now ADE was in a bind, able to mandate assessment policy but powerless to fund statewide training of teachers to adapt to it. Some wealthy districts with philosophies consistent with ASAP did invest considerable resources in local capacity development, but these districts were in the minority. In a state with considerable disparity in taxing ability, the already rich and poor districts reproduced disparities in staff development for ASAP as well. As an ADE official reported later, the department chose to underplay the technical and administrative problems that had surfaced along with capacity building needs:

> We should have gone back to [the Legislature] and said, "we're going to need some more training money, we need more field test money." The Legislature was saying let's get going, let's get going. At that point what should have happened is we should have said, we need two more years. We need another statewide pilot, we need more of the psychometric people to make sure the thing is

ready to go, and we need additional district training budgets so when they come on line with this they could train their teachers. We had underestimated the profound training effects that this would have, clearly underestimated what it would be.

Because it was a political project, ASAP had limited the amount of time provided to develop the capacities of teachers and schools or to develop sound psychometric instruments. As a result of political pressure, it was necessary for the ADE and the test publisher to produce the various performance test forms in weeks rather than years. Form D-1 (the first integrated state performance test) was commissioned and administered before all the psychometric and administrative kinks of Form A (the preliminary version that the districts administered) were worked out. D-2 (the second integrated state performance test) was commissioned and administered before the problems of D-1 were corrected or even known. Nor was there an equating study to show whether Form D could function as an "audit" of Form A.

An ADE official would later recall that the development of D "was done in a fairly shabby way, without adequate field testing." An ADE insider at the time agreed:

> Now, the problem there was that the first Form D was used, we tried it out, we reported the results, but Riverside ran a concurrent field test on the form D. The concurrent form D-1 field test was returned to the department in late '93, or the fall of '93 sometime. And what it said is that the D form didn't match the A form well enough. But, for whatever reason, the staff of the Department kind of took that report and put it on the shelf. Politically, the thing was developing its own momentum down there. Nobody wanted to stop the process, nobody wanted to pull it back. Riverside staff was saying you've got to stop this because the D now needs to be revised and re-field tested to be sure that it matches the A that it's auditing. Wasn't done. [The report] was shelved.

In June of 1993, ADE released the initial results of ASAP Form D-1. The newspapers published the results by school and grade level and ranked them in much the same manner as they had always reported results of state standardized tests. Headlines in the *Arizona Daily Star* read, "Tests say schools are failing." The Superintendent called the results disturbing and distressing, but said nothing to indicate that technical problems (associated with any test undergoing its maiden voyage) likely explained the scores. She criticized schools and teachers for not adapting fast enough and for failing to teach "the way kids learn." Educators were shocked and dismayed at ADE and media reaction. Many had believed that the state had intended ASAP to leverage changes, not to embarrass and punish them. The state had used the results of standardized tests that way. ASAP was supposed to be different.

But time and political capital had begun to run out for the reform faction in ADE. The State Board of Education, prompted by key legislators, demanded action. They wanted to use ASAP scores to determine high school graduation.

To that end the Board appointed the Task Force on Graduation Standards to make recommendations about how to turn ASAP into a graduation test and to set "proficiency levels," that is, the cutoff scores for dividing those who graduate and those who do not. The Task Force recommended (and the Board adopted) the following level of proficiency for graduation: "A student shall demonstrate competency in reading, writing, mathematics, social studies and science . . . by attaining a score of 3 or 4 on each question or item of each Form A assessment [of ASAP] . . . scored with the corresponding Essential Skills [ASAP] generic rubric. . . ." The Task Force had met a number of times, and taken the twelfth grade Form A, and used the generic rubrics to score their own responses.

However, the Task Force failed to examine technical data available on Form A (for example, standard errors around cut scores), failed to consider the consequences—that is, how many students would likely fail if the chosen proficiency levels were enacted. It failed to consult experts on established procedures for setting cut-scores. It ignored the Riverside technical report, which had warned that Form A was too unreliable to determine the fate of individual students. A member of the Task Force later described its decision-making. They considered the rubric scores in terms of percentages, as if the assessment was like a competency measure. That is, since four was the highest score on the rubric, and since 3 out of 4 was close to 75 percent correct, and since the public would judge any mastery level less than 75 percent as too lenient, therefore, a 3 would be the cutoff between mastery and non-mastery, between graduation and non-graduation. Such logic would undoubtedly amuse most psychometricians but strike most politicians as appropriate.

Her ear now tuned to the legislature, Bishop paid no attention to the technical recommendations of Riverside and continued in the direction of making ASAP into a high-stakes graduation test. ADE could have commissioned a serious evaluation or independent analysis of ASAP (some states have done this) but it chose not to do so. And by then reports came from the field that ASAP had serious implementation problems, having to do with glitches in administration, the burden of purchasing test materials, poor wording of test questions insufficient time limits, inadequately prepared scorers, vague scoring rubrics, and lack of time and training. If rationality had been less of an illusion (that is, if ASAP had not by then have been swamped in the political spectacle), the state could have slowed down, analyzed and corrected these problems, and quieted the growing resistance from educators.

However, Bishop and ADE staff reacted defensively to any criticism of ASAP. At a meeting of educators sponsored by ADE and AEA, she warned that if teachers complained too much, the conservative policy actors would likely move to reinstate universal standardized testing. Since educators dreaded that possibility, they quieted their resistance, but as a result, open debate over assessment policy never happened.

1994 Elections

In a move that took everyone by surprise, Bishop bolted the Democratic Party in 1994 and campaigned for Governor Symington's reelection and supported his voucher policy. After his election, he created a position of education advisor and appointed Bishop to it. Her voice in matters of school policy was thereafter muted.

Taking Bishop's place, Lisa Graham Keegan, the successful candidate for state superintendent, was a bright, attractive, articulate woman in her thirties, a Stanford-educated speech therapist. Newspapers referred to her as the "Voucher Queen" during her two highly visible terms as state legislator.[13] They also wrote of her as the strongest candidate for governor in 1998, a designation that later turned out to prove significant.

Keegan's Agenda

As a political conservative, Keegan supported policies of less government, less regulation, greater efficiency, decentralization, and choice. As for her perspective on assessment policy, in public Keegan supported the ASAP "process." Privately, to her conservative supporters, she promised to return to standardized tests. Before audiences of teachers' organizations and school advocates, she used the inclusive pronouns "we" and "us". She shared the concerns of her corporate supporters, however, that the schools were underachieving, bureaucratic, and failing to produce graduates that could plug into jobs in the corporate world. According to the corporate view, the problem with public schools was a lack of accountability.

Very quickly, Keegan gained visibility in educational policy in the national arena as well as the state. On the national scene, she broke ranks with the Council of Chief State School Officers, the organization of most state superintendents, to form a more conservative group. In an *Education Week* article,[14] she expressed her opposition to federal assessment policy (Goals 2000) and her skepticism about the quality of public schools:

> We believe that true education reforms are those that center on the needs and choices of families, empower parents and teachers to work in concert to chart the course of a child's education, increase accountability in America's schools, and restore local control over school policies and practices. While all of that separates us from the education establishment, we believe it unites us with parents and the vast majority of American teachers and school administrators

who share our exasperation with the nationalized business-as-usual approach to reform, and our fear that unless we act quickly and boldly to restore excellence to all schools our nation at risk will become a nation of ruin. . . . Too many [children] are stuck in failing schools. We haven't lost our zeal to free them. . . .[15]

One month after taking office in January 1995, Keegan announced the reorganization of ADE. Various informants used words such as "purge," "hit list," and "litmus test," to describe changes in the department.

They came in and they decimated the department, is what they did. Anybody that wasn't on permanent status was history—gone. That was 90-something people, as I understood, overnight. Anybody with a doctorate—gone, or moved to a marginal position.

On January 25, 1995, Keegan issued a press release announcing the suspension of ASAP "for one year because of concerns about whether it accurately reflects what students are learning" . . . after questions were raised by the company that developed it. "The results we have so far have been called into question. I can't say with confidence that it's a valid test. It hasn't been verified enough to determine whether it correlates with how much kids know." Keegan also announced that she and ADE staff, along with the test publishing company would study ASAP in an effort to improve it. She described this process as an "affirmation of ASAP and nothing less. We are not abandoning the process."

The technical report (*Arizona Student Assessment Program: Assessment Development Process/Technical Report*, published by Riverside Publishing Company) that Keegan referred to had in fact been available since June, 1994, but had not been made public.

The report (which few people saw) began this way:

Form D is a statewide audit of student achievement on a subset of the Essential Skills. As an audit, the content and the specific skills addressed has to be secure. Form D was developed by addressing a selection of Essential Skills in reading, mathematics, and writing each year over a four-year period, for each of the grades 3, 8, and 12 with all the Essential Skills being measured over the four-year span.[16]

The report described the development of Form D-1, a process that apparently took less than three months. Fairness and content validity checks were performed by convening "focus group discussions" (p. 11) and incorporating the comments of participants in subsequent revisions of the tests. The content group evaluated the match between the assessments and the Essential Skills. Based on this review and "informal tryouts" to determine if instructions were clear and to estimate time requirements, the report declared that Form D assessments were content valid and free of bias. In the annals of the testing profession, this much validation does not amount to much, nor does it meet the standards of the profession. But so what? This is the political spectacle that we are demonstrating.

Although few—perhaps no one—read the report, policy actors responded to Keegan's announcement in ways consistent with their prior political stance on ASAP, some expressing regret about the demise of ASAP and others expressing glee. Their statements also indicated a dismal understanding of the technical aspects of testing:

> In the Form D that we weren't getting an accurate reading of the overall assessment of ASAP. And it made it impossible to absolutely certify the results. So if we couldn't do that, then basically the overall aspect means that it was worthless from a standpoint of being able to say, here's what's this data is doing compared to another state.

Keegan and her allies on the Board of Education considered the report both definitive and damning. Asked about whether she had ever considered an effort to improve the assessment rather than kill it, Keegan replied:

> I don't have that kind of patience. I mean I can't fathom my representing the state exam as a valid measurement of the Essential Skills which were mandatory—are mandatory—when I knew for a fact that the test was not a representation of ability in that area. It's dishonest. So I mean, no amount of time gets you over dishonesty.

But others believed the technical report served as a pretext for political action. That is, since there was such rampant misunderstanding of psychometric principles and conventions and the relative absence of technical advice, the state could not possibly have been using the data rationally. Only a political use of the report remains credible.

A Riverside representative opined:

> It's a wonder they correlated at all. One of the problems with so many of these State-mandated programs that, you know, somebody comes out here with an RFP [Request for Proposal], and where the impetus for this is coming from either the Legislature or the Governor, policymakers have this just [clicks fingers] I mean completely unrealistic idea about the difficulties in building tests in terms of time and money. . . . And so inevitably these mandated programs always have too short of a startup time associated with them. Which means there's no question but what the materials suffer in quality. You just can't do things that fast. And so when I say given, what I think of the comparison of these materials to other similar kinds of materials, they're fine. They're—but they're not near as good as they would be. And reliability and validity? They're just words to policy makers.

An official in the Bishop administration thought that the technical qualities were adequate even in light of the suspect methodology of the study, stating:

Well, it gave people a place to stand if they didn't like ASAP. But I think nothing was so severe that would require completely scrapping the examination. I mean it could have been corrected; if there was a technical flaw, it could have been corrected. . . . Reliability and validity are very good words to use when you want to take an action as she did to end the test. As a new chief, she has to make her mark.

A Democratic legislator agreed:

I don't believe for one second that it was this great revelation that this testing didn't jibe. . . . So this trumped-up, great revelation that this is all out of whack and we have to put a moratorium on testing and we have to re-tool the instrument, I think it was done with a lot of dramatic flair.

Keegan assembled a technical committee, which advised her to correct the technical and administrative problems of ASAP rather than abolishing it altogether. But by May she began hinting at a more radical move to remedy Arizona's assessment policy. On a local television program, Keegan recommended sending the Essential Skills to the scrap heap along side ASAP. Most of the skills were not measurable, she claimed, and the documents were so long, convoluted, and filled with educational jargon that parents could not possibly understand them or hold schools accountable for achieving them. In addition, the Essential Skills failed to embody world-class standards and emphasized process rather than outcomes. Worse, ASAP was still not being used to enforce graduation standards. Her tone was derisive, as if she had already made up her mind. Two months later, on May 25, 1995, ADE announced a revision of the program as a whole, and a new name with the old acronym: the Arizona Student *Achievement* Program [italics added]. Keegan commented, "What we expect of our students is what we will get. . . . Our expectation must be for both high academic achievement and lifetime employment. . . . We remain committed to high-stakes graduation requirements for our students." The release noted that the state would continue to require norm referenced testing. The new ASAP test would be piloted during 1996–97. Subsequent to the press release, the Board of Education approved her proposals.

Although Keegan originally planned to take five years to revise the Essential Skills, members of the Board wanted a graduation test and they wanted it immediately. So Keegan put aside her plan for a patient, collaborative process of standard-setting in favor of an Academic Summit and rapid pace for developing a whole new set of tests—tests with her stamp on them.

Edelman wrote about the political spectacle that policy actors construct themselves as leaders by promoting policies that seem innovative and appear to rectify the failed policies of their adversaries and predecessors. They offer to the public symbolic solutions to crises that they themselves construct. Meanwhile, they allocate tangible benefits to themselves and their political allies, obscured from the spectators. Keegan's allies included corporate donors and business insiders that sought a reduction in public expenditures and a future workforce trained to their specifications. Chapter Six in this book explains in detail the corporate agenda. In addition to her corporate allies, we must also count prominent neoconservatives such as Dennis Doyle, who would help design—and later evaluate—the new Arizona Standards, and Arizonans of the religious right who, as we show in a subsequent section, opposed in the most extreme terms the progressive reforms of Keegan's predecessor.

Blitzkrieg Standard-Setting

The Academic Summit took place in a Scottsdale resort in October 1995. The nine Design Teams, one team for each of the nine content areas for which standards were to be developed, had two prior meetings to become acquainted with each other and the task before them. Summit planners believed it would be possible to form a team, write a three-page list of clear, measurable standards, present them to the other teams, get reactions during public hearings in December, and write a final draft to present to the State Board in time for its January, 1996 meeting. The Board planned to approve the standards and issue a request for proposals to test publishers. The winning bidder would then construct pilot assessments to be administered in March of 1996.

A Board member who represented the interests of the corporate community offered this influential perspective:

> I have always been concerned that "seat" time should not be a graduation requirement. Ever since I was in high school, seat time was all you really needed to get a diploma. And we all agreed that we wanted a diploma to mean something, to have some stakes to it, some risks to it, perhaps even get to the point ultimately where there could be a guarantee to the business community that if our students have a diploma that they can count on them having certain skills.

Each of the nine Design Teams was comprised of nine members, plus one or more facilitators. The participants included parents, teachers, students, and laypersons who had been appointed by ADE from a list of self-nominations. Curriculum specialists were conspicuously absent. This seemed to be both coincidental and, perhaps, intentional. Many of the participants had nominated themselves based on Keegan's informal comments during a fact-finding trip. Later, when she announced the Summit officially, the teams were already full of the self-nominees. ADE made clear that loading the teams with non-specialists would have the effect of reducing educational jargon and making the standards clear and measurable. During a Board meeting, one member said about curriculum specialists,

"We don't want to know what they know. We deliberately cut them out of the process."

Whether by accident or intention, ADE did not pursue a strategy of representation on the teams, except to include laypersons on each. They did not invite experts in curriculum or assessment. They did not invite representatives of ethnic groups.

We were able to watch most closely the language arts team and follow its waxing and waning of tensions. Although the summit directives attempted to guide participants away from constructivism toward the simple, clear, and measurable, a few educators attempted to introduce constructivist principles derived from the standards of the National Council of Teachers of English. The resisting educators tried to deal with issues of equity and quality education for second-language learners. Despite their pleas, the Superintendent resolved that:

> Without question, the standards you are creating are for proficiency in the English language. Assessment of the standard will be in the English language.

On the language arts Design Team, 20 planned hours became, by some estimates, approximately 200 hours of meeting time, spread over nearly a calendar year, plus countless hours spent in reading, writing, and reflection. (The language arts standards would not be accepted by the Board until the summer of 1996, and even then, only the reading and writing components were approved). Standards in science and social studies were still incomplete in 1997.

The language arts team eventually overcame their diverse perspectives to arrive at common understandings. They took their "work seriously and produced draft standards with integrity, focus, and balance." The team incorporated constructivist principles in several ways, for example by writing standards that could not easily be tested with multiple choice tests. In addition, they attempted to inject issues of global literature, cultural comparisons, reading for pleasure, and self-assessment of students as writers. The team believed that it had incorporated progressive ideas by designating four varieties of standards within language arts: listening/speaking, visual representation, reading, and writing. Many progressive ideas such as content integration, projects, thematics, and problem-solving were in those latter parts of the draft language arts standards.

Revising Draft Standards

During the third week of December, after the nine draft standards documents had been distributed, ADE conducted 11 public hearings. The audience for most of these meetings consisted primarily of organized constituencies:

members of Parent-Teacher Associations, teacher associations, university content specialists, and conservative political groups, plus a few parents and teachers on their own. The meetings were all of a type—ADE described the history of the standard-setting process and allowed questions. Then it orchestrated a series of controlled, three-minute speeches from members of the audience who had signed up to speak. Those at the podium listened politely but took no notes, suggesting that the comments would not affect the department's actions.

Contenders over such issues as Outcomes-Based Education, bilingual education, and phonics instruction argued against each other or against the state. There was no reasoned debate; the contenders failed to share basic assumptions. Instead each speaker ran out his or her three-minute opportunity in the spotlight. This was performance, complete with claques, stage whispers, and catcalls, but nothing one could recognize as democratic participation.

Following the public meetings, further reactions to the draft standards came to ADE by mail and fax. No one could say, however, just how extensive was the distribution of the design drafts or how representative were the comments that were sent back. If state teacher organizations had an official response, it was not reported in the newspapers. ADE later claimed that extensive teacher input had been sought and received. Many were dubious. A national representative of the American Federation of Teachers compared the drafts with AFT criteria for evaluating state standards and found them deficient and the process "absolutely flawed from the beginning."

ADE appointed review teams for each set of draft standards, adding people to the original Design Teams. Two members of the State Board appointed themselves and some of their friends to the review teams and assumed dominant roles, pressing the Board's and Keegan's agenda. This was a critical event, as a team member explained:

> This is where you see a tightening of examples and leaving out the "fluffy stuff" and the multicultural stuff and all that. And this is where you see all the concessions about how much emphasis to give to phonics. There was this constant refining and rewriting and paring down. "Is this tight enough? Is this clear enough? Can this be tested? Is this a one-answer thing?" It was a constant movement in that direction, a constant struggle.

Revisions were made and passed back and forth from review teams to ADE and the Summit facilitators over the next several months. The evolution of the language arts drafts reflected the tensions already evident at the Summit: the Board and ADE emphasizing the simple, brief, measurable, and ambitious; the Team leaning toward the complex, process-oriented, holistic, integrated, and influenced by the national standards. Between drafts three and four, the Superintendent wrote a long memo to the review team, recommending additional components to the standards, as well as clarifications, elaborations, and rewording. Although the team resisted many of her intrusions, one resulted in the substitution of the standard for writing, "Perceiving themselves as writers," to "spells simple words," and "writes the 26 letters of the alphabet." ADE's insistence on measurability also resulted in the deletion of standards related to developing students as "life-long readers."

The Board had two interests that opposed the Team's work. First there was the pressure of time and the need to show that *something* had been accomplished. The second interest was to undo the old ASAP reform agenda and move the policy toward a more traditional pedagogical and accountability orientation.

Over the months of sending drafts of the language arts standards back and forth, Keegan modified her position, accommodating some progressive principles. But while Keegan compromised, the legislature worked toward eliminating the final vestiges of progressivism.

In September, 1995 Governor Symington called for radical restructuring of the state school system, doing away with districts altogether and allowing site councils at individual schools to hire principals, who would in turn "negotiate individual contracts with teachers." He announced his plan to eliminate unions and certification. He pledged to free public schools from regulations, institute parental choice, and place into receivership those schools that consistently failed to educate their students. In addition, Symington proposed to abolish the ADE, or, failing that, to restructure government to make ADE report to the governor.

A week before his dramatic intrusion into the Board of Education meeting (the subject of the vignette at the beginning of this chapter), Symington declared personal bankruptcy. He was also at that moment faced with criminal indictment for fraud. The *Arizona Republic* editorialized, "If Gov. Fife Symington had set out deliberately to divert public attention from his personal financial travails, he couldn't have picked a better strategy than getting his critics, and others, focused on something else."[17]

Other significant shifts occurred during 1996. The Board approved ADE's recommendation of the Stanford-9 achievement test as the state-mandated standardized test for grades 3–12. The Board failed to articulate the reasons for the change from the ITBS. Although an ad hoc advisory committee reasoned that the Stanford-9 provided a better fit with the developing state standards, conservatives later protested the decision. They reasoned that the ITBS focused more on basic skills and less on problem-solving, which was important to them.[18]

In 1997, ADE released a request for proposals for the development of the Arizona Instrument to Measure Standards (AIMS), the proposed successor to ASAP. The request included no ceiling on budgets, but required that items be written in formats that would maximize efficiency. Test items were to reflect the Standards. With no public participation, ADE selected CTB/McGraw Hill and National Computer Systems, two organizations that operate test development, implementation, scoring, and reporting of assessments in many other states. ADE directed these corporations to be ready with a pilot version of AIMS in spring of 1998 and the first version ready for administration in spring of 1999.

In October 1998, 76,000 students took the pilot version of AIMS. Enough problems were experienced that, by November, the Board decided to delay (from the class of 2001 to the class of 2002) the use of AIMS to determine high school graduation. The Board decided in December to reduce the battery of math tests from 5 to 1. The Board had pressed for a fast development process, and, just as had been true in the ASAP era, had underestimated how complex and difficult developing and improving such a test can be.

Throughout the history of AIMS, Keegan and the ADE repeated the mantra that AIMS is a reliable and valid test to measure state standards. But just what evidence bolstered that claim?

An undated technical report prepared by CTB/McGraw Hill described the test development process, and referenced the process that it had used to scale the items and set the cutoff scores to determine whether students had met the standards. It devoted only a few brief paragraphs to the technical merits of the tests. It listed the various ways that the reliability of a test could be indicated, but reported only the weakest form of reliability analysis. AIMS demonstrated internal consistency, but reliability over time or consistency across different test forms was not determined. The report promised that those more important aspects of reliability would be determined in the future by ADE. Validity, or the evidence that AIMS really was testing what it is supposed to test and correctly performing the function assigned to it (determining who met the standards), was also given short shrift. Content validity (the weakest form of validity) had been judged by whether the content standards panels and others believed that particular test items matched the standards they purported to measure.[19] To be plain, there was much less evidence about the validity of AIMS than there had been about ASAP, which Keegan had scrapped for its inadequacies.

Fast forward to the spring of 1999 to find the state's first official administration of AIMS, and to August, when the Board received the dismal results and chose to withhold them from the public. Although a few commentators attributed the low passing rates to the weakness of the tests themselves and the difficulty of the math content being tested, more often the controversy was political rather than technical. Critics of public schools demanded the immediate release of these scores, citing laws and regulations and the public's need to know. Arguing for the delay, the Board President wrote that she considered this version of AIMS to be a pilot test and not intended to determine which students would graduate. She argued that the public would misconstrue such low scores. Keegan argued that the public paid for the tests and therefore had a right to know the scores. She failed to mention any problems with the technical aspects of the test or its too-rapid development. Nevertheless, the Board appointed a 30-member panel "to review some questions" on the AIMS. Billie Orr, spokesperson for ADE denied that political panic over low scores motivated this review. In her words, the committee had "to re-evaluate how it initially categorized them." In other words, the committee was formed to fiddle with the way that certain items were categorized. Although no documents came out of the committee, such a process likely produced higher passing rates.

Finally, in November 1999, the AIMS scores were released to the public. Nine out of ten students failed to meet the standard on the math test. Keegan attributed the low scores to poor teaching and admonished teachers to align their teaching with the Standards. She recommended adding a third year of math to the required high school curriculum. She also asked the legislature to add $1,200 per student to the education budget to prepare students to pass the test. Legislators laughed. "Just what are we throwing the money at over there?" asked one. "We can keep fooling ourselves or we can face reality," said another.

Critics of AIMS, however, offered several alternative explanations for the low scores: (a) sophomores (who might not have completed their math courses) took a test meant for juniors and seniors; (b) students had not tried hard enough because they thought their test scores would not count against them; and (c) test developers had falsely assumed students would be allowed to use calculators. Gene Glass, an expert on statistics and measurement, stated that the level of math being tested was unrealistically advanced and inappropriate for most students. He also blamed the test development itself: "All it shows is the incompetence of the people who put together this test and determined the passing score."

Mesa School District, noted for its high scores on standardized tests, immediately adopted a course (that students could take for credit) on how to pass the AIMS. The *Tribune* quoted a district official who said that "the state has forced them to make extra provisions [to prevent subsequent AIMS failures] like the review courses because so much is at stake. You have to teach to the test. . . . The ramifications for not passing says it all."

By the end of November, the Board, which once had taken such a hard line on testing and accountability, softened. The Board president asked her colleagues to listen to educators who said the math test was too difficult—even gifted and accelerated students had failed it.[20] But Board member Todd Bankofier, a national sales director for a telecommunications company argued that the state should hold the line. "It's too early to talk about backing down. . . . When we fired this missile, we knew we'd have to guide it." And a newspaper columnist added his scorn for critics such as Glass who decried the disparity of scores of white verses nonwhite students. "The time for whimpering is over. Is the test discriminatory? This argument has taken on the stench of victim politics at their most rancid." And Board member Janet Martin wrote that, "It is a travesty of justice to lower expectations on some due to socioeconomic or racial statistics of past performance. These are the very ones who need to be held to a high bar of expectation."[21] And Governor Hull said, "No matter how many Arizona students fail. . . . No matter how many students drop out," the state should not decrease the difficulty of the tests. Keegan added, "AIMS is here to stay."

But was it? Late in the year 1999, the press became aware of the growing costs associated with AIMS, which was already one million dollars over budget. The state budget for AIMS was around $10 million over five years. Districts reported that they absorbed at least that much of their own funds. The *Republic* estimated that nearly two million dollars each year would be required just to re-enroll students who had failed the AIMS graduation test.

Sometime in spring of 2000, ADE discovered that the National Computer Systems had used the wrong answer key to grade an algebra item, affecting the scores of 12,000 students. Thirteen students who had been told they had flunked the math test, were now informed that they had passed it. An ADE official said, "It stinks when you see this." Adding to the controversy, a research study[22] on dropouts revealed that, as was the case in many state assessment programs, the AIMS program had increased the dropout rate in Arizona. But Billie Orr, ADE spokesperson, had this to say: "You can't fall out of bed when you're already on the floor." Referring to the already high dropout rate in Arizona, she opined that the state's tougher standards would actually encourage students to stay in the classroom because they "will be getting a diploma that's worth the time they've spent in school."

The first half of 2000 marked an important turning point in the history of assessment policy. The popularity of Governor Jane Hull, who had assumed the office after Symington was removed, assured her re-election and stifled Keegan's local ambitions. Keegan turned her attention to the national arena. Her commitment to charter schools, vouchers, and tax credits for private schools and her record of success impressed Republicans. Her highly visible AIMS program provided a model for the national testing policies adopted by presidential administrations of both parties and fit perfectly with George W. Bush's educational platform. Conservative columnist George Will recommended that Bush name her as his running mate. Her support of John McCain of Arizona for the presidential nomination, however, dimmed her chances. After the election, she remained a front-runner for Secretary of Education right up to the day that Bush named Rodney Paige instead.

The second administration of AIMS took place in April of 2000. But Keegan and the Board began to express doubts about the scores those tests might yield. Keegan recommended that the Board delay the application of the graduation requirement. Janet Martin said that if this year's scores turn out to be as bad as last year's, "it would be the only ethical thing to do." Kenneth Bennett, by now a state senator, said that "But the last thing we need in this whole process is a bunch of overreaction. The emotions are high enough as it is." The Board appointed a task force of 30 educators, which found that 40 percent of Arizona students had not taken algebra or geometry before taking AIMS as sophomores. In other words, there was a substantial mismatch between what the test covered and the typical math curriculum.

Ignoring the report of the commission it had itself appointed, the Board determined that the classes of 2001, 2002, and 2003 would still take all parts of AIMS. All students would have to pass the reading and writing tests in order to graduate. Although those classes would not have to pass the math test to graduate, their scores would appear on their transcripts. The class of 2004 would have to pass all three parts, including math.

The newspapers published more dissenting editorials about AIMS. Activists, parents, and other members of the public began posting on websites and list serves to express their opposition and to disseminate information that often escaped the papers. As schools began adapting their curricula to the AIMS test and increasingly gave up regular curriculum not covered by AIMS (as in the Mesa case mentioned above), school programs narrowed and standardized. Proponents of charter schools and other public schools of choice felt this pinch. A director of a charter school based on the Montessori model despaired: "Slowly but surely, we are being forced to alter our pure Montessori approach. . . . I can see our dream fading." All because of the high stakes placed on AIMS.

At its June 2000 meeting, the Board, still smarting over the massive failure rates, voted to reduce the number of topics on the AIMS test, dropping, for example, trigonometry.[23] It also approved Keegan's recommendation to adjust the system used for scoring the writing test and to lower the score that would count as adequate to pass the test. She denied, however, that the test burden was too high ("Kids are not being tested enough") or that AIMS had made things worse.

In September, 2000, the Board released the scores of the second administration of AIMS. Nearly 70 percent of sophomores failed to pass the writing test. Thirty percent failed the reading test. Eighty-three percent of sophomores failed the math test. As was the case in the previous year, the scores provoked strong reactions. Testing expert Tom Haladyna called the rate of failure "cataclysmic. . . . What are we going to do with those kids?"

Worse, perhaps, was the failure rate of those who had taken the test for the second time. Of those juniors who were retaking the test, 80 percent failed again. Sixty percent who had failed the reading test as sophomores failed again on the second try. On the math test, 88 percent of those juniors who had failed it as sophomores failed again. The *Republic* quoted one sophomore as saying, "If you have to take the test to graduate, then some of us will be here until we're 50."

At this failure rate, some experts said, more than half of seniors in 2002 would not be allowed to graduate based on the reading and writing tests alone. Some districts took heed. Some began preparing certificates of high school completion that could be given to seniors who had successfully fulfilled the state course requirements but had not passed AIMS. Others began planning and budgeting for the impact of providing programs for students who could possibly continue taking classes until they attained the age of 21.

Mounting evidence to the contrary not withstanding, Keegan stuck by her program: "Parents of students who failed must recognize that time has run out on hoping that this will be taken care of [that AIMS would be revoked] and must demand help from their schools." She reiterated her philosophy of external motivation: "Without a penalty for poor performance . . . students and schools will have no incentive to take tougher standards seriously." She took some comfort in an increase (small but not significant) from 12 to 17 percent in the passing rate. Governor Hull again cautioned against overreaction and panic.

The gap in passing rates between white and nonwhite students provoked consternation. Because of their low AIMS scores, up to 80 percent of minority students were in danger of not graduating. In one heavily minority district, for example, 100 percent of the Hispanic students who took the test failed some part of it. The *Republic* recalled that in 1999, 97 percent of the African-American, Native-American, and Hispanic students had failed the math test, compared to 86 percent of white students, and the achievement gap was even worse in reading and writing. Keegan called the gap "shameful" but offered no solutions to the problem.

After the elections of 2000 and the nomination of Rodney Paige as Education Secretary, Keegan seemed to blunt her wholesale promotion of

AIMS and to take a defensive position. Dissent had reached such a point that by November, Keegan decided to conduct a survey to find out the extent of negative opinion and solicit suggestions about how soon schools would be ready to require the graduation test. After the survey research results came in, Keegan announced a delay in imposing the graduation mandate until the class of 2004. The *Republic* editionalized that Keegan "waved the red flag," attributing her action to relentless criticism.

ADE contracted with WestEd, an independent policy research group, to analyze the survey results and conduct Town Hall meetings. And although the state would not allow the researchers to report the number of naysayers, the *Republic's* own analysis showed that 25 percent of respondents said that AIMS should be abolished altogether as a graduation hurdle. Only 11 percent of respondents agreed with ADE's timetable.

Critics used terms like "giving up the ship" and "the beginning of the end" to describe the latest state decision. Even the Greater Phoenix Chamber of Commerce recommended a long delay. Nevertheless, Keegan stood by AIMS as "a good measure of progress and . . . necessary to raise academic standards." She invited educators and representatives of the "business community" to a series of forums to study the program and make recommendations. But she stopped short of holding public hearings because, she said, "Unfortunately these town halls do turn into food fights."

Pressure emerged from the Senate. A new senator (who was also a university professor) introduced legislation that specified a public referendum on the future of AIMS if a legislative panel could not come up with solutions to the problems that had arisen. The *Republic* reported (3/3/01) "The political posturing kicked off" when the bill was introduced. ADE policy director John Shilling spoke against the idea of the public voting on AIMS. Assessment policy ought to be the province of ADE, not the legislature or the public. "We don't see why a public vote is necessary. I think polling has consistently shown . . . that the public is very supportive of AIMS. . . ."

By that time, Keegan seemed less in the news, less often in the state. At the end of April, she announced her resignation and intention to work full time in the right-wing think tank that she had developed. Departing from her post, she answered questions from the *Republic*. She was asked why she was always labeled as polarizing. She replied, "If you disagree with folks about private-school choice, they'll find a way to demonize you." When asked why AIMS is so controversial, she replied, "It wouldn't have mattered what assessment it was. . . . The education community is strongly anti-test."[24]

Governor Hull appointed her own information officer as the new Secretary of Public Instruction to fill out Keegan's term of office. She explained her choice this way, "I wanted to look at someone who has some experience with tough love."

Almost from his first day in office, the new Secretary announced his intention to reconfigure Arizona's assessment policy.

For months the stage went dark, but a new production was in the works. The 2002 race for the state superintendent was waged as a referendum on AIMS, when one nominee vowed to eliminate it and the other vowed to enforce it even more vigorously.

Assessment Policy on the Stage of the National Theater

We have shown in this chapter the symbolic value of assessment policy in the Arizona political spectacle. Other states may not be quite so melodramatic, but Arizona is far from unique. Here and elsewhere politicians ride assessment policies to higher office and greater acclaim that they can trade in the economy of careers. Politicians make plenty of press by warning of a crisis of achievement and accountability that they alone can solve. This crisis will yield, they claim, to a new, relatively simple and cheap testing program.[25] Opinion polls support assessment policies. And the persistent voice of corporate interests provides them with a discourse and images that further push policy makers in this direction.

By proposing an assessment policy, the politicians give people a reassuring impression that they are doing something about the "crisis" that threatens the state or nation. Unfortunately, few researchers document the effects of such policies, leaving the public without evidence about the crisis, the policy, or the policy maker. It is past time to probe whether this most prevalent educational policy has advanced, retarded, or been irrelevant to the fate of American schools. Here we begin to ask the questions.

What Effects?

What has happened, if anything, to schools as a result of assessment policies? Although documented effects on the outcomes of schooling are few, unanticipated side effects are obvious. When things go wrong (like the high failure rates of AIMS), states flounder around, changing passing rates, revising test items, breaking from test contractors—all trying to get something done and preserve the essence or symbolic values of the policy. The resulting policy flux has already been documented in Arizona and several other states.

Chaotic Effects

In Arizona, Massachusetts, Ohio, Virginia, and Wisconsin, grass roots resistance to high-stakes tests has forced states to delay, revise, or retreat from their assessment policies. Delays or changes have occurred for other reasons in Alabama, Alaska,[26] California, Delaware, and Maryland.[27]

As of 2001, at least 19 states had experienced major errors in their testing programs. For example, in New York City, CTB/McGraw Hill made errors in scoring and reporting of promotional gates tests. These errors led to 8,700 students being required to take summer school when they had (it was later discovered) actually passed the test. Mayor Rudy Guiliani, who strongly supported high-stakes testing, declared that these students needed the extra academic work anyway and should thank the city for the chance to go to free summer school. Because of errors of scoring, equating, and reporting, 3,600 students were mistakenly required to spend another year in their grade.[28]

In the market for state tests, demand greatly exceeds supply. Only a handful of organizations possess the capacity to develop and validate tests that fit states' standards. Representatives of these organizations admit they cannot keep pace with states' demands for their services. They attribute their difficulties and errors to politicians' demands for fast test development and immediate reporting of results. As we saw in Arizona, politicians often fail to foresee the complexities of large-scale assessment.

Limited budgets and the need to rush tests into operation preclude the lengthy and serious work that is required to validate tests. The ease with which political values swamp technical values is remarkable.[29]

The professions of psychometrics and educational research have established standards for validating tests for use in high-stakes circumstances, but politicians and policy makers routinely ignore or neglect them. Together, policy makers and testing contractors settle for the weakest forms of reliability (internal consistency of items) and of validity (face validity, wherein focus groups compare state standards to test items and decide the two are congruent). They settle for weak methods of detecting test discrimination among ethnic groups. They rarely pursue more robust forms of reliability (stability of scores from day to day, for example) or of validity (correlation of scores with other indicators of achievement). Yet despite these compromises, politicians can still claim that the state test is valid— clearly a case of "symbolic validity." The lip service analyses provide political cover to both policy makers and testing contractors. Yet tests with deficient reliability and validity have tangible effects on students. As in the New York City case just cited, poor testing practice results in wholesale misclassification of students in which it becomes possible that some qualified students were failed instead.

Four corporations dominate the market for large-scale assessments: Harcourt- Brace (Psych Corps), CTB/McGraw Hill, Riverside, and National Computer Systems (which scores about 20 million tests per year). These four often enter into each other's contracts as well. This supply is hardly up to the task.[30] The private corporations are joined by a number of non-profit agencies such as College Board (Educational Testing Services) and Apt Associates. Because the list of providers is so short, no matter how egregious the errors one of them makes, state policy makers have few options. One state severs its contract with Company A, and the next day, a different state enters into a similar contract with Company A, having been burned by Company B, and so on.

The *New York Times* analyzed the pattern of errors in state testing and found that the corporations employed untrained workers at minimum wage to score responses to essay questions and failed to maintain quality control over their work. The companies blame the policy makers and their demands for instant, error-free work. But if the corporations were so hard-pressed, one wonders why they do not simply refrain from bidding on subsequent contracts, once they have met their capacity. The answer is money. In 1996 the states spent $165 million on testing services. By 2001 that figure grew to half a billion dollars.[31]

Add to that figure the profit to be made by selling texts. The same corporations that develop tests also sell texts and materials that match their items. Assessment policies also have been a boon to for-profit test preparation companies and consultants. The *New York Times* reported that an on-line test preparation company charges schools a $250 license fee plus $4–7 per student. David Bacon wrote in *Z* magazine of an emerging education-industry complex and of the influence of corporate leaders such as Lou Gerstner in pushing its testing agenda from above:

> Publishers are very secretive about the money they make on testing, hiding it within the income figures they report for educational publishing generally. [When Pete Wilson was governor of California he cut short the state's efforts to write new standards and] insisted on adopting the Harcourt test specifically, and school districts around California were forced to sign contracts with the company—worth $12 million a year—for a guaranteed period of 5 years. . . . Obviously, the test didn't assess the real knowledge and skills of those children [whose first language was not English]. But the kids fulfilled a more important function. They consumed the product.[32]

So, the tangible benefits to corporations are clear. But have tangible benefits of assessment policies to students, schools, and society been documented? Real effects are hard to find, and states themselves rarely even look for them. Research may disappoint those who claim state tests cause academic performance to rise.

Apparent Effects

Many states' assessment policies use one test to serve two purposes. First, the state uses a test to bring about change, to reform schools toward greater achievement. Think of that as the "Gadget" test. The second purpose is to measure the change that the Gadget is supposed to bring about.

Let us provide a hypothetical example. Imagine that a particular state determines that third graders must attain a certain score on the Stanford-9 reading and math tests in order to pass from third to the fourth grade. The state assumes that the existence of this test and the promotional gate that lifts and lowers will, by themselves, motivate students to study harder and teachers to focus their attention on the basic skills of reading and math. This is the Gadget test. Later, after the initial use of Stanford-9 as a gadget, the state measures the effects of the gadget by administering the Stanford-9 and notes its rise or fall in each subsequent year. Here the Stanford-9 functions to measure the effect of the gadget. During the first year of this policy and the first administration of Stanford-9, average scores are lower than what would have been expected based on the previous year's perfor-mance on, say, the Iowa Test of Basic Skills. The second year, however, Stanford-9 scores soar. Based on the rise in average scores, state officials claim success for its policy. In this example, the Stanford-9 was used both as a gadget (the cause of change) and a measure of change. When a state uses the same test as both the means to increase achievement and the mea-sure of achievement, the evidence looks positive.

Research on this topic almost inevitably reveals this pattern in the above example: low scores the first time a state-mandated test is given, substan-tially higher scores in the second year, and a leveling out in subsequent years. This pattern emerges whether or not the schools are doing better or the pol-icy is having any real effects. Instead the increase in scores has more to do, say the researchers, with the teachers getting past the novelty of a new test. By the second year both teachers and students have grown more familiar with the format of the test. Schools have adopted texts and materials that match the new test. Perhaps teachers learned how to teach to the new test.[33]

Real Effects

To provide a more trenchant probe of the effects of assessment policy re-quires that researchers demonstrate on some other indicator besides the Gadget that the standards and testing program caused achievement to rise. Continuing the example above, researchers ask whether scores go up from year one to year two on an alternative test, say the Comprehensive Test of Basic Skills (CTBS). The latter test purports to measure the same domains as the Stanford-9. But because the state attaches no stakes to scores on the CTBS, teachers see no need to adapt instruction to match it. Nor do they teach to its specifications. If scores on the CTBS rise as they do on Stan-ford-9, we count that as evidence that the policy had real effects. What this means is that something the schools did in the interim made a difference in deep achievement status. Apparent effects changed only the superficial pe-culiarities of the two tests, like measuring the ability to solve a math prob-lem arranged vertically on the page rather than horizontally.

Research on this question casts doubt that assessment policy has much in the way of real effects. William Mehrens reviewed the literature and found no credible, independent evidence for the positive gains on any measure other than the test being used as a lever of change.[34]

Audrey Amrein and David Berliner probed for real effects by looking at the longitudinal pattern of scores on Scholastic Aptitude Tests, American College Tests, and other indicators of achievement. Of the states that had introduced tests to determine high school graduation, the level of these alternative indicators rose significantly in only one.[35]

Thomas Kane and Douglas Staiger analyzed the pattern of scores over time in North Carolina (the only state in which Amrein found positive effects) and concluded that the change from year to year was not due to real improvements that the schools made. Instead the changes were due to sampling errors and normal fluctuations. They estimated that most of the change (from 50 to 80 percent) was inflationary rather than real.[36]

Dan Koretz and his colleagues addressed the question of whether gains on tests used both as gadget and measure of effect generalize to a different test of the same content domain. They compared the results of two tests, one a high-stakes test and the other a test of the same academic skills. Scores dipped initially and then gradually rose in subsequent years, but only on the test used as both gadget and measure. Scores on the other test scores stayed level. The researchers believed that intensive teaching to the high-stakes test explained the difference. That is, because low scores led to bad consequences, teachers drilled students on work sheets that looked very much like the items on the high-stakes test. Intensive test preparation increased scores on the gadget test but had no effect on a parallel test. In the researchers' words:

> [S]tudents are prepared for the high-stakes testing in ways that boost scores on that specific test substantially more than actual achievement in the domains that the tests are intended to measure. This suggests that the results on the "taught-to" test do not generalize across tests for the same domain.[37]

Studies such as these explain incidents where test scores rise dramatically when high stakes are introduced. In Tacoma, Washington, the district hired Rudy Crew and directed him to solve its chronic problems with achievement. Crew in turn hired a consultant firm that trained teachers how to boost scores by teaching to the test. Test scores rose twenty percentile ranks, and newspapers referred to it as "the Miracle in Tacoma." New York City was impressed enough with this record to hire him as superintendent. After he left, the scores regressed to their previous level. Journalist Peter Sacks, helped by an evaluation conducted by Apt Associates, showed that the spike in scores was simply the result of intensive teaching to the test. He referred to the precipitous rise and fall of test scores as "the Rudy Crew Effect."[38]

The difference between apparent and real effects epitomizes political spectacle. Apparent effects are inflationary, illusory. But they serve the purpose of enhancing political and professional careers.

Adverse Effects

Do assessment policies produce adverse consequences? Under the cloud of high-stakes assessment policy, schools can actually get worse. How can one explain this apparent anomaly? The time that schools spend administering the tests and drilling students on test preparation materials subtracts substantially from instructional time, sometimes amounting to a month or more of school. Test preparation displaces topics and whole subjects from students' education and turns instruction into test-like learning activities. Teachers lose their capacity to teach in ways other than handing out work sheets that look like test items.

Negative effects of high-stakes testing policies fall most heavily on students of poverty and color. Since achievement tests discriminate against these children, average scores of their schools will be lower. As a consequence, the state will put most pressure on those schools to raise scores. Those schools then devote more time teaching to the test and neglect broader content.[39] They spend their limited funds on test preparation materials, software, consultants who hold pep rallies, Saturday and after-school "academies," and so on, even when their available text books are decades out of date and their library shelves empty.[40] States with high percentages of poor children are the ones most likely to have high-stakes testing policies. The stakes are more often punishments than rewards.[41]

One of the most perverse long-term consequences of high-stakes testing policies is that they decrease the likelihood that poor students will graduate from high school. Research on this relationship could hardly be more consistent and clear: getting behind in school, repeating grades, being held back from promotion and graduation because of low test scores increases the likelihood of a student's dropping out of school. One study found that students that are held back are eleven times more likely to drop out of school than comparable students whose age was consistent with their grade level.[42]

Can adverse impacts be justified, offset by the greater good? Defenders say they do. They claim, for example, that negative effects ought to be weighed against the renewed legitimacy that public schools have purchased by implementing programs to promote accountability through testing.[43]

Other assessment advocates say that even though assessment policies have shown long-term harm to children of color or poverty, they draw attention to schools that serve them.[44] Lisa Graham Keegan warned the public against giving credence to warnings about adverse consequences of assessment policies. She demanded that critics prove the harm they believe tests cause.

The National Academy of Science assigned the National Research Council to study high-stakes testing and make recommendations for future assessment policy makers.[45] Scholars and experts considered the evidence and reported as follows:

No single test score can be considered a definitive measure of a student's knowledge. . . . Research shows that students are typically hurt by simple retention and repetition of a grade in school without remedial and other instructional support services. In the absence of effective services for low-performing students, better tests will not lead to better educational outcomes.[46]

Tests should be used for high-stakes decisions about individuals only after implementing changes in teaching and curriculum that ensure that students have been taught the knowledge and skills on which they will be tested. . . . Test results may also be invalidated by teaching so narrowly to the objectives of the test that scores are raised without improving the broader set of academic skills that the test is intended to measure.[47]

It is also a mistake to accept observed test scores as either infallible or immutable. When test use is inappropriate, especially in making high-stakes decisions about individuals, it can undermine the quality of education and equality of opportunity. For example, the lower achievement test scores of racial and ethnic minorities and students from low-income families reflect persistent inequalitites in American society and its schools, not inalterable realities about those groups of students. The improper use of test scores can reinforce these inequalities. This lends special urgency to the requirement that test use with high-stakes consequences for individual students be appropriate and fair.[48]

From this most expert panel of experts in psychometrics and education policy, who had no vested interest in assessment programs, came pronouncements quite at variance with assessment policies in most states. Some education policies and programs fit comfortably in our common sense, taken-for-granted assumptions. Tests are easy; tests are cheap; tests provide immediate political payoff to their authors. Any policy with a prayer of making authentic change, on the other hand, is hard—it implies examining the social structure surrounding schools, and its course extends beyond the typical term of political office.

Notes

1. Parts of this chapter have appeared in the *Teachers College Record* (Smith, Heinecke et al, 1999).
2. We are limiting our analysis to just the current wave of school reform. However, in the 1970s many states went through a cycle of accountability policies. An example is the New York City Schools and their promotional gates tests. Current discourse about testing policy almost always neglects that experience. This historical amnesia is fascinating because evidence about the effects of those policies has been consistently negative. It is also worth noting that Britain mandated competency testing during the 19th century (Glass, 1978); (House, Linn, et al., 1982).
3. McDonnell and Elmore (1987); McDonnell (1994).
4. Practice differs from the ideal, yet it is important to recognize the professional ideals. See, for example, Heubert and Hauser (1998).
5. Stone (1997).
6. Edelman (1985).
7. Cronbach (1979).
8. National Commission on Excellence in Education (1983).

9. At the 2001 meeting of the American Educational Research Association, the incoming president of the association said in reference to some particularly bad urban schools, "if intrinsic motivation hasn't helped, a little extrinsic motivation can't hurt." But the outgoing president said that research shows extrinsic motivation depresses intrinsic motivation. That is, threats of punishment through high stakes testing produce perverse consequences.

10. However, even this is contested. See Heubert and Hauser (1998).

11. Quality Counts (2001).

12. National Commision on Excellence in Education (1983).

13. Arizona Chief (1996).

14. Keegan and Root (1996), p. 39.

15. Keegan and Root (1996).

16. Arizona Student Assessment Program (no date).

17. Murphy (1996).

18. Marianne Moody Jennings, a conservative columnist for the *Arizona Republic* called the "good old Iowa [Test of Basic Skills] . . . the final vestige of classical education and the one no-holds-barred method for determining whether our children are actually learning." She attributed the demise of such tests to "market forces generated by educrats using their theories of integration, open-ended questions with flexible rubrics and tests as the destroying angel of self-esteem." She characterized the Stanford-9 test as disdaining basics and oozing creativity. It is geared toward standards. "Standards are part of the goals 'every-child-a-functional-illiterate-net surfer by 2000.' " The "beauty of a true standardized test is that there is nowhere to hide when assessment time rolls around. . . . The traditional pencil-pushing, mind-bending, sweat-inducing, computer-graded, knowledge-based, right-and-wrong-answer test has given parents, legislators, and concerned educators the single most reliable piece of information about children's mastery of basic skills. . . . Educational malpractice is rampant, but with these new tests, no one will ever know." (Jennings, 1997).

19. Reliability of AIMS was judged based on internal consistency rather than test-retest consistency. The report also described a rater agreement analysis done on ratings of open-ended items. As for validity, at the very least, one would want to know how a student's AIMS math score compares to his scores on other measures of math. The test publisher conducted an analysis of this issue, using the scores of a sample of 10 students. This is inadequate evidence to support high-stakes decisions. The report claimed that there was good convergent validity between AIMS and the Stanford-9 reading tests because the proficiency levels to which students in the validity sample were the same on both tests. However, the technology available to establish proficiency levels, such as "proficient" and "basic," is far from being conventionally accepted, even among the profession of psychometrics. More importantly (but often overlooked by assessments in the policy domain), one would want to see how the students that AIMS named as meeting the standard vs. failing the standard managed to achieve in college math courses or in math-related jobs. Did students identified by AIMS as failing the standard end up doing good work or bad work in such real-world situations? What CTB-McGraw Hill did in the name of reliability and validity constituted the bare bones of validation. As for fairness, the publisher used a technology of test item discrimination between white and nonwhite students and the judgments of a diversity committee about whether the content of each item might unfairly bias performance by minority groups. Once again, even among the practitioners of technical rationality, such procedures are inadequate to gauge the group bias in the test as a whole. The latter is reflected in group differences at the level of the test rather than the level of the item (Camilli and Shepard, 1994; American Educational Research Association, 1999).

20. Gene Glass wrote in an *Arizona Republic* op-ed piece that NCTM standards (after which the Arizona math standards were modeled) were a "math teacher's wish list. . . . Little did the NCTM group know that . . . Arizona would adopt its goals as requirements for all high school graduates: solve two-variable inequalities, master exponential algebra, learn to graph quadratic functions, or you're not fit to carry an Arizona diploma. . . . Arizona Academic Standards might be appropriate for fewer than one in five high school graduates."

21. The paradox of racial attitudes in the interpretation of disparate test score results resounds throughout the assessment policy literature. But official assessment policy continued to ignore problems of social justice, language diversity, and ethnicity. The official line on equity

for ethnic and language minority and disadvantaged pupils was that the state must set the bar high and equally for everyone, and that it is racist to think that all children cannot vault it successfully with the available pole. In an interview conducted in 1997, Keegan responded to concerns that minorities may suffer adverse impact because of test bias:

"It is one of the reasons that you set the bar even for everybody. I think that is a pernicious and quite frankly sort of a racist view that particular students don't deserve a high expectation, and that's what I read that as. I mean I've listened to that for years about school choice; you can't give poor parents or minority parents a choice because they don't know how to use it; the parents won't profit from it. I don't believe it. Where there is high expectation of that student, they rise to the level of expectation. And I just don't believe that the problem with our minority kids is capacity; I think it's expectation. And so everything from my philosophy, if I won out, it's going to be—what it will look like is a clear expectation for all students, and then we're going to have to figure out ways to expect better things of all students. I don't think there's any question if you've looked very hard at public education that we have a lower expectation for certain groups of students than others. That's not news to anybody. And our problem is how to get over our expectation problems, not how to lower the bar. So I've read the same stuff, and it makes me angry, because it's failing to do well by the kids and then excusing ourselves for that."

22. The study by Dean Lillard, professor of economics at Cornell University, showed that high-stakes testing programs increase dropout rates from 3 to 7 percent over the rate before the tests were instituted (Lange, 2000).

23. Keegan had persistently denied up to that point that AIMS had included items testing trigonometry.

24. *Arizona Republic* summary of interview with Keegan (May 6, 2001, B1).

25. Testing policies are simple and cheap compared to policies that reduce class size or level up financial and intellectual resources to the schools of the poor so as to match those of schools of the rich. In absolute terms, of course, testing programs are expensive.

26. A legislator from Alaska called the delay "academic child abuse." He further said, "we need accountability. We need tough love" (Bushweller, 2001).

27. Amrein and Berliner (2002).

28. Amrein and Berliner (2002).

29. For example, see McDonnell (1997).

30. Achieve, Inc., a private sector group tied to the Business Roundtable, later launched its own for-profit test development corporation. ETS also spun off a for-profit agency to enter the market.

31. Henriques and Steinberg (2001); Steinberg and Henriques (2001); Olson (2001a).

32. Bacon (2000).

33. Shepard (1991); Koretz, Linn et al. (1991); Linn, Graue, et al. (1990).

34. Mehrens (1998).

35. Amerin and Berliner (2002).

36. Olson (2001b).

37. Researchers conducted a comparative study of student achievement in high-stakes and low-stakes conditions of in reading, vocabulary, and mathematics. The large urban, high-poverty district in which they conducted their study had used a standardized achievement test (Test 1) from 1980 until 1986. In 1987 the district switched to Test 2, used in high-stakes conditions. The study was conducted in 1990 and reintroduced Test 1, which of course no longer was subject to high-stakes, and compared median scores of students on Test 1 and Test 2. The difference between the current high-stakes Test 2 and the now low-stakes Test 1 was a robust 6 academic months in math, 6 months in reading, and 4 months in vocabulary, all in favor of Test 2, the high-stakes test. An additional comparison was made between Test 2 and Test 3, the latter made up of items especially constructed by the researchers to sample the same content domains and parallel Test 2 in difficulty. The difference between Test 2 and Test 3 was 7 academic months on math and 3 months on reading, again favoring the high-stakes Test 2 (Koretz, Linn, et al. 1991).

38. Sacks (1999).

39. Camara and Schmidt (1999).
40. McNeil (2000); McNeil and Valenzuela (1999); Madaus and Clark (1998); Madaus, West, et al. (1992): Sacks (1999).
41. Amrein and Berliner (2002).
42. Grissom and Shepard (1989); Lang (2000); Rumberger (1995).
43. McDonnell (1997).
44. Skrla (2001).
45. It is not clear whether governments paid the slightest heed.
46. Heubert and Hauser (1998), p. 3.
47. Ibid., pp. 6–7.
48. Ibid., p. 4.

CHAPTER 3

School Choice and the Illusion of Democracy[1]

What the best and wisest parents want for their own child, that must the community
want for all its children
—John Dewey

HOBSON'S CHOICE (A VIGNETTE)

Martha drank her second cup of coffee and looked west—beyond the clothes hanging on the line, beyond the cyclone fence, beyond her back neighbors' camper—to her spectacular view of the pink morning light on the Flatirons, the signature backdrop to Boulder, Colorado. Just below the mountain, also within her view, million dollar homes in the Devil's Thumb neighborhood overshadowed the half-million dollar homes further down the slope, the great dividing line of Broadway, and finally Martha's neighborhood, perhaps the last bastion of the lower-middle class. Martha was satisfied with her thirty-year-old brick house, which in any case was about all her family could afford on her nurse's salary and her husband's computer contract work. She liked the idea of living in a real neighborhood where the families knew each other and watched out for the kids. Her children could easily make the walk from home to school, and she was close enough to stop by once in a while after work to check out what was happening there.

But she wondered just how long she would feel this way about her school, Adams Elementary. A couple of years ago, the school district had informed the staff that they were considering whether to close Adams, because its enrollment was dropping. Of course it was dropping, she thought—the district had moved all the sixth-graders out of elementary schools into middle schools. Those empty chairs were like a vacuum. They drew in the big shots, and the first thing the big shots thought about was closing schools. No matter that small schools are better for kids. No matter that the school served as a unifying point for the neighborhood. The district had other values, like efficiency. More than that, Martha had been told repeatedly that there was tremendous pressure on the Board of Education to build new schools in the eastern part of the district, outside the city limits where the new housing developments were booming. This year some of those eastside kids had been bussed into the Adams building. Soon their new school would open and they would leave Adams to the mercies of the district axe. All the schools on the west side with declining enrollment (which, because of the middle school reorganization, was all of them) were being considered for closure. Martha could predict, though, that some of those schools in the best neighborhoods would escape the axe because of the activism and clout of the parents there. The Adams neighborhood was different. Most of the mothers needed to work full time. As much as they cared about their kids' education, they had little time for activism—even if they had known how to fight effectively. Well, she was smarter now.

Last year, though, the district offered the Adams parents a choice, if you could call it that, either to close Adams altogether or to become one-half of a school-within-a school. In this latter plan, which seemed already to be in progress, the two schools would share the building, but remain, as organizations, separate. It wasn't much of a choice, but the Adams parents grew excited about the prospect. So, Apex Focus School was assigned, and the two schools began their side-by-side operations. As Martha understood it, focus schools were like charter schools, only focus schools had to follow district rules, although each could establish a distinctive program. Parents could have more of a say in programs their kids would get, staffing, organization, and so on.

So Adams parents got to choose. It wasn't a difficult choice—they wanted to save their school. At first, Martha and her neighbors had been intrigued. Choice! Some parents, like her neighbors the Floyds, could opt for a traditional curriculum for their kids, and enroll at Apex. Martha and others could stick with the more progressive program their kids enjoyed. And they still could all go to school together.

But the Adams community was in for a surprise. Apex filled up to its maximum capacity with students from outside the neighborhood. By the time the Floyds heard about Apex, they were already too late. Its roster was full. Apparently, the Apex parents had been planning for two, three years (who knew how long?) for a school of their own, one that they could control. They could hire the teachers or get them transferred if they did not fit the Apex profile. They could pick the books and materials (they chose the Core Knowledge program that E. D. Hirsch published) and raise funds for the extras that they would need. Eventually, if all went well, they would find their own building (Martha knew that the Apex parents already had their eyes on the Adams building itself) and fill it with the children of parents like themselves. As long as there was a waiting list, Apex could pretty much select the students that fit its profile and deny admission to anyone else. Allowing for the fact that Boulder is not the most diverse place around in any case, Martha could already tell that Adams had a more diverse population than the Apex group. When pressed on the issue, Apex parents pointed to its Asian students (the children of University scientists) as evidence of its diversity. And as if to reinforce Martha's growing sense of us-versus-them, it hadn't taken too long before the Apex parents demanded separate lunch periods, and separate areas and times for recess, so the two groups wouldn't mix with each other.

Then there was the issue of fund-raising. Apex parents raised an enormous amount for computers and such, but drew a line in the sand about distributing any of it to Adams. Martha, who took on the extra job of organizing bake sales, had given up trying to generate even a quarter of what Apex had raised (although, it seemed to her, the Apex bookkeeping was being kept close to the vest). The Apex mothers were often present at school and seemed to attend every school board meeting. Either they didn't have jobs or they worked professionally and could afford nannies. The fathers also helped Apex. They provided legal services, set up bookkeeping and accounting, did research studies and surveys, monitored phone and E-mail lists. It just went on and on. The group even had its own Website, but Martha couldn't access information from it without a home computer. Apex parents seemed to have connections on the school board, played tennis with people in city government, rubbed elbows with the newspaper editorial staff. They spoke each other's language, always anticipating what was up. Martha's group never seemed to know about school-board actions like the Apex parents did. The politics were a mystery to her. It wasn't that they hadn't tried to protest, but important policies seemed to be made behind closed doors. By the time her group had lined up to testify before the board, the deals had all been made.

So now Martha's kids had to watch from their side of a wall the Apex kids in their smaller classes, working with their science equipment or computers connected to the Internet, helped out by a bevy of mothers and even fathers; watch as those kids boarded buses for special outings. Kids can compare. They can recognize the differences. But when Martha protested about the differences in privileges between Adams and Apex, she was scolded, told that everyone was free to choose and only bad parents failed to make the right choices for their children. It wasn't the fault of Apex that Martha's group hadn't been smart enough or caring enough to figure out the system and play the game. Sometimes life isn't fair. To Martha, it was the accusation of being a bad parent that hurt the most.

Martha put on her coat to walk her kids to school. It was too dangerous now to let them walk alone, what with the Land Cruisers and Range Rovers speeding by, on their way from Devil's Thumb to Adams/Apex, mothers driving with cell phones clamped to their ears, their eyes straight ahead so as not to encounter the neighborhood kids or meet the eyes of their parents.

This is school choice, she sighed. But unlike the rain that falls alike on the just and unjust, the benefits of school choice don't seem to fall the same on everyone. Some are choosers and some are losers.

School Choice in Theory

When George W. Bush took office in 2001, he proposed legislation that would require all students in grades three through twelve to take a national test. A student's scores would determine whether he or she could pass to the next grade or stay in the same grade for another year. Scores would also determine whether high school students graduate. Average test scores of a school's students would be used to determine whether the school itself was improving. Schools that failed to improve would be held accountable to "market forces." Parents of children in failing schools would be given a sum of money ($1,500 was the amount usually mentioned) to spend on tuition at schools of their choice, whether public or private, sectarian or not, other than the neighborhood school that their children would normally attend. In theory this plan would be good for everyone, because parents could opt out of schools that were failing and go to the schools of their choice. Faced with the threat that families might leave, administrators of neighborhood schools would have to take steps to improve. Those who did not respond to these market forces would eventually find the school doors closed permanently, the parents exiting with their $1,500 to spend elsewhere.[2]

To Bush advisors, it was important that the press refer to this policy as "school choice." To his critics, it was important to call it "school vouchers." In the political spectacle, language serves important functions. It obfuscates real benefits for the few behind a fog of ambiguous language. Choice sounds like a good thing. Choice sounds American. If we can choose a Hoover upright canister from the array of vacuum cleaners on the market, why shouldn't we be able to choose the schools that satisfy our individual preferences and needs?

Milton Friedman, noted economist and advocate for applying the free market to all aspects of political and social life,[3] introduced the concept of choice as a remedy for underachieving schools. He reasoned that public schools were ineffective because they belonged to the State. As creatures of government they became bureaucratic, entrenched, and unresponsive to parents. Overall, they were inefficient, especially compared to private and parochial schools, producing less achievement for greater cost.[4] Like the

U.S. economy of the 1970s, public education underperformed and under-achieved. Conditions were bad enough, he argued, that fundamental reform was only possible by injecting the discipline of market forces. Freed of obligation to send their children to neighborhood schools, parents would educate themselves about options and then select the ones that would best meet the needs of their own children. Public schools, forced to compete, would improve and diversify their programs. Parents with options would be more likely to participate in the education of their children. The key policy issue, however, was to divert public funds for private use. A pupil's state allocation should be given to parents to use as they saw fit. The invisible hand would move across the landscape of education and improve it for everyone. So thought Friedman, who created a large following among neo-liberals. Along with Friedrich Hayek, Friedman's work made a significant impact on Margaret Thatcher, British Prime Minister, and spread to many parts of the world. *A Nation at Risk*, the lengthy report released by the Reagan administration in 1983, mentioned market choices as a response to the crisis in public schools (although that report concentrated most of its attention on making public schools better by mandating higher standards and accountability).

School choice (as we will call it here) gained adherents in several categories.[5] Together, these groups bought choice policy space in the national discourse about schools.

Political conservatives viewed choice policies in light of their general distrust of, and antipathy toward, all government institutions. Since they believed that the size and power of government should be constrained, they also slanted their discourse, calling public schools "government schools," monopoly schools, or even "socialist schools." They likened the privatizing of education to the fall of the Berlin Wall and the collapse of the Soviet Union.

Religious conservatives viewed school choice policies as ways of escaping the wickedness—sex education, secular humanism, assault on family rights and values, absence of school prayer, and promotion of homosexual and other nontraditional life styles, even satanism—that to them was evident in public schools.

Cultural restorationists (or neo-conservatives) such as E. D. Hirsch (whose Core Knowledge curriculum package played such a heavy role in the Boulder debates), Allen Bloom, William Bennett (speaking on behalf of the Reagan and Bush administrations), and others viewed choice policies as a way out of the quagmire they believed progressive "educationists" and "educrats" had made of public schools. Advocates of home schooling and traditional pedagogy made common cause with them.

Existing parochial schools, in light of declining enrollments, identified choice policy as a way for their institutions to survive.

Activist parents in some predominantly non-white urban neighbor-hoods, having lost faith in the schools their children attended, identified choice as a way to escape those schools. Groups such as the Black Alliance for Educational Options in Milwaukee often received funding from foundations such as the Friedman and Walton Foundations to press their case.[6]

Another set of advocates for choice policies emerged from the private sector in the form of for-profit private schools as well as corporations that market products and services to public, choice, and private schools alike (see Chapter Six).

Although the aims of these groups sometimes diverged, they forged an effective coalition to provide political support, funding, and discourse in favor of various policy instruments under the school choice umbrella. A number of conservative think tanks provided strong communication networks for these groups to pool their ideas and resources. Several researchers did studies that seemed to provide an intellectual justification for choice. James Coleman, who analyzed achievement test scores of public and private school students, concluded that public schools reward teachers for characteristics (e.g., seniority, college credits) that are unrelated to school achievement and therefore lacked incentives to make schools truly productive. The book *Politics, Markets and America's Schools* by Chubb and Moe, and early (and controversial) research on the first voucher program in Milwaukee provided a semblance of empirical support for these ideas.[7]

The choice coalition favored vouchers because they epitomized the free market ideal. However, most states failed to adopt this policy. Given the chance to vote, citizens of most states rejected vouchers. Perhaps most people still endorsed public schools (in spite of the cries of crisis). Perhaps they worried that vouchers would undermine public education. With vouchers unavailable, the choice coalition pushed for several "second best" alternative policy instruments. These included charter schools, magnet schools within districts, tuition tax credits, inter-district and intra-district transfer policies, as well as incentives for education corporations that arose from the private sector.

Magnet and charter schools took center-stage in the choice movement. The coalition believed that charters provided a point of entry. Today, charters, tomorrow, vouchers. The opposite theory also gained credence. Some advocates of public schools embraced charter and magnet schools because they believed that charters were a way of defending against vouchers. As states turned down legislation and referenda on voucher programs, advocates pursued these other alternatives. Some advocates of public schools, on the other hand, adopted magnet and charter schools as a way of avoiding vouchers. Critics of choice policies disputed the arguments of the coalition. For example, some critics argued that a free market depends on fully informed consumers and a broad and diverse group of producers. Neither assumption is tenable in American schools at present. Without openings and available seats in the various schools of choice, parents would not be able to exercise choice. Instead it would be the schools that have their choice of students and, unfettered by policy, choose those students who fit a particular profile. As a result, critics argue, schools become more segregated, stratified, and homogeneous, while good options elude children of poverty and color.[8]

The United States lags behind the United Kingdom, Australia, and New Zealand as well as Chile in the adoption and implementation of market options to neighborhood public schools. The experiences of those countries can shed some light on the consequences that might occur here. Stephen Ball, a policy scholar in Great Britain, wrote extensively on choice policy there, attributing it to the regimes of Thatcher and Majors, ardent followers of Friedman and other advocates in free market mechanisms for public institutions. Ball claimed that most advocates of choice idealize the market model and caricature the public system. Ball claimed that evidence in Great Britain bears out this contention. He wrote that the government (continuing under the Blair administration) paid "systematic inattention to the plight of the losers" of choice policies. Ball also introduced the idea of cultural capital as a way that upper-middle-class parents can manipulate policies and programs to benefit their children and put poor children at a comparative disadvantage:

> The role of cultural capital . . . is general in the sense that certain types and amounts of cultural, social, and economic capital are required in order to be an active and strategic chooser: for example, knowledge of local schools, access to and the ability to read and decifer the "promotional" activities of the schools . . . the ability to maximize choice by "working the system" (making multiple applications, applying for scholarships etc.) and the ability to engage in activities involving positive presentation of self. . . . It is specific in the sense that the making of "successful" choices, getting your first choice, can depend upon direct engagement, advocacy and pursuit of your choice. There are key points of articulation in the choice process, when certain kinds of cultural and social capital are crucial. . . . Choice presupposes a set of values which gives primacy to comparison, mobility and long-term planning; it ignores those cultures which give primacy to the values of community and locality.[9]

Great Britain and New Zealand sought privatization schemes for many reasons. Among those reasons, they identified school choice as a way to fill seats in some under-enrolled schools and close down schools nearby. The researchers cited above, however, found that under-enrollment related to social class. They found that school choice, school capacity, and social class formed a nexus. Without understanding this nexus it would be impossible to probe the assumptions of advocates and critics in Boulder, Colorado or anyplace else.

School Choice in the Perfect Town[10]

In 1989, the Boulder Valley School District could boast of the full program of progressivism. Teachers and parents made many important decisions, including curriculum. Bilingual education was a priority. The district provided professional development so that many teachers became proficient teachers of conceptual math and whole language, and they were supported by curriculum specialists in all content areas. Scores on achievement tests were high, as one could expect from the district's demographic profile. Up to that time, the public was generally satisfied with the quality of schools and demonstrated this satisfaction by passing most bond issues the district proposed.

Typical students in the valley attended public schools in their neighborhoods. Two small, expensive, and elite private schools, one parochial school, and a residential school for problem students drew only a tiny percentage of eligible students away. The town of Boulder proper had long ago reached icon status, a desirable place to live, a place of natural beauty and liberal politics. Years of focusing on the preservation of its environment and quality of life had led city councils to adopt open-space ordinances and to control growth.

Demographic trends, including an in-migration from the west coast infused new money and contributed to vast expansion outside of the city in the communities east of Boulder, filling existing schools. East side parents pressured the district to build new ones. Inside the city limits, housing costs skyrocketed. Young, middle-class families moved out as costs rose, so that, as the children in city schools grew up, no new children took their desks. City schools found themselves short of students and at risk of being closed. Increasingly, students from one neighborhood were bussed to another. Children most likely to be on the buses lived in mobile home parks or low-income housing (Boulder's sole link with low-income families). In the schools with the most affluent parents, the periodic threats of closure were successfully fought off—even when many of its chairs remained empty.

Deep currents of social change began to threaten the apparent consensus on education. The small university town of the 1950s and '60s and the laid-back liberal sanctuary of the 1970s and 80s had begun to give way to a much more affluent and conservative population, people with different ideas and expectations for the education of their children. Conspicuous consumption altered the previously egalitarian social landscape. The school district, however, did not yet feel this local social current as it occupied itself with implementing a complete package of progressive reforms.

Progressive School Restructuring

In keeping with its progressive policies and in response to nationwide restructuring efforts in public education, the Boulder Valley School District (BVSD) adapted a middle-school philosophy in 1989. The middle-school restructuring, to be phased in by fall 1992, followed the report of the Carnegie Commission entitled *Turning Points.* That policy document recommended that schools for young adolescents be reorganized so that students from sixth through eighth grade could be placed not in homogeneous ability groups but mixed with students of all types and levels of prior achievement. Instruction was to be delivered in blocks, so students could spend longer periods of time with teachers who covered more than one curricular area. The centerpiece of the middle-school philosophy was its focus on practices appropriate to the developmental needs and characteristics of young adolescents. The resulting programs were designed to feature thematic and integrated instruction designed around students' interests. In its restructuring plan, BVSD aimed to make schools more effective for all students. Most teachers and parents who participated in restructuring plans called this "the middle-school model." Conflict over the middle school philosophy would soon erupt into broad institutional changes over the next decade in Boulder.

In January of 1990, the district hired Dean Damon, a known innovator and progressive educator, as superintendent. Damon set up School Improvement Teams (SIT), the Institute for Development of Educational Activities schools (IDEA), and Site Based Management (SBM). The alphabet soup of his restructuring involved teachers, parents and administrators at schools throughout the district. They met regularly to envision a new direction for education with a focus on site-based decision-making and progressive reforms. By that time the district had a full staff of specialists on various aspects of progressive curriculum as well as a thoroughgoing program of professional development for teachers. Things seemed to be going well and headed in a particular direction.

Choice Options Introduced by the District

The initial school choice options that the district launched matched its vision for progressive education. For nonconformist students the district had already opened, in 1988, an alternative school based on William Glasser's philosophy of reality therapy and integrated pedagogy. For its patrons who favored a wholistic and student-centered program, the district opened an elementary school in 1991. For parents wishing bilingual education for their children, the district opened an elementary school in that same year, where Spanish-speaking children would learn English (and English-speaking children could learn Spanish) along with their academic subjects. Each of these schools operated as a magnet school that any parent in the district could select over their neighborhood schools. And in each instance, designing, planning, and implementing were conducted by professionals in concert with the parent groups, with rich contributions from the experts in curriculum and pedagogy at the district office.

First Sounds of Discontent

District reforms ran counter to the national discourse exemplified by *A Nation at Risk*. Whatever the condition of public schools elsewhere, Boulder schools were not in a state of crisis. The message of national school crisis was first brought to the Boulder consciousness by Janet Jones, a parent from the affluent southwest corner of Boulder. She believed—and a considerable number of other parents believed with her—that the district plans would de-emphasize rigorous academic preparation. She focused her attention especially on the plan for converting junior high schools to middle schools. She believed that the plan for reorganization would exacerbate "declining" academic performance of Boulder schools, and more especially, would end up detracting from her own children's education. She based her complaints on her analysis of district achievement test scores. Not receiving any attention or satisfaction from the district, she next took her statistics to the local newspaper, the *Boulder Daily Camera*, which not only published her analysis but also endorsed its findings and recommendations:

> The excellence of Boulder Valley schools is widely taken for granted, but this analysis by a parent and informed critic suggests a deepening mediocrity. Her prescription: Take the system back from the education "experts" and restore a real commitment to academic excellence.[11]

Media Created Spectacle

If the *Camera* had taken a balanced position on the subject of school achievement it would have reanalyzed test scores to confirm or disconfirm Jones's interpretation. Or newspaper staff might have interviewed internationally recognized experts in testing who worked at the university. If the *Camera* had requested clarification and reinterpretation, it might have provided a more sensible picture. The *Camera*, however, did none of these things. Instead it accepted Jones's claim that achievement was declining in Boulder and even referred to her as an "informed critic." It punched up the message of discontent and crisis by printing a half-page cartoon depicting a student with a dunce cap in one hand and a mortarboard in the other. Although the *Camera* printed a variety of letters to the editor on both sides of this debate (more perhaps of the critical ones), a response from Superintendent Damon did not appear until a month later. When he did respond, Damon justified the district restructuring on the common good and the goal of improving education for all. In his op-ed piece, he showed that, by using the correct metric recommended by the test publisher, most of Boulder schools exceeded expectations and were high overall. In contrast with the torrid and emotional language of Jones and her group, Damon's language was measured, rational, and tepid, almost offhand.

Aware of the threat that lay behind Jones's analysis of Boulder school achievement, the district hired Lew Romagnano, associate professor from Metro State University, to analyze math achievement test scores from 1987 to 1995. His analysis showed that, contrary to the Jones conclusion, "the district's efforts to improve the mathematics education of its students have already begun to show positive results."

But you cannot unring a bell. By the time Professor Romagnano pointed out the fallacies of Jones's analysis, the picture of mediocrity she constructed had impressed itself on the public consciousness.

The Jones episode illustrates some principles of political spectacle theory and the role of media. First, a political agenda is usually launched by an actor who bases his or her message of crisis on statistics more dramatic than technically accurate. The apparently scientific reports provide the illusion of rationality so necessary to policy makers. In this case, Jones intended for her analysis to serve as a pretext for adopting school choice policies as well as exclusive programs for the top students. Second, newspapers construct and reinforce a sense of crisis in policy matters. As noted above, the *Camera* could have checked to see if her analysis created or reflected a factual decline in district performance. Third, the media reduce complex situations to simple sound bites and visual symbols, such as the mortarboard cartoon and the table of scores that Jones created. Fourth, the media take strong perspectives on policy issues and craft news articles and select or solicit opinion pieces that reinforce those perspectives. They do not—as they claim to do—simply observe and report from a disinterested stance. It seems clear that Jones's opinion piece reflected a point of view that was held by the *Camera*. From 1991 to 1997, few articles and opinion pieces that the *Camera* published were favorable to district schools. Fifth, the perspective that local newspapers take is often consistent with corporate interests nationally rather than local concerns.[12] During these years the *Camera* took an anti–public school and pro-choice perspective that echoed the national discourse about the decline of schools. In addition, the newspaper seemed to align with the elite critics of public schools, irrespective of local evidence to the contrary. Paraphrasing David Berliner and Bruce Biddle, choice advocates and the local media had "manufactured a crisis."[13]

The Rise of the Local Elite

Scholars define "elites" in various ways. For example Harold Lasswell defined elites as "the influential."[14] Ronald Bruner wrote that "political elites struggle to organize public opinion and mobilize public support by circulating symbols that purport to diagnose the causes of the crisis and to prescribe solutions."[15] Amy Stuart Wells and Irene Serna defined local elites as "those with a combination of economic, political, and cultural capital that is highly valued within their particular school community."[16]

Call people elitists or show how they manipulate symbols, and some will bridle. But, as Edelman argued, in the political spectacle it is essential to appear to be both democratic and rational, even though one's true intentions and actions point toward private benefits backstage and out of sight. In the conflict that followed in Boulder, critics of choice often used the word "elite" to refer to the programs that Parents and Schools (the group that formed to resist Superintendent Damon's progressive reforms) created. The elites, meanwhile jeered the use of this label. For example, when choice parents crowed about high test scores, choice critics attributed those scores to the privileged status of "elite" students. Angry choice parents countered:

> This is misinformed at best, and a deliberate lie for the purposes of political attack. . . . Their [Adams parents'] xenophobia is the true elitism and prejudice.
>
> No one active in his or her child's education, whether through Parents and Schools, a school committee, a booster club, or otherwise, needs to apologize for trying to "get what they want for their kid." Many of the interests of each of our children are not for everyone, but this fact should certainly not diminish our commitment. If the school district has a problem with that, so be it.

On the other hand, some members embraced this designation, as one can see from the following letters to the *Camera*:

> The argument for denying the option for hard academics seems rooted in the notion that a sense of inferiority will be engendered in those students who do not avail themselves of the opportunity. The entire program thereby grovels for inferiority. . . . The above observation will draw charges of elitism. Yes, and the world is based on elitism, delineated by those who can and those who can't process and communicate information.[17]
>
> Radical egalitarianism has become the basis for a scorched-earth policy when it comes to academic rigor. Something happened to public education a few decades ago, around the time that the federal government injected itself and social engineering into the process. A cannibal joined the family picnic and calmly began to eat the children. Perhaps in a couple of decades . . . we will all conclude that certain things, like war and public education, are too important to be left to the experts and politicians.[18]

Credit Janet Jones for tapping into a reservoir of discontent among affluent parents, particularly about district plans to convert junior highs to middle schools and to eliminate tracking students by ability. Why? To track and sort by ability results in opportunities for the favored students to move quickly and efficiently up the hierarchy in the race for credentials. Research shows that tracking places students in the lower tracks at an unfair disadvantage.[19] Among the well-educated and affluent parents whom Jones enlisted was Nobel prize-winning chemist Tom Cech, a professor at the University of Colorado. Cech added his voice and prestige to Jones's group and recruited other well-educated, powerful parents, many from the scientific community. This core group called a meeting in March of 1992 to challenge Superintendent Damon and the Board of Education. Five hundred people, almost all critical of district programs, attended this meeting. The core group administered a questionnaire. The results of this poll showed that the majority in attendance favored academic rigor, doubted the middle school philosophy and claimed that the district was unresponsive to the concerns of parents. Thus the activists formed the group, Parents and Schools. Soon the group was making headlines. For example, a *Camera* headline read, "District Is Under Siege: Organized Parents Posed to Change the School System." Local and national political and educational experts said that the group possessed the characteristics of a "powerful political movement:"

> Its message is broad. It uses both passionate rhetoric and quantitative research. Its leaders are well known and have captured community attention.[20]

In April, Parents and Schools circulated a petition that reflected the themes of the March poll. It presented this petition, with over 3000 signatures, to the school board. The board, however, refused to back away from its plan for middle school restructuring. Undaunted by the board's decision, the activists continued organizing.

Parents and Schools aimed first to organize political action that would force the district to offer school choice. To this end the group began a campaign to recruit and expand its membership to others who were critical of schools. Indeed, the rhetoric of Parents and Schools was almost exclusively critical, even damning and derisive. With Jones as its leader, Parents and Schools put together an e-mail network. It regularly published a newsletter that disseminated reports and letters critical of the schools and promoted its stance on curriculum and school organization. Through this communication network members were encouraged to speak out to the district administration, school board members, teachers and the public about the lack of academic rigor in the school system. One Parents and Schools newsletter solicited "horror stories":

> Stories Sought: What is your favorite example of the lack of challenge to students in our schools? Please send your "horror story" to Parents and Schools.

A letter-writing campaign was organized, and the *Camera* published dozens of letters critical of the district's plans.

Parents and Schools enlarged its power through networking. Many members also participated on school governance groups and site-based teams. They used these groups as platforms to express their complaints about the district and recruit more parents. With help from the *Camera*, the group had convinced many that the public schools in Boulder were failing and that immediate action was necessary. One of its first action items was to pressure the district to institute an International Baccalaureate (IB) program at one of the high schools. The IB program would offer students a rigorous curriculum and an internationally recognized diploma. For Parents and Schools, this program was an antidote to what they saw as the watered-down district curriculum and just the thing to provide an edge for their children into the most desirable college. Always the group used the threat of voucher legislation and charter schools to push their agenda of academic rigor.

Finally realizing the heat of dissatisfaction but suspicious of its extent and distribution across the entire district, Superintendent Damon asked the League of Women Voters to solicit a broader range of views from the community as a whole. Meanwhile the district fulfilled its plan to open the middle schools by the fall of 1992. It assigned ninth graders (who previously would have been assigned to junior high) to high school and students in grades six through eight to middle schools. Among other consequences, the restructuring decreased elementary school enrollments by fifteen percent—a decrease in enrollment that would later prove to be significant in arguments about school choice.

A comment from Superintendent Damon in school-board minutes illustrates the district perspective at the time—that "focus schools" and open enrollment indicated district responsiveness and offered parents choices in curriculum while leaving most district governance in place.

> The whole issue of focus schools was begun in this community as a way of being responsive and at the same time, good stewards of resources, responsive to a community that increasingly sees value in choice in public education. They (the board) have done a number of things to try to accommodate the community's interest in choice. One of them is the open enrollment policy which has been liberalized incredibly in the last three years because of legislative interest as well.

The Boulder Case, Choice, and Political Spectacle

The story so far seems to support the arguments for school choice. Perhaps the "government" schools of Boulder had not responded well to the demands of this group of parents. But the story can also be told through the lens of political spectacle.

Parents and Schools adopted the rhetoric of national achievement crisis, even against the evidence of the local test scores. Edelman points out that policy makers and political actors often invoke crises—whether real or not—to justify actions on behalf of private rather than public values. In this case the parent group wanted schools to return to homogeneous ability grouping and the most advanced and accelerated academic courses. They wanted these options so that their children would receive the most advanced and accelerated curriculum and preparation in academic subjects that would pay off, they believed, in higher college entrance test scores and enhanced transcripts. Parents and Schools lobbied the district to initiate a weighted grade system so that students who took advanced classes could still attain perfect grade averages. Whether the consequence of their proposed policy changes disadvantaged anyone else's children did not concern them. They wanted to return to the way things were before the progressive restructuring. This was cultural restoration and social reproduction writ small.

Was the reaction of the elite parents rational in its pursuit of individual interests? Probably. Would attaining private goods accrue to the common good, as market theorists claim? Would it not be more valuable for the society as a whole for the best students to attain the best and highest academic slots? Would it not be more efficient? In the political spectacle, one must always speculate about differences between the onstage and backstage benefits of policy decisions. Parents and Schools regularly claimed that the common good would be served if the group attained its goals. After all, they reasoned, every parent would have the right to choose, so everyone would benefit. It seems clear, however, that its members pursued private, individual goals through the manipulation of public policy and public institutions.

David Labaree argued that a retreat from broad public interests toward private ones is a feature of a society that is driven by the values of social mobility rather than democratic equality or even human capital. At a time when the number of people attaining any given level of educational credential (junior high graduation, high school diploma, junior college certificate, college graduation, and so on up the educational pyramid) is increasing, the market value of that credential goes down. The newly dominant perception in American society identifies education as a commodity that individuals can acquire and then use to exchange for better positions in the occupational or educational world. Furthermore, the credential race is a zero-sum game; one person only gains relative to another's loss. As more people gain a credential, the elite of society press for higher standards and more selectivity at the next level, because they want to preserve their existing standing in a hierarchical social order whose topmost places become ever more scarce as the population size increases.[21]

Labaree's argument implies that elite parents in Boulder were trying (whether intentionally or unconsciously) to position their children more favorably to compete for the best spots at the next educational level. A rigorous and exclusive academic experience at junior high might get their children into the honors track at Boulder High, which would position them to gain admission to a prestigious university, which could then lead to better law schools, and so on. But acquiring these commodities for their own children also had the consequence of denying them to other children. Pursuing credentials to the detriment of others, however, was not part of the discourse onstage.

Local and Non-Local Discourse on School Choice

By 1992, Parents and Schools had tapped into an abundant source of pro-choice discourse. Communication and consultation networks provided advice, canned arguments, and "research" that supported "solutions" to "crises" of school achievement—more educational options—different choices. It tapped into both national and local advocacy resources. For example, Professor Richard Kraft of the University of Colorado wrote a report advocating school choice which the Independence Institute, (a conservative think tank designed to do the political work of the Coors family) published and distributed. In it, Kraft recommended that Colorado adopt a choice policy. The purpose of the paper was to influence state legislators who were then considering various plans including vouchers. Citizen groups had brought forward several initiatives, and Kraft's paper and many others galvanized support for choice across the political spectrum.

In November 1992, Colorado voters defeated a measure that would have provided school vouchers statewide. Heeding polling results, advocates for choice realized that sufficient support for vouchers was lacking, they instead concentrated on the next best alternative: charter schools. Advocates showered legislators with papers and briefs put out by various foundations and think tanks. They pushed newspapers to promote the values of choice. They sponsored a Charter School conference designed to win over enough legislators to pass the bill. Through their efforts, a long list of legislators in both houses sponsored the bill, which passed in 1993 with strong majorities.

Unlike charter school legislation in, for example, Arizona, Colorado's was not particularly permissive (or, as choice advocates usually describe it, "strong"). The law in fact placed charter schools within district governance. That is, private groups or individuals inside district boundaries could propose charters, but the local board would have to approve those proposals. A result of this devolved decision-making about charter schools created substantial variation among districts in both the number of charter schools they approved and the extent of oversight each district imposed.[22]

Subverting Participatory Democracy in Boulder

In his attempt to get a handle on the extent of the public's criticism of the progressive reforms underway, Damon asked for help from a respected outside agency, the League of Women Voters. The League attempted to address this request by hosting a conference to discuss the direction of public education and propose a new plan. They wanted democratic participation by all the community, every constituency. To accomplish this the League appointed parents and educators to a planning committee. After the initial planning sessions, however, Parents and Schools staged a protest, withdrew its members from the planning committee and threatened to withdraw its members from the conference itself. In a letter to the League president, Parents and Schools stated that the proposal for the conference "smacks of the kind of manipulated, impotent 'process' that has frustrated many parents and contributed mightily to the district's current plight."

Apparently, the League's efforts were too democratic for Parents and Schools, which then began planning a conference of its own. Despite its earlier withdrawal, when the League-sponsored conference finally commenced in February of 1993, Parents and Schools turned out in force.

The conference agenda called for dividing into small groups, each with a separate issue to discuss in regard to the future of education in Boulder. One of those groups was "Choice Vision" whose assignment was to discuss the possibility of choice schools in the district. More than one-third of the members of the group of thirty-three was affiliated with Parents and Schools, including Janet Jones and her husband. After the conference, a spin-off of the Choice Vision group was formed, made up of primarily Parents and Schools members. The stacking of the committee precluded open debate about both the pros and the cons of charter schools and other choice options. The self-selected composition of the subgroup co-opted the agenda and transformed itself into an advocacy committee. Thereafter, this subgroup was absorbed by Parents in Schools, but still retained the semblance of a fair-minded deliberation.

The spin-off Choice Vision Action group planned a second conference three months later that they called the "Conference on Magnet Programs for BVSD." Putting the district name in the conference title made it appear to be district-sponsored, but it was not. This time there was not even the semblance of district involvement that might have assured a broader perspective or any voice to represent the good of all. To symbolize its autonomy from the district, the group invited the superintendent to attend as just another conferee, like parents or other invited guests. Because the

Choice Vision Action group relied on Parents and Schools to publicize the Conference on Magnet Programs with its well-organized network of parent volunteers, the composition of the magnet school conference, its agenda, and guest speakers were all controlled by Parents and Schools. The mailing address for the conference was also the Parents and Schools mailing address, the home of Janet Jones. The group prepared summaries and full news releases for the media. Most of the names listed as further contact resources were Parents and Schools members. Two of those members were employees of the Colorado Department of Education. Another member sat on the Governor's Advisory Council for Math and Science. Nineteen days after the Conference on Magnet Schools was held in Boulder, Governor Roy Romer signed the Colorado Charter School Act of 1993.

Focus Schools in Boulder: Threats and Opportunities

The district was already changing. The hard work and diligence of Jones and Parents and Schools paid off when the district approved adoption of the International Baccalaureate program at Willowbrook High School. To Parents and Schools, "this is just the beginning."

In the summer of 1993, anticipating the effects of the new charter school legislation, Lydia Swize, Executive Director for Administrative Services for the district, assembled a group of parents and administrators. Their task was to design a process by which schools or private groups could apply for a new kind of school: a Focus School. Focus schools would function much as magnet schools. Like magnets, focus schools would draw students from throughout the district to schools with a specific curricular emphasis.

Both district administrators and choice advocates defined focus schools as alternatives to charter schools. District employees imagined that focus schools would satisfy advocates of charter schools (the more extreme solution) as well as redistribute students to under-enrolled schools. Choice advocates, on the other hand, imagined that focus schools would be the thin edge that would eventually widen toward charters.[23]

The contrasts between charter and focus schools were ones of relative autonomy and application of market ideology. In the public arena, choice advocates concentrated on those values. A charter school had to be approved by the district, and if approved, the district had to fund it. Once the money was assigned to the charter school, the district would have little control over day-to-day operation. A charter school could waive the district policies and contracts. In contrast, to establish a focus school in Boulder, the parties did not have to adhere to state oversight, and the application process was much simpler and more streamlined than what one had to do to apply for a charter. Once approved, the focus school would have to provide students with the district curriculum as well as any specialized curriculum inherent in the focus application (e.g., Montessori or Core Knowledge). It would be funded by the district, and would have to comply with district policies and the teacher contract. The budget of the two options differed as well. Funding for focus schools remained under the authority of the district. Students who joined charter schools, in contrast, took the amount of their expenditure with them. In retrospect, it is easy to see why the district favored focus schools.

Five administrators, three parents, and one teacher sat on the Process Design Committee for Focus Schools in late summer 1993. In addition to these members, Dr. Lydia Swize functioned as the group's facilitator. Although charter schools were intended to allow teachers and parents to design effective schools, the focus school committee had only one teacher member, the president of the Boulder Valley Education Association. In any event, all three parents were active members of Parents and Schools—including Janet Jones. The group constructed a process that individuals would need to follow to develop a focus school.

"Designing Our Dream School"

Looking back two years, while the political movement for choice developed, Parents and Schools served as a focal point for individuals disenchanted with their neighborhood schools for various personal reasons.

Back in 1991 Jane Barillo blamed the teaching of whole language for her daughter's inability to spell or write. When she asked her daughter's teacher to provide spelling instruction, she was told to buy her daughter a spell checker. Later, Jane's husband Jeff campaigned successfully for membership on the School Improvement Team in the hope of influencing school practices and found the staff intransigent on the question of basic skills versus whole language. The staff believed that instructional decisions should be made by trained professionals, but Jane began to dwell on what she and her husband defined as absence of accountability. By an absence of accountability she meant that the school, principal, and teachers had neglected her family's preferences.

Jane's neighbor happened to be Janet Jones, the founder of Parents and Schools, who shared her analysis of test scores with Jane and Jeff. This seemed to confirm their growing belief that district schools were declining. Jones also gave them information about the emerging options of school choice in the district and state.

Jane ran into Maria, an old friend, while shopping for groceries. Maria had been frustrated by the district's failure to provide the services required for her gifted child. Maria had to fill in the void with academic activities at home. She had complaints about the music teacher. Since the school would not remove the teacher, Maria removed her daughter from music class and even showed up during music period to supervise her daughter. She campaigned to remove a principal she didn't think was effective.

Together the two friends discussed their frustrations and the declining test scores. They began meeting periodically to discuss what could be done. Jones put them in touch with Kay Harbruck, whom Jones had pegged as a critic of the district, but in her case it was the vocational programs that she deemed a failure.

Dot Enwall was a well-respected teacher, having taught foreign language at the secondary level in BVSD for 14 years. For a frustrating year and a half she had worked as the foreign language coordinator for the district. She believed that teachers had too much autonomy and not enough accountability and that they jumped too quickly on any new fad that came their way. Now that her daughter neared school age, she began to pursue the idea of an alternative school. Janet Jones introduced Maria to Dot and Jane.

After much discussion, they decided to propose a focus school rather than go through the tedious work of applying for a charter. The group then turned to curriculum and teaching methodology. Although the four parents seemed sure of what they didn't want for their children, formulating a plan for what they did want was more difficult. Reasoning that the district would be more likely to respond favorably to a program with a national cachet, they fixed on Core Knowledge, a program that Parents and Schools targeted as promising. As the group studied the literature that Jones provided, the women discovered that their beliefs matched those of its creator, E. D. Hirsch. The package that Hirsch sells focuses on basic skills. After children master basic skills, the program takes them to ever-higher levels of knowledge—to facts that every student in America should know. The women began to think of themselves as the Core Knowledge group. With the help of Parents and Schools they arrived at a school name, Apex Elementary School. News of their plans spread through the affluent southwest corner of Boulder where they all lived.

In the summer of 1994, district Executive Director Lydia Swize met with Apex founders and seemed satisfied with its proposal for Core Knowledge. Now came the question of where to put the school. Swize suggested that the founders hold meetings to gauge which schools might be interested in inviting Apex to share its facilities. Of course, the founders would have preferred their own building, but this did not seem to be a reasonable possibility. Swize named the buildings that were then or would soon be under capacity: Stonegate, Franklin, and Adams Elementary schools, all on the south side of town.

Capacity was a central issue in the district, which had to balance the demand for new schools in the east suburbs with the needs of each city school to survive. In the previous year Swize had met with the staff of each school in the district whose enrollment approached the threshold ratio of enrollment to number of seats. When she met with Stonegate staff and parents, she let them know that closure was a distinct possibility. In the alternative, Swize said, the staff and parents might consider the possibility of inviting a Focus School into its building. The schools would thus operate as two different entities within a single school building. She hinted that a group of parents were in the process of designing such a focus school for south Boulder.

Versions differ about what happened at that meeting, whether Swize had merely hinted about or in fact had formally notified the staff and parents that the board had already pegged Stonegate as the primary site for Apex.

The Apex founders held their initial meeting in August 1994 at Stonegate. The meeting was well attended. Although its stated purpose was to provide information about the proposed focus school, the Stonegate community believed that Apex parents had staked it out. The defenses went up.

Stonegate staff and parents strongly opposed any action that would threaten the integrity of their school. They had explored, since Swize's meeting the previous spring, alternative means for increasing enrollment or otherwise warding off this, as they saw it, attack. By October, when the board announced that Stonegate was a likely choice for siting Apex, a full counter-offensive was under way.

Stonegate's well-educated, affluent corps of active parents held neighborhood meetings, gave short speeches at school board meetings, wrote letters and phoned members of the school board and Superintendent Damon. They engineered a letter-writing campaign to the *Camera* and distributed flyers and letters to all the homes in the neighborhood. In addition, a "Town Meeting" was held at Stonegate two days before the board was scheduled to consider the Apex proposal and a second proposal for a focus school based on the Montessori approach. When the board met on October 25, most of Stonegate's teachers and parents showed up to press their case. Thirteen of them spoke of their concerns: that Stonegate had been left out of the planning phase of placement; that plans for placement had been rushed through; and that sharing the building would have a negative impact on both programs. They also brought with them a plan to turn their school into its own focus school, operating as a magnet for families throughout the district to choose. In contrast with the Apex focus, Stonegate Focus would retain its identity as a student-centered school with progressive curriculum and pedagogy. It would remain a neighborhood school but attract additional students whose parents wanted a progressive curriculum but who lived outside its boundaries. More important from Stonegate's point of view, it would be teachers and parents who worked together to plan and implement the Focus School. This contrasted with

Apex Focus School, where the parents alone would develop and run their school.[24]

The Board decided to find another place for Apex, citing several reasons for dropping Stonegate as a target. But Stonegate's successful defense lay mainly in the economic and political clout of the families in the neighborhood who overwhelmingly supported Stonegate as it was.

With its new insights about allegiances between staff and parents of neighborhood schools, and without any guidelines to follow for siting focus schools, the school board turned its attention toward other schools with unfilled seats. Franklin Elementary, which was part of the less-affluent part of south Boulder, proved to be an inviting target. Enrollment at Franklin had been declining for years, but the board had kept it open to provide temporary housing for the overflow from the suburbs. Trying not to repeat the Stonegate mistakes, Swize convened meetings between the Apex planners and Franklin staff and parents (which were no less unhappy than Stonegate had been about the prospect of Apex being sited there).[25] By then the board was fully aware that, although few had ever raised objections to the idea of choice, the siting decisions were turning into political nightmares.

Finally a solution was proposed. The first two focus schools approved (Apex and Montessori) would be sited at an annex of Madison Elementary School. The annex would be empty the following fall. The Madison community had planned to add new language programs to be housed in the annex for its considerable population of children of foreign students at the university as well as a magnet bilingual education program for children bused in from the rest of the city. Last minute notification prevented the Madison community from pressing its case.

The board's next move foreshadowed problems to come. It appointed Claire Sauer as principal of both Apex in the Annex and of Adams Elementary School. The board reasoned in public that Adams would soon lose its bussed children from the eastern suburbs to their new neighborhood school. As a result, Adams enrollment would then shrink by half. Clare Sauer could surely handle both assignments.

Following months of planning and staffing, Apex and Montessori focus schools opened their doors at the Madison annex. But everyone acknowledged that neither school could stay there for long. Both were filled to capacity and already planning to expand, and the Annex had no more space. So the politically charged process of siting them more permanently began. But this time, Apex had an advantage: a sympathetic principal.

To the school board, siting Apex at the Adams building made sense. Nevertheless, it put off the political conflict until the election in November.

In September, a new east side school opened and 300 previously bussed children who lived in its catchment area, along with their prized teachers and fund-raising parents, moved out of Adams. As eagerly as the Apex group looked to its future, Adams staff and neighborhood somberly contemplated its own. Sensing the inevitable course of policy, Clare Sauer, shared principal, suggested that the Adams School Improvement Team meet with the Apex group, as a friendly, welcoming gesture. The early meeting went well as the three parent leaders discovered what seemed to be similar goals for their children. There was no reason to believe that the two schools could not form a productive relationship.

Sometime before the November school board election, however, Adams parents had a change of heart. Principal Sauer hinted about the desire of Apex founders to maintain a "separate identity" from Adams. Ensuing phone conversations between representatives of the two schools confirmed the rumor that Apex parents did not want the two school populations to mix. To the Adams parents, the phrase "separate identity," was really a code for segregation of children from the two schools. Mutual wariness and suspicion clouded subsequent relations. With little time before the school board made its final siting decision, Adams parents attempted to organize its opposition. They wrote letters to the school board, superintendent, and the *Camera*, and held neighborhood meetings, but it was too late. Unlike the parents at Stonegate, Adams parents possessed little ammunition—what some writers refer to as cultural capital—to effect the course of politics in the district and city.

While the Apex founders pursued its "separate identity," Parents and Schools directed its political activities toward the next election and the composition of the school board.

Colonizing the School Board

The school board election in November 1993 added two new faces and shattered the board's consensus with regard to progressive restructuring. Although not among the founding members of Parents and Schools, Stephanie Hult and Kim Saporito were certainly sympathetic to its mission, always keeping "academic excellence" at the forefront of any debate. This was not the board majority they had hoped and campaigned for, but Parents and Schools finally placed some advocates there. As long as they were in the minority, they could not change policy. They could, however, radically change the style of discourse in board meetings. And change it they did, making civility a thing of the past.

In 1994, as the focus school drama played out, one school board member resigned, leaving room for an appointee to complete the term. Of the fourteen who applied, the board voted unanimously for Don Shonkwiler. It soon became clear that Shonkwiler's ideas about education were closer to those of Hult and Saporito than to the board's majority.

The diligence of Parents and Schools, meanwhile, began to pay off when an International Baccalaureate program opened at Willowbrook High. In addition, one high school opened as a focus school and a middle school applied for a charter. Parents and Schools viewed the IB program as having a "ripple effect" on the rest of the district. Right away, the group began to push for a pre-IB program in a middle school that would prepare students for the IB program.

Parents and Schools went to work in earnest as they planned for the 1995 election. Professing interests in equity, its candidates practiced stealth techniques, keeping much of its platform out of public view. In November, an incumbent and another candidate that Parents and Schools endorsed won the election and shifted the board majority. Within its first five weeks, the new board, which everyone referred to as the Hult board, approved seven applications for focus schools and one charter school. The placement of Apex at Adams was one of those decisions.

Relations between the board and founders of Parents and Schools' changed drastically. The new board majority appropriated Parents and Schools goals for its own. The Hult board made no secret of their disdain for the past reforms (e.g., middle school restructuring, inclusion, heterogeneous grouping, collaborative, site-based decisions made by parents and teachers, and progressive pedagogy). Empowered by the "will of the voters," the school board immediately focused on the agendas of the new majority, spending most of its time approving various focus schools, schools-within-schools, "strands" within schools, and wholesale adoption of basic skills curriculum for elementary schools. So much choice activity went on that the board finally had to declare a moratorium to catch its breath. And even after that, groups approached the board behind the scenes to press for additional choices; in some cases, they got them.

Within the administration building a new type of "restructuring" was occurring. Since the 1970s the district boardroom placed the board members and the superintendent at a long, slightly elevated table in front of a small auditorium. Soon after the election, Superintendent Damon's seat was lowered to spectator level. This gesture symbolized the Hult school board assumption of control over decisions that the "educrats" had formerly made. The Hult board established curriculum Councils meant to supersede the curriculum specialists. It appointed four teachers—all white, all male, and all experienced in high schools—to lead the Councils. Similar shuffling took place throughout the administration, with specialists in curriculum and professional development demoted, sent back to the classroom, or fired. The board ignored the protests of the teachers association. It micromanaged even the smallest details. Administrators with many years of experience in the district were fired or resigned.

No one was safe from Hult's caustic comments, even at public board meetings:

> It's the teachers' union and entrenched administrators and the school of education at CU that grind out this pap on education. Their number-one priority is to ensure the continuation of their own jobs. We come smack up against this bureaucracy of educrats. The teachers' union gets the teachers worked up, and they do the same with the students.

Despite the district's own evidence to the contrary, the Hult board kept beating the drum that Boulder schools were declining academically and needed more choice. Hult herself was fond of claiming publicly that charters and focus schools were antidotes to the threat of vouchers. Outside the public eye however, she was recorded at a meeting of the Independence Institute saying:

> I'm in favor of vouchers but don't let that leave this room because in Boulder that is really serious stuff.

By June 1996, the district had bought out superintendent Damon's contract and appointed Lydia Swize for a one-year term. Later that summer minority member Susan Marine resigned, stating her frustration with the Hult board's new direction. Dorothy Riddle, whose philosophy was closer to that of the Hult board majority, replaced Marine. In her formal resignation speech, Marine charged:

> Late this spring the board majority gave in to a small, vocal group of parents who demanded a new Core Knowledge site. We created even higher expectations for special-interest groups that do not want to work through the system and abide by established procedures.
>
> Many of the problems I have with board conduct now occur in the back rooms at the Education Center and out of public view. Indeed, I am not directly informed when, for instance, some board member is trying to exercise control over hiring. If I am not gathering my own information, I may never know what is going on. Since matters like personnel are cloaked in executive privilege, the public remains largely ignorant of the way this board is operating.[26]

After leaving the board, Marine galvanized citizen opposition, although the effort failed to recall Hult. The board, however, ignored its opponents and single-mindedly pursued its goals.

The district mission statement was rewritten to echo the academic emphasis of the Hult Board. In March, the focus school moratorium was lifted officially, although it never stopped anything in fact. The Apex parents petitioned the board to expand further into the Adams building, thus displacing the neighborhood students. Adams offered a counterproposal, requesting that it be allowed to operate two "strands," one adopting Core Knowledge and the other continuing its progressive classes. The board, follwing the wishes of Apex, rejected the Adams proposal. Adams as an entity would be phased out.

After a national search, the board hired Tom Siegel, a retired navy officer with no education background, in June 1997. Some observers claimed that the superintendent's lack of education background would make it easier for the board majority to continue to micromanage the district.

Public concern about the Hult school board majority continued to grow and Susan Marine formed the Coalition for Quality Schools to unseat the Hult board majority in the fall 1997 school board election. The campaign funds for the election reached mammoth levels. The political strategist hired by the Coalition focused campaign rhetoric on the need for greater civility on the part of school board members.

Hult gave the critics plenty of ammunition. Shortly after she was elected, Hult created public furor when she made a negative comment to a *Daily Camera* reporter about the presence of a Downs Syndrome child in her daughter's English classroom. "I think those children are wonderful, but don't tell me it's a good mix." Parents of special education children took umbrage. They had fought many years for their kids to be educated in the mainstream. Although their effort to recall Hult failed, the group kept up its scrutiny of the board's actions.

However, the Coalition's focus on civility took attention away from more substantive issues. The topic of school choice was absent from much of the campaign discussion. After unseating Hult, Saporito and Riddle in a landslide, the Coalition lost its edge and failed to scrutinize closely the tremendous changes already made and the consequences of the Hult agenda on district organization and curriculum.

As the Coalition celebrated its victory, Parents and Schools contemplated a future without three of "our four" school board members. That very night they began to plan for a new dream school, a stand-alone charter school for K–12, which founders hoped to operate without any district interference. They named the school Zenith because it represented the peak of their aspirations.

Even with a different philosophy, the new board could not undo the policies and directions of its predecessor. The new superintendent was ill-equipped to lead, and most of the former administrators and specialists had left the district during the Hult restructuring. Moreover, most of the Hult board decisions were now part of the district structure. In a sense, it didn't matter so much that Parents and Schools did not have a compatible board. The group held enough power to communicate privately, enough power to operate almost completely out of sight of the public, enough power to control staff, curriculum and the selection of most of the students it wanted, enough power to conduct its financial affairs independently. With the opening of Zenith, all of its dreams had come true.

The new superintendent faced the persistent problem of excess capacity in the south and west parts of Boulder coupled with overcrowding and demands for new schools in the east suburbs. He floated again the necessity of closing schools. But when the public protested, he and the board withdrew their proposal and placed a public moratorium on any school consolidation. Behind the curtain, however, plans for consolidation proceeded.

The post-Hult school board refused to examine the hard questions— the possible perverse consequences of choice in Boulder and whether to revise the policies of its predecessors. Instead it focused on the more ephemeral issue of restoring civility.

Whose Dream Schools?

Long before Zenith, while macropolitics played out at the district level, micropolitical conflicts proceeded at school. Back in the fall of 1996, Apex moved into the Adams building with one classroom each for kindergarten through fifth grades. Apex parents had chosen a "Lead Team" as its form of governance equivalent to the Site-based Team of Adams. The Lead Team acted as the executive body for a network of subcommittees that mirrored the organizational structure of Parents and Schools. The Core Knowledge Liaison Committee worked with the national Core Knowledge Foundation. The Goals and Accountability committee made recommendations to the Lead Team regarding student achievement and faculty evaluation. The Budgeting/Resource and Staff Allocation Committee made recommendations to the Lead Team on personnel selection and utilization, curriculum and staff development, leadership and school resources. The Enrollment and Publicity Committee worked directly with the district on enrollment issues, contacted potential parents and provided marketing for the school.

The team interviewed candidates for its teaching staff, and the district approved its choices. It oversaw acquisition of materials and equipment. It did almost all the things that a principal normally does. But in this case the principal merely attended the meetings of the Team as one of seventeen members. Only one teacher (who was not also an Apex parent) served on the Lead Team.

As a matter of course, Parents and Schools made its resources available to Apex. For example, Parents and Schools counted among its membership lawyers, statistical consultants, management consultants, accountants, and doctors, all ready and eager to lend their expertise. Pierre Bourdieu defined cultural capital as "the hereditary transmission of power and privileges."[27] The cultural capital that Parents and Schools transmitted may not have been hereditary, but it was power and privilege nonetheless. Furthermore, the Lead Team created a private nonprofit organization that, they argued, was not subject to state public-records laws nor to the district policies on financial matters. As time went on, less and less of the business of running the school was conducted by the Lead Team and more was conducted in the private meetings of the nonprofit board. Minutes of Lead Team meetings grew shorter (10 pages as contrasted with 100 pages of minutes of the Adams site-based decision-making committee), and the minutes of the nonprofit board could not be accessed by anyone not affiliated with Apex.

Apex, in contrast with its neighbor across the firewall, raised enough money to purchase a computer and video equipment for each of its classrooms. The teacher of the Gifted and Talented Program, who was supposed to divide her time equally between Apex and Adams, spent most of her time tutoring math in Apex classes (she was an Apex parent as well as teacher). Apex kept its class sizes low, and parent volunteers were everywhere in evidence. In one year when statistics were kept, Apex parents volunteered over 10,000 hours. Not only did they assist the teachers in delivering the curriculum and individualizing instruction, they provided transportation to various events and also drove fifth-graders to accelerated math classes at the middle school. They enhanced the per-pupil allotment from the district with donations to offset the costs of various extras. Although the publicity for Apex called this donation voluntary, no parent seemed to avoid it. District policy prohibits such fund-raising, but officials did nothing to oversee it, let alone stop it. Apex parents steadfastly refused to share any of this bounty with Adams. The differences in resources and opportunities that the extra money provided, however, could hardly escape the notice of Adams parents, teachers, and children. When the Adams fourth-graders went on a field trip to the Museum of Natural History in Denver, Apex fourth-graders flew to the Smithsonian in Washington, D.C.

School Choice or School's Choice?

At Apex, the Lead Team interviewed prospective teachers to determine whether they would adhere to the Core Knowledge curriculum. Reversing the culture in the district, the Apex Lead Team made sure that its teachers had little autonomy over what and how they taught and no control over the operation of the school. Core Knowledge is a curriculum package that is meant to be "teacher-proof," that is, standardized and prescriptive. Since parents were so often in the classrooms, they could monitor how well teachers followed the prescriptions, and within the first six months, two teachers were pressured by parents to leave the school for teaching "Core Lite," or a softened form of the real thing. When asked about how this happened, a founder responded, "Oh, the parents take care of them." Another commented, "I don't care what teacher I step on as long as my kid's interests are being met."

The Apex Lead Team also chose students. During the first two years, there were many more applicants than there were openings. Left unsupervised (it could always adjourn its meeting and reopen in its nonprofit entity), the team chose whomever it wanted. Since it was also able to conceal its records, no one could discern until later how its choices affected the diversity or past academic achievements of the Apex population. Later it was discovered that Apex played fast and loose with both district and state policy.

Colorado Revised Statutes (§ 22-1-102) requires that "Every public school shall be open for the admission of all children, between the ages of six and twenty-one years, residing in that district without the payment of tuition." The relevant district policy prohibits discrimination in admissions decisions. Federal regulation promises that schools violating nondiscrimination clauses will be denied federal grants. The Colorado Department of Education regulations limit the priority pools outside the lottery to ten percent of the school's enrollment. And although each level of authority professes fairness in principle, none monitors fairness in practice.

Contrary to both district policy and state statutes that forbid discrimination, choice schools set up priority pools which limited free access. The Lead Team prioritized applicants into the following groups, or "pools": (1) children of Apex founding parents; (2) in-district children of Apex teachers with a half or more appointments for the current or next school year; (3) in-district siblings of current Apex students; (4) in-district siblings of Apex graduates; (5) in-district children of Apex staff who are employed as half time or less; (6) all other district applicants; and finally, if any spots remained, (7) out-of-district applicants.

Children in Adams' neighborhood were not included in any of Apex's priority pools.

The stated selection process read this way. If there turned out to be more applications than spaces available in a grade level (after exhausting the priority pools), the applications went into a lottery. Each application was assigned a number, the Lead Team transmitted those numbers to the district, a district official randomized the numbers, and then returned the randomly ordered list of applicant numbers to the Lead Team, which thereafter announced the names of the students it selected. The district relied on an honor system to assure that all students had fair access. But the Lead Team did not always follow even these liberal rules. It regularly made exceptions for children who matched the school profile. Crude analyses after the fact revealed that half or more of the Apex enrollment was made up of children from the priority lists.[28] Even assuming that the Lead Team followed the lottery results, half or fewer families applying for the choice program would even enter the lottery.

Choice advocates extol the virtues of the free market and claim that informed parents can make the best choices for their own children. However, when demand exceeds supply, as it did in Boulder, it is the schools that get to choose, not the parents. In this kind of market, the schools are likely to choose those families that can best fit its profile or contribute to its continued symbolic success by adding the value of the selected students' high test scores or other accomplishments.[29]

Expanding the Colonies

Since the opening day of the schools-within-a-school, tensions were high and trust was low between Apex and Adams. Although the district administration and board knew about the worsening conflicts, they failed to intervene.

Before the board voted on the placement of Apex, the superintendent arranged for an open forum so the two groups could air their respective grievances. On short notice, the Adams team scrambled to prepare its arguments. At the forum, while Adams complained, the Apex group sat calmly. Kay, its leader, merely reiterated Apex's cooperative attitude and hopes for rapprochement. Later she had this to say about the reaction of the Adams parents and teachers when they found out about the district's plans.

> They seemed to be outraged when they came to the board. . . . And we were kind of surprised because we felt the board had indicated the direction it was going to go a year earlier and so I am still not quite sure why there was a lack of understanding.

Apex's calm was probably based on the group's awareness that most of the decisions about placement had been made. District administrators and some board members had made these decisions out of the sight of the public and especially the Adams community, as much as a year in advance of when they were announced. As one of the Apex founders admitted, the principal "certainly knew [what was going to happen] by the time she showed up that June (1995) before we opened."

After the 1995 election the new board voted to place Apex at Adams and appointed a Transition Team from the two schools to draft a "transition agreement" that would work out their difficulties. The board hired a mediator to make the transition "less bloody," claimed an Adams parent. In February of 1996 the first Transition Team meeting was held with the mediator. Negotiations continued for four months. Meanwhile, Damon instructed school principals throughout the district "to always be positive about these opportunities to provide exciting new educational choices and to make the best use of facilities." This memo effectively took the Adams principal out of the role of advocate for Adams. Thereafter the principal tried to keep things calm and remained in the wings. Apex pushed on toward the inevitable while Adams tried to hold it off.

The transition team eventually reached some agreements and resolved disputes concerning heavy street traffic, teacher aides, and use of facilities. Fund raising, scheduling of lunch and recess, and the role of the principal remained contentious. For Apex, the primary concern was autonomy as reflected in its separate identity and its definition of the role of principal as more of an observer and consultant to the Lead Team. The Adams group believed that the principal was the main authority in the school, the overseer of curricular, pedagogic, organizational, and human matters. At Apex, the Lead Team and parent volunteers took those jobs. The Lead Team once considered eliminating the principal all together, but the board rejected that idea. Apex parents were insistent about what they wanted. It was an "in your face" kind of thing, reported an Adams parent about the demands of the Apex transition team.

The transition agreement brought no peace. Shortly after the two schools signed it, the board asked Damon to resign. Lydia Swize replaced him on a temporary basis and promoted her friend, the Adams/Apex principal, to the central office. To fill the vacant principalship, the board appointed William Hart, formerly head of a prestigious private school. Although Apex liked his credentials, the Lead Team was upset that the group had not been consulted about his appointment. The Lead Team worried that the new principal would not fill the subordinate role that it had assigned to his predecessor (especially regarding the power of the Lead Team to select curriculum and teachers and control finances). The Team took these concerns to the Assistant Superintendent (the superior of principals) who offered reassurance that he would personally serve as a go-between for Apex to make sure that district personnel would make no further decisions without consulting them. He also promised to maintain the Lead Team organization as it was. Members of the Lead Team interpreted his promise to mean that it could make most of the decisions. But at that point even Apex teachers had begun to complain about excess parent control.[30]

While Adams parents and staff tried to adjust to their circumstances, Apex thrived and made noises about expanding. In response to Adams's concerns the superintendent sent them a memo stating that "no such plans for expansion were under consideration" (which was, as we have noted, untrue). In fact, board member Saporito had already intervened in behalf of Apex expansion. She coached the Lead Team in how to package enrollment data in such a way that it would seem that the demand for Core Knowledge exceeded the current capacity at Apex-in-Adams. She also guided them on how to advertise and to target advertising toward parents of children then in private schools and other parents known to be critical of their current school.

Despite the official moratorium on additional choice schools, the board had been working behind the scenes with Parents and Schools to restructure Cherry Middle School as a Core Knowledge focus school so that, when the Apex students advanced into grades six and beyond, they would have continuity of curriculum throughout their school years. The tentacles of the Core Knowledge expansion then advanced on Eagle Elementary School, which, like Adams, fed its students into Cherry Middle School.

When the Eagle community got wind of this plan and knew that the Hult board meant to expand choice, the Eagle Parent Teacher Organization invited Adams parents to speak to the group. The Adams group minced no words. They made clear the difficulties they experienced with Apex under the same roof and especially the backstage/onstage actions of the board, the interim superintendent, and Parents and Schools. As a result of this meeting, the Eagle community put up a concerted fight against such expansion plans.

Naturally this unmasking of the collaborative duplicity outraged all those who perpetrated it.

On stage at the February 1997 board meeting, Saporito spoke on behalf of "the many concerned citizens who want Core Knowledge" and urged the district to be creative in accommodating their needs. She brought statistics with her that purported to document that need. No one asked where those statistics had come from. Parents and Schools had made estimates of the demand from applications of parents for choice programs. If the parent listed four desirable choice options, that parent was counted four times to inflate the statistics. These pleas for fairness and rationality from the Hult board can be read as a cover for what transpired out of public view, offstage.

At the last minute, Adams teachers and parents heard about the proposal for Apex to expand further into Adams's space. In desperation, Adams presented a counter-proposal: merge the two schools into one school that offered the Core Knowledge curriculum. What a good idea, they thought. This way the popular Core Knowledge curriculum could be grafted onto Adams, keeping it as at least in part a neighborhood school and adding to Apex the richness of Adams's Title I, special education, and English as a Second Language programs. Even the Apex teachers supported this plan— until the Lead Team found out about it. This was one kind of richness that Apex did not want. Overnight, the Apex teachers withdrew their support and declined to sign the proposal. Whom the Team had hired, the Team could fire, or at least make their lives miserable until they quit.

For its part the Lead Team expressed derision toward Adams and its proposal, which, they claimed, smacked of desperation and insincerity. Apex didn't believe that Adams teachers knew enough Core Knowledge to teach it effectively. But very likely this proposal threatened the autonomy, the separate identity, and the exclusivity of Apex. One parent requested that the Board vote against the Adams proposal because it represented an "initiative as a disguised effort to kill Apex by converting the term 'core knowledge' into a vacuous advertising slogan and assimilating the program into business as usual."

The discourse of derision was nothing new from Apex, which had from the beginning characterized the Adams community as poorly behaved, silly, immature, inarticulate, liars, and troublemakers. An Apex parent said,

> I think the Adams community that were so vocally opposed to us took it to a
> level that was really nasty. They made accusations about us that were absolutely

and emphatically wrong. They spread rumors about us that were wrong. . . . At Stonegate they never did that. They never fell to that. They just talked about what they were going to do. Adams just dwelled on all the things that they thought we were going to do. . . . Adams was never able to give a vision. They still don't have one.

According to Edelman, the political spectacle involves the rhetorical construction of friends and enemies. The Boulder case supports his view. Anyone who opposed any decision about choice on any principled basis was branded as an advocate of the status quo and an enemy of Core Knowledge, or choice in general. Parents and Schools referred to Superintendent Damon as feeble, weak, incompetent, and "the Wizard of Oz." In an editorial cartoon, the Parents and Schools newsletter depicted the district as a Tyrannosaurus Rex. Anyone who was not a believer was viewed as an adversary. Anyone challenging Parents and Schools as elitist or discriminatory invited a barrage in the next day's news. One member wrote about criticism from Adams parents as xenophobic and misinformed, even as outright lies.

Critics of Parents and Schools complained that Apex systematically selected students and denied entrance to students from the full spectrum. Parents and Schools countered by defining diversity, not as a school's inclusiveness of students of poverty, color, or handicap. Instead they defined diversity as a school's openness to different curricula or to students from various parts of the district. One wrote:

> Diversity means more than just being from different ethnic backgrounds, although multicultural diversity is certainly part of the mix. Respect for diversity also means respect for people with different goals and desires for themselves and their children. . . . We must pass on to our children the common heritage and shared values that hold our nation together as one.

Efforts of Parents and Schools to portray itself in a good light exemplifies Edelman's theory of the social construction of self, friends, enemies, and leaders. The group did not forbear from manipulating symbols and statistics to promote its image and mission. Beginning with Janet Jones's misleading analysis of achievement scores in 1991, there followed a series of other such attempts. For example, Jones often cited studies that she claimed demonstrated the effectiveness of Core Knowledge and of its effectiveness for disadvantaged children. She did not provide the foundation for her claim.[31] In another example, Parents and Schools compared the achievement scores of children in schools of choice with children in neighborhood schools and attributed the advantage to superiority of the curriculum of choice schools. It ignored the selectivity of choice schools and the well-known correlation between achievement test scores and socioeconomic advantage. It ignored the lower class size and the amenities at choice schools that surely explained some of the difference in scores. Instead, it attributed the higher test scores of schools of choice to parent involvement and superior programs. No matter how fallacious such accounts are constructed, the public seems not to question their validity. Nor did experts try to correct the misleading use of statistics. When ordinary citizens raised doubts, Parents and Schools called them amateurs, statistical illiterates, or enemies of school choice. This is how research is used in the political spectacle, as a rhetorical sword for partisans to wield, a way to appear rational and technical without utilizing the discipline and even-handedness of science at its best.

District Accommodation

Parents and Schools could not have been so successful if the school district had not accommodated its values and interests. By accommodation we mean acquiescence—the gradual adaptation of the institutional values and the common goals of the representative body of decision-makers and administrators to the goals of a special interest.

This case study presents compelling evidence that district officials accommodated choice parents. The election of pro-choice school board members constitutes legitimate political activity. The accommodation by the district of political activities—both public and private, both conscious and unconscious—constitutes the politics of spectacle, bifurcating onstage and backstage actions. District officials accommodated simply by looking away. Perhaps they accommodated out of fear of reprisals, political or institutional. The Hult board's firing of administrators who challenged its pro-choice and anti-progressive policies represents an institutional reprisal. The following quotation from Parents and Schools literature represents a political threat of reprisal:

> If the local school board refuses to approve requests for magnet programs with merit, we will elect better representatives in November. There is growing, powerful support for magnet programs in the state legislature and in the Colorado Department of Education. If the charter schools legislation is approved, as expected, during this session, we will have the option of appealing local school board decisions on magnet programs. Parents have the right and responsibility to define the education they want for their children.

Perhaps district accommodation can be thought of as a way of avoiding trouble from part of the community that had political power, as this quotation from a frustrated critic suggests:

> The Apex parent leadership has become absolutely intoxicated with the power the board majority increasingly bestows upon them. . . . Why is the board majority willing to wholesale turn over the education of our children to these zealots?

The district accommodated by failing to adjudicate conflict and weigh in with factions with less power. Instead of substantive help the district offered only symbolic democracy. An Adams parent commented on the conflict between the Adams and Apex transition teams. Meeting of these committees

> made this appear to be a decision that the school governing body, teachers and parents, had actually made. But really we were just duped by the whole process. . . . But the administration knew what was happening and they left it up to her to maneuver it through. We were just a rubber stamp for a decision that was already made. It had the appearance of a democratic process but it really wasn't.

But was district accommodation inevitable? To answer we describe contrasting cases of districts that acted differently.

In Boulder's closest neighbor to the north, the St. Vrain Valley School District, elite parents did not exert enough pressure on the district administration to obtain special treatment. The superintendent and board took a strong stand when they declared that any charter school in the district would be subject to strict oversight. In particular, the board made known its intention to take legal action to counter any attempt to establish schools that would select a single stratum from the student population. When asked to compare the St. Vrain district with Boulder's, the board president later stated that the St. Vrain community was generally satisfied with its schools. Two applications for elementary charter schools and one application for a charter high school were submitted. The board ruled that since the two elementary school proposals were substantially the same, they should be merged into one. That charter was subsequently approved and the school opened. The board denied the only application for a charter high school because the proposal failed to include a "responsible" fiscal plan. The charter school applicants appealed the district's decision to the Colorado Board of Education, an appeal process built into the Colorado law. The State Board overturned the district's decision, and the school opened. Less than one year into its operation, the school's poor management had culminated in financial shortages, and the district took over the school's operation.

The Cherry Creek District south of Denver, with demographics similar to those of Boulder, also provides a relevant comparison. The board approved only two choice options because other proposals duplicated the district's existing programs. Elite parents exerted pressure, but a Cherry Creek administrator, responding to a question about why so few choice schools operated there, said, "We know how to say no."

These two examples show that, even considering the pro-choice policies at the state level, capitulation to the elite parents in Boulder was not inevitable. There were alternatives that the district could have pursued that would have led, potentially, to a more even-handed outcome. First, the district could have insured that all students had an equal opportunity to enroll in choice programs. The district could have required that choice schools enroll the same percentage of free-lunch students as reflected in the district. Second, the district could have monitored enrollment procedures, particularly to insure that enrollment priority pools of choice schools conformed to state law and district policy.[32] Third, the district could have required choice school applications to provide unique programs that did not duplicate existing district programs. BVSD has many programs that market themselves as academically rigorous. Fourth, the district administration or the board could have closely scrutinized the business and financial plans and operations of the choice schools. Although most choice schools in Boulder have not had financial problems, prudent monitoring by the district would have required schools to follow policy regarding fund raising and private donations. The district could have insisted upon broad and fair discussions involving all constituency groups with a stake in the policy. It could have intervened to make the discussions more equal. The district could have analyzed the potential costs and risks of choice schools to the broader community. The district could have performed an evaluation of the schools after they were in operation. The district did none of these things.

Choice Effects in Boulder and Beyond

Parents and Schools echoed neo-liberals worldwide when they claimed that choice benefits all parts of society. They scoffed at the idea that choice policies actually exacerbate existing inequalities in social life generally and school achievement specifically. They discounted the possibility that families with fewer resources and less cultural capital might lack complete information on which to make a choice or might value schools in their neighborhood. They went further to label as "racist" any such doubts. They held fast to the notion that free-market solutions were preferable to government-imposed neighborhood school boundaries, which tended to isolate poor children in bad schools. They ignored issues of community, transportation, and disposition that might discourage the willingness or ability of some people to make such choices. So deep were the beliefs of the members of Parents and Schools that they readily ignored equivocal or negative evidence, or they found reasons to discredit it.[33]

In the political spectacle, one set of claims is made onstage (e.g., enhancing equity) and another is hidden behind the scenes (e.g., maintaining privilege).

In Edelman's words:

> In politics, moreover, the incentive to preserve privileges or to end inequalities is always crucial, offering fertile psychological ground for using language and action strategically, including slippery definitions of means, ends, costs, benefits, and rationality.[34]

Clearly, elite parents in Boulder manipulated the instruments of choice policy. And they were not alone. Research by Elizabeth Graue and Stephanie Smith showed that elite parents used backstage political pressure to undermine progressive reforms in math classes. The educators had attempted to remove ability grouping and implement problem-solving and cooperative learning. But the parents believed that homogeneous classes with traditional instruction had successfully prepared their children to win the "credentials race," as Labaree described it.[35]

In their study of schools that attempted to eliminate ability grouping, Amy Stuart Wells and Irene Serna identified four strategies that elite parents used to undermine this reform.[36] First, elite parents threatened to withdraw their students from the "detracked" school if their children were not given the specialized curricula they demanded. Second, elite parents co-opted institutional elites by directly influencing school administrators, pressing their case until they gained advocates from within the school to create specialized placements for their students. Third, high-status parents recruited the "not quite elites" to press their case for them. Parents of students in Advanced Placement classes convinced the parents of students in the next highest track to lobby for a return to tracking. Schools offered bribes to elite parents to keep their children in a de-tracked school or a magnet school. For example, a school promised small classes or the best teachers to elite parents to convince them not to withdraw their children and send them to another school that offered high, homogeneous, and selective tracks.[37] Graue and Smith believe that such strategies to restore the hierarchically arranged classes and schools have the effect of increasing stratification among schools and diminishing the quality of educational opportunities for the poor.[38]

Donald Moore and Susan Davenport found that students, after the introduction of magnet schools, seemed to have a broader array of schools and programs from which to choose. But many of these options were open only to select groups of students. Choice schools were less than fair in their admission practices. Students at risk were much less likely to apply to or be selected by the schools that advertised themselves as academically advanced. Most working class and poor parents did not comprehend the application process to select schools. They were less likely to catch on to what elite parents knew: that if the schools were pushed hard enough they might well admit students who fell below the required admission standards. Junior high school counselors, even when they were available, tended to direct low-income students into less selective high schools. Schools with programs like the International Baccalaureate advertised only to students with the top academic records and scores. Academic schools systematically excluded special education students and students whose first language was not English. The high-track, academically selective schools also attracted the best teachers and the most resources from the district. Even when admitted to an academically selective school, students who failed to conform to its profile found themselves forced out. Finally, districts pressured school administrators to raise and maintain high test scores, lest elite parents remove their high-scoring children.[39] All of these practices further segregated children of color and poverty in the least desirable schools or tracks or schools-within-schools, and thereby consigned them to the fewest educational opportunities.[40]

Hugh Lauder and David Hughes conducted research in New Zealand where school choice policies have had more influence than they have in the United States.[41] Their research was conducted in an urban setting where available transportation to schools outside the students' neighborhood facilitated their choice of schools (in contrast to American settings where the lack of transportation hinders exercise of choice). Lauder and Hughes tested hypotheses they gleaned from both critics and advocates of school choice. They examined the relationships between the social class and ethnicity of students and the level of academic achievement in four high schools (of students prior to admission and during subsequent attendance). They found that most lower-class students in high academic schools were there not because of successful application, but because they lived in the schools' catchment area. Of the students who applied to the high-status academic schools, there was a strong relationship between their successful admission and their social class. Furthermore, the following conditions exacerbated stratification of the schools:

> Students from [a] high SES background have the greatest opportunity to avoid working class schools, and most take it.... Students with the highest SES background in a neighbourhood [sic] are most likely to exercise choice.... Exit from working class schools induces a spiral of decline ... whereas schools with more applicants than spaces effectively insulate themselves from the effects of the market.[42]

The authors argue that stratified opportunities result in disparities in subsequent achievement, and that such effects accumulate over multiple years of disparate opportunities.

Despite the remarkable consistency of findings among the studies of the effects of school choice, we do not have to look beyond Boulder to get a reading on the effects of the choice movement. In 1999 the board of education finally decided to commission an independent analysis of the ramifications of its decisions about school choice. As a result of that analysis, Ken Howe and Margaret Eisenhart concluded that the district's policy had resulted in 16 choice schools attended by 20 percent of the district students. But families that availed themselves of choice options were not representative of the district as a whole.

> This deserves the name "skimming" because some schools are drawing a disproportionate number of students from the high scoring pool . . . whereas other schools are losing a disproportionate number.[43]

Their study also showed that "Race/ethnicity is a prominent feature of open enrollment patterns . . . students are leaving regions with higher percentages of minorities. Whites are disproportionately requesting open enrollment in schools with high test scores."[44] Boulder schools have become substantially more stratified by ethnicity since the district adopted school choice policies.

Howe and Eisenhart concluded that the process by which choice schools recruit families contributes directly to increased stratification. For example, applications that are contingent on donations, requirements that parents volunteer a certain number of hours, and transportation costs, all discriminate against families with low incomes and constrained schedules. They took to task priority pools, stating that giving priorities to founders' children and others produces unfairness.

Howe and Eisenhart pointed out that, because of the district's system of funding schools, when advantaged families leave their neighborhood school for a charter or focus school, district funds follow. This drains the budgets of the neighborhood schools, thus exacerbating the disparity in resources. Those schools then enter a downward spiral for those who are left behind.

Although surveys showed that parents of both neighborhood schools and schools of choice were satisfied with their schools, the majority of respondents also believed choice had negatively affected both the sense of local community and the collegiality of the professionals. Finally, the authors recommended that the district oversee the application process, particularly of the lottery, to increase fairness.[45]

But in Boulder, the decisions had already been made by the usual political process—not a democratic process—unaffected by the research study that the district itself had commissioned. All five neighborhood schools in the city that the district closed because of low enrollment have since been converted to schools of choice. Stratification continued to the benefit of the few and as a risk to the many.

Notes

1. The material for this case study came from Linda Miller-Kahn's masters' thesis. Her paper contains extensive references to evidence she collected. We will not repeat such references here. They may be obtained from her directly. Epigraph is by John Dewey (1902).
2. The legislation that finally became law in 2002 lacked the provision of vouchers for families in failing schools. However, a sum of money would be provided to purchase remedial services at approved sites, including religious and secular private schools.
3. Friedman (1962). Also see Hayek (1944).
4. Coleman and Hoffer (1982).
5. See distinctions drawn by Apple (2001).
6. Other parts of the coalition invoked these parents of color whenever they needed to counter the claims of critics that school choice favored the already advantaged parts of society. It is worth noting that these foundations favor radical right-wing causes. They are also referred to in Chapter 6.
7. Coleman and Hoffer (1982); Chubb and Moe (1990); Peterson and Greene (1996). We note that vouchers experienced an earlier avatar in Alum Rock California. In the contemporary era, however, Milwaukee is recognized as first.
8. Cobb and Glass (2000) demonstrated that charter schools in Phoenix were more ethnically homogeneous than the neighborhood schools nearest them.
9. Ball (1994), p. 119.
10. A reference to Schller's (1999) book about the JonBenet Ramsey case in Boulder.
11. Blackmon (1991).
12. At the time the parent corporation of the *Cameria* was Knight-Ridder. We take up the roles that media play in the political spectacle in depth in Chapter 4. Note that examples and tallies are available in Miller-Kahn (2000).
13. Berliner and Biddle (1995).
14. Lasswell (1965), p. 40.
15. Bruner (1995).
16. Wells and Serna (1996), p. 94.
17. Smith (1995a), p. 3B.
18. Smith (1995b), p. 4C.
19. Labaree (1997).
20. Taylor (1992).
21. Labaree (1997).
22. State statute and district policy also must conform to Federal law, specifically the Improving America's Schools Act of 1994. Part C—Public Charter Schools, allows for federal grant money allocated to states for Charter schools. The exact language follows: "In General—The Secretary may award grants to State educational agencies having applications approved pursuant to section 10303 to enable such agencies to conduct a charter school program in accordance with this part."
23. These disputed images of focus schools vis-à-vis charter schools echoed the disparate images of charter schools vis-à-vis vouchers. Choice advocates see charters as entrees to the more preferable alternative of vouchers whereas public school advocates see charters as a way to preempt vouchers. Parents could use the Charter School Act as a "threat" to force the district to create magnet schools. Districts propose the lesser evil from their point of view to cool out or dampen the determination of parent advocates of choice.
24. One year later Stonegate was approved as a focus school in its own right. Active parents at the school believed that the designation protected them from advances from other focus school proposals and a school board sympathetic to school choice.
25. Swize and the Adams principal (also a close friend of Swize) met with Apex's founders to discuss the eventual situating of Apex at Adams but parents and teachers were never informed of the meetings.
26. Hult proposed deleting Marine's resignation speech from the board minutes but that motion failed.
27. Bourdieu and Passeron (1977), p. 487.
28. At the Montessori Focus School, priority-listed students also took most of the available slots. The founders of Zenith, the K–12 charter school, adopted similar guidelines but defined as "founder" anyone who paid a fee to get on the list of applicants. That way, any fam-

ily on the list would be exempt from the lottery and there would be fewer slots determined by lot.

29. Labaree (1992); Lauder and Hughs (1999).

30. Apex teachers threatened to walk out on two occasions because parents interfered with professional decisions. The district knew of the problems and once again paid for a trained mediator to help teachers and parents work out their problems. The mediator found that the teachers' concerns were real and suggested that the governance structure be revamped to include more faculty representation on the Lead Team.

31. A further investigation of the Core Knowledge Foundation website listed its own research to support the claim that Core Knowledge curriculum was superior to the curriculum of most school districts. The website did refer to a recent, "independent," longitudinal study on Core Knowledge conducted by John Hopkins University. The study was funded by the Walton Foundation, a group that has issued grants to Core Knowledge schools across the country for several years. In an abstract written by a Core Knowledge employee, the researchers claimed that in schools where Core Knowledge was consistently implemented, the results were promising. They did, however, state that the positive results were not necessarily due to the Core Knowledge curriculum, but more likely the result of a consistently applied program.

32. Nine months after the CU report on open enrollment that recommended the district handle all choice applications to insure an equitable process, the Zenith website still instructed parents to send two applications directly to the school. One application was for school purposes and the other would be turned into the district for oversight.

34. Edelman (1988), p. 109.

35. Graue and Smith (1996); Labaree (1997).

36. This study focused on de-tracking within schools. Only two of their ten cases were magnet schools per se. Nevertheless, their findings are relevant here, because schools of choice in a position to select their students will select the students that best fit their profiles, whether arts magnets or accelerated academic achievement magnets. Selecting within a school building for homogeneous groups of successful students follows the same principle. (Wells and Serna, 1996.)

37. Wells and Serna (1996).

38. Graue and Smith (1996).

39. Moore and Davenport (1990).

40. Both of the studies just described—Moore and Davenport (1990) and Wells and Serna (1996)—emphasized the negative consequences involved with the use of achievement tests to select students or to establish accountability. Most standardized tests are systematically biased by socio-economic status. Therefore, to use test scores as the basis of admission to special schools or programs is automatically to produce schools stratified according to social class, and by extension, to race.

41. Lauder and Hughes (1999).

42. Lauder and Hughes (1999), p. 101.

43. Howe and Eisenhart (2000), p. 10. By 2003, almost one third of district students attended "schools of choice."

44. Howe and Eisenhart (2000), p. 10.

45. Howe and Eisenhart (2000), p. 10.

CHAPTER 4

The Contribution of Mass Media to Desegregation Policy

The media has been great. They call us the Merchants of Hope.
Almost like being a magician, where you create an illusion that we're working
in the best campus with the most wonderful kids in the city.
—A principal

SOUTH HIGH AND THE EYE IN THE SKY (A VIGNETTE)

Turn on the television to catch the Diamondbacks. A news flash interrupts the baseball game. It's the video camera view from the Channel 33 news helicopter. You recognize the pilot, know his name. He has a hard-rock theme song and music video that hints at war journalism or at least manly courage and his skill at reporting traffic accidents. His helicopter hovers over the schoolyard (you recognize South High, or the filmed images of the school, though you've never been there in person). Maybe a couple dozen teenagers mill around. Almost as many police are there, costumed in riot gear, wearing masks to protect themselves from the wafting tear gas. You watch the television news trucks arrive and the attractive blond reporter set up to conduct interviews—live, on-the-spot. In tones and facial expressions a little out of proportion (it seems to you) with the basic story, that a rock or two got tossed. School security officers called in police. Reporters intercepted the radio call. As she speaks to the camera, kids mug, jumping up and down to get into the shot with her. It seems as much a carnival as a riot. Seeing the images on television, parents have rushed over to make sure their children are okay. Finally, the public information officer for the police department pronounces the incident finished. But television coverage goes on. The images play over and over, making you feel each time that the events themselves are recurring, over and over. Something about the camera angle from the helicopter reminds you of the rampage killing that day at Columbine. You're glad that your daughter doesn't have to go to that school in the video frame, what with those poor kids and the gangs and guns (you don't let your thoughts go further). Your attention wanders. Your eyes drop from the screen to the newspaper in your lap, at the tiny headline on the back page of the *Arizona Republic.* In 10-point font it whispers that a scuffle broke out at the Scottsdale school nearby—where the country-club kids go. It seems that a few rocks got thrown. The principal soon had things under control. It happened last week.[1]

Media and Political Spectacle

A spectacle requires promotion and publicity. Someone must write the advertisement, yell through a bullhorn from the back of a pickup truck, and tack up the posters. Without the media—newspapers, magazines, television, billboards—the public would not know when a theatrical production comes to town or what to expect of the show. Political spectacle requires the media.

In Chapter Three we showed how the local newspaper did not limit itself to reporting the news in the way we ordinarily imagine the press to do (with neutrality, more or less). The *Boulder Daily Camera* had a political agenda of its own that mirrored one set of issues and one set of constituents and treated with prejudice anyone with a competing point of view. By so doing, it abetted the political spectacle by disguising the real values that the policy of school choice allocated to the few. Meanwhile it trafficked in symbols—anxiety over a nonexistent crisis and reassurance that school choice policy will fix it—to the rest of the public.

In this chapter we consider further the relationship of media and political spectacle and show in more specific terms how the web gets spun and how that web entangles policy. We use the case of desegregation in urban Arizona to reveal the particulars.

Consider the word "medium." It suggests a neutral conduit of information from source to destination. But the state of journalism today and the state of policy in political spectacle suggest that this medium distorts, glosses, and obscures the signal and prevents the public from obtaining the information it needs to participate effectively.

The media bias and distort the message, not usually because of some explicit political ideology (left or right), but because media act in the vested interest of the cultural and economic institution in which they operate. Mass media operate according to certain conventions called "media logics." They employ leads and hooks and angles, without which an incident is not considered newsworthy. Without a hook a piece of information is not a story. Journalists must make deadlines, sell newspapers, and increase market share. To accomplish such ends, media favor the dramatic, the novel, the deviant, the sensational, mythic imagery and completed narratives.

Television adds its favorites: vivid pictures, artsy camera angles, eyewitness accounts, celebrity reporters.

As a cultural institution, media dominate and transform other institutions—the military, the church, the schools, and the state itself. All these institutions must adopt media logics to attract any attention from news agencies.

To prosper and maintain legitimacy and authority, schools have adapted themselves to the needs of the media. Schools, like other organizations, produce "suitable symbols . . . processed and prepared for possible uses by journalists."[2] Journalists have a format that defines what is reportable news. School officials who work with journalists adapt journalistic frames and angles if they want good press. So schools hire public relations staff to dress up school news, such as reports of test scores or the advent of new programs, into formats that the media recognize and can use. Once journalistically framed, these accounts thereafter serve the interests of the institution. News organizations then make use of institutional accounts as a basis of subsequent stories. A process of mutual shaping of interests and discourse then transpires. For schools, interests include disseminating information and managing positive impressions as well. Eventually "news" about schools cannot be distinguished from public relations. Yet the media still enjoy the cultural cache of objective reporting, independent investigations that serve the interests of the public. The process continues. Institutional actors then incorporate the "news" accounts into "sign-work," in newsletters and program brochures that the school sends to parents and the community. In those outlets the school can quote and attribute the positive report to the magazine or newspaper, even though the school itself framed the original information. Political success soon becomes intertwined with media success.[3]

Journalists and policy makers engage in similar modes of discourse. Both simplify social reality for audiences that have neither specialized nor direct knowledge of the policy. By the process of simplification, media affect policy intentions and interpretations at all levels of the policy process. The media contributes "to the policy process through selective coverage and interpretation of events by media professionals like journalists and program makers. Their values about what makes a story newsworthy, lead to a consistent bias or 'refraction' in media output."[4] Contemporary journalists are interdependent with source organizations. Reporters rely on public relations staff for quotes and leads. School officials rely on reporters to represent their schools in favorable ways. Journalists restrict themselves to sources that are the most accessible and convenient. They rely on institutional press releases and interviews with handlers and experts in public relations rather than investigating leads, exploring counter claims, or attempting to achieve a comprehensive perspective. Thus media become part of the knowledge reproduction efforts of the school.[5]

Edelman defined news reports as central to political spectacles. Politics is driven by people's interpretations of facts and events and as a result "much political activity is an effort to control interpretations."[6] Policy language promises future benefits that will flow once the policy is implemented or threatens what will transpire if it is not. It is the symbolic language about political events rather than the events themselves that people experience. In the vignette at the beginning of this chapter what the narrator will remember will be images on the television screen, which represent only a portion of the real event and only that specific portion that fits the needs and formats of television. Frames of tear gas draw more viewers than the reasoned arguments.

Politics and policy involve constructing meaning in a persuasive manner. Since policy involves the continual conflict over preferred signs and meanings, the media provide to policy makers the principal way "to mobilize support and immobilize opposition."[7] According to Edelman, "Officials, interest groups, and critics anticipate the interpretations of particular audiences, shaping their acts and language so as to elicit a desired response."[8]

In a society dependent on knowledge, journalism constructs and distributes information in such a way as to exacerbate social inequality. Control over information is unequally distributed, and this inequity translates directly into inequitable power. Journalists give voice to certain sources as authoritative. Others have little chance of affecting the social construction of reality. News serves as a central arena in which organizations attempt to construct an organizational order that is partial to their own interests.[9]

Catherine Lugg invented the term "Prolicy"—public relations public policy —to describe this new form of policy dominated by media. Prolicy emerges, not from democratic deliberation or elected officials negotiating and compromising for the public good, as we commonly think. Instead, Lugg wrote, "unelected media specialists who are well versed in the techniques of symbolic manipulation formulate Prolicy. Constant polling, the use of focus groups, and the tailoring of strategic sound bites for reporters' daily consumption are but a few examples of Prolicy techniques employed by politicians and their handlers."[10]

As the public adjusts its expectations to media formats, it comes gradually to think about the social world differently. The world that mass media presents to the public is a world that appears to be in constant crisis, threatening chaos at every turn. Policy makers too are changed, more often addressing the symbolism rather than the substance of policies. How will the policy play in the newspapers? What can we do to make it seem like schools are improving? Impression management assumes a greater proportion of their strategies and tactics. What will the television stations make of armed security guards? When policies are framed in terms of images, perceptions, sound bites, and headlines, then media images themselves stand in place of tangible evidence about the tangible workings and benefits of a program.

Our brief summary of theories about the media's effects on policy applies credibly to desegregation policy in Phoenix District and South High School.

A Case of Mediated Desegregation Policy[11]

In 1954, in Brown v. the Board of Education, the United States Supreme Court ruled that African-American children receive education that is deficient compared to that of white children. The court declared that schools made up exclusively of children of color could not, by definition, provide equal education. Thus began a vast policy experiment—school boundary changes, two-way busing, one-way busing, open enrollment, magnet schools—all in the name of desegregation, which at the outset was meant as a proxy for providing equal educational opportunities for African-American children.

In 1954 the Phoenix Union High School District (hereafter called the district) opened a new high school across the Rio Salado, south of downtown in a predominantly agricultural area where a mixture of ethnic groups lived in adjacent, but separate, neighborhoods. Although the racial composition of South Mountain High School (hereafter called South or South High) did not concern the district in 1954, Phoenix has a history of de jure segregation. A school exclusively for African-Americans operated downtown until the 1960s. The racial climate, we were told, was "just like Mississippi."[12] As demographics and land-use policies changed, South's catchment area tipped in the 1960s to a majority of African-American students and later to a majority of Hispanic students. Throughout the 1960s and 1970s, white families fled to the more expensive and exclusive outer edges of Phoenix and to the suburbs where their children could attend "good," safe schools with others like themselves. For a quarter century, because its land values and housing costs were lower than the rest of the city and because of local government actions that segregated communities, South's enrollment soared. As South became more segregated (the federal government termed such schools "racially identifiable" or "racially isolated"), the district began to neglect its facilities and programs. The grounds deteriorated. They were reminiscent of prisons with concrete hardscape and little green landscape, and 30 unmatched, cobbled together buildings, high fences, locked gates, and security guards.

In the process South High acquired a reputation—a mediated reputation. Newspapers, magazines, and television reports amplified the racial angle. They dramatized the problems that occasionally arose at South, focusing public attention on disturbances like gunfire in the neighborhood or campus demonstrations after Martin Luther King was shot. Since most

Phoenicians never crossed the river—and still don't—they lacked direct information that would enable them to evaluate for themselves the conditions at South High. Instead they absorbed the dramatic images and soaked up the narrative plot lines that the media constructed for them. When most people thought about South, they visualized gangs, guns, and incompetent teachers. Knowing only the mediated image, the public pictured unmotivated students whose poor (in both pocket and spirit) parents cared little about their children's education.[13]

Contrary to that reputation, many non-Anglo parents cared deeply about what the school offered their children. They well knew that middle-class parents in other neighborhoods would not have tolerated what South offered. African-American parents protested to the district. The district ignored them.

In 1978, the local chapter of the National Association for the Advancement of Colored People filed a complaint with the Office of Civil Rights against the district on behalf of the parents. The complaint alleged that the district had engaged in discriminatory practices and policies that produced segregation, such as gerrymandering boundaries of some schools and closing some others. Schools that served mostly non-Anglo students failed to offer complete academic programs and channeled their students into low paying jobs. Thus, the complaint charged, the district had acted in violation of the 1964 Civil Rights Act and the equal protection clause of the U.S. Constitution.

After the court issued its findings in 1984, the Office of Civil Rights entered into negotiations with district administrators and lawyers to devise a remedy. Because the federal executive had by then scaled back its desegregation efforts (magnet schools displaced busing) and because the state legislature fought against any federal mandates, all parties to the negotiations rejected busing as politically unacceptable. They settled on magnet schools as a solution to segregation in the district. More importantly to the story of political spectacle, the parties to the negotiation settled on a numeric criterion that the court could use to determine whether each school in the district had achieved racial balance. A numeric criterion (the percent of a school's population that was non-white) gave the appearance of rationality and fairness, but turned out later to be nothing but hollow and cynical symbolism.

Neither the African-American parents nor the NAACP participated in this negotiation, a fact with subsequent ramifications.

By 1988, as a consequence of the magnet school program, the district had met the criterion of racial balance in all its schools—except for South. At South alone the magnet programs had been designed to attract white students exclusively. Neither racial balance nor school achievement had improved. So the district initiated a compensatory reform for students left out of South's magnets. Everyone called this reform "the Plan."

In 1994 the federal judge found South had attained the numeric criterion for racial balance and terminated the desegregation order. But look at the daily life at South at the end of the century and you see that neither the degree of segregation nor education quality and achievement had changed from conditions in 1978.

This thumbnail sketch above fails to capture how a policy meant to solve unequal educational opportunities transformed into something quite different. Nor does it show how media affected beliefs about what the problem was, beliefs about what the solution should be, or beliefs about how the effectiveness of the solution should be judged.

We present in this chapter the case of a high school at which a desegregation policy was implemented in order to show how the media played a significant role in defining for the public both policy problems and policy solutions. We show how institutional actors used the media to support the implementation of a symbolic response to court-ordered desegregation. In providing a symbolic solution, the district neglected the underlying reason for the policy—to make schools more equitable and effective for non-Anglo students.

How did this happen? We have to backtrack to show how the history of desegregation policy at the national level shaped responses locally.

Desegregation Policy from the Top Down

In the decade following the *Brown v. Board of Education* decision, the Federal government failed to implement policies or fund programs that might have diminished school segregation. Desegregation policy was symbolic until President Lyndon Johnson addressed racial composition of schools as part of his "Great Society" programs to help the poor. Between 1964 and the early 1970s all three branches of government supported desegregation and enforced court orders by mandatory bussing throughout the South, where it had a lasting impact. In political spectacle language, the policy developed substance and allocated tangible benefits.

Although policies during this era were effective in the South, they failed to address the underlying structural relationships among housing, education, and family income. In other words, poor and minority people were concentrated within neighborhoods, and school authorities assigned pupils to schools according to their neighborhoods. Although these patterns came about because of government policies and traditions (land values and building codes, deliberate housing segregation and the like), policy makers believed that equal access to schools would be enough to break apart these underlying structural relationships.

This logic—that equal access to schools would break the patterns and improve the economic prospects of the poor—had its detractors. Harvey Kanter and Robert Lowe claimed that the Federal desegregation policy, like Great Society programs such as Head Start, legitimated claims for equal education but at the same time neglected education policies that African-Americans wanted most.[14] Policy makers also feared a backlash by white Americans and sought solutions that, while appearing to do something about school segregation, did nothing to challenge the underlying structural inequality in society. That is, even the best program to integrate schools would run into a barrier of housing discrimination and income disparities.

The administration of Richard Nixon determined to dismantle desegregation policies and diminish Federal enforcement and the pursuit of new cases, particularly in the western U.S. As well, the Supreme Court ruled that voluntary desegregation should supplant mandatory desegregation. It disallowed bussing plans that crossed district boundaries into the suburbs. Bussing was replaced by magnet schools as the preferred policy to correct the problems that minorities faced.

Except for a brief period of renewed interest during the Carter administration, federal policies weakened and the number of enforcement of court cases dwindled. Desegregation policies lost their substance and became symbolic. This policy trajectory provided the context in which the Phoenix case developed.

Phoenix District Before the Court Order

To desegregate schools in Phoenix required that federal policy overcome decades of local policies and cultural traditions that reinforced segregation. Discrimination against ethnic groups had been built into state law from the state's beginnings. In 1909 state law mandated segregation in elementary schools and permitted high schools to practice segregation if they chose. A local historian described Arizona's constitution as the creation of Southern men who wanted segregated schools.

An informant characterized the racial climate in Phoenix after World War I:

> When the cotton growers came to Phoenix . . . they didn't want their white kids to go to school with any black kid at all. . . . The first black kid to go to high school . . . he was treated very shabbily. He couldn't be in the library when the white kids were there and he couldn't eat with white kids. When he was graduated he wasn't permitted in the commencement. . . . It was not just that the school district in 1980 was guilty, but the history of Phoenix and the history of society in the state was guilty.

In 1942 and after twenty years in operation, the single high school for African-Americans still had no library and no musical instruments, art, or shop equipment. Calling the conditions "appalling," a community leader began orchestrating protests, lobbying the legislature, and filing lawsuits. Although the state supreme court eventually declared school segregation laws to be unconstitutional, attitudes toward race remained the same, and segregation continued in housing and employment. The state government failed to follow up the court declaration so that school segregation increased, simply by the lack of enforcement. Meanwhile, the minority population of Phoenix grew at a faster rate than the white population.

By 1980 the majority of Phoenix district students were non-Anglo, making it a "majority minority" district. And non-Anglo students were concentrated in three of the nine high schools, schools that were increasingly neglected over the years. As in Newark and other cities, covenants and land-use policies, segregated housing, and actions by banks to redline neighborhoods concentrated poor and minority families in particular sections of Phoenix. The district, reacting to pressure from advantaged parents, drew school boundaries in ways that tightened the noose. Financial problems and out-migration of white families (at a rate of three percent per year) created pressure on the district to operate more efficiently. The district reacted by closing schools, again in such a way to appease Anglo parents and isolate non-Anglos in targeted schools. The district dressed up these decisions as necessary to economize. Racial attitudes played their parts.

In this spirit, the state legislature created a policy of open enrollment, spinning it as a benefit to poor and minority pupils. However, it was mostly used by white students' families to allow them to transfer out of schools that primarily contained students of color. When enough minority students transferred to a target school, the white students exited. As schools became recognizably minority, the district's support of those schools diminished.

The growing restiveness on the part of minority parents eventuated in the Castro order, which invalidated the open-enrollment law, but the legislature ignored the order, and students continued to transfer out of the district and take their per-pupil allocation with them. The district also found ways around the Castro order.

But African-American leaders believed that racial isolation and segregation were less important than the experiences of their children in schools. They were more concerned with discriminatory hiring of teachers, the treatment of their chidren by Anglo teachers, and a decent, quality, and more equal education. Desegregation was merely a means to those ends, a pragmatic interim solution. One recalled,

> And the inner-city schools were in terrible shape. You would go in and the kids would be throwing erasers and chalk and all the teacher was doing was sitting there. They didn't have those [academic] courses. . . . The schools did not have the supplies needed. . . . The average non-minority hasn't had the experience it takes to understand minority students.

Another leader recalled:

> And then we tend to blame the children . . . the victim, "His momma's in jail, his momma's on crack." And we excuse our lack of attention. Teachers come to class with such low expectancy that the children never rise above the low expectancies, and they don't teach so the children will rise. There are no black teachers.

In 1985, the typical freshman was more than two years behind the national norm for achievement. Only about half of that group remained to graduate. Thirty-eight percent had failed at least one course. Eighty-eight percent of South students were non-Anglo, and many lacked fluency in English. These statistics set South far apart from the rest of the district.

After the Court Order: School/Media Reactions

Arizona politicians opposed any federal decree, and the court order to desegregate the district was no exception. The district mounted a vigorous legal defense, and as a result relations between district and the Office of Civil Rights remained adversarial throughout the period of negotiating remedies. The district even resisted OCR attempts to study the schools. The media wrote "war." Open-enrollment policies that increased white flight and more school closures actually increased segregation. More legal action, claiming intentional discrimination on the part of the district, was settled when the district agreed to disallow any transfers that did not improve ethnic balance. The superintendent resigned amid the pressures from both sides.

The court gave little guidance to the district as to how to fund the desegregation programs, creating a vacuum for agencies to redefine and weaken the order. The OCR, for example, encouraged the district to focus on improving the public image of South by means of magnet schools which other districts under desegregation orders had used to improve racial balance and school image. Magnets could attract white students to South and minority pupils to schools that were then predominantly white. In this negotiation, therefore, OCR moved the district in the direction of symbolic goals rather than to face head on the underlying problems of financial neglect, poor educational opportunities, and educators' discriminatory practices.

These suggestions fit the district's agenda perfectly. Magnet schools appeared to provide choice, a value that always resonates with Arizona's political culture. Magnets offered benefits to white students, who could pursue special curricular interests or more advanced programs like the International Baccalaureate. Most important from the state standpoint, programs gave the appearance of efficiency, in that they did not require wholesale bussing or expensive reforms for all students. Magnet schools made the state and district appear to be doing something about a significant problem.

Desegregation policy also became a money-maker. The state regularly failed to fund inflation costs to schools and even passed a revenue control limit that restricted the level of revenue that districts could raise without voter approval. Because Arizona schools were financed by local property taxes, because the neighborhood's property was of low value, and because the district's enrollment was dropping due to white flight, the district had few financial resources to implement court-ordered remedies. To forestall a lawsuit threatened by the plaintiffs, the legislature later passed a bill to exempt the district from the statewide revenue control limits until the court order could be lifted. The district exercised authority over how this new money would be allocated, and district officials used some of it to further their own interests, not those of the court order. For example, the district used some of these funds to open magnet programs at other schools that attracted white students away from South. In other words, the money was not directed specifically toward the policy targets. It paid for public relations, promotion of its programs, and recruitment of Anglo students from other schools.

The OCR also redefined and weakened the court order by specifying a numeric target that it could use to determine when the district had complied with the order. That target specified that the ratio of minority students to the total student body at South was to be no worse than the ratio of minority to white students in the district as a whole. And moreover, when the composition of South reached within 20 percent of the district composition, OCR would declare the district in compliance with the court order and remove it from its jurisdiction. So, if minority students made up 50 percent of the total students in the district, South would be judged in compliance when its minority percentage fell below 70 percent. As one can see, this was not only symbolic but lenient for the district, and it failed to foresee the looming disproportion of minority students in the district as a whole. Still, the solution seemed reasonable at the time.

Once the target was negotiated, OCR failed to evaluate or monitor how well the district implemented it. Parents of minority pupils, who were most interested in substantive improvements, were denied a role in monitoring what the district carried out.

Media and Constructed Images

What role did the media play? Phoenix newspapers and television accentuated the dramatic parts of South's reality, and drama sells papers and advertising.

An African-American reporter for the local newspaper covering the education beat in the 1980s recalled that most Arizona journalists had never crossed the river into South Phoenix to write a story, were generally insensitive, and lacked experience with ethnic minorities. Stories in the media emphasized South's low achievement and high dropout rates. South was viewed as the school that turned out losers.

News stories focused on race, violence, and gangs. Rather than investigating closely or questioning a variety of sources for their news stories, journalists relied on police sources and district public information officers. A teacher at South recalled:

> There were always articles about South in the paper about student achievement being low and about racial tensions, always in the news.

After decades of such news coverage, it is little wonder that policy makers focused on the image and reputation of South. Policy makers could have taken the long, courageous approach; that is, by making the real South a better place, an improved image would inevitably (but eventually) follow. For policies in the political spectacle, policy makers must act fast, before the next election or their next career move. Think body counts, cure rates, intensive preparation for high-stakes tests: all fall into this category of flawed indicators that can be tweaked, inflated, manipulated for political purposes. So, too, images are managed more easily than substantive reforms.

The media created a negative image of South, only partly based in fact, then dramatized and simplified it. As the OCR, the courts, and district officials came to see it, the negative image was what caused white flight, hence segregation, hence the court order. And if image was the problem, they reasoned, then they must effect a change in the image the media relayed to the public. Substantive improvements in the education they provided to minority students gave way to improvements in mediated images. First, district officials adopted magnet programs to bring white students back. Second, they worked directly on the image problem building a bureau whose sole responsibility was to work the press.

Thus the media entered into policy. South's poor reputation even made its way into desegregation court orders and civil rights enforcement. A 1984 OCR document claimed that, unlike the other schools, the district had failed to dispel the poor image of South or improve its programs:

> Further, because of student protests and discipline issues during the 1970s, which were highly publicized in Phoenix, widespread attitudes were formed that the minority high schools did not offer a positive learning environment. It is apparent that these attitudes continued to exist. A great deal of media attention was focused upon, for example, fears of students and faculty at Center High over the influx of minority students; predictions of violence after the closed-zone policy went into effect; threats of parents refusing to comply with new policies; predictions of failure. . . .

A positive program should be developed by the district to address any real and perceived disparities in services, and to change any continuing negative community perceptions. Such a program could potentially alter the resistance among some Anglo students to attending [South].

Magnets

The public image of the school became the official policy target of the Federal agencies involved in policy development. A significant portion of the subsequent court-ordered desegregation plan centered on improving the image of the school through magnet programs. Once this occurred, the policy shifted to a management of signs and symbols rather than changing substantive educational practices.

About the time that negotiations between the district and OCR came to a resolution, the superintendent resigned.

To find a new superintendent who could handle the fractionalized environment brought on by the desegregation order, the district hired a public relations firm, which then involved itself in school operations and politics.

The search for a superintendent ended when the district chose a charismatic "idea man" who understood media and impression management. Right away, the public relations firm arranged for an informational session between the new superintendent and the education reporters of the major newspapers. From among these reporters, the superintendent hired one as Assistant Superintendent of Public Relations. Thus, the media affected the organization of the district, and the district reshaped itself into an organization that could use the media to change the image of South High School. The reporter cum assistant superintendent later recalled:

> I did not realize at the time was that he was interviewing me and that's how I came to work for the district. The next time we talked he offered me the job. He took the only person in the media who knew more about that school district and was in a position to hurt him more with the reporting . . . and hired him. That was brilliant . . . that was the strategy he used. He elevated that position to a cabinet-level position and I was put in as one of his advisors and all of the things I knew about the district and what was wrong with the district were put to work for the district.

The superintendent then hired an external organizational consulting firm to reorganize the district and clarify goals. The consulting firm also gave advice to the public information officer, who said of the superintendent:

> He got everybody speaking the same language and then he moved them in the direction of using magnets as an educational tool—not as a desegregation tool. And he got desegregation funds to use for the magnet program.

The district offered the following explanation of the continued problems at South and how best to fix them:

The public's perception of South, true or false, had to be altered sharply; parents do not transfer their students to the "worst school in the district" regardless of how good the magnet programs are. The public's perception of South included the following: (1) neither students nor their possessions were safe or secure on campus; (2) test scores were the lowest in the District and under national norms; (3) drop-out and absenteeism rates were the highest in the District; (4) the faculty and support staff were inferior and lacked dedication; and (5) the plant and physical environment were sup-par, the least attractive in the District. For the [remedies] to succeed at South all the above perceptions need to be changed . . . . South is a safe school to attend. This message repeated over and over again is being presented to the public via newspapers, radio ads, parent support groups, and the students themselves. It flies in the face of twenty years of misperception.

The superintendent later explained:

> I think it was primarily the image of South. . . . South has always had a tough reputation its entire existence. It was very difficult to convince parents . . . they didn't think it would be safe . . . it took no mental giant to figure that out. All you had to do was listen to parents on the phone, listen to legislators, listen to the business community, everybody heard this. There was no debate on the matter.

From the OCR's point of view, South's problem was segregation. The federal theory of change assumed that equal educational opportunity would result from numerically racially balanced schools. Furthermore, the primary way to balance the racial mix was to change public perceptions. The way to attract white students to South would be to offer magnet programs or other educationally desirable benefits. Both the OCR and the district favored impression management over other programs that might have improved school quality for non-Anglo students and families in the neighborhood. Aligning their discourse and action to each other, the two organizations aimed, not to upgrade staff and facilities at South to approximate those of the rest of the district, but instead to play the numbers game—racial balance. The superintendent later said:

> The law didn't require quality education, the law required that we ethnically balance and not segregate certain schools over those other schools. . . .

The solution that OCR and the district negotiated was the following: To rid itself of the designation "racially identifiable," South must be no more racially segregated than the district as a whole. It is remarkable in retrospect that such a weak standard could have been accepted. Clearly, the solution fits into the category of a symbolic policy. It fit the media's need for a simple, numeric solution to a problem, and a narrative end of a story. Furthermore, the media accepted as the public relations officer's account. It did not investigate further the anomalies and implications of this solution.

The OCR staff had first mentioned magnet schools, which seemed to offer values to whites as well as African-Americans—more educational opportunities, more choice—would eventuate. The judge who supervised the school district's desegregation case said:

> I was willing to try it [desegregation] on the basis of magnet schools, but I am not convinced even that works. In fact, I think generally today, as someone once said, there's a feeling of malaise about race problems. . . . The latest *Time* magazine has a whole article on how people are giving up on integration. And how the judges are getting worn out and all that kind of stuff.

Although the district educators knew little about magnet schools, they pressed ahead to learn, taking field trips to Kansas City and other places where such programs had been established as a means toward voluntary desegregation. In his pitch to the media and Anglo families, the new superintendent soft-pedalled desegregation and emphasized choice. In most people's minds, desegregation implied mandates and bussing. But magnet programs connoted a more palatable image of voluntary participation and choice of a high quality, highly specialized educational program. And while the superintendent emphasized quality, exclusivity and choice to the Anglo parents, he often used the threat of bussing as a way to ward off criticisms and concerns that staff and non-Anglo families had about magnets.

The assistant superintendent for public relations described the process of altering the organization and practices of the district in its attempt to get good press:

> He [the new superintendent] basically initialed the desegregation program and got it started. He conducted a series of meetings to get parents to understand what he was trying to do and I thought it was a stroke of brilliance that he no longer sold the magnet programs as a desegregation tool, he sold them as a viable educational option that was going to raise the level of education throughout the district by concentrating instruction in certain areas on certain campuses. And it worked.

When a journalist was named assistant superintendent for communication, a new post, he began a campaign to distribute packaged, positive information to reporters in formats they could use. Meanwhile, he passed along his inside knowledge about the media to district administrators:

> We increased the communications and I used some of my skills as a reporter to get the word out. Because a lot of times there were valid stories coming out of school districts that parents were interested in but were not sexy enough to compete in the paper. . . . Then there were stories that got coverage in the paper because we wrote them in the newsletter. We put politicians on the mailing list and reporters on the mailing list and it all came out of my office. The transition [from journalist to public relations officer] was not as difficult as I thought it would be.

So far as the reporters, we had a very good relationship with the press and not only print but also the electronic media. The reporters came to me. My job was to work with the media —you don't handle the media, you open it up and let the media in . . . you answer questions. You can suggest stories. It's the wrong terminology to say "feeding." As the information about the magnets came available we let them know because the magnets were new to the whole area and a lot of reporters didn't know what they were and so we educated them as far as what a magnet program is and what it is supposed to do.

You work with people in the school district and tell them, 'this is how you act during an interview, don't do this, don't do that. Give them the information, get them to trust you' . . . sort of an informal training for everybody.

I would write press releases. If you want to talk to someone, you speak their language. So I didn't write them like puff things but like news items. You gotta find a hook. Most of it and if you talk to most PR professionals, most of it we did face-to-face. You don't do it with news releases. . . . You sit down when they call you, you touch base, you call them if you hear about something happening not even in your district or in education but something happening you think will help them . . . you call them. You build good media relations. I was doing the tipping some, yeah. . . .

A hook is a news angle. That's basically if you had a program you wanted to sell you would not sell it like, oh, the [district] has initiated this program, you know, for students and the administration said this about it and that about it. No, no. What is this program you are going to do? Ok this program is designed to increase the graduation rate amongst minority students. . . . You would maybe quote the superintendent once, but you talk to the people going to be affected by this. . . . The hooks and angles on desegregation were education program, education program.

The result of these public relations strategies attracted positive attention both nationally and locally for the school. A Hispanic state legislator said:

Two things happened as a result of the magnet programs. As much as I see it as a failure, it did attract some national attention and some attention from the state and it started getting a fairly decent reputation.

But this legislator went on to describe how the magnet programs did not enhance the education of non-Anglo students. He said:

I have to believe that when we started it was more in the nature of rhetoric and pursuing something in that respect rather than having a program that would have objectives and goals and monitoring.

The African-American community that brought the suit in the first place did not follow the logic or accept the appeal of magnet schools. An African-American leader said that the purpose of the magnet programs was to bring Anglo students into the predominantly minority school but that segregation was only half the problem. He asserted that the real problem, the problem as defined by minority interests, was holding the mostly

Anglo teachers accountable for effectively teaching minority students. He asserted that the magnet programs were symbolic: "It was about images."

> Nor did the magnet program deal with the organic needs of blacks. It dealt su-
> perficially. . . . What it sought to do was to bring black children from here to
> any of the schools up north. . . . White kids from up north could come here to
> these special programs and of course the selling point was you [Anglo stu-
> dents] don't come in contact with them [minority students] anyway and you
> are an island in this great sea of humanity.

The district's choice of a performing arts magnet for South incensed the African-American leaders as well. They viewed the decision as the result of stereotyping and believed it would solidify that stereotype.

In spite of the enormous work put into magnet programs, they remained separate from the rest of the school. Teachers in magnet and non-magnet programs barely interacted or even walked into each other's spaces. Funds were unequally distributed. Non-magnet students "feel like step-children and they are not given the challenges or the chances with boring classes and teachers that don't care," according to an evaluation report. Most of the non-magnet school population believed that they were not eligible to enroll in the magnet programs and therefore did not bother to apply. Most of the staff believed that the magnets existed solely to restore racial balance. The same report concluded that the district had never been centrally concerned about improving in concrete ways the educational experience of non-white students at South.

These strategies included a concerted effort to use the media as a key resource in the struggle to promote the district's definition of the problem and the solution. The notion of desegregation and magnet programs was sold to Anglo parents as an education reform that would benefit them. As a result of the district's communication office, media coverage of the magnet programs and subsequent reform programs at the school were overwhelmingly positive and supportive during the 1988–1992 period.

From the Magnets to the "Plan"

In 1988, despite several years of the magnet programs in the district, only South remained racially out of balance, according to the court's formula. Among the students not in magnets, achievement was still too low. Dropout rates were still too high. Once segregation had been the separation of white and non-white students into different schools. Now segregation had migrated to program versus program *within* a single school. The magnet remedy had failed to change segregation at South and certainly had had no effect on educational quality and opportunity. Enough rumblings were heard—from the leaders of the non-white groups as well as the less than sanguine findings from evaluations—that the district had to take action. Since the district still had to hit its numerical target for judging racial balance, it still had to work on its image and efforts to draw in and keep Anglo students. To do that meant that magnet programs must be continued. Yet the district now had also to find some other solution for the students who were not part of magnets.

What the district installed was called "the Plan." It featured organizational restructuring. It assumed that restructuring would lead somehow to better instruction for minority students, and thence to higher achievement. For example, teachers involved in the Plan had fewer courses than they usually did, and the ideas was that they would use that extra time to attend to students' psychological and social needs and oversee their academic progress. Further, freshman and sophomore students were assigned to "cores," small groups with teams of teachers for the purpose of interdisciplinary program planning and the like.

Once again, the district assumed that by changing the way that South was organized, the day-to-day educational experiences of non-Anglo students would improve. Events proved otherwise; the hoped-for transformation of education did not take place. Organizational changes were not enough to guarantee that substantive changes would occur in the classroom. For example, the school required all students to take algebra (and this requirement garnered much favorable publicity). This change in organization-by-mandate failed to provide relevant professional development to teachers or to evaluate classroom instruction. Many teachers in courses called "Algebra" were in fact teaching basic arithmetic. But no one—plaintiffs, Office of Civil Rights, attorneys, district officials, the media—watched closely enough to know this until too late.[15]

The absence of evaluation and professional development left to chance what the teachers did with their greater freedom and new roles. Most of them knew nothing about how to counsel or how to make home visits. The restructuring came to them as a top-down mandate, both ambitious and extremely ambiguous. To decrease student-teacher ratio required hiring many new teachers, who differed from the teachers already there. The new guard was committed to reforming education. The old guard remained pessimistic about reform in an environment where (the teachers believed) parents didn't care, students lacked the requisite academic background, and the administrators failed to exercise consistent leadership. Morale decreased as internal dissent and conflict increased. The organizational changes failed to raise the low expectations many teachers held for minority students. The teachers might comply, but either they didn't know how to do what they needed to do or their hearts were not in it. Many teachers recalled that era with frustration. It seemed chaotic. "We were doing 10,000 things. We were meeting-ed to death."

To enhance the image of the school and change the perceptions of the Anglo population, the Plan established an organization with two principals. One of the co-principals had responsibility for media relations and publicity. The other ran the school. Both seemed obsessed with obtaining national and state awards as ways of generating positive media coverage. One co-principal said:

> One of the terms that I like to use is "caretaker of the dream," that we are care-takers of the dream that all our students here can achieve academically. An-other one that a [reporter] from Channel thirty-three coined for us and we've latched onto it is "Merchants of Hope". . . . Part of it as caretaker of the dream is almost like being a magician as far as creating an illusion that "gosh, look at how wonderful these kids are. . . . So that's part of the dream, that part of the . . . merchants of hope, where you create an illusion that they are working in the best campus, not only in our district but also in the city . . . and the state . . . and pretty soon, nation-wide. . . . So every little thing that's done academi-cally, Al and I make a point to go out and sell, and Al's a great salesman. He does that. I think its one of his real major skills, just being a salesman. . . . "

From the quote above it is clear that this man was thinking in sound bites and imagining how certain things would look in the media. The other co-principal also began to measure the success of the school by the extent to which it received positive media coverage:

> The area I am most enthusiastic about the success is the positive public rela-tions. I think it has been really, really good. And that's one of three major arti-cles we've had in the last . . . month or two. And there have been a number of smaller things, both on television and in the newspaper. So the media has been great.

Most of the awards had been garnered by students in magnet programs, an inconvenient detail the principal failed to reveal. He continued to trum-pet these accomplishments in his comments to the media, parents, and the students:

> The other thing that speaks to the success of the program is individual awards both for individual students, staff, and the school in general. As you know, we were selected by the Department of Education as an A-plus award recipient. That was significant. That was a real positive thing. Many of our teachers have received awards this year. Rod Comfort was selected as Teacher of the year by the Black Scientists and Engineers Association; Bob Andrews, the NFL teacher of the month; and a number of other individual awards. Our students have re-ceived many awards. . . . We just took honorable mention top-ten in the national mock trial competition; we won the state in that. We had sport suc-cesses. . . . Our academic decathlon team made it to the state for the first time in history. Our foreign language competition at the state level . . . received su-perior ratings. Our programs have been getting a lot of recognition for their

excellence in success, as have our kids. You know I was selected as one of the principals of the year this year, top six. So there have been a number of accolades and successes. All of the press that we have received this year has been positive press as opposed to the previous years.

As the above quotations indicate, media helped transform desegregation policy from substance to an elaborate public display of symbols. The success of the program came to be defined as the level of media coverage the school received. School administrators engaged in a strategy of "impression management," using the media to persuade key audiences of program success. Their strategies worked. Between 1988 and 1992 media coverage was overwhelmingly positive. But nothing was helping minority students.

An analysis of news articles from that period reveals that journalists relied primarily on official or friendly sources. Thus, the district screened teachers, parents and students so that reporters would only hear comments that supported the Plan. Almost exclusively, news articles quoted only students who were enrolled in magnet programs and thus those who benefited disproportionately from the infusion of funds for special programs.[16] The majority of staff that the news articles quoted also had vested interests in the Plan. Critics of the Plan rarely rated any space in the papers.

The way in which media frames promote administrators' characterizations of South and the Plan can be viewed as instances of symbolic compliance. Take, for example, the following statement of the principal concerning the goals of the South Plan, in which he reveals his awareness of the distinction between symbolic and instrumental policy:

The school board responded to desegregation to increase the white population at South. We have come close. On any given day we might achieve the court-ordered desegregation. . . . But part of desegregation means having white and brown students interacting as well and respecting each other. This is a big order we may decide not to take on. All the court order says is that we have to have the numbers.

According to Ericson and her colleagues, media sources align their reports to journalists' demands for news of deviance. Phoenix officials and public relations officers gave them what they wanted: an Horatio Alger success story of heroic school leaders overcoming huge odds to save kids otherwise doomed to fail by the system. News accounts characterized the Plan as an extraordinary cure for the ills of the surrounding community, which they portrayed as a barrio suffering from drugs, unemployment, high mobility, and gang violence. Articles framed the pre-Plan school as "plagued" by violence, low achievement, dropouts, and truancy. Students were characterized as being "potential dropouts," low achievers, and chronic truants. But in the "success against great odds story," the magnets and the Plan changed all that.

Having been satisfied in their demands for sensational stories, the media looked no further for the more complex and problematic facts of life at South—at academic quality or even at integration. How school officials characterized the school became the authoritative version of the progress of the South Plan in fulfilling its mandate to desegregate.

The media described previous problems at South from the national angle of educational crisis, evoking the warnings of academic and economic ruin in *A Nation at Risk*. The media defined the solution (supposedly based on "research") as enhancement of parents' participation in education. Newspapers focused on school choice as a solution. Magnet programs seemed to fit that solution. Such a predilection fit the ideology of the parent corporations of the newspapers, which advocated for free market solutions to educational and social problems. So all these traces fit together: media need for sensational stories, the preference in the political culture for school choice, and the district administrators' need for legitimacy.

Through the media, the district attempted to convince Anglo parents that the Plan was meant to benefit their own children. It downplayed any message (if such an aim even existed by that time) that those programs emerged from policies meant to benefit non-Anglo students.

The media characterized the South Plan as effective simply because it existed and jibed with school choice. They failed to question or investigate the Plan's effects. Instead they reported the positive anecdotes and statistics that the district spun out. For example, the school sold the media on a decline in the rate of dropouts between the 1987–88 and 1988–89 school years. Archival data show that no such decline occurred, that an artifact of measuring and reporting these data created the illusory decline. Articles rarely attributed school problems to administrators or to the institution itself, perhaps because of the interlocking among the administrators, the public relations department, and the media. Reporters failed to investigate the self-serving anecdotes. No one asked, for example, who exercised choice, who benefited from the magnet programs, what alternatives exited, how the money was spent, or how the programs addressed the problems for non-Anglo students.

Media reports centered on the theme of "turning the school around," likening school policy to the Super Bowl in which the underdog football team miraculously comes from behind to win. Reporters depicted the school as "award-winning" and "nationally recognized." In addition, local media covered national media reports about South. National media picked up local reports. Then both local media and school officials quoted the national reports, eventually reifying the reputation of South as award-winning. Journalists missed the grubby details that many of these reports came about as a result of concerted activity of the public relations office, which applied for any and all competitions, basing its application on self-reported data and anecdotes. Sheer recognition translated into "success" and external legitimacy but overlooked the flat horizon of student achievement and integration in the school as a whole.

News accounts were used by administrators in organizational communications to maintain control over the definition of the situation with staff. In repeated instances at key meetings of the school, administrators referred to media reports as evidence of the legitimacy of the reform plan and their actions. At meetings the administrators reported on news coverage of the school as if it was evidence of the success of the school under their leadership.

At a student assembly at the beginning of the year the principal stated:

> As you know, South High School has been recognized during the last two years for excellence in education in many areas. We were designated one of the top three high school in [the state] when we received the A-plus award by the state department of education. Last year Redbook Magazine recognized South High School as the best in Arizona.

South teachers usually expressed accord with administrators' reports to the media. However there were instances of conflict. At a staff meeting one teacher stated that substantive educational improvements should lead reputation, rather than reputation being an end in itself: "We should change public perception by becoming more up to par on academic achievement, not by lying about what we are doing here." The principal responded to this challenge by saying, "Let's worry about how we feel about what we do, how students feel about what they do."

Presentations of media reports favorable to the school were used as evidence in regular reports to the federal district court judge supervising the desegregation case. Press releases about the magnet programs were included in the annual reports to the court as evidence of district compliance.

A district report (annual reports were required by the settlement) to the court on the progress of the magnet programs at South High provided further evidence of the "spectacle" nature of the desegregation policy. "Since June, South has had some 300 inches of favorable newspaper copy." Press releases were scheduled every month.

The report rationalized the district's failure to budge achievement and integration, claiming that major innovations require at least three years to bear fruit. It made, nevertheless, optimistic promises for the future:

> The Anglo population at South has jumped 55% in the past 3 years. Yet South remains our most unbalanced school. It will not continue that way. . . . The upgrading of the appearance, safety, and security of the campus . . . the continued success of students . . . and the new and unified community relations plan to

publicize all of the above . . . the racial imbalance can be reduced by 3 to 5 % a year. In 4 to 6 years, relative racial balance at South could be a reality. The machinery is in place.

Both the increase in the number of minority students attending South from within its home-attendance zone and the increase in pupil transfers from outside the South's attendance zone are directly attributable to improvements in academic courses, to better security measures, and to additional publicity efforts.

The district added magnet programs to South that were intended to attract white students and enhance the school's image: Communication Arts, Law, and Aerospace. Its original Performing Arts magnet sent students around Arizona to put on productions. The media covered these theatricals as if their mere existence counted as solid evidence that desegregation policy was working. These images of success emanating from the media substituted for information about the true state of achievement and integration, which would have revealed little improvement. Desegregation became performance art.

Back to the Future

In 1994 it seemed clear to everyone that all the efforts and resources devoted to magnets and the Plan had failed to improve educational quality, achievement, or integration. The plaintiffs had given up on desegregation as an effective method of attaining good, equitable schooling for non-Anglo students. An attorney for the plaintiffs said this:

> Hispanic parents are saying, "we don't care about desegregation." Our kids are going to hell in a hand basket, quickly. And not only are they going to hell in a hand basket, they're going to hell in a hand basket despite thirty-five million dollars that the district is receiving annually. And that, my friends, is not doing us any good. It has not done us a bit of good. So as far as we're concerned, give us a good school that's going to teach our children the basics. And whether we have Anglos, and whether we have orange, green, whatever, we just want our kids to learn . . . . Neighborhood schools are what we need . . . bricks and mortar so that we can look back and say, this is what we got.

A new district superintendent agreed with the Hispanic community that the previous efforts to desegregate had not achieved either equal opportunities or better quality education. With a cold eye, he examined the evidence emerging from district census and school test data. He soon began dismantling the Plan and moving toward a traditional school organization. The rosy view of conditions at South soon petered out of media accounts. The district's compliance with the court order could be attributed, not to program effectiveness, but to demographic changes in the city. Moreover, he disdained the original criterion that the district negotiated with the court:

> Improving the racial ethnic presence at the school within 20% plus or minus
> . . . is extraordinary. It allowed for compliance to occur with very little [of sub-
> stance] occurring. That bewildered me from the beginning . . . They [the pre-
> vious administration] just sat back and said, "This is good stuff. We hit the
> number without having riots."

One of the evaluation reports found that students' test scores at South remained around the 35th percentile and "test scores declined on standardized tests the longer they were in school." Moreover, students were still segregated—magnet programs consisting mostly of Anglos and the rest of the school mostly non-Anglos. Students of different ethnicity rarely crossed paths and rarely socialized. Yet in spite of this poor record, South reached its symbolic, numerical target of racial balance—not because of program improvements, an influx of Anglo students, or even good press management. No, the target was reached because, by the mid-1990s, the rest of the district schools had become just as racially unbalanced as South.

The school board, citing the negative evaluation reports, terminated the Plan in 1994. Frustrated by the lack of district activity but pressured by the conservative legislature, the judge issued an order to terminate the desegregation order and declare unitary status for South. But this was a mixed blessing for the district, which had come to depend on the desegregation tax levies of over $30 million per year.

Finally, the district assigned funds to build a new high school in the territory covered by South. It would serve, because of its assigned boundaries, mostly minority students. The book on desegregation closed.

Other Places/Same Fate

The Phoenix desegregation case demonstrates the intersection of policy and the media as a contemporary institution in the political spectacle. Among desegregation cases, however, Phoenix is not alone in the impact of media accounts.

Gary Orfield and colleagues asserted that the media has played a role in dismantling desegregation across the nation. They argued that the local press ignores the persisting conditions of inequality and isolation, or simply treats the symptoms of school failure. In some cases, journalists accept without examination exaggerated claims about the success of re-segregated schools.[17] "The local press tends to accept uncritically whatever the local school bureaucracy says without any of its normal skepticism about improbable claims."[18] The national press has reported only the worst cases of desegregation and glorified the best cases of segregationist programs.

National media promote the choice-oriented magnet school remedy to desegregation. They frequently refer to Prince George's County, Maryland as a positive example. President Reagan's promotion of the County's successful magnet programs was "echoed in two typical newspaper articles describing the improving achievement in the school system."[19] This type of media attention lent legitimacy to the District's actions. The media enthusiastically reported rises in standardized test scores and attributed the improvement to the magnet programs. But the positive publicity eventually waned when the state changed its testing format. A former school board member indicated that the superintendent had distorted the connection between test results and the magnet programs.

> Prince George's school system, which received national acclaim for its "success," has no reliable evidence that would show that there [was] substantial improvement that kept pace with nationwide achievement or that magnet schools improved academic achievement.[20]

The magnet programs and the public relations campaign initiated by the superintendent did restore faith in the school system. An assistant superintendent said: "John Murphy was a mastermind at being able to woo the public. We advertised profusely. Billboards, TV shows, we went all over the place." The district hoped to use its magnet program to change the district's negative image and lure Anglo parents. The magnet programs were a symbolic policy as they appealed to many diverse interests:

> Policies set in Prince George's County could be claimed by both liberals and conservatives. Conservative policymakers may have liked the fact that magnets emphasized the populist "choice" concept and rejected mandatory student assignment for desegregation. Liberal politicians may have seen magnets as an example of the capacity of big public school systems to reform themselves. And in many cases the press simply increased the visibility and credibility of local claims. One of the clear lessons of this case is that the appearance of great success may be more the results of politics and public relations than of educational accomplishments. . . . As a result of demographic changes the schools have become more racially identifiable and less integrated. . . . The concept of racial integration has ceased to have any serious meaning in Prince George's County.[21]

We believe that these two cases implicate the media and their function in the political spectacle. First, the media have a perspective. They are not, as the word suggests, a neutral medium through which flows unalloyed information. Moreover, media follow their own logic, emphasize the timely, the glossy, and the easy. Reporters take the simpler route. Ordinary people who read and watch the news are thus screened from information that would allow them to participate effectively in education policy.

Media Theory and Political Spectacle

Educational institutions and organizations adopt media formats to maintain legitimacy and promote their interests in the policy process. Because journalism emphasizes conflict, drama, and currency, it neglects whether and by what means policy produces lasting, inequitable effects on peoples' lives. Hiding behind a facade of objectivity, journalists provide entertainment—narratives about people and issues removed from most people's daily lives. According to Edelman, the policy narratives that journalists construct offer probable outcomes in the future (story endings). Journalists' predictions of policy benefits reassure the public and increase the chances they will support the policies. By the time "the future" arrives, however, journalists have moved on to the next policy narrative.[22]

Edelman asserted that the "privileged benefit more than the disadvantaged from spectacle construction." And "the dominant ideology that justifies the extant inequalities. They divert [attention] from historical knowledge, social and economic analysis, and unequal benefits and suffering they might raise questions about prevailing ideology."[23]

In *Rich Media, Poor Democracy*, Robert McChesney wrote that about ten mega-corporations dominate all the media. As a result:

> media fare is ever more closely linked to the needs and concerns of a handful of enormous and powerful corporations. . . . These firms are run by . . . billionaires with clear stakes in the outcome of the most fundamental political issues, and their interests are often distinct from those of the vast majority of humanity.[24]

Now, news divisions are seen as potential profit centers, and journalists "cater to business interests" and "are discouraged from examining their corporate operations."[25]

These efforts have decreased the amount of hard news that television, radio and newspapers report; they have also corrupted the level of investigative journalism. As evidence of the connections among global media, government policies, campaign contributions, and the two-party system, the *Columbia Journalism Review* reported that the ten largest media corporations and associations contributed $27 million to candidates in 1999. They paid out lobbying fees in the amount of over $111 million. The legislative issues that most concerned the corporations were taxation, intellectual property rights, and deregulation.[26] Media corporations oppose campaign finance reform because most campaign expenses go to purchase advertising. They have little incentive therefore to provide free ads or air time for independent candidates.

The trends that McChesney pointed out have ramifications on how well ordinary people can participate in policies and debates about public schools. The media played a significant role in the definition of the policy culture surrounding the development of desegregation policy in both the Phoenix and Prince George's County cases. Key actors used the news media to construct symbolic responses to the problem of desegregation. School officials use news to display a certain semblance of a policy agenda and obscure the daily life and tangible effects of policy. They thus maintain support for it and deflect criticism or bury the information that potential critics might use. As Edelman stated, media accounts best serve the interests of the already powerful—not the public interest. The parents and community of South High School wanted quality and equality. What they got instead was flimsy symbolism—a school no more segregated than the rest of the district, a school that had met its numerical standard.

American public schools have not served children of color very well. The great national commitment to racial balance began with good intentions and gradually diminished in implementation and effect. Conditions of educational opportunity are no more justly distributed now than they were a half-century ago. Yet the political spectacle—spun out by governments, courts, school officials, public relations experts, and the media— shrouds their actions from the public. The tangible evidence is out there, but in Phoenix, no one bothered to search it out.

Notes

1. This vignette fictionalizes a viewer's experience of the media coverage of an actual incident at South High in Phoenix and a subsequent incident at a Scottsdale high school. The Scottsdale incident resulted in one injury; the South incident, none.
2. Ericson, Baranek, et al. (1989), p. 377.
3. Altheide and Snow (1991).
4. Wallace (1994).
5. Ericson, Baranek, et al. (1989).
6. Stone (1997), p. 21.
7. Edelman (1988), p. 104.
8. Edelman (1988), p. 95.
9. Altheide and Snow (1991).
10. Lugg (in press), p. 5.
11. This case study was originally published as Walt Heinecke's (1997) dissertation. For complete references to his quotations, please see the original document.
12. In their treatment of state policy culture, Marshall, Mitchell, et al. (1989) characterized Phoenix as a southern city in a southern state.
13. During the settlement of the area, news reports characterized minorities in a negative light.
14. Kantor and Lowe (1995).
15. A swing to the right at the national level brought about federal intentions to dismantle desegregation and cut back on both OCR enforcement and federal funding to aid districts under desegregation orders, so that OCR could not monitor as it should.
16. "(A)lthough there is an enormous array of knowledge sources available—official documents, academic texts, survey and trend statistics, and direct observation . . . the journalist seeks a source in the know to say it is so, and has a routine, predictable supply of such sources in established organizations." (Ericson, Baranek, et al., 1989), p. 1.
17. Orfield and Eaton (1996), p. 87.
18. Orfield and Eaton (1996), p. 87.
19. Eaton and Crutcher (1996), p. 277.
20. Orfield and Eaton (1996), p. 285.
21. Eaton and Crutcher (1996), pp. 285–288.
22. Edelman (1988), p. 94.
23. Edelman (1988), p. 125.
24. McChesney (1999), p. 50.
25. McChesney (1999), pp. 52–53.
26. Lewis (2000).

CHAPTER 5

Research and the Illusion of Rationality[1]

Facts are simple and facts are straight
Facts are lazy and facts are late
Facts all come with points of view
Facts won't do what I want them to
Talking Heads, "Cross-eyed and Painless," *Remain in Light*

SHE BLINDED ME WITH "SCIENCE" (A VIGNETTE)

She certainly looks the part. She dressed herself like a researcher who presents her research at a conference of researchers. She adjusts the overhead projector so that its light illuminates what we expect to see at research conferences: numbers, statistics, trend lines. With her laser pointer, she points out the "before" part and the "after" part of her graph and follows the upward trajectory of points across time. She tells us about the significance of the significance tests she used. She helps us make our interpretations. Before the governor's accountability policy school achievement had been low—too low. Just two years later, see how it rises! The policy has increased achievement across the state. Test scores went up—research proves it. Good research, too, university people did it—Professor X, Professor Y, and herself. She tells us that her governor had been elated when he saw that graph. Standing in front of us at the conference she is so pleased she blushes, as if she is about to take a bow. But her face grows serious, almost sad for the doubters, as she alludes to "some people at this conference who think that test scores went up just because teachers wouldn't let bad students take the test. But I just can't believe that any teacher of ours would do such a thing. And anyway, their data is just stories and our data is scientific."

I leave the room, needing a shower. What would Edelman think?

That in the political spectacle research occupies a world more like George Orwell and Lewis Carroll's than Marie Curie and Albert Einstein's?

A world where anything other than rationality—emotion, self-delusion, Pavlovian reactions, unconscious ideation, blind loyalties to the community, the family, the sacred text and priests, ignorance or carelessness—govern actions and meaning? Where no amount of contrary evidence can sway a person from his convictions?

Where the players shout down all pleas for even-handedness, for broader perspectives, for respectful dialogue about the presumptions, methods and findings, or even the good faith of researchers outside the fold? Where invoking "science," "objectivity," and reliability amounts to little more than another dance move, another costume, another trick of lighting?

Where the phrase "Research shows . . ." or the phrase "According to the scientific evidence" is an epigraph, a prologue to the show, an advertisement, a stratagem that brings the audience to a willing suspension of disbelief?

Power Speaking to Truth

"Speaking Truth to Power," was a phrase once used to characterize policy research. Its truth depends on particular and peculiar definitions of both truth and power. In the political spectacle, is it possible that power talks and truth listens?

Research,[2] scientific research, presents itself as the modern embodiment of rationality. Research now enjoys a powerful cachet. We treat research as rational, objective, fair, and conclusive. We honor researchers for being dispassionate, disinterested, and scientific. In the last few decades, theorists have deconstructed that image.[3] But outside the Academy, people in Western culture hold on to the ideal of objectivity. Most people believe that scientists occupy an exclusive domain and produce unvarnished truth about the effects of policy. At worst, the eyes of ordinary folk glaze over at the first mention of technical details or complex procedures. If they question at all, they tend to go to the other extreme, toward radical skepticism of all research, and they make the researcher an object of disdain. "You can prove anything with statistics," they say. Either reaction takes citizens out of the knowledge business, which then takes them out of the democratic participation business.

In the political spectacle, research functions in quite different ways from the cultural ideal. Edelman scorned the commonsense, romantic notion that

> . . . citizens who are informed about political developments can more effectively protect and promote their own interest. That response takes for granted a world of facts that have a determinable meaning and a world of people who react rationally to the facts they know. In politics neither premise is tenable, a

conclusion that history continually reaffirms and that observers of the political scene are tempted to ignore.[4]

Edelman believed that in politics there can be no consensus on the meaning of events. Even the notion of "fact" depends on premises and assumptions that the polity cannot resolve. However, those partisans who deploy messages disguised as scientific facts have no incentive to reveal hidden assumptions and glosses.

The politicians who authored A Nation at Risk took for granted that test scores and national productivity are related and did not bother to reveal their presumptions as such. They equated college entrance test scores of a limited, unrepresentative group (those seeking admission to college) to school achievement of students throughout the nation. Their failure to identify underlying presumptions promoted a particular construction of data as truth, and a crisis as real. The report set the terms of a political movement in that every subsequent article on policy and achievement had to refer to it. Some say that A Nation at Risk was meant to discredit public schools and restructure them for the benefit of the private sector. If not so intended, it was so used. While critics occupied themselves reanalyzing and critiquing the reported decline of test scores, they could not pay attention (or direct the attention of politicians) to the underlying social and economic inequality latent in the same data. Furthermore, attempts by scientists to rebut government interpretation of data were met with political censure.[5]

Citing scientific evidence and rationality bemuses the public, according to Edelman:

> . . . the phrase "rational choice" is one more symbol in the process of rationalization rather than the path to enlightenment . . . neither precision in observation nor rigor in deductive reasoning will yield . . . generalizations. They offer an appearance of doing so as long as attention is diverted from the problematic premises. . . . Reasons for support or for doubt are all mortals can hope for. Final conclusions, like final solutions, are for dogmatists.[6]

Yet politicians continue to use policy research both to establish the need and rationale for new policies and to portray the consequences of policies already undertaken. When a political actor quotes research, it establishes her as a wise leader, someone who makes rational choices based on scientific evidence. However, wrote Edelman:

> . . . leaders' reputations do not hinge upon a ledger account of the consequences of their acts. . . . A confident manner, ebullience, an appeal for sacrifice in the public interest, or a narrative account about the past or the future . . . becomes a substitute for demonstrable improvements.[7]

Edelman described policy research as mired in the "myth of rationality." As stated in Chapter One, we do not go so far. Research can yield conclusions that are warranted and useful. Even if researchers follow the best norms and practices of their disciplines, however, they do not get a free pass from political spectacle. At every step, they act out roles. However pure their intentions, they serve political purposes and interests.

Deborah Stone included scientific research in what she called the "rationality project" and found the presumptions of scientific ideals problematic. Instead, she argued, research findings depend on numbers; numbers depend on measurement; measurement depends on categorization; and establishing categories depends on political negotiation or exercise of power.

How Politics Confound Rationality

Categories Depend on Political Negotiation

Determining which children are handicapped and which are not is an example of problematic definition and categorization. The basis of slotting children into such groups is never certain, in spite of claims to the contrary. Yet counting the number of children depends on first constructing categories, the meaning and boundaries of which are ambiguous. The process of "counting as" depends on a dynamic of interests, ideologies, and political tactics of the persons involved. The accountability movement teeters on a fragile system of categories such as pass and fail, or "exceeds the standard," or "approaches but does not reach the standard." Typically political entities perform this task and make such categorizations—not by technical or statistical procedures, but by political processes. In the Arizona case described in Chapter Two, representatives of interest groups settled on a cutoff score of 75 to determine which kids passed and which did not. They picked that particular cutoff because it was politically acceptable and credible to the public—not too easy and not too tough. They did it without technology or science.

Even when political entities use statistical procedures to establish levels, categories, and cutoff scores, results are problematic[8] and the application of those levels is political. Consider the levels set for the National Assessment of Educational Progress, sometimes called the "nation's report card." Its "basic" level of proficiency was set high, so high that the majority of American students—who do well on other measures of achievement—fail to attain it. Critics of public schools often use this "failure" in their rhetoric. However, those levels, as Gerald Bracey wrote, "have been rejected by everyone who has ever studied them," including the General Accounting Office, the National Academy of Sciences, and the Center for Research on Educational Standards and Student Testing.

Why would these groups dispute NAEP levels? Bracey answered:

> In the 2000 NAEP reading assessment, only 32% of fourth graders attained proficient or better, but American 9-year-olds were second in the world among 27 countries in the [International Educational Assessment] reading study.[9]

About thinly disguised political acts such as these Stone wrote:

> The rational ideal presupposes the existence of neutral facts—neutral in the sense that they describe the world, but do not serve anybody's interests, promote any value judgments or exert persuasive force beyond the weight of their correctness. Yet facts do not exist independently of interpretive lenses, and they come clothed in words and numbers.[10]

When we read that one-third of American children do not meet standards of reading proficiency, do we pause to ask who defined proficiency and who categorized students as having it or not having it? What did these categorizers intend to accomplish?

Quantification Depends on Measurement

Stone argued that entities cannot be counted until they are measured, and in the polis, political actors select measures to project a particular image. The rational ideal, in contrast, treats measurement as a pristine viewing of the world as if through a clear window. However,

> people, unlike rocks, respond to being measured. . . . . Measurement, like a mirror, triggers the natural desire to look good . . . to present themselves as they want to be seen.[11]

Once measured, entities can be counted. But numbers have political purposes. Stone argued:

> Numbers are invoked to give an air of finality to each side's opinions. . . . Every number is an assertion. . . . No number is innocent, for it is impossible to count without making judgments. . . . Every number is a political claim . . . . Projections, correlations, simulations and every other fancy manipulation of numbers all rest on decisions about "counting as". . . . Measures imply a need for action, because we do not measure things except when we want to change them.[12]
>
> Counting . . . is an essential instrument of political mobilization . . . . numbers offer the promise of conflict resolution through arithmetic . . . once a phenomenon has been converted into quantifiable units . . . it can be added, multiplied, divided, or subtracted, even though these operations have little meaning in reality. Numbers provide the comfortable illusion that incommensurables can be weighed against each other, because arithmetic actually "works": arithmetic yields answers. . . . Numbers are symbols of precision, accuracy, and objectivity, even though all counting involves judgment and discretion. . . . Numerals hide all the difficult choices that go into a count. And certain kinds of numbers—big ones, ones with decimal points . . . advertise the

> prowess of the measurer. . . . To offer one of these numbers is by itself a gesture of authority.[13]

Consider this hypothetical example. School A, when it administers the state's mandated assessment, excludes learning disabled students. School B includes students of the same type in its tested population. Since learning disabled students typically score lower than others, School A ends up looking as if it were the better school. Its average test scores appear objective and compare favorably to the other school, yet the two sets of numbers depend entirely on alternative underlying assumptions and procedures that are invented locally and effectively hidden from the public. Consider this example from the record of experience. Texas officials claimed that its accountability policy had raised achievement as indicated by the increased numbers of students who took Advanced Placement courses.[14] These officials failed to point out, however, that, during the same time interval, Texas had decreased the fees students must pay to take those courses. In the political spectacle, everything depends on what gets counted and what gets discounted.

Establishing Causality Depends on Quantification and Logic

Using research to establish the causal connection of policy to outcome presents significant political problems. Establishing cause suggests who or what is to blame for a situation. It also points to the group that ought to be responsible for correcting it. As Stone argued,

> In the polis, causal stories are strategically crafted with symbols and numbers and then asserted by political actors who try to make their versions the basis of policy choices.[15]

Stone wrote that even the "gold standard" of the experimental trial in medical research fails to meet the requirements of a rational process free of politics.[16]

Even in the natural sciences, research studies cannot always shake loose from politics. Indeed, the formation of factions of scientists, each addressing and producing rival claims, creates a level of ambiguity and public bemusement that exacerbates the political spectacle. Take global warming for example. In the body of evidence on global warming, what is "Truth"? Is there a single truth? Or is there one truth for those who want to save the planet by reducing emissions from factories and another truth for those who want to develop industrial capacity and believe that restrictions on emissions will stunt that development? Each group has its own researchers and its own body of evidence. Whose science is junk science? Medical science has reached consensus that smoking causes cancer. Yet scientists employed by tobacco corporations disagree. Since no one has conducted a true experiment by assigning people at random either to the smoking or non-smoking treatment groups and measuring later cancer rates, then one cannot prove cause and effect—so goes their argument. And because such a design is unethical, the critical experiment will never be done.

Conflicting results and less than definitive claims, which characterize social science (and significant parts of medical science as well), contribute to ambiguous methods and results, and ambiguity is the soil in which political spectacle takes root.

Education Research and Political Spectacle: The Case of Reading[17]

The prototypic case of politics confounding research is the tawdry history of research on how to teach children to read. It encompasses all the elements mentioned in the previous section: ambiguous, politically determined categories, problematic measurement and counting, and weird and conflicting logic about cause and effect. Most of all, this case shows how political dynamics—the ebb and flow of power and authority—govern what appears on the surface to be rational and scientific.

How could policies about reading instruction generate political controversy? Doesn't everyone pursue the same goal—to expand and improve literacy? Yet the media now depict disputes—over what seems to outsiders as a straightforward dialogue over best methods or core understandings—as "reading wars." How is the public able to understand this dispute well enough to participate in education policy?

Disagreements about how one teaches another person to read have always existed. Disagreements took on added valence as the stakes rose. As public schooling expanded through the ranks of society so did the market for texts and materials. Early on, public and professional debate broke into two broad categories of belief and practice. Persons identified themselves with one or the other and rarely found points of agreement. The differences hardened into Manichean categories—two cultures, two sets of professional associations, two sets of journals, two markets for materials and training, and—more to the point of this chapter—two sets of scholars and modes of research. Pleas for reconciliation or pluralism or even a balance of approaches to teaching reading are met with scorn and suspicion. Pleas for eclecticism and balance become grounds for the next round of disputes.

The crux of the difference between these two perspectives is whether to teach children to read 1) by first teaching them the separate skills that are believed to underlie the act of reading (parts to whole) or 2) by engaging children in meaningful literacy activities and introducing the separate pre-reading skills as students need them to make sense of texts and literature (whole to parts). At the risk of further oversimplification, we label these categories as "phonics-first" and "whole language."

Teachers divided themselves along these lines long before researchers studied reading formally. Now researchers are combatants, operating out of separate paradigms, with different intentions and approaches. Standing outside of this bifurcated culture, we had assumed from second- and third-hand accounts in the media that research evidence favored the efficacy of phonics-first. When we examined that literature ourselves, we were surprised to find that it was replete with equivocal findings, shaky methods, unwarranted conclusions, and dramatic pronouncements about research findings and their implications for policy.

Despite how this research is portrayed, it is anything but one-sided in its evidence about the superiority of one or the other of these two approaches. How then could one side of a debate on reading have succeeded in the rhetorical and policy arena out of proportion to its relative success in the research arena? How did one side capture the coveted label of scientific when its studies were, in close-up, so problematic? How did it happen that the federal government now requires schools to adopt phonics-first reading programs and why it justifies its mandate on the claim that only phonics-first programs meet the standards of scientific proof? Only political spectacle theory resolves this contradiction between the evidence and the pageant of "evidence."

"Phonics First"

Phonics-first is a theory of how children and adults learn to read and a methodology for teaching reading. People become literate, according to this viewpoint, by learning a fixed sequence of separate skills. They are first taught to recognize that words comprise phonemic units and that there is a relationship of sounds and alphabet letters. Then they are taught how to put these sounds together into words. And only after they master these separate and sequenced skills (sometimes called constituent skills or sub-skills) are they taught about ascribing meaning to the words. Comprehension depends on a foundation of constituent skills, as April follows March. Because the basic elements and their sequencing are so standard, teachers must impart them systematically and in order. If teachers allow children to skip steps or read books too soon, those children are apt to develop reading problems later. To prevent reading problems, therefore, teachers must follow scripts—literally—that arrange instruction in a lockstep sequence. Comprehension of real texts comes later, the culmination of a long walk down a single path. Even then, the only texts children encounter are highly structured ones that include only those sounds, symbols, and words that have already been systematically trained by the teachers and mastered by the students. Until students master the core skills, they should not choose books or try to read them, although teachers are encouraged to read stories aloud to children. To follow the phonics-first logic, "writing" means handwriting, penmanship. Therefore, teachers postpone classroom opportunities for students to write (in the way most of us think about writing, like writing a description of a pet).

If teachers follow the prescriptions, children ought to be successful. However, those children who do fail to master the constituent skills the first time they are trained must go through them again. The recycling process necessitates that teachers group students into high, medium, and low reading groups. For the low group, teachers do not change the nature of materials and lessons. These students simply go through the same materials for a second or third time while the high group proceeds to the next level.

Thus, tracking (also known as ability grouping) is the norm in phonics-first classrooms. Testing of skills also assumes a prominent place in those classrooms. Only by frequent testing can teachers ascertain the mastery level of students. The tests and the standards for passing them are predetermined by the curriculum developers and not by teachers. That feature makes it possible for the school to construct a hierarchy of curriculum and student performance, so that observers moving from class to class and school to school would see the same skills taught in the same sequence of steps. Standardization of elements and sequences in phonics-first pedagogy necessitates structured materials and texts that are common to large groups of students.

What is the core process in learning to read? Phonics-first theorists believe that certain neurological and perceptual mechanisms underlie mastery of discrete skills. Thus, blood flow to the brain (measured by CT scans) and eye movements reveal the physiological elements at work and constitute important foci of the scientific study of reading. The core process in reading, it is said, is "phonological processing."

Researchers in the phonics-first culture seek to elaborate on the existence of the core, physiological processes involved in learning to read and the teaching methods that respond best to that developing core process. For example, they identify groups of children previously diagnosed as reading disabled and non-disabled. Then they correlate the children classified as reading disabled with those children's scores on various tests of reading's constituent skills. Researchers typically find that reading disabled students have poor skills. They assume from such findings that skills underlie reading ability and disability.[18]

Because of the competing paradigms, phonics-first researchers also design studies to refute some premises of whole language. Whole language theory suggests that beginning readers search the context (illustrations, chapter headings) of a story for cues to its meaning, make predictions about meanings from these cues, and that they often skip words they don't yet know. To refute that hypothesis, phonics-first researchers measured eye movements to prove that subjects focus on every syllable in every word in order—rather than scanning for cues and skipping words.[19]

As well, researchers conduct comparative experiments, either in laboratory conditions or in classroom settings, to pit phonics-first against some other approach to teaching children to read. We deal in detail with the experimental model in the next section.

Periodically, scholars have summarized and synthesized the results of the studies about the effects of phonics-first. Jeanne Chall's book, *The Great Debate*, summarized studies that compared phonics with other methods. Her work is frequently cited as demonstrating the superiority of phonics over whole language.[20] However, she failed to contrast these approaches because she mislabeled the treatments. The studies she reviewed actually compared phonics methods with the "whole word" method, an approach that whole language experts explicitly reject.[21] Thus Chall contributed to misconceptions and fallacious labeling that already plagued the field of reading. Rather than settling the great debate, the book created even more ambiguity.[22]

"Whole Language"[23]

Whole Language is based on a theory of how language is acquired and used. It holds that children construct meaning from interactions with texts, with teachers, with parents and with other children. People become literate through writing as well as reading texts, through listening and speaking. The texts that people draw on to acquire literacy are authentic texts: stories with beginnings, middles, ends, and illustrations. Children use multiple cueing systems—including, but not limited to, the sounds and alphabetic symbols—to work out the meaning of a word or sentence or passage. Teachers support and assist students as they read by pointing out those multiple cueing systems, including the sound-symbol relationships of the words themselves. At many moments during classroom interactions with text, teachers do teach phonic skills, show how words from the story are made up of phonemes, demonstrate with the text how to use the alphabet to sound out words, and the like. Whole language educators oppose regimentation, work sheets, and rote learning because children come to the classroom with many different literacy experiences and needs. Rather than teaching all children the same skills first, teachers arrange materials and activities so that students make their own interpretations of text, make choices, and engage in dialogue about books. "Parts" are learned in the context of "whole" texts.

Part of a larger idea of progressive education, whole language theory and practice put children's activities, choices, interests, and interpretations in the foreground. Progressive education treats both children and teachers as active agents with intentions and emotions. It follows a principle of "knowledge construction"—that people interpret text and information in many different ways and come to their own understandings of it. Teachers try to discover what interests and engages students and what students already know. Then teachers help students select reading materials and activities that match and extend those interests. Teachers provide students environments rich in reading materials and in opportunities to write and talk about what they read, about their interests and experiences. Teachers aim to enhance not only the children's comprehension of text, but also their enjoyment of reading and writing and their ability to think and question what they read and to grow intellectually and personally from it.

Whole language extends the educational philosophy of progressivism into the domain of psycholinguistics, sociolinguistics, and critical literacy. Throughout the school day teachers help children to use multiple cueing systems such as the syntactic properties of sentences and the semantic properties of longer texts as well as the phonological and phonemic characteristics of words.

Whole language developed in part as a renunciation of the part-to-whole method of teaching reading. Whole language educators resist the standardization of basal reading series and other highly structured reading and testing programs. They resist any policies that diminish the skills and professional discretion that teachers must have to respond to the diverse learning needs of the children before them. That is, they oppose the requirement that all teachers follow scripts mandated from outside the classroom by textbook corporations or public policy makers. They oppose the compulsory and compulsive use of worksheets to teach anything and everything.

Educators in the whole language tradition do not oppose phonics instruction, but they do oppose a slavish, concentrated regimen of phonics training before or instead of literacy experiences such as reading and writing. Standardization and denial of teacher discretion are what whole language educators do oppose, a fact that has significant consequences on the status of whole language research.

Whole language educators avoid standardization. But standardization is exactly what experiments require. In an experiment, all children selected for one treatment are exposed to the same learning activities and materials in the same sequence. The experimenter—in principle at least—thus has control over the treatment. The absence of standardizing inherent in whole language makes experimental research difficult. In contrast, experimental designs are more consistent with phonics-first methods since all children in a group are treated the same and teachers follow scripts.

Whole language researchers have investigated the claims that mastery of phonics skills is the sole cause of reading ability. Steve Krashan found that students who made many mistakes on discrete skills (that is, they had poor phonics skills) often turned out to be good readers anyway—no worse certainly than children who mastered the discrete, component skills first and made few errors on tests of those skills. He concluded that mastery of "foundational sub-skills" was not a sufficient or even necessary precursor of reading comprehension.

Researchers have shown through rigorous statistical studies that when students have good early reading experiences and literacy experiences inside and outside the classroom, they develop better reading comprehension and love of books. In his synthesis of such studies, Steve Krashen found research that showed Sustained Silent Reading (a practice wherein all students in a class or school devote themselves entirely to "free" reading) enhanced students' level of comprehension. In 51 of 54 comparisons with other treatments, he found that practice in reading begets reading comprehension.[24]

Jeff McQuillen summarized the statistical studies that examined the relationships among phonological tasks, reading comprehension, and the amount of free reading that students do. Using regression analysis, he found a high correlation between the time students spent in "free reading" and students' level of reading comprehension. In contrast, he found a low correlation between a student's phonological skills and that student's reading comprehension.[25] He concluded that the more students are allowed to read real books, the better their comprehension will be. However, students' ability to use phonetic skills did not predict very strongly how well students could read—in the commonsense meaning of the term reading.

McQuillen also found evidence that the more children have access to reading materials (in home, school, and public libraries) the better their comprehension, their vocabulary, and their writing will be.[26] Such a finding introduces a societal element into the conversation about reading. Students in poor schools and neighborhoods have substantially less access to books and other texts. Poverty, not defective phonological skills or whole language teaching, may therefore explain reading failure. He called schools for the poor in California a "print wasteland," which explains low achievement scores there.[27]

Adversaries of whole language dismiss studies such as those described by McQuillen and Krashen because they are not experimental and do not therefore meet the official standards of "reliability and replicability." Yet these studies meet the tests developed by methodologists for use with regression analyses of quantitative evidence where the researcher examines alternative explanations by using statistical controls—which is the mode of analysis in medical research on the effect of smoking on cancer. It is a tiny slice of the field that uniquely places experimental designs in the categories of "rigorous" and "scientific."

Whole language researchers acknowledge that teaching phonics skills can be shown to increase students' achievement test scores when tests measure only those limited skills. But longitudinal analysis shows that the initial advantage to students on even these simple skills did not persist over time. More importantly, studies that showed the positive effects of phonemic awareness training on phonemic skills did not show that phonemic awareness training translates into better reading comprehension.

Why should this be? Much hangs on one's definition of reading and how one chooses to measure it. The word "reading" taps into a wellspring of cultural images: the child who is absorbed in one of the Baby Sitters Club books, the fifth-grader devouring *Harry Potter and the Sorcerer's Stone*, the high school junior struggling with the texts in the National Merit Exam, the parent reading the newspaper over coffee, book groups chatting about what they like about *White Oleander*, the new immigrant trying to make sense of the state's drivers license exam book, the novice poet reading his work at the poetry slam, people using books for thinking and feeling new things—for reaching out to new worlds and experiences. To most of us, these are the concrete referents for the word "reading."

But those common images of reading are not how researchers define and measure it. The "reading" that phonics-first researchers refer to is something considerably smaller. They define reading as the number of times students can correctly pronounce unfamiliar words on a list. "Reading" amounts to whether a student can correctly identify the first phoneme in the word "cat" or the similar sounds made by the words cat, bat, and hat. Drill and practice may include children chanting in unison to the teacher's prompts. Later, as children progress through the hierarchy of reading sub-skills, researchers may also define reading as filling the correct words in the open space of the sentence: "The best title of this story should be ———." Whole language researchers define and measure different concepts of reading: the amount of time a student is engaged with a book, a student's access to textual materials, a student's ability to use the cueing systems to understand a text, a student's ability to explain a story to another student, or a student's performance on assessments of reading comprehension. These are more complex indicators of reading, often more difficult to measure, but nevertheless closer to cultural concepts and images about real reading.

In addition to statistical studies of observed variables (such as Krashen and McQuillen presented), whole language researchers use research models such as micro-ethnography, discourse analysis, and qualitative research. These models fit better the unpredictable flow of interactions in whole language classrooms, which may confound standardized treatments in experiments. Phonics-first advocates argued that experiments and only experiments possess validity that qualitative research models lack. That is, phonics-first advocates tried to differentiate their own research studies from qualitative and correlational research by using value-laden terms such as hard vs. soft, objective vs. subjective, replicable vs. not replicable, universal vs. local and contextual. The federal mandate for researchers to use experimental and quasi-experimental methods as the "one right way" to validate instructional approaches emerged out of the controversy over the "one right way" to teach reading. Methodology itself emerged as a choice of weapons in a political argument.

Politics of Resaerch in Reading

Although the political fighting between supporters of progressive education and phonics instruction goes back at least to the beginning of the twentieth century, the division between phonics-first and whole language cultures took on political overtones in the 1950s. Rudolf Flesch claimed in his best-selling book, *Why Johnny Can't Read,* that reading failure was widespread in America. Among the culprits he blamed for widespread illiteracy were reading teachers who used the "whole-word" method (also called the look-say or sight-word method) rather than the phonetic method.[28]

Flesch blamed progressive educators such as John Dewey, whom he labeled the Lenin of education, for misleading teachers and guiding them away from sound, systematic, linear training—first of sounds, then of association of sounds and letters, then of words, then of meanings. The conservative right took up this cause and spread his message.

Political uses of research were evident during the California debates about reading policy. Advocates for phonics programs capitalized on test scores that seemed to show a decline in reading achievement. They blamed whole language. The media readily accepted this view. Jeff McQuillen later demonstrated that a testing artifact—the tests themselves had changed—had resulted in the apparent decline of scores. On the only test that remained constant for the period in dispute (1984–1990), scores remained stable or climbed higher. According to the 1992 and 1994 NAEP survey, those students whose teachers reported that they used whole language instruction showed small but consistent advantages on reading comprehension.[29] It seems clear that the NAEP data made no impression on the political debates or in the subsequent policy. Nor did the studies reviewed by Krashen and McQuillen. Phonics-first proponents were selective about what studies to present to policy makers and how to spin their results. The winning side produced comparative studies that seemed to support phonics. That was the information that policy makers wanted to hear. Thereafter state policies supported phonics instruction and basal series, professional development, and materials acquisition that exclusively involved phonics.

NICHD Research

The National Institute of Child Health and Development (NICHD) is a department within the U.S. Department of Health, congressionally authorized and federally funded. Reid Lyon, who holds a doctorate in special education, has (as of 2003) the title of Research Scientist and Chief of Research and acts as principal spokesperson for the program of research that the Institute funds and disseminates. He is also the person most likely to testify to congressional panels, consult with state education authorities, and speak to the media about the results of the research on reading.

A *Wall Street Journal* article reported that in the first four years of the Clinton administration, Lyon traveled 10 times to Texas to push Bush's reading policy there. He reinforced the message about phonics that Barbara Foorman, a Houston researcher, had been providing Governor Bush for several years. During the Clinton years, congressional allocation for reading research doubled, all this money going to NICHD. Lyon convinced congressional Republicans to reject Clinton's proposal to pay volunteers to read to children, because such a program would be, in Lyon's opinion, a waste of money. Instead the $2.5 million was redirected to the Reading Excellence Act to teach phonemic awareness and systematic phonics. "You ought to see his schtick," said a Bush adviser about Lyon's slick presentations.[30] By the end of the Clinton administration, Lyon had involved himself in reading reforms in half the states, and he was well situated to assume a prominent position in the Bush presidential administration. Some called him the "czar" of reading.

When George W. Bush became president, he asked Lyon to recruit likeminded people to fill top positions at the Department of Education and Department of Health. Locating reading policy and research in the Department of Health defined illiteracy as a public health issue, which in turn drew attention toward neurological explanations about individuals and away from social explanations such as poverty, children's access to books, or their early literacy experiences. According to the Institute's core theory, neurological factors cause reading failure and phonemic awareness and systematic phonics provide the cure. Teachers must train children in the relationship between sounds of words and parts of words, and if they do not, then it is the teachers that are to blame for creating reading failure.

The Institute focuses on dyslexia and quotes statistics that 20 percent of the American population suffer from that "disease" and that 40 percent of American adults cannot read.[31] NICHD disseminates bad news about schools that it gets from any source. It blames all declines on the failure of schools to provide systematic training of sound-symbol relationships.

NICHD speaks with a single voice about reading and research and funds a small group of researchers who share its core perspective. It defines reading narrowly, believing that the central element in learning to read is phonological processing. Thus, the Institute funds research on tracking eye movements and brain activity while a subject is engaging in, for example, recognition of phonemes in nonsense words. The Institute focuses on the genetic underpinnings of normal and disabled readers. It funds no projects that involve research on emergent literacy, for example, or on the social and economic conditions that bear on reading, or indeed on any subject such as those McQuillen and Krashen reviewed. It funds no projects investigating comprehension of extended text passages (similar to the NAEP definition of comprehension) or of real books or magazine articles. There is no government agency like NICHD to distribute research funding to whole language researchers or to disseminate their results to policy makers and practitioners.

The Institute restricts research methods as well as topics of research. To receive Institute funds, proposed research must be "reliable and replicable," which means comparative studies, preferably experiments. Research at the Institute purports to follow the methodological standards used by medical researchers in clinical trials of drug and psychological interventions.

From the framework of political spectacle, NICHD has mastered the art of symbolism and theater. Affiliates work in concert so that the researchers themselves can claim the academic high road. When conversing with the academic community, researchers invoke science and address the scientific community with appropriately cautious empirical claims and generalizations but often overstate findings to policymakers and practitioners.

The Institute provides a research cover for what policy makers want to do on other grounds. Its discourse invokes the aura and cultural authority of science and medical research to persuade groups with small capacity or inclination to look behind the words to their concrete referents, that is, to the factual performance of the researchers themselves. Only the opponents of the NICHD studies look closely, but they are then labeled as cranks, flailing about, incapable of understanding or appreciating real science.[32]

To support our statements we offer the case histories of two Institute projects, Barbara Foorman's Houston study and the National Reading Panel's meta-analysis of research studies on reading.

The Houston Study

Perhaps the best-known study of the effectiveness of phonics instruction was conducted by Barbara Foorman, a frequent recipient of funds from NICHD and prominent consultant with policy makers in the states, the federal government, and test publishers. She is the director of research at the Center of Academic and Reading Skills at the Texas Medical Center. She also collaborated in the writing of the reading series called Open Court, a product of McGraw Hill. The Institute made an $11 million grant to Foorman's group to conduct a "reliable, replicable, scientific" study to compare the effectiveness of different methods of teaching reading. After the study was finished, the media referred to it as definitive proof that phonics-first methods are the superior way to teach reading.

Even before the study was completed, affiliates were using it to advise policy makers in Texas and California, where legislation to mandate phonics was being considered. Later, when the study was completed, Institute researchers and affiliates used the conclusions of the study to influence national legislation on reading and accountability. The findings influenced policy makers in several states including California during the time when policy makers were designing penalties for districts that would adopt curriculum packages other than those that focused on intensive, systematic phonics. California authorized funds for teacher training and professional development—only if that training focused on intensive phonics. The state required that trainers be certified and compliant with the phonics mandate and it refused to certify whole language consultants and trainers.[33] Eventually, many districts adopted Open Court, one of three reading programs on the state approved list and one of two that the state would fund. It was the districts most strapped for funds that most felt the pressure to take advantage of the state's largess. Districts with sufficient revenues could afford to deviate.

Although the Houston study made headlines and influenced policies even before it was published in a peer-reviewed forum, researchers outside the NICHD circle found it difficult to get access to the preliminary report. Its authors claimed that the government had placed an embargo on it. A preliminary version eventually appeared on the Internet. Critiques followed soon after. Denny Taylor, a researcher interested in the social and economic aspects of literacy, heard about the Houston study from newspaper accounts. Her subsequent book, *Beginning to Read and the Spin Doctors of Science,* describes her attempts to ask questions and clarify ambiguities in the report. She was told to be patient and wait for the peer-reviewed, published version. When she persisted, her motives were questioned. Meanwhile the results of the study were being used to inform policy.[34] The study went through the process of scholarly peer review and was finally published in the prestigious *Journal of Educational Psychology.*[35]

A person would have to chop through a considerable thicket of technical detail to see the flaws in the report. One would have to care enough to look closely to see the ways that the study fell short of the ideals of science it espouses, to find that it would be nearly impossible for independent researchers to replicate (if they could obtain the funds to do so), or to know what exactly produced the effects or to what situations and classrooms one could generalize the results. Instead of clarity, there is buzzing confusion.

In an earlier section we contrasted the common sense meaning of reading with the simplistic measures of the components of reading that phonics-first researchers use. This contrast implies that when the study concludes that phonics instruction (or Open Court or Direct Code—the various labels used in the Houston study) produces greater effects than whole language (or Implicit Code) on "reading," one needs to "read" between the lines. One needs to understand the political symbolism and the

political tactics that researchers use to induce the reader to make unconscious generalizations—from the narrow measures they use in their studies to the broad images in our minds.

But does it matter, in a rational sense, that the highest scientific ideals
had not, in fact, been followed in this study? In the interval between the
preliminary version and the final version, the Houston study made a substantial impact on policy. And McGraw-Hill could advertise its product,
Open Court, by citing Foorman's research as proof of the superiority of
phonics instruction. "The program is based on the latest scientific research. . . . Research shows that 11 to 15 hours of training in phonemic
awareness is the key to reading success."[36]

The National Reading Panel Meta-Analysis

When George W. Bush became president he brought his reading policy
from Texas as a plan to the nation. The Reading Excellence Act was based
on the notion that scientific, evidence-based research had established the
superiority of phonics for teaching children how to read. As he had stated
to Texas business leaders back in 1996, "We do not need trendy new theories. The basics work. If drill gets the job done, then rote is right."

Not all legislators were so sure, however. Congress commissioned the
NICHD to review and synthesize existing "scientific research" and make
recommendations about national reading policy. This commission would
have made good, instrumental sense had not another report recently been
issued on the same topic by the National Research Council (NRC), an arm
of the National Academy of Science. The National Academy relishes its
status as the primary voice of science to the government. It accepts commissions from the legislative and executive branches of the federal government to make policy recommendations based on the best available
scientific evidence. It follows the norms of science by naming to its commissions only scientists with excellent credentials and by submitting commission reports for scholarly review.[37]

The NRC report presented a review of research and made recommendations about the teaching models best able to improve achievement and
prevent reading failures. It concluded that research supported a balanced
approach to teaching children how to read.[38]

Some critics have suggested that the NRC's recommendations were too
"balanced" and not sufficiently clear about the superiority of phonics-first.
Hence, the National Reading Panel (NRP) was commissioned.

The NRC seeks a balanced membership for its panels and seeks nomi-
nees from the scientific community. NICHD, in contrast, chose individuals
who were its affiliates or were known to support its perspective on reading.
The NRP was made up of researchers who study the genetic origins of

reading disability, specialists in special education, dyslexia, and the like. Experts in classroom literacy, socio-linguistics, economics, or anthropology were excluded. Only one panelist with an alternative point of view was appointed, and she was not a researcher. Joanne Yatvin, long-time educator and teacher educator disrupted the consensus on the panel and later published a minority report that shed light on the ways the panel functioned to skew its review toward the NICHD perspective.[39]

Key to understanding the recommendations of the Panel were the initial decisions it made about topics and procedures. Under the guidance of NICHD staff, the panel members themselves selected the topics to be studied and then divided themselves into subcommittees that focused on the chosen topics. The largest subcommittee consisted of just five members, plus some assistants from the NICHD staff.

To synthesize the research within the chosen topics, the Panel decided to use meta-analysis. Meta-analysis is a method that medical researchers often use to combine the results of "primary" research studies in which separate researchers examined the comparative effectiveness of, for example, a drug like Prozac for decreasing depression or the effectiveness of massage to relieve arthritic symptoms. Meta-analysis provides a solution to the common problem in medical, psychological, and educational research that different primary studies produce different results. On a particular topic, many researchers conduct primary studies; some show one thing and others show the opposite, or are inconclusive either way. A single study is never definitive. Therefore, a person seeking to base or judge policy decisions must look to reviews and summaries of research rather than to single studies. Meta-analysis emerged from educational research. It was invented by Gene Glass, now professor at Arizona State University, and was first applied to the large and disparate literature on the effects of psychotherapy.[40] As Glass envisioned it, meta-analysis solves two problems. First it helps scholars reduce the sheer amount of information which a large body of studies produces to a manageable amount, and in a quantitative, statistical format. Second, it provides a systematic way for research reviewers to document their process of synthesizing the studies, to reduce the chance of selectively biasing their conclusions by including only the subset of studies that confirm a hypothesis.

In rationalist terms, the Panel's work fell short on both grounds. It winnowed what some said were 100,000 studies to somewhere near 40 studies per subcommittee. With only 40 studies, was a meta-analysis even necessary?[41] Or did it add another set of technical terms to bedazzle the audience? Arcane technical procedures provide more symbolic punch.

The Panel set what it called "stringent" methodological criteria for selecting which studies it would include in the meta-analysis. The small and select membership of subcommittees applied those criteria and winnowed down the population of studies to a small and select sample. They did not document the winnowing process. No technical advisers or practitioners oversaw those decisions or weighed their impact on the ultimate conclusions of the Panel.[42]

Moreover, the Panel adopted such a narrow definition of reading that whole bodies of relevant evidence were omitted because the studies employed other than experimental methods (omitted were ethnographies, discourse analyses, regression analyses, and the like). Important substantive content was missed as well. For example, panel members excluded studies on the effects of phonics on writing. They excluded studies that examined the effects of teaching methods on students' ability to comprehend extended, authentic texts. Nor were there studies on the effects of writing or early literacy on reading skills. Nor were studies included on the effects of such programs of Sustained Silent Reading. By excluding the latter studies, a reader might draw the conclusion that only phonics and phonemic awareness training had been proved—when it was only that other methods had been excluded from the calculations.[43] The subcommittee reviewing studies on comprehension decided not to do a meta-analysis. Its narrative results never got the attention received by the statistical findings of the phonics meta-analysis.

Once the Panel selected the studies to be analyzed, the crucial tasks of classifying and coding studies and calculating effect sizes was contracted out to an affiliate of NICHD and his team of graduate assistants.[44] Congress had given the panel such a short time to do its work that many panel members never actually read the studies.[45] Nevertheless, the physicist who had been appointed chair of the Panel maintained that he was sure that scientific standards were followed because, as he said to a reporter later, "I know what good research looks like."[46]

The Panel did its work in 1999–2000. Unlike the National Research Council report, however, the National Reading Panel did not seek review by independent scholars. NICHD developed three formats for its reports. First, it posted an extensive technical report on the Internet. Second, NICHD chose Widmeyer Communications, a public relations firm in Washington, D. C., which also worked for McGraw-Hill and the Business Roundtable, to write the summaries and conduct a public relations campaign. Third, Widmeyer also crafted promotional materials including a videotape for even broader distribution to textbook publishers, practitioners, policy makers, and others.[47] Perhaps the choice of a public relations firm rather than scholars to disseminate the findings was responsible for the discrepancies among the resports. Whatever the cause, the conclusions in Summary and promotional materials—that is, the ones that most people were likely to see—differed substantially from the conclusions listed in the long technical report.

Table 1 Comparison of Wording in the National Reading Panel Report of the Meta-Analysis of Results on Systematic Phonics Instruction with the NICHD Summary of that Report (after Garan, 2001, p. 506).

NRP Conclusions by Panel Members as Listed in the Technical Report	"Summary" of NRP Conclusions as Reframed by NICHD & Public Relations Firm
"There were insufficient data to draw any conclusions about the effects of phonics instruction with normally developing readers above first grade"	"The meta-analysis revealed that systematic phonics produces significant benefits for students in kindergarten through sixth grade and for children having difficulty learning to read"
"The effect size [on spelling] was not significantly different from zero"	"Across all grade levels, systematic phonics instruction improved the ability of good readers to spell"
"There were insufficient data to draw any conclusions about the effects of phonics instruction with normally developing readers above first grade"	[Meta-analysis] "results indicate what can be accomplished when explicit, systematic phonics programs are implemented in today's classrooms"

In her critique of the Panel's study, Elaine Garan[48] demonstrated the political use and misuse that can be made of research. She compared the Panel's conclusions with the NICHD summary, using the exact words of both forms of reporting. We place these side by side in Table 1.

The differences amount to distortion. Panel members concluded that phonics affected only children in first grade and that phonics did not produce benefits in spelling. The summary and video display no such reticence, claiming that phonics improves spelling and improves reading for normal students from kindergarten to sixth grade. To get a flavor of the extent of distortion moving from statistical findings to conclusions to summaries to policies, read this account of the Panel's work by NICHD affiliate Marilyn Adams. Adams's statements to a group of policymakers purport to represent the Panel's findings yet directly contradict them. We have placed in italics the worst of the contradictions:

> The NRP located 52 studies of the value of phonemic awareness instruction and children's reading and spelling growth. In fact the results of these studies [were] *uniformly positive . . .* where that *includes reading comprehension as well as word recognition*—explicit instruction of phonemic awareness was shown to

> be of significant and *lasting benefit* for all students, including normally devel-
> oping readers, *children at risk for future reading problems, disabled readers,
> preschoolers, kindergartners, 1st graders, children in 2nd through 6th grade . . .
> children across SES levels, and children learning to read in English.*

Adams continues with claims based on the phonics meta-analysis.

> . . . the NRP was able to conclude that both reading and spelling growth are
> significantly and positively influenced by systematic phonics instruction. The
> panel's meta-analysis . . . affirmed this conclusion across students' socioeco-
> nomic backgrounds and especially when such instruction was provided at the
> outset of children's reading careers, in kindergarten and grade 1.[49]

As warranted statements based on instrumental rationality and science, the above conclusions approach fraud.[50] But as instances of political rationality, they are pure gold.

Repeatedly, NICHD and NRP affiliates and officials from the Bush administration repeated the claim that 100,000 studies entered the NRP analysis and that the sheer weight of evidence in favor of phonics made the NRP findings solid science. Donald Langenberg, the physicist and university administrator who headed NRP, testified to Congress thusly:

> . . . Phonics instruction produces significant benefits for children from
> kindergarten through sixth grade and for children having difficulty learning
> to read. The greatest improvements were seen from systematic phonics
> instruction. This type of phonics instruction consists of teaching a planned
> sequence of phonics elements, rather than highlighting elements as they
> happen to appear in a text. Here again, the evidence was so strong that the
> Panel concluded that systematic phonics instruction is appropriate for rou-
> tine classroom instruction.[51]

By looking at the only peer-reviewed version of the NRP study,[52] however, one can see that only about 1,500 studies were uncovered by using the relevant indexing systems, and most of these were not comparative studies and were eliminated based on information from their abstracts. Only 38 studies were actually included in the phonics meta-analysis. By looking at the tables in that report, one can see that studies in which the researcher examined the effects of phonics on reading real texts number only nine (most studies measured basic skills but not real reading). Considering studies on normal kindergarten and first-graders, the population for whom the Reading First legislation is primarily intended, the body of evidence shrinks to only ten studies (most of the studies in the phonics analysis used reading disabled or otherwise "at-risk" subjects). Of these ten, one lacks a control group, which violates one of the panel's selection criteria. Of the remaining nine, only one study is a true experiment, the gold standard and the basis of extravagant claims that the literature is scientific.

Education Week, the primary outlet for news and opinion about education policy, quoted from the Summary, failed to examine the details, and led with headlines about how phonics triumphed in "reliable, replicable" research. Furthermore, because of the notoriously low attention span of policy makers, none is very likely to have investigated what the research really states, let alone the presumptions and definitions and methodological minutiae of the study itself. Instead, they took the opinions of staff or lobbyists on what speech to make and how to vote, appropriating only the words "reliable, replicable, evidence-based" without understanding what those words mean to research methodologists and practitioners.

Despite the limitations of the NRP meta-analysis, phonics advocates used it to persuade policymakers to require that all teachers incorporate 11 to 15 hours of phonemic awareness training into their classes. The summary of the NRP meta-analysis was used to convince states and districts to adopt structured reading programs such as Open Court. They claimed that such a move would make reading instruction "science-based" or "evidence-based." They urged universities to incorporate phonics-first instruction into teacher preparation programs and threatened the universities that failed to comply voluntarily. The political campaign disguised as scientific research synthesis triumphed with the passage of the Federal Reading Excellence Act, later incorporated into the No Child Left Behind legislation signed into federal law in 2002.

The political outweighed the scientific. Nevertheless and ironically, the NRP meta-analysis and many of the studies included in it fell short of NICHD's own avowed research standards. Rather than following the modest findings of the technical report of NRP, NICHD followed the highly crafted and misleading summary to establish phonics-first as the sole, official method of teaching reading[53] and the most far-reaching Federal education policy in history.

Enforcement of Reading First has been heavy-handed. Susan Neuman, officer of U.S. Department of Education, admonished state education chiefs that their reading programs had to be "science-based." That is, they must include systematic phonemic awareness training and phonics instruction, fluency, vocabulary and comprehension. Otherwise, the federal government would conduct audits and withhold moneys from the Reading First initiative. Newman was quoted as aiming to "change the face of reading instruction across the United States, from an art to a science. . . . From science it becomes a mission."[54]

Why "Phonics First" Won

If the research results themselves were so equivocal, why then did phonics-first win the rhetorical war over reading instruction and over research?

Beyond rhetoric, how did it happen that federal policy should mandate one form of reading instruction? Why did whole language not stand a chance? The reader should not be surprised to see us rely on political spectacle theory for a way to resolve the conundrum of how reading research relates to reading policy.

Reason Number One. Phonics-first has powerful and visible political allies. Former Secretary of Education William Bennett was quoted in the *Wall Street Journal* that phonics is the "vaccine for preventing reading difficulty" and that it needs to be administered immediately to everyone. But, he posited, "most state education agencies, schools of education, and school districts march under the banner of balanced instruction which is just whole language in disguise, equivalent to treating polio with aspirin."[55]

Reason Number Two. Media also seem to favor phonics (or at least their vision of phonics) and to mock whole language. Perhaps a thorough public relations campaign and training programs conducted for education writers by phonics enthusiasts resulted in this proclivity toward phonics-first. Or perhaps journalists simply reflect society more broadly. Many Americans endorse—at least for other peoples' children—forms of instruction that involve repetition, testing for mastery, tracked classes, and believe that skills must be acquired in order; the simple first, and then the more complex.[56]

Reason Number Three. If one believes that reality and knowledge are social constructions, it is inconsistent to claim, as whole language advocates do, that a research finding could represent the single, authoritative, definitive truth. Nor does whole language yield its complexities to sound bites like "hooked on phonics" or "rote is right." Nor is there a way to transform the reading process into a medical process. One cannot blame reading problems on a brain glitch if one believes, as whole language theorists do, that literacy emerges through social interactions involving texts. Nor is there much chance that whole language educators would conduct experiments because experiments require control and standardization of instruction. Because they believe that literacy is a process of joint construction between readers and texts, they value carefully done, intensive and ongoing analyses of classroom life. But to describe and analyze the subtle flow of events across time (as ethnographies do) means to forego state-approved and narrow notions of reliability and control over treatment variables.

Follow the money to discover the fourth reason why phonics-first won the research race. Whole language does not provide mass markets or opportunities for capital growth and private fortunes. Phonics-first provides these opportunities, although they are taken largely out of the public eye. From policies that require a small and sensible amount of phonemic awareness and phonics training, it is but a short step toward requiring schools to adopt one of the big programs such as Open Court or Direct Instruction. These curriculum packages consume large chunks of the school day, and their high cost diminishes the discretion that schools might exercise to purchase materials that "balance" the reading programs. This exclusion is most likely to be felt in schools of poverty. The huge curriculum packages also dominate professional development by spending staff development resources to train teachers to follow their scripts exactly. An official in the Bush Department of Education recommended that poor districts take that next step and adopt one of the total packages. She justified this recommendation on the results of NICHD research showing that Open Court had established itself scientifically. To adopt an alternative program would mean that the district had to present its own evidence that its favored program met scientific standards.[57] Districts with too few financial resources are unlikely to draw off scarce funds to do research, so they comply.

For corporations to make big money on selling reading programs they rely on the integration of products such as texts, tests, worksheets, audio- and videotapes, and teacher manuals. To be highly profitable the publishers must have standardization, mass production, efficient distribution, and mandated adoption in big states like Texas and California. But there is little standardization or mass marketing involved in whole language education. Whole language educators reject standardization and insist that it is a mistake to make all students learn the same things, in linear order, or read the same materials and books, or take identical tests. Instead students should pursue a variety of content and goals and demonstrate their learning with authentic performances of multiple and varied tasks.

In phonics-first classrooms, teachers stick to scripts and materials that textbook corporations develop and administrators pass along to them. To follow such scripts requires less training overall and more training and supervision that are carefully targeted to carry out the standard packages. In whole language classrooms, teachers must know more about curricular content, pedagogy, and assessment than do teachers who only adhere to scripts. Teachers have more discretion in the classroom. Whole language requires highly competent and knowledgeable teachers. Experienced teachers cost more. When neo-liberals look at experienced teachers, they see higher labor costs, a situation to be avoided in the global economy.

There is no big money to be made off of whole language. In contrast, big curriculum packages like Open Court, the statewide adoption of single textbooks and curricular packages, and state and national testing programs (along with the materials that prepare students and teachers to pass them) have provided opportunities to enhance corporate and individual wealth.

The fortunes of the corporate leader of McGraw-Hill, which publishes Open Court, illustrate the potential profit to be made from big, commercial, phonics-first packages. Harold McGraw III, besides directing the publishing giant, also serves as vice president of the National Council on Economic Education, chair of the Emergency Committee for American Trade, and a member of the Education Task Force of the Business Round-table. In 1999, McGraw-Hill sales from its educational products exceeded $4 billion. As each additional state adopted one of its products, Open Court or Reading Mastery, McGraw Hill's profits rose precipitously. Despite a weak economy in 2000, McGraw-Hill's profits rose 28 percent in six months, and its income rose to $874 million.[58] Its subsidiary, CTB-McGraw Hill (one of the three top providers of large-scale testing) also reaped profits from state testing programs. In *Business Week*, Harold McGraw III praised Bush's reading initiatives. "It's a great day for education . . . We have an unprecedented opportunity to bring meaningful improvements in education."[59]

Reason number five. Profiteers aligned with the radical religious right, which detests whole language and favors phonics.[60] Groups such as the Moral Majority, the Eagle Forum, and the Right to Read Foundation oppose whole language and progressive education, which are grounded in ideas about students' ability and power to construct their own knowledge and come to their own interpretation of texts. But these ideas challenge right-wing theology, which maintains that the Bible is the single source of truth not open to interpretation. The idea of children constructing knowledge for themselves, the idea of multiple knowledge claims, the idea that multiple interpretations of texts are possible—all ideas fundamental to whole language—are anathema to the religious right. What is more, the Christian right believes that children are sinners by nature and must be controlled by their parents. Teachers, according to this view, are the interlopers who attempt to wrest control away from parents. The public schools fail to provide safe havens for Christians and promote evil ideas about sexual permissiveness, cultural diversity, and anti–family values. The religious right demands discipline, order, phonics and explicit, structured instruction under the control of parents, not professionals.

The agendas of religious right and corporate executives converge with long-time developers of scripted curriculum packages. Overlooking internal contradictions, corporations and the religious right pool money to fund research, to commission policy papers, and to conduct public relations campaigns. At the hearings at the California board of education prior its adoption of the phonics-first reading policy, only these constituencies were represented. No dissenters were allowed.

Individuals migrate among these constituencies. An official in the Moral Majority founded the conservative Right to Read Foundation, then joined the staff of a congressman just in time to advise Congress on the superiority of phonics as demonstrated by reliable, replicable research, then received an appointment in the U.S. executive branch. An author of a reading curriculum package became a reading researcher, and a reading researcher became an author. Researchers receive royalties, consultant fees. Conservative Internet sites have links to NICHD research summaries. Money flows in all directions. Research provides the cover.

How Research and Political Spectacle Intersect

In the political spectacle, politics comes costumed as science. Here we list the ways in which research functions in the political spectacle.

Political Actors Demand that a Particular Policy Be Studied (While Another Policy Escapes Scrutiny)

The mere act of doing or commissioning or quoting research defines the actor as rational and scientific. Political actors strategically manage impressions to advance their interests and ideologies. When political actors call for research or evaluation, the call symbolizes that a problem or crisis already exists.[61] Policy research rarely grows out of a researcher's curiosity or the demands of her discipline—a hallmark of the scientific ideal. Instead it comes about because a client commissioned it. Often the client is a government agency, and sometimes a foundation, professional association, or think tank sets the study in motion. What gets studied is a political decision, and these decisions depend on who controls power and resources. Studies almost always flow from ideologies and interests, no matter how technically adequate or apparently rational and scientific they might be.

Likewise, the absence of calls for research on a particular policy may indicate that the program is above scrutiny or its benefits are taken for granted. Programs for "gifted" students are rarely evaluated; programs for the economically disadvantaged, almost always. Political actors also commission studies to delay action or diffuse opposition. When spoken by a politician, the words "We don't know enough about X" usually mean "I oppose X" or "We can't afford X." Such was the case when the Tennessee legislature commissioned an experiment on class size rather than make a policy to reduce the size of classes for all children in the state.[62]

Ernest House argued that research conveys not simply scientific knowledge but also legitimacy and power to political actors:

> Legitimacy should not be understood as those in power controlling or determining the thoughts of others. . . . [Rather, policy research and evaluation are new forms] of cultural authority based on persuasion, cultural authority being manifested in the probability that descriptions of reality and judgments of value will prevail as valid. . . . In practical terms, the government can say to antagonistic parties, "Look, we have subjected the situation to a fair determination of the

facts and arrived at this decision objectively. What more can you ask?" It is important for governments to demonstrate their impartiality and ability to adjudicate among competing interests.[63]

Schneider and Ingram distinguished different contexts in which research intersects with politics. When the scientific research is equivocal and particularly when findings contradict each other, policy makers and their political allies exploit the debate by aligning with the faction that provides a rationale for what they were going to decide in any case. In most instances, the results favor the powerful and neglect the interests of the less advantaged parts of the public.

> Even though policy actions may be taken primarily to satisfy powerful groups ... politicians must articulate some sort of instrumental reasoning that connects policy actions to substantive results.[64]

Furthermore,

> The elements and rationales in scientific and professionalized designs reflect the utilitarian rationality of science yet often confer benefits that further the interests of the scientific and professional communities themselves.[65]

When researchers define a policy problem they tend to make it more complex and technical than it need be. Researchers often end their report by recommending additional studies to resolve the complexities and inconsistencies. Schneider and Ingram wrote that when that occurs, ordinary citizens are pushed out of the deliberation over policies that affect them, further alienating them from politics. Debate becomes more insular, a contest among experts.[66]

Political Actors Selectively Recruit Researchers

When clients of research have a clear political intent, they make simple choices of whom to hire and fund. They can look at the biographies and institutional affiliations of researchers to find the ones most likely to provide support for their favored policies. Research is also done by employees of think tanks or by researchers whose livelihood depends on a flow of contracts from such agencies. Think tanks particularly operate outside the scholarly community and do research in which the scientific value of its knowledge claims assumes a lesser priority than ideological compatibility.[67] In Arizona, if the Goldwater Institute commissions a study or assigns it to one of its own staff, a reader can safely predict that the results of that study will be consistent with a free-market and anti-public institution perspective. Organizations and government agencies have long commissioned studies. Now they commission particular results.

Even if clients choose a researcher who is not an insider, proclivities of researchers who work at universities and research and development organizations are known from their biographies and records of their work. Voucher promoters would hire Harvard's Paul Peterson, advocates of tracking policies would avoid UCLA's Jeannie Oakes. We don't mean to suggest that all contracted research is by definition biased toward the interests and ideologies of the client. Many researchers work hard and successfully to preserve more than just the semblance of neutrality when conducting and reporting their studies. Many researchers place a higher priority on the integrity of their discipline and their own reputations than they do on confirming the values and interests of their clients.[68] However, the political implications of choice of researcher can no more be ignored than can the rigor of the study's design, sampling and measurement.[69] In a labor market in which many researchers and evaluators are trying to make a living and build a career while clients are few and powerful, one must examine potential managerial or client bias.[70] Researchers also risk, when they lose sight of the client's values and interests, losing access to data or the chance to do more research. There is only one decision-maker in school districts such as Philadelphia, Chicago and Los Angeles who controls school data and gets to pick from many hungry researchers.

According to scientific ideals, researchers operate outside the fray of politics and policy and gaze on the policy arena from a neutral, independent vantage point, separated from the action, as through a one-way glass. In the political spectacle, researchers are themselves actors, testifying to Congressional committees, talking to the media, attaching themselves to commissions, advising politicians, lecturing interest groups, and competing for research grants. All of these acts add political capital, cultural authority and financial status to the researchers themselves, and all forms of capital can be converted from one form into another. It is tempting to view the NICHD staff and affiliates in this way.

NICHD officials did not select researchers at random but picked known commodities. It granted Barbara Foorman eleven million dollars to conduct a study on the comparative effects of phonics-first instruction. Having such massive grants not only permits researchers to do research. It also purchases enormous clout for those researchers in their institution and puts them in line for further funding, lectureships, endowed chairs, opportunities to consult with publishing companies, contracts to write textbook series, and the like. Such stardom also provides a researcher access to powerful decision-makers—a place at the table, as many policy researchers describe it.

An interesting variation of this theme is the strategic selection of experts to review existing research, advise policy makers, and confirm the imprimatur of science on the results. The National Reading Panel that conducted the meta-analysis of reading research serves as an example. Congress and the President asked that the NICHD research director appoint the panel.

With a single exception, he appointed panelists who shared the perspective of the institute. By confining the range of issues narrowly, the majority on the panel ruled out studies of literacy and text comprehension. By failing to draw on such literature, The National Reading Panel produced an unrepresentative portrait of reading research and less than comprehensive set of conclusions and recommendations to congress.[71]

Testimony to state and U.S. legislatures also seems to have been arranged to present one-sided evidence and recommendations. When the California policy makers changed from local control of curriculum to mandated programs, they heard testimony exclusively from experts quoting NICHD's version of research and recommending intensive phonics and programs like Open Court. The chosen experts did not, as far as we can learn from the transcripts, reveal their connections to the publishers under consideration or reveal their financial interests in the very programs they promote in the name of fair- minded expertise. Nor were potential conflicts of interest mentioned. Not only were whole language advocates not allowed to attend, in their absence they were castigated and ridiculed as being the cause of the state's achievement crisis.

If political actors selectively choose researchers and reviewers of research, they also can establish awards and sinecures for persons they know will testify favorably to the political agenda put forward. For example, NICHD officials often point toward the awards that their researchers have won, without noting that those awards are targeted, not open-ended.[72]

Officials Make Tactical Choices of Methods and Approaches to Research

No study is perfect or perfectly comprehensive. No single study can address all the important issues or measure all the important aspects of a policy and its effects. All researchers make choices. For example, one researcher decides to measure immediate but not long-term effects of policy. One researcher limits the study to a single measure of effect while another uses many measures. Some neglect questions of cost or justice. Some researchers actually examine the workings of the policy in the field while others treat the policy as a black box. Some interrogate the meanings and practices of people who deliver the policy; others claim that alternative meanings are subjective and random, and therefore exclude them. Some interpret statistical findings conservatively; others allow themselves more latitude. Some reveal missteps in conducting their studies; others conceal them. In representing their studies, some use generous or speculative language; others choose more circumspect language.

In the political arena, however, researchers and sponsors of research gloss over the choices they make and conceal the limitations of their studies, so that the researcher appears more objective and detached, and the study itself more scientific. Each choice provides an opportunity for political values to intrude in the research process.

Researchers and political actors make a virtue of recommending a particular methodology or way of doing research. Researchers do so to appear objective, competent, the members of elite clubs. In education, those researchers who are influenced by laboratory psychology and medical research often claim the superiority of field experiments. Economists, on the other hand, prefer the logic of production function analyses. Anthropologists and sociologists cleave to participant observation and survey methods. The discipline a researcher represents conveys a cultural authority to herself and also to her study if she follows the norms of her discipline.[73] The differences among disciplines, however, are metaphysical, incommensurate, and beyond resolution.

To claim otherwise—to proclaim one's approach and methods as exclusively scientific—amounts to scientism (an irrational dogma or orthodoxy), not science. Such a claim works in the political spectacle to promote oneself as a powerful actor on stage, one with a commanding presence, irrespective of the underlying truth of one's pronouncements or the interests at stake behind the curtain.

Government Censors Research that Counters Key Interests and Ideologies

Who owns the results of research and controls the right to release them to the public or scholarly community? In the rational and scientific ideal, scholars are accountable to their community of scholars and to the ethical and scientific standards of their fields. When they accept grants or contracts from a government agency, they transfer part of professional accountability to the state and reduce the scope of their independence. State agencies can embargo reports temporarily (as happened in the case of the ASAP Technical Report described in Chapter Two) or until such time as the dominant political agenda is achieved or overtaken by events.

Once again we return to *A Nation at Risk* for an example. In 1990, the Secretary of Energy under George H.W. Bush asked the Sandia National Laboratories to turn its attention to science education. Sandia Lab receives the bulk of its funding from the U.S. Department of Energy. It ordinarily studies nuclear physics, alternative energy systems, information technology, and the like—not education. Sandia scientists decided to conduct a comprehensive review of public school performance. After conducting their analysis the scientists submitted their report to the Energy Department. The report concluded that American public schools were not failing, were not even substandard when compared to the schools of other nations. The researchers at Sandia later reflected (the President and cabinet heads having changed by then): "To our surprise, on nearly every measure we found steady or slightly improving trends."[74]

Their conclusion contradicted *A Nation at Risk* in nearly every particular. The funding agency responded by placing an embargo on the report and a gag order on the scientists who wrote it. However, the report was leaked, causing some risk to the scientists' careers and to the federal funding of the lab, which was heavily dependent on it.

We believe this story illustrates an important aspect of the intersection of a political agenda and research. In this case, perhaps the Bush administration wanted to provide a rational basis for its perspective that public schools were in crisis or perhaps it wanted to squelch perspectives and evidence that contradicted the alleged decline. Rigorous studies that show the benefits of print access and experiences with books on children's reading comprehension were excluded from the NRP meta-analysis, and this too illustrates a form of government censorship.

Results of Research Are Strategically Represented

Advocates and even researchers tend to overstate the findings consistent with their cause and generalize their findings far beyond what can be justified by the procedures they used. They understate the limitations and problems in conducting the study. They tend to ignore the underlying assumptions on which the study was based. They disseminate their results to people within their faction, to the media during press conferences, and to policy makers. Such a means of dissemination bypasses the usual avenues that their scholarly community uses to report their findings. When media or policy makers misinterpret or overstate research findings, advocates seldom correct them.

Political researchers tend to portray their findings as definitive, as the last word on the subject. They rarely put their findings in the larger context of all other relevant research. Yet single studies never provide final answers. In the body of research studies, findings are rarely consistent with one another, thus necessitating reviews and syntheses of the collection of studies. Research reviewers can also tip the scales toward a favorite outcome by selecting only the favorable studies to synthesize.[75] Like the National Reading Panel members, reviewers sometimes develop and rationalize arbitrary criteria for selection of studies to synthesize, thus biasing the conclusions from that review.

Validity Is Determined On Political Rather than Disciplinary and Methodological Grounds

Who decides whether the knowledge that a study gleaned is valid? In the scientific disciplines, the standards worked out by the disciplinary community are the core criteria by which a study is to be judged. Although factions within disciplines argue among themselves, at least they have a forum or institution within which to argue. A scientific discipline rests on whether the issues can be joined.[76] That is, the factions agree to disagree about the key categories of valuing credibility, but at least they jointly recognize the categories themselves. Factions within archeology might disagree about whether the Anasazi practiced cannibalism, but at least they can agree on the rules of evidence on which the question turns.

There is no consensus in the educational research community that experimental designs equate exclusively to truthful knowledge claims. Nevertheless, in reauthorizing ESEA Title I, Congress appropriated NICHD language to impose its narrow view of research methods and validity. The bill requires that schools select programs that are "evidence-based." Research, according to the language that defines such evidence:

> . . . involves the application of rigorous, systematic, and objective procedures to obtain reliable and valid knowledge relevant to education activities and programs; and . . . employs systematic, empirical methods that draw on observation or experiment; involves rigorous data analyses that are adequate to test the stated hypotheses and justify the general conclusions drawn; relies on measurements or observational methods that provide reliable and valid data . . . ; is evaluated using experimental or quasi-experimental designs in which individuals, entities, programs, or activities are assigned to different conditions and with appropriate controls to evaluate the effects of the condition of interest, with a preference for random assignment experiments, or other designs to the extent such designs contain within-condition or across condition controls; ensures experimental studies are presented in sufficient detail and clarity to allow for replication, or at a minimum offer the opportunity to build systematically on its findings; [and] has been accepted by a peer-reviewed journal or approved by a panel of independent experts through a comparably rigorous, objective, scientific review.

That the state should equate one form of research with all valid research, that the state should appropriate the term science and attach it to one form of science and to one segment of scientists, that the state should wrest authority over standards of research from a professional body is a remarkable—even a breath-taking feat. The profession of education scholarship, represented by the American Educational Research Association, has since the 1970s published and respected a wide range of research approaches, methods, and models for generating knowledge claims. Experimentation is only one of those approaches. Researchers have constructed and debated standards to substantiate knowledge claims appropriate for each one of the approaches. Indeed, the National Research Council of the National Academy of Sciences issued a report in 2002 that endorsed a variety of research approaches and included them under the umbrella of "scientific research."[77] The voice of the scientists on the NRC panel was drowned out by the much more narrow view expressed about science in the federal legislation. By the time the NRC issued its report, the power to define science had already been lost—legislated away by the No Child Left Behind bill.

Critiques of experimentation and statistical hypothesis testing are many, and they are developed by quantitative and qualitative researchers as well as by philosophers. Yet Federal and state governments now mandate both the approach that researchers must take to be scientific and the standards that they must meet. "Evidence-based practice" is the term that medical researchers use to denote that part of physicians' treatment that has been confirmed by controlled trials, that is, by experiments. By using the phrases "reliable, replicable research" and "evidence-based" practice, NICHD attempted to distance itself from educational research and identify itself with medical research.[78]

Does it make sense to apply the same criteria to educational research as to medical research? Or is this identification yet another political intrusion into the endeavors of truth seeking? Whether education experiments share sufficient characteristics with medical experiments is anything but settled, and there is no institutional forum for considering the issue. In identifying with the medical research profession and equating science with experimental trials, NICHD affiliates ignore several basic principles learned through research experience. First, medical researchers are able to exert greater levels of control over treatment conditions. Controlling the treatment variable in studies of effects of drug A is much more clear cut than controlling the treatment variable in a study of instructional methods. The former requires that the same dosage of the same chemical compound be administered to all subjects. Experimenters can control intake to make sure that subjects comply. If effects in a randomized experiment are found, say, between drug A and drug B, researchers can be fairly sure that drug caused the effects. Researchers can also be relatively confident about how to generalize the findings.[79]

Compared to medical trials, comparative experiments on instructional methods present additional complications. Many aspects peculiar to the context alter and compromise the nature of any instructional treatment, no matter how explicitly that treatment has been described. Instructional treatments are always mediated by teachers. But, do the teachers understand the method well enough to deliver it and are they favorably disposed to do so? Does the treatment fit with the characteristics of the subjects? In most experimental studies (the Houston study provides ample evidence) school realities intrude to frustrate the needs of experimenters to keep things under control. Uncontrolled and uncontrollable variations and glitches are typical of educational experiments, as the field knows based on the Follow Through Planned Variation Study that was conducted in the 1970s.[80]

However, if NICHD sought to emulate medical research it neglected two critical aspects of medical experimentation. One is the requirement that trials be conducted with double-blind controls. Neither the experimenter, the person who measures the effect, nor the patients themselves, know which treatment group they are in. Second, all investigators must divulge any financial and institutional interests they have in the treatment that was investigated. The winning side on research and reading wars did not seem hampered by these professional restraints. Researchers, policy makers, and people making money from texts and materials were part of the same network.

But the latter arguments are rational arguments, and one must look further into the political rationality that underlies the apparently principled and scientific debate.

Irrationality and Policy Research

This chapter concerns rationality and irrationality in education policy and how research and policy confound each other in the political spectacle. We have shown that researchers are actors in the drama, not the dramaturge that stands outside, gazing at it from above. Research wars are political conflicts. Yet, to win one of these wars it is necessary never to acknowledge that one is a combatant. Instead, to be taken seriously as a rational actor, one must succeed in portraying one's own evidence as technically adequate and scientific; while portraying one's opponent's evidence as nothing other than the product of defective methods, ideology, and self-interest. Thus we can consider **political rationality**, the logic that ties selection of topic, researcher, methodology, and dissemination of findings together with political interests and ideologies. Within the context of political intentions and assumptions, political actors proceed logically.

So, should science be abandoned because it is constituted in part by irrational, political elements, because evidence is a product of social construction and not factual truth, because studies all have flaws, holes, motivations; because researchers have values that intrude on their work? Never has it been more urgent for the public to know about what is happening in the everyday life of classrooms. Never has it been more urgent to discover the consequences of policies such as the No Child Left Behind act. Never has it been more urgent to learn who benefits and who loses in the allocation of material values backstage. In this book we lament the decline of rationality in the political spectacle. We believe that rational and technical analysis must be applied to research studies with differences debated in (as Schneider and Ingram called it) occasions of **communicative rationality**.[81] However, judging the technical merits of studies and their empirical warrants is no more important than political analyses to determine the function of politics in those same studies.

In defending the Houston study against the assault of a team of critics in the *Educational Researcher,* Foorman and her team wrote this:

> . . . we patiently suggest that our time and that of our colleagues . . . would be better spent focusing on generating research and not on imagining the motives of other researchers.[82]

In the political spectacle, motives—and more—are exactly what we should investigate.

Notes

1. We believe that strong language is warranted by the fact that we ourselves and our colleagues are implicated as researchers in the political spectacle. Perhaps readers might interpret this vignette as evidence for postmodernism, where everything is constructed and nothing is real and all facts are up for grabs. Yet we assert (and we think Edelman would agree) that real, material benefits are dealt backstage, resulting in real and material consequences. The audience, meanwhile, is absorbed in the fantastical magic acts onstage.
2. In this chapter we conflate policy research with evaluation research and applied research. We follow Lee Cronbach's categorization (Cronbach, 1979).
3. See, for example, Knorr-Cetina (1981).
4. Edelman (1988), p. 1.
5. Bracey (2001c).
6. Edelman (1988), pp. 4–5.
7. Edelman (1988), pp. 43–44.
8. The NAEP levels were set by using the "modified Angoff method," which requires a panel of experts to look at test items and judge them in terms of whether and how well "proficient" students ought to perform. Then these judgments are statistically aggregated to arrive at levels of basic, proficient, etc. The No Child Left Behind legislation requires all states to move all their students to the NAEP proficient level by 2012 or face financial penalties. Two problems emerge from this policy. First, the policy treats NAEP levels as scientific reality when they are little more than aggregate judgments. Second, states have their own ideas about the meaning of proficiency and have various methods of judging it. *Education Week* reported its analysis that the results differ substantially from NAEP to state definitions. In North Carolina 84 percent of fourth graders reached the proficient level on the state test, but only 28 percent of them reached the NAEP proficient level. States differ among themselves in how stringent to set levels of proficiency. Thirteen percent of Delaware eighth graders met their state's standard for proficiency. Eighty-three percent of Georgia's eighth graders met Georgia standards. According to Lorrie Shepard, who did a comparable analysis on Colorado standards, standards can be set high or low in a distribution of test scores. She said, "Unfortunately policy makers are not aware of how high some standards have been set and are inclined to treat all standards as if they were the same" (Olson, 2002a). See also Pearson and DiStefano (1993).
9. Bracey (2002c).
10. Stone (1997), p. 307.
11. Stone (1997), p.177.
12. Stone (1997), p.167.
13. Stone (1997), pp. 174–177.
14. Personal communication, Audrey Amrein, May, 2002. This was not the only discounting engaged in by Texas officials to make it seem that TAAS had been effective. They failed to account for children exempted from testing because they were re-classified as English learners or special education students or because they had been retained in grade rather than advanced to the grade that the state tested.

15. Stone (1997), p. 189.
16. What is widely acknowledged to be the best example of field experimentation in education is STAR, the Tennessee study of the effects of class size on achievement. (See Finn and Achilles (1999); Mosteller, Light, et al. (1996); Nye and Hedges (1999); and Ritter and Boruch (1999).) Yet in spite of its high quality methodological elements, STAR was political in several respects. For example, the legislature substituted the experiment for a policy that would reduce class size throughout the state and failed, ultimately to implement its positive conclusions.
17. Research on the efficacy of vouchers is hopelessly embroiled in politics, with researchers and think tanks on both sides of the political issue lobbying methodological grenades at the other.
18. But as all the world knows, correlation does not prove causation. Researchers use this data to assert that good skills predict (and cause) good comprehension, but the direction of effect could be opposite—ability to comprehend text may cause children to master skills (like sounding out words) better.
19. Recent studies by whole language researchers suggest the contrary.
20. The term whole language was not often used before the 1970s, after the Chall review. Instead proponents called it "meaning-based" or "comprehension-centered" instruction. Despite this anachronism, people later cited Chall's book as if it had proved the superiority of phonics over whole language. (personal communication, Carole Edelsky).
21. Chall based her conclusions on four studies that supported intensive phonics and four favoring look-say or whole word methods, two favoring "some phonics"—a much more equivocal finding than advocates subsequently admitted. See Chall (1995).
22. McQuillan (1998).
23. Much that calls itself whole language is a caricature. Whole language has been confused with "whole word" sight-reading, and language experience approaches. The label is so politically charged that even its experts and advocates have begun to disavow it.
24. Phonics-first advocates made clear that since Krashen's studies were not based on random assignment of children to treatments that they did not measure up to "evidence-based" methodology. Refer to Krashen (1993, 1999).
25. McQuillan (1998).
26. McQuillan (1998), p.71, concluded that "those who read more have better reading comprehension, better vocabulary and better writing skills" even after statistically controlling variables like socio-economic status.
27. McQuillan (1998), p. 81.
28. Flesch (1986).
29. For example, the average reading proficiency score for classes in which reading workbooks and worksheets were used everyday was 208, and for classes that used reading workbooks and worksheets less than weekly was 222. Scores of classes with heavy emphasis on literature-based reading averaged 220 and those classes with little or no emphasis on literature-based reading averaged 211. Classes that used primarily basal readers was 214 while classes that used primarily trade books averaged 224. Finally, classes that emphasized structured subskills averaged 200 while classes that emphasized integrative language averaged 220. However, the positive correlations between wholistic practices and reading proficiency are also jointly influenced by the socioeconomic status of students. Students in low-ses schools are more likely to be taught with structured programs. Students in high-ses schools get the wholistic approaches (McQuillan, 1998).
30. Davis (2001).
31. The survey used to establish the rate of dyslexia came from a small sample of poor readers in Connecticut. Institute materials cite the National Adult Literacy Study to the effect that 40 percent of adults cannot read or write (although another section of the survey shows that of the supposed "illiterates," half read the newspaper daily).
32. Foorman, Fletcher, et al. (2000). Also see a *New York Times* article that quotes Reid Lyon in a way that illustrates the contempt for whole language held by the "winning side": "Dr. Lyon says that much of the antagonism toward the new call for evidence-based instruction—often taken as code words for phonics—springs from inertia, laziness and occasional corruption on the part of education bureaucrats.

   "He said: 'A lot of this is about people investing in careers, in products, in ways of making a living that have frankly been found to be wanting. And it's hard.'" (Schemo, 2002c).

33. This description is taken from Taylor (1998), who also noted that the right-wing Packer foundation provided enormous sums to districts that would adopt Open Court.

34. Taylor (1998).

35. Foorman, Francis, et al. (1998).

36. Taylor (1998), p. 2.

37. In his book, *Science on Stage*, Stephen Hilgartner (2000) deconstructed NRC reports on health to show how scientific authority is constructed rhetorically and functions as aspects of theatrical performance, even in the most prestigious scientific reports.

38. Burns, Griffin, et al. (1999).

39. Yatkin (2000).

40. Glass (1976); Smith, Glass, et al. (1980).

41. The psychotherapy meta-analysis involved 500 studies.

42. For example, an independent committee could have analyzed a sample of excluded studies to show the kinds and size of effects produced. In general, one would want the processes involving the most judgment, but also the most well-documented and confirmed by independent scholars.

43. National Institute for Child Health and Human Development (2000a).

44. National Institute for Child Health and Human Development (2000b).

45. In their analysis of panel meetings and its presentations to the public, Shannon et al (2000) found that, despite the panel's declaration of rigorous standards for including or excluding studies, it made exceptions. For example, some studies that confirmed the perspectives of the panel were included even though those studies used less than rigorous methods. Their process resulted in the rather odd selection of studies that were conducted in Finish and Norwegian. If one were to eliminate some of these incongruities, the small advantage reported for phonics and phonemic awareness would probably drop further. Shannon, Edmundson et al. (2002).

44. Garan (2002), p. 73.

46. Chenoweth (2002).

47. Metcalf (2002).

48. Garan (2001), p. 506.

49. Adams (2001), p. 67.

50. We maintain that the scholars on the panel ought to have challenged the discrepancy between the technical report and the disseminated accounts. The fact that they did not reveals their status as actors in the political spectacle, perhaps with their own interests served backstage. Therefore the term "fraud" is warranted.

51. Langenberg D.N. Testimony before the U.S. Senate Appropriations Committee's Subcommittee on Labor, Health & Human Services, and Education.

52. Ehri, Nunes et al. (2001).

53. Patrick Shannon and his colleagues called the National Reading Panel report a "de facto policy document" since so much of the research findings were incorporated in the federal legislation (Shannon, Edmondson et al., 2002). For a complete analysis of the methodology of the phonics meta-analysis, see Camilli, et al. 2003).

54. Schemo (2002a).

55. Bennett (2001).

56. Contrary to the ideas they endorse, their own experience would likely be the contrary. Garan (2002) pointed out that most people over the age of 30 were instructed to read by the sight-word method rather than phonics.

57. "This July, the Department of Education will send education officials around the country guides that will 'carefully content-analyze all core reading programs to see whether or not they are scientifically based' on the National Reading Panel's findings.' Dr. Neuman said. Poor school districts that do not use a standardized reading curriculum 'would have to provide evidence they work,' she said, adding, 'I suggest they purchase a core reading program.'" (Schemo 2002c).

58. Garan (2002).

59. Quoted by Metcalf (2002) http://www.thenation.com/doc.mhtml?i=20020128&c=1&s-Metcalf.

60. Paterson (2000); Lugg (1996).

61. For example, see Weiss (1998).

62. Ritter and Boruch (1999).
63. House (1993), p. 18.
64. Schneider and Ingram (1997), pp. 6–7.
65. Schneider and Ingram (1997), p. 7.
66. Ibid. (1997), p. 7.
67. Greider (1992); Molnar (2000).
68. The policy research organization, Mathematica, withdrew its participation from the research on Florida voucher program, noting that the researcher, in his zeal to present positive results, misstated warrantable claims (Bracey, 2001c). Also see Bracey (2002a).
69. The question of independence or dependence of researchers has long been discussed in the theoretical literature of evaluation. In their professional standards, for example, the choice and institutional position of evaluators must be taken into account in judging the credibility of the study. In principle, the community of evaluators could reach consensus on the independence of the scholar and the value of the study (House, 1993).
70. House (1993), p. 18.
71. Yatkin (2000).
72. See Foorman's mention of Stanovich's awards (Foorman, et al., 2000).
73. Ernie House wrote that "The research disciplines focus on particular and highly specialized problems. Workers in these disciplines ask each other questions, challenge each other's ideas, and test each other's answers, a process of discourse captured by the term discipline. Through disciplined inquiry, workers build a body of specific knowledge about limited topics. It is this disciplined mode of inquiry that produces new knowledge." (House, 1993), p. 57.
74. Carson, Huelskamp, et al. (1992), p. 259. Also see Berliner and Biddle (1995); Miller (1991).
75. Slavin (1987) invented an a priori, selective method for statistically integrating studies—"best-evidence synthesis."
76. House (1993).
77. Shavelson and Towne (2002). The report on the status of "scientific" research was commissioned by the Office of Educational Research and Improvement. At the time OERI was under considerable criticism and danger of being phased out. In contrast, the agency that commissioned NRP and the standards for science set down by No Child Left Behind was cabinet level. The NRP was commissioned at a much higher level of government and given more latitude than any work of NRC.
78. As an example, Reid Lyon admonished educational research to change its ways.
      "Educational research is at a crossroads. We can choose to be part of the modern scientific community or isolate ourselves and our methods from mainstream scientific thought and progress. Not decades, but centuries of scientific discovery attest to the enduring value of the process of scientific thought and experimentation. . . . In order to develop the most effective instructional interventions, we must clearly define just what it is that works. . . . This requires experimental methods. . . . If educational research is to participate in, and contribute to, the scientific community and the lives of our children, leaders within the academic educational establishment must show the next generation of educational researchers the way" (Lyon, no date).
79. Outside the drug area, however, studies of the effects of procedures such as mammograms or prescribed behaviors such as exercise have shown the same kinds of uncontrolled and contextual glitches as studies of educational variations. In any case, experimentation is only one of a complex of methods used in medical research, and is distinct from "observation" and "case-control" methods. Controversies and micro-politics have formed around the different methods. Advocates of experimental methods complain about the absence of randomization in studies, for example, of the mammography, without which causal claims are not warranted. Researchers close to the tobacco companies make the same criticism of the causal link between smoking and cancer.
80. House, Glass, et al. (1978). Also note Cronbach's (1982) critique of the experiment as the gold standard of research methods to determine causal claims.
81. Schneider & Ingram, 1997.
82. Foorman, Fletcher, et al. (2000), p. 35.

CHAPTER **6**

Education Policy, Inc.

The business man has, of course, not said to himself, "I will have the public school train
office boys and clerks for me, so that I may have them cheap," but he has thought, and
sometimes said, "Teach the children to write legibly, to figure accurately, and quickly, to
acquire habits of punctuality and order; to be prompt to obey and not question why; and
you will fit them to make their way in the world as I have made mine."

Jane Adams, 1897

WHAT'S GOOD FOR MOTOROLA IS GOOD
FOR THE SCHOOLS (A VIGNETTE)

She sits in the audience with the officers of professional associations and
the teacher educators. She has a great deal of experience helping teachers
become expert, progressive professionals, but she holds no illusions that
anyone on the "Teacher Certification Summit" will call on her or the other
spectators, irrespective, or maybe because of, her expertise. The most she
can do is witness and record as the Summit, heavy with corporate leaders,
considers policy changes. She muses, "Why are they always male?" Well,
not exactly true, "but it seems true."

She realizes that the policy changes recommended by this Summit will
follow the spirit of deregulation, the ideology of the free market—competition as the prime fix—for everything. Industrial metaphors infuse the policy
makers' talk. She's heard it before. They call the universities "our suppliers."
They call students "our products." "Volume" refers to the number of people
who want to become teachers. Teacher training programs must be subject to
"fines and penalties for non-compliance" if they fall down on "quality control." By "labor costs" they mean teachers' salaries. Anecdotes provide evidence for "customer complaints." Principals are "middle management."
Accountability means testing students against national and international
"benchmarks" and holding teachers, students, and schools responsible for
attaining and increasing test scores.

191

To the men at the Summit, standards for teacher certification are equivalent to standards for accountants or pilots or contractors. Forget about those standards for the national teacher professional license (they just raise labor costs). After all, the panelists claim, anyone with a willing heart and the ability to control a classroom and deliver the state curriculum can teach. Training teachers is somewhat like training horses, says a rancher/ businessman. Another declares, "'I run a family oil company business and so I think about standards there—whether it's the octane standards or whether it's the standards of the oil that you put in your engine."

A guest speaker, the CEO of one of the biggest corporations in the state, does not depart from the tenor of the summiteers.

> 'We are losing our competitive edge. We are competing in the international market. Our job is to make sure that each employee helps us remain competitive with every person in other firms around the world. I have talked to CEOs of major corporations . . . and some of them are moving their operations to other countries because they have more competent work forces. There is a relentless force of competition. Educators have to prepare for the changes that are occurring in our society and around the world. Educators often say, but schools are different. We can't say that schools are different . . . we must assume a competitive mindset where we ask how can we improve, how can we learn from our competitors. . . . We should learn the lessons of TQM . . . how to reach down all the way to your suppliers to improve the quality of your raw material. That's how you work with your poorly qualified students. . . . A competitive mind-set says, if you can't measure it, you can't be sure that you are producing anything. The status quo can never be an option."[1]

She waits in vain for a competing point of view about teaching, accountability, or professionalism. But none is offered and none would have been welcome. She wonders, what kinds of teachers do these men seek for their own children? She predicts, rightly as it turns out later, that the new policy on teacher certification will involve tests. The state will use a test to determine who will teach and who will have to find another way to make a living. The test is doubly useful to the state, because it will screen candidates and also make the university teacher ed. programs more accountable. If a certain program does not put out a healthy proportion of candidates who pass the test, the state can decertify the program. Then private institutions like the University of Phoenix can train teachers. Or school districts can train teachers. And prospective teachers can even get their training on the Web. They won't have to go to a university where those pesky professional certification requirements slow them down. The test will then sort out which programs are best. Accountability. Competition— that's the business way.

Big Business and Education Policy

Over the past two decades, no single entity has influenced education policy more than the corporate sector. If this bald assertion surprises you, attribute that surprise to the political spectacle. A curtain of symbols renders almost invisible the exchange of material values between government and the private sector. Most people are unaware that the increased influence of corporations has decreased the authority that the public ought to have over all public institutions, including public schools.

In this chapter we address the ways that business affects education policy. We begin by describing the metaphors that are borrowed from corporate and industrial culture and applied to schools. We touch on the economic theories that underlie corporate influence on schools and that also conceal behind a façade of friendly language—"partnerships" for example—the raw pursuit of the political agenda of the largest corporations. We then show examples of that agenda: what corporations want and how they go about obtaining it.

How Corporate Metaphors Influence Education Policy

The business sector exports its guiding metaphors, models, and practices to schools. When people speak of parents of school children as "customers" they apply a business metaphor. Metaphors work unconsciously at the level of emotions, outside the realm of reason, evidence, and deliberation. Metaphors, myths, narratives, and rituals are all forms of non-discursive symbolic activity. Metaphors have power over thought, bypassing rational argument. A metaphor encourages the audience to think of one thing in the terms of another. Policy makers employ metaphors to influence the ways the public thinks about a phenomenon. To write of immigration as an invasion, for example, is to encourage readers or listeners to apply all they know about wartime aggression to the actions of Mexican people crossing the border at Nogales. To see immigration as invasion evokes all the associations the public might have about war: enemies, weapons, defensive positions, infantry, and the like. Without direct access to the actual events and being unable to untangle the complex amount of information purveyed through the media, the public uncritically takes in the metaphor. Without feedback, the public feels a threat to national security and acquiesces to policies such as internment camps and the use of the armed forces to quell the "attack." The metaphorical work of politicians and the media, wrote Edelman, injects the public "into an artificial universe or semblance" and diverts "attention from cognitive and rational analysis."[2] Out of conscious awareness, the public fails to consider alternative metaphors that might be applied to immigration. For example, one might symbolize border crossings as a labor queue in which unemployed workers line up for jobs that native-born people reject. Defining immigration as a labor queue instead of an invasion provides quite different language and images and suggests contrastive policies.

To Edelman, symbolic politics are inevitably tied to the images that people hold about the state. Political symbols "condense into one . . . event, sign, or act of patriotic pride, anxieties, remembrances of past glories or humiliations, promises of future greatness."[3] Although political symbols "evoke the emotions associated with the situation . . . the constant check of the immediate environment is lacking."[4] Declining achievement test scores symbolize a threat to the nation's economic competitiveness and thus evoke feelings of anxiety in the public. However, chances are remote that the public can examine for themselves the relationship between test scores and economic health. The public cannot probe the plausibility of the symbolic referent. The public lacks grounding in the world of direct experience and concrete particulars. Without that grounding, only the feelings of threat remain. Thus, the public feels it must call on the state to solve the crisis through some action or policy.

Cognitive psychologists George Lakoff and Mark Johnson described metaphors as "understanding and experiencing one kind of thing in terms of another."[5] Metaphors go beyond poetic language, and even beyond language itself, to include action: "our conceptual system is primarily metaphoric in nature. . . . [Our ordered concepts] "govern our thoughts, structure what we perceive, define our realities."[6] People organize their actions according to these metaphors, which "are so natural and so pervasive in our thought that they are usually taken as self-evident, direct descriptions. . . . The fact that they are metaphors never occurs to most of us"[7] [Within a culture] metaphors are the terms in which we organize our thoughts and actions."[8] Thus, political discourse has the character of common sense in that we do not recognize that some core metaphor underlies most of our political ideas.[9] Because a person in the grip of a metaphor experiences it as common sense, metaphors are more influential than research studies. Contemporary policy makers, many of them, think that it is simply common sense that schools are like businesses, and that both should be treated the same way.

Industrial/Business Metaphor

For a policy maker to invoke the industrial metaphor is to see teachers' work as industrial work and to see schools as factories. To invoke the industrial metaphor is to see students as raw materials, passive and malleable to the strategies of managers (administrators) and the actions of workers (teachers). This metaphor has a long history. Nevertheless, schools are not by nature either factories or hospitals or families. Metaphors are social categories constructed within a culture, and our culture has constructed the industrial, factory metaphor for schools.

According to Raymond Callahan, the industrial metaphor arose in the United States around the turn of the twentieth century, a time of vast industrial and economic growth, population growth, immigration, and urbanization, and in a symbolic culture that lionized industrial leaders such as Andrew Carnegie and Henry Ford. While the economy grew, budgets for public institutions did not. School superintendents adopted industrial discourse and industrial practices for several reasons. First, they shared the prevailing ideology that U.S. industries were so successful because of the methods by which they were organized. If schools could be organized and managed like an industrial shop then perhaps they could be run efficiently within limited budgets. Second, school boards were often made up of business leaders who pressured the superintendents to operate more efficiently. Third, their jobs depended on it, for the superintendent held his job at the discretion of the businessmen on the board.[10] These influential business leaders applied the principles of Frederick Taylor and his methodology of industrial efficiency.

Industrial leaders urged school superintendents to replace teachers' traditional practices with Taylor's "scientific" methods. Superintendents aligned themselves with the industrial ideology, hoping for the same kind of legitimacy and authority that the public bestowed on the lions of business and industry. Thus, seeds of political spectacle in education policy were sown long ago.[11]

Taylorism triumphed, and efficiency became the primary goal of schools. The industrial metaphor was strong enough to withstand war. It withstood the criticisms of progressive educators such as Dewey. It even withstood periods of economic decline and catastrophe.

The industrial metaphor has several associated beliefs: that people are lazy by nature and need specific direction, close management, and material incentives to work most efficiently; that teachers are just like other workers; that schools are just like any other plant or work place that need to be organized to maximum efficiency; that school organization should be hierarchical and patriarchic; that administrators should be separate from, and superior in authority to, teachers; and that the outcomes of schoolwork could be measured, and the measures could be used to compare schools and teachers. The achievement products could thus be related in straightforward ways to costs, and therefore to efficiency. All these beliefs manifested in how schools were organized and operated.

Callahan illustrated with the words of a prominent expert in school management:

> Our schools are, in a sense, factories in which the raw products (children) are to be shaped and fashioned into products to meet the various demands of life. The specifications for manufacturing come from the demands of twentieth-century civilization, and it is the business of the school to build its pupils

according to the specifications laid down. This demands good tools, specialized machinery, continuous measurement of production to see if it is according to specifications, the elimination of waste in manufacture, and a large
variety in the output.[12]

In promoting the industrial metaphor, experts such as the one quoted
above advocated a focus on "products" which they understood as units of
costs and achievement, narrowly defined so that they could be measured.
They decomposed learning into small components, sequenced them in a
linear flow, and standardized them. Once they had standardized the sequence of learning activities, they could intensify teachers' work (for example, by adding more children to a teacher's class or assigning teachers to
tasks like monitoring lunch). Teachers were besieged with work they had
not had before. They had to account for expenses and materials as well as
students' progress through the standardized curriculum. School systems
created management and staff positions such as efficiency experts, record
clerks, researchers, and specialists in public relations. The new managerial
staff insisted that "scientific," reliable, and objective data should govern
curriculum decisions and the evaluation of teachers.

The success of the industrial metaphor created a workplace that was almost completely divided according to gender. Teachers were almost always
female, and faceless—perceived as people without agency or individuality,
viewed as throughputs in the industrial process. Like businessmen, school
administrators were almost exclusively male. Women were viewed as passive, compliant, as temporary workers. Status, agency, income, gender, and
ethnicity all intertwined with each other and constructed a patriarchal organization that still structures teachers' work and stature.[13]

The success of the industrial metaphor pervaded curriculum theory
and became for granted as natural and right, invisible as common sense, its
origins obscured. Ralph Tyler extended Taylor's system and applied it to
curriculum and evaluation. Tyler's formula started by taking as given those
goals that the system stated, translating those goals into detailed objectives,
developing measures of those objectives, comparing results against objectives, and then refining curriculum. Tyler's principles spawned variations
such as behavioral objectives, goal-based evaluation, computer-based
learning, and competency-based education. The Tyler model inspired the
competency teaching and testing models initiated in the 1970s that continue into the present.

Alternatives to the industrial metaphor exist, of course. To see teachers
as professionals is to fit them into a category—not with workers on an industrial assembly line—but with doctors, lawyers, and professors. These
professions are distinguished from other occupations by, among other
things, the existence of a specialized knowledge base, autonomy and con-

trol over their practice and over how aspirants may join the group, and authority and autonomy over how their practice is evaluated. To use the metaphor of the care-giver is to see the school as an institution "based on reciprocal relationships between teachers and students," which provide the "basis for all learning."[14]

Both the professional and care-giver metaphors compete weakly against the industrial metaphor, which dominates education policy. Policy makers and educators continue to import ideas, methods and fads from industry and apply them to education. The names of the methods have changed, but their function persists. Planning, Programming, Budgeting System, Management by Objectives, Zero-Based Budgeting, Total Quality Management, Reinvention, Six Sigma, Market Competition, Pay-for-Performance Incentives, Find-and-Fix, Command and Control, System-Wide Accountability. Fixation on techniques in the industrial model leaves little room for considering the moral or teleological substance of teachers' work.

Major policy events of the 1990s (culminating in the No Child Left Behind legislation) represent the triumph of the business metaphor. Those policies treat instruction, academic standards, testing, and accountability as business practices. They fulfill the dictates of America 2000, part of the policy of President G. H. W. Bush to reform schools toward a business model. America 2000 represented pervasive business influence over government stemming from the years of the Reagan administration.[15] A watershed document, the 1991 report of the Secretary's Commission on Achieving Necessary Skills (SCANS), showed the influence of large corporations on federal government policy. The intent of the commission was to focus the attention of schools on a set of skills that would prepare students for the workforce. The SCANS report demanded that all schools teach the skills to all students, even students who intend to go to college. Frequent testing would be necessary to insure that teachers teach these skills. The report quotes a cabinet official who proclaimed, "America 2000 is not a program but a crusade." The report imagines, from the vantage point of the 1980s, the schools of 2000:

> Students of all ages learn more per hour in schools. . . . The emphasis on quality means fewer drop-outs and fewer rejects from the assembly line.[16]

Economic Theories

Business people try to influence education policy because they believe that schools and the economy are related. They believe that a better-educated and prepared set of students produces economic productivity and growth—human capital theory. Politicians, policy makers, and business leaders who subscribe to that theory blame the economic recession of the 1970s on the low educational productivity of the public schools. Both business and government were alarmed by the achievement test scores of the U.S. compared to those of global economic competitors. Both government and the business sector espoused policies that would result, they thought, in better achievement. The policies were higher academic standards, tests, and school choice.

The fallacies of human capital theory revealed themselves in the 1990s when the economy recovered without any corresponding change in the level of achievement. What is more, the Japanese economy declined during the same time that Japanese educational achievement stayed level. Evidence against the human capital theory did not deter policy makers. The business-government alliance then modified its language to fit the new economic picture: achievement scores are not rising fast enough to equip American students for the high-paying, high technology jobs and the global economy of the twenty-first century. By this standard, schools are still in crisis, and policies of high academic standards, testing, and choice are still needed to create coherence of curriculum across U.S. schools and to spur them and their students to higher levels of achievement at the same or lower cost.[17]

Because human capital theory puts so much importance on schools, many people outside the business sector embraced it. Professional associations recognized that, in human capital theory, education assumes a high priority in public policy. Organizations such as the American Federation of Teachers began to recite the rhetoric of human capital theory. Many of the voluntary reform organizations like the New Standards Project followed suit.

But not every economist endorses human capital theory. Henry Levin found evidence to contradict a guiding idea behind human capital theory—that the new jobs of the near future will require better education. He showed that most new jobs are projected to arise in the service sector rather than the higher paying technology sector. Thus, raising academic standards and achievement will have little effect on the future economy. In fact, the number of jobs that require a college education barely rose over the previous few decades. Among college graduates, 20 percent have jobs that require only high school education. The new technical jobs have been swept away by globalization to places like India where highly trained and educated people work for a pittance.[18] Levin also found that test scores bear little relation to supervisory ratings. He stated,

> Despite the claims that the new educational standards movement has established criteria that are closely related to the needs of modern workplaces and will improve productivity if they are met in the workforce, there is nary a bit of validation.[19]

As Ernie House wrote, focusing on problems of school productivity distracts the public's attention away from failing business practices as well as deep structural problems in the economy and society.[20]

The corporate community and their allies in government also adhere to the theory of free market capitalism, which provides the entry point for business ventures into education policy. Of the many theories in the field of economics, laissez-faire capitalism (also referred to as market capitalism, advanced capitalism, late capitalism and—by its critics—extreme capitalism, corporate capitalism, and robber capitalism) justifies policy work by businessmen.[21] This theory holds that the market is the most efficient and effective way to organize society because it allows people to pursue their rational, individualistic self-interests. When governments make policies, they interfere in this process and create inefficiency and distortion. All public institutions—including public schools, public transportation, and public health and welfare—interfere with the market. To pay for programs, government must tax its citizens, and, by reducing their wealth by the amount of tax they pay, it inhibits their freedom to pursue their self-interests. Indeed, market capitalists look on taxation as an unwarranted seizure of private property. Taxation and government regulations also interrupt the smooth operations of markets. As applied to businesses, a market free of regulations undergoes a Darwinian process in which the best succeed and the worst wither.

Advocates of free market capitalism seek to apply the discipline of markets to public institutions like schools. Their primary goal is privatization. Under privatization, parents receive vouchers directly from the government to pay the price of schools they choose. Vouchers serve several tenets of free market capitalism. First, a partially privatized education system removes public institutions that stand between government and parents, thus making schools more efficient and responsive to individual preferences. Schools that remain in the government system must compete or pass out of existence, thus improving the level of education overall. In a partially or fully privatized system, parents choose aspects of schools that satisfy their individual preferences, whether or not those aspects meet current government regulations. A parent might choose to send her child to a school without a playground or without certified teachers because she does not feel playgrounds are necessary or does not believe that teachers need special training. If enough parents eventually select schools that offer bilingual education instead of English immersion, then the English immersion schools must adapt or eventually shut down. Thus, market forces substitute for government regulations, making schools more efficient and more effective in matching customer preferences.

Critics of free market capitalism point to the inability of the market to address issues that bear high costs to the community but low costs to individuals, environmental pollution being the paradigm case. Critics show that laissez-faire capitalism inevitably leads to excesses and inequality. It leads, according to critics, to concentration of wealth in the hands of a small section of society. Then this privileged group uses its wealth politically to secure its self-interests at the expense of ordinary people. Some critics claim that public institutions are needed to temper the excesses of capitalism and care for the needs of its victims as well as for the community at large. Critics of market approaches to education point out that privatization schemes thus far have further stratified and segregated schools (as noted in Chapter Three). These critics also note that any Darwinian evolution that leads to closing ineffective schools occurs so slowly that generations of students are sacrificed until market forces do their work. There is no independent evidence to show that competition makes schools work harder or perform more efficiently.

In pursuit of policies consistent with free-market capitalism or policies that bring the discipline of the market to bear on public schools, there is a substantial element of political spectacle. Advocates of free-market capitalism create a false dichotomy, the idea that the only alternative to the market is socialism. Advocates promote a chain of associations: the Soviet empire failed because of the form of its economy; its failure epitomizes the triumph of capitalism; all societies and institutions not organized by market forces are thus failures; public schools are such "socialist" institutions; hence public schools have failed. This chain of associations is itself a script meant to instill anxiety and create an anxious and ultimately pliant public. The dichotomy is fallacious because it obscures the many forms of capitalism less extreme than laissez-faire capitalism, all of which blend market forces with government institutions that soften the most harmful consequences of extreme capitalism and consider the social and educational commonweal.[22]

When one hears or reads that laissez-faire capitalism is the only alternative to a socialist state, one must recognize the statements as very successful scripts that political actors recite when they seek something tangible behind the scenes. So successful is this script, however, that it usually goes unchallenged. Actors use this script to control conversation and silence alternative ideas and speakers, as if it is the last true word on the subject. Of course, many theorists make these claims for the superiority of the free market out of honest analysis. Others flying under the banner of the free market have less honorable motives and intentions.

Edelman would say that use of the word "free" in free-market theory is gauged to achieve public compliance to actions that the rich take to enrich themselves further. What is hidden in the plea for capitalism is really a pursuit of corporatism—the fusion of corporate interests with government. Unfettered capitalism (late capitalism, advanced capitalism, laissez-faire capitalism) frees up opportunities for a few people to gain great wealth. Ordinary people are "free" to pursue such opportunities (if one ignores the social structures that inhibit them). In their unprecedented access to government officials and media, corporate leaders themselves become political actors and work on-stage and backstage in the political spectacle.

What Do Big Corporations Really Want?

The business sector has long been involved in public schools. Businessmen have often served on school boards and provided internships to students seeking occupations. Businesses donate money, recruit volunteers to mentor and tutor students, and help in myriad ways to help schools pursue their many purposes—not exclusively those purposes that relate to productivity and preparation of a labor force.

But the business sector also has its particular agenda, and as we have already detailed, its own way of looking at the world and at schools. The business sector seeks to influence the policies of the state to enhance its special agenda. The success of political influence of business over policies is astonishing. Corporate leaders have sponsored or been a major part of nearly every summit and conference on education policy of interest to the state. In contrast, look in vain for ordinary people or professionals at the Charlottesville conference that resulted in Goals 2000 where leaders of the largest corporations pressed the government to adopt policies promoting high standards and high-stakes tests. Corporate leaders command unprecedented access to political leaders, not only because they share a common vision of human capital and free market theories, but because corporations contribute massively to the campaigns of all elected officials of both major parties.

Some of their success can be seen in the strategic use of the political spectacle. The business sector can operate effectively on both sides of the curtain, deploying symbols out front and bidding for material benefits backstage. Onstage, business leaders profess to want to improve education for everyone and make schools more effective and accountable. They also provide funds and equipment to enhance school's technological capacity. They also desire a better educated, better prepared work force. To pursue ends like these only makes sense.

The symbols portrayed are clearly designed to foster allegiances among policymakers and evoke support from those who look to schools to serve society's (via their children's) needs. Some examples of these ambiguities generated by prominent national business groups include the following:

> The Business Coalition for Education Reform supports efforts to: raise academic standards for all students; ensure standards reflect the knowledge and skills needed for workplace success; and help the public understand the critical need for world-class academic standards and necessary changes needed for school systems to deliver them.[23]
>
> As business leaders, we know we can't improve what we don't measure. Tests are vital tools for managing and evaluating efforts to ensure that all children receive a high-quality education that prepares them for college, for the workplace, for participation in the nation's civic life and for lifelong learning to keep up with the rapid pace of change in the 21st century.[24]

> The business and education community are working together to ensure that students, parents, schools, and the public are aware of the crucial link between school performance and success in later life.[25]

The argument appears logical, emphasizing as it does the welfare of students, their families, and the community. It seems nothing if not altruistic and civic. It engenders allegiance among many constituencies involved in and affected by education and silences critics. Messages like these tend to generate high degrees of support or at least public quiescence.

But the agenda of the business sector has little to do with "working together with educators" as equal partners. It has little to do with enhancing the civic capacity of all pupils. Statements such as the following provide cover for a corporation seeking private profitability.

> The grant-making program in education developed by the Philip Morris Companies 45 years ago is built on our company's most deeply held values—a dedication to diversity and equal opportunity, a commitment to training and preparing the future workforce, and the support of the best possible education for every citizen.[26]

The posturing of public interest in the above quotation contrasts with corporate action against government attempts to remove advertising away from school children—the tobacco industry's future customers. Recent court rulings extend the constitutional right to free speech to industry's right to advertise in schools. In 1991 the U.S. Supreme Court ruled that a state may not impose its own advertising restrictions on tobacco. A *Washington Post* article, "Supreme Court Strikes Down State Tobacco Ad Ban," declared:

> The unanimous but tangled ruling was a victory for a group of cigarette makers that had fought proposed ad restrictions in Massachusetts as both a violation of federal law and an unconstitutional limit on the companies' free speech. . . . Massachusetts proposed banning outdoor advertising of all tobacco products within 1,000 feet of schools and playgrounds, including ads outside stores and those inside stores that can be seen from outside. The state law also required that tobacco products be kept behind store counters, and it prohibited advertising at children's eye level. The state cited reports by the

Food and Drug Administration and the surgeon general that tobacco advertising significantly influences children's tobacco use.

"From a policy perspective, it is understandable for the states to attempt to prevent minors from using tobacco products before they reach an age where they are capable of weighing for themselves the risks and potential benefits of tobacco use, and other adult activities," Justice Sandra Day O'Connor wrote. "Federal law, however, places limits on policy choices available to the states."[27]

The ruling makes it difficult for schools to protect students from intrusion by corporations. It shows how the pursuit of corporate profits trumps children's health and welfare. Yet one would never know it just by reading the ads paid for by industry. Public statements by corporations and business alliances provide cover for important agendas that might seem crass if expressed in bald, plain-speaking forms.

Stephen Metcalf noted that groups like the Roundtable push so hard for accountability and standards because reforms like high-stakes testing are relatively cheap when compared to reforms like class size reduction. The Roundtable believes that schools already have adequate support or perhaps squander what they have.[28] Profits, according to the Roundtable, depend on freeing up as much money from the public sector as possible.

If profits are the ultimate goal, what are some proximate goals that the business sector pursues on the path to profitability?

Tax Avoidance
One important goal that drives corporations' involvement in education policy is to reduce its tax bill. Corporations lobby the state to reduce their contribution to the public treasury. Every reduction subtracts from the resources from which public schools draw.

The Business Roundtable places a high priority on fiscal and tax policy, as the following quotation about its goals reveals:

> Present an effective voice for the business community on major tax issues affecting the economy and promote sound tax policy to ensure that American business and its workers can compete on a global basis. Advocate improvements to the federal budget process to secure a more accurate measurement of current and future government liabilities to permit prioritization of federal spending and revenue programs based on realistic fiscal projections.[29]

As corporations push for lower taxes, lost in their message is that detail that they already contribute much less than at any time in the past 100 years. They paid 33 percent of total federal tax during the 1940s and 10 percent in the 1990s. Individual rates have risen to compensate, as have property and state income taxes. Furthermore American corporations pay far less in federal taxes than do corporations in other modern nations. In truth, corporations receive public funds through various subsidies. Corporations induce communities to compete with each other. Which town or state would kick in the most tax abatements, tax credits, and other incentives in return for placement of a factory or corporate headquarters?[30]

Besides reducing their tax contribution, corporations seek to use the tax code to redirect funds from public schools to private schools. Contributions to private schools are framed as grants that make them tax deductible. Therefore, money that might have been available to public schools is reduced while private and charter schools flourish.

Deregulation

The business sector pushes government to remove regulations that cut into efficiency, control, and profitability. In the energy industry, regulations include penalties for unsafe workplace conditions and for harmful emissions. In education, regulations have to do with protecting children's health and safety, for example, by requiring a certain ratio of bathrooms to kindergartners. According to Business Roundtable and other advocates of privatization, the sheer number of regulations on schools builds a huge and unnecessary bureaucracy and creates significant inefficiencies. Among economists, public-choice theorists point out that private and parochial schools are more efficient (in a ratio of costs to achievement tests scores the school yields) than public schools. They press for school choice policies to test this assumption. As a result of this policy work, states have relaxed building codes for charter schools. In some states, charter schools are not required to provide playgrounds or transportation. In some states, private schools that receive vouchers are exempted from tests and other reports that are mandated for public schools. A major goal of deregulation of schools is removing states' requirements to hire certified teachers or to pay them according to state or local scale. State regulations involving inclusion of handicapped, minority, and English learners are deregulated de facto when charter schools fail to disclose their selection practices or when states fail to monitor them.

Off-load of training costs

The corporate community seeks to reduce the amount of money it spends on training new employees. It intends to transfer training costs to the schools as well as to the trainees themselves. The rhetoric of Business Roundtable and the National Association of Manufacturers made this clear. When the supreme goal of a corporation is short-term profitability, then it seems reasonable that it should attempt to remove employee training from the cost side of its ledger.

America 2000 was the policy directive of the early 1990s designed to force schools to teach basic job skills to students so that business and industry would not have to train entry-level employees. One hears the common complaint that schools fail to provide job-related skills to students and therefore businesses are forced to invest in training. This complaint may serve as a cover for corporate interests. The report of the condition of public education conducted by the Sandia National Laboratory found that the private sector in the U. S. spends little on training overall, and what it does spend goes to training managers, professionals, supervisors, and salespeople, and to upgrading skills of established workers, not blue-collar entry-level workers. Furthermore, no more than six percent of large companies provide remedial training in the basic skills of reading, writing, and math.[31] The SCANS report, therefore, was predicated on the false assumption that entry-level workers lacked fundamental academic skills and workplace know-how. Few policy makers questioned those assumptions.

The logic of reducing labor costs is by no means universal. Many European and Japanese corporations accept the responsibility to fund training and believe that a specially trained work force contributes to stability and profits in the long term. The Sandia project reported that autoworkers in Japan received three hundred hours of training and U.S. autoworkers receive about 50.[32] Facts to the contrary not withstanding, the goal of off-loading training costs feeds into the education policy work of the business sector.

Union busting
American corporations perceive organized labor as a drag on profitability and an obstacle against reforms. The conflicts between corporations and labor extend back to early American history, with government policy intervening, sometimes on the side of labor, but more often on the side of corporations. Complaints of corporations against teachers' unions are particularly virulent and figure prominently in education policy work. Referring to the National Education Association, the leader of the Center for the Study of Popular Culture said, "We want to take them out of politics, not just in California, but in every state in the union." The anti-union groups promote policies that allow union members to reject any union activity that went against voucher campaigns.[33]

Dorothy Shipps told an illustrative story of the education policy in Chicago, where antipathy to teacher unions animated much of the agenda. The corporate community believed that unions were a major obstacle in the way of corporation-friendly reforms and convinced the Illinois legislature to authorize the mayor to take over Chicago's public schools. Mayor Daley restructured the system into the "CEO model" so that the lines of accountability would be clear and administrators would have more complete control over hiring and firing teachers and principals—outside union contracts.[34]

Reduction of Labor Costs
The agenda of the largest corporations includes reducing labor costs through privatization and deregulation, and this goal provides an explanation for

education policy work. In the 1990s the Business Roundtable and other corporate alliances sponsored the Secretary's Commission on Achieving Necessary Skills (SCANS). Proposed initially by the Hudson Institute, SCANS,
Workforce 2000, and Welfare-to-Work policies were all part of an effort to
make schools conform to the needs of corporations. What they wanted
from the public schools was to restructure them into two tiers. The top tier
would be made up of a small, elite group of students destined for college,
the professions, and for corporate leadership. The next tier was to be made
up of the majority of students who would receive an eduction for acquiring
minimum academic skills so that they would fit well into entry-level positions. The purpose of such a system was to create a stratified labor market
tailored specifically to the needs of the corporations.

Corporate Cultural Capital
Participation of corporate leaders in the policies of public schools has
often been cited as a way for schools to regain legitimacy in the eyes of the
public. At the same time, corporate leaders use this policy work to position
themselves as public celebrities and to provide opportunities for themselves to receive jobs and consultant fees. The media help corporate leaders
to promote their image as saviors of public institutions, as advisers to
politicians, as wise leaders whose only interest is civic. While corporate
leaders gain power, others lose it, so that ordinary people have less chance
to participate in the policies that most affect their lives.

Roslyn Mickelson's case study of IBM's Reinventing Education Program
in North Carolina provides insight into the onstage/backstage workings of
the business community at the state level. IBM's program has been touted
by many as being one of the most visionary examples of how business can
improve education.

Onstage, IBM's official stance about its efforts looked like this:

> The Reinventing Education grant program forms the centerpiece of IBM's
> global commitment to education. Through Reinventing Education, IBM is
> working with school partners throughout the world to develop and implement
> innovative technology solutions designed to solve some of education's tough-
> est problems.[35]

> To each grant site, IBM is contributing more than just money; we are dedicat-
> ing our world-renowned researchers, educational consultants, and technology.
> Through these contributions, we are finding new ways for technology to spur
> and support fundamental school restructuring and broad-based systemic
> change to raise student achievement.[36]

Mickelson provided a closer look at what went on backstage in North
Carolina. She described the Charlotte-Mecklenburg Education Village as a
four school (elementary through high school), high-technology complex
adjacent to IBM facilities. According to the original plan, once children

were admitted to these schools, they and their siblings attended until they graduated from high school. IBM provided a $2 million grant to the school district for the Village. Over half of the grant was earmarked for development of Wired for Learning software developed by IBM. At a cost of $6 million, the district purchased the land from IBM to build the Village. The construction costs supported by public funds amounted to $82 million, and because IBM's contributions were in the form of grants, they could be written off as a tax deduction. What did IBM gain from their investment? The school served as a "workplace magnet" for the corporation to recruit employees in a highly competitive technology market. In addition, because children of employees of IBM had "reserved" places, the corporation could control its composition, essentially obtaining a private school at mostly public expense. Mickelson quoted a local activist:

> So, at a cost of $2 million, they [IBM] bought a seat for the children of their employees at the newest, highest technology school in the county. . . . IBM is putting up 2 to 2.5 percent of the total cost of the village to buy one-third of the seats for the children of their employees—not a bad investment on their part.[37]

Based on her study of this and other business-supported initiatives in North Carolina, Mickelson asserted:

> It is no secret that business involvement in school reform, especially at the highest levels, springs as well from no small amount of long- and short-term strategic self-interest.[38]

In this case, the "interest" was to create a set of private schools at what was mostly taxpayer expense and present a positive public image. True to political spectacle, that special interest goal could be effectively hidden behind rhetoric involving the public interest.[39]

Shaping Education Policy for Private Profit
Profits are the primary motives behind businessmen's policy interests. There are many avenues toward profits in schools.

Profits from Advertising and Commercialization Children and schools make up a relatively untapped, tantalizing, and captive market. Established taxation mechanisms guarantee revenue. With a free-market ideology, everyone is a potential buyer. "There's plenty of gold in U.S. schools if you know how to mine it," wrote Alex Molnar in his stunning portrayal of how businesses effect the commercialization of America's schools.[40] Molnar named several areas of commercialism in schools. First, corporations purchase sponsorships, paying schools a fee in return for attaching their names to school events or programs. Second, corporations enter into exclusive agreements with schools; for example, in exchange for a fee the school agrees to sell only the products distributed by that particular corporation and not those of its competitors. Third, schools enter into incentive programs with corporations. For example, a school signs a contract promising to sell a certain number of units and if successful, receives a bonus in cash or goods. Fourth, schools agree to display corporate logos, for example, on the scoreboards of basketball arenas. Fifth, schools agree, for a fee, to use instructional products and materials of a corporation. An example is the "Count Your Chips" program mentioned below. Sixth, corporations provide electronic gadgets to schools in exchange for the right to advertise their products. Molnar showed that the number of times such activities were mentioned in newspapers rose from 991 in 1990 to 4,909 in 2000.[41]

A few examples of corporate programs are illustrative. Channel One (formerly Whittle Communications) provided free televisions, VCRs, and satellite dishes to schools. In return, schools signed a three-year contract guaranteeing that students would watch their programming daily, ten minutes of current events and two minutes of advertising. Technology is an expensive commodity for most schools; opportunities to get it "free" are difficult to resist. But California's state superintendent, Bill Honig, determined that having students watch commercials for candy, cosmetics, and sneakers for a few minutes daily adds up to approximately one school day per year. Over a three-year contract, that would cost California taxpayers over $48 million dollars, even after deducting the value of the "free" technology.

Molnar explored numerous other examples of how businesses make profits by tapping into public funds and still hide their economic self-interest behind the facade of improving education for all. Typical of this pattern is Lifetime Learning Systems (the owner of the Weekly Reader and Channel One), which provides "free educational programs." Count Your Chips, a program about potato chips and how students can sharpen their computational skills through counting them, is co-sponsored by the Snack Food Association. Gushers Wonders of the World is another Lifetime Learning program, sponsored by General Mills, the maker of Gushers fruit snacks. General Mills referred to this as a science lesson. It purports to help middle school students learn about geology and earth sciences—geothermal dynamics—by having them bite into a snack.

Profits from Assessment Policy Under every presidential administration since Carter's, federal policy defines a successful school as one with high achievement test scores. The provisions of the No Child Left Behind legislation require states to test the achievement of students in reading and math in every grade from third to eighth. Tests must be developed for this purpose. Tests must be printed and administered. Students' answers to tests must be scored and their scores analyzed and reported. When the stakes on test results are high, schools must do special training so that students pass. These tasks don't come cheap, and the organizations that perform them are profit-making entities with strong incentives to influence policy. The testing industry thus does policy work operating backstage as a special interest group and partner with government officials. Out front, however, the message is that they simply want what is best for schools.

The Educational Testing Service provides examples of how this works. Although the ETS had been directed by educators and testing experts in the past, the organization took another direction during the 1990s, getting rid of Professor Nancy Cole and replacing her with Kurt M. Landgraf, past CEO of DuPont Pharmaceuticals. The ETS board of directors recognized the opportunities afforded to the testing industry by state and national testing policies and decided to spin off a profit-seeking entity.

Landgraf lost no time or opportunity to show his support for the President's policy:

> The ambitious education agenda released today shows that President Bush and Secretary Paige are committed to pursuing multiple approaches toward meeting these challenges," said ETS President and CEO Kurt M. Landgraf. "It is clear that they understand the high-quality testing and assessments can be valuable tools to help identify what students know as well when students need help to achieve their best. The Bush administration has said it wants to leave no student behind, a sentiment that echoes the values upon which ETS has operated or more than half a century. We look forward to helping the Education Department achieve those goals."[42]

Landgraf's half-page ads in *Education Week* and *The New York Times* regularly coincide with policy-making events. The quotation above was published during congressional deliberation over national testing. The ads emphasized civic virtue and the public interest, but neglected to acknowledge the enormous profits that would be made by ETS if the government selected National Assessment of Educational Progress as the national test or even the benchmark against which state tests could be compared.

ETS also assumed a greater share in the market to develop, administer, and score tests for the states. It joined the other two corporations dominating the testing industry. CTB/McGraw Hill and Harcourt-Brace together controlled about 80 percent of the test development and scoring business. State assessment policies resulted in such a rapid and vast expansion that the industry leaders often stretched themselves too far and made many mistakes and experienced many delays. Nevertheless, assessment policies are likely to generate unprecedented profits.

Besides the test industry, state and national assessment policy creates profit potential for other kinds of service industries. Organizations such as the Princeton Review, Kaplan Learning Services, and Sylvan Learning project enormous growth through demand for tutoring and test preparation as well as training for teachers who must train their students how to pass the various high-stakes tests. The same firms anticipate windfalls from another provision of the Bush policy—that government must supply remedial training for students whose schools fail to make progress on academic standards.[43]

That the principals in these corporations do not try to influence policy is a possibility too remote to accept. Yet their special interests are cloaked in a public display of altruistic concern. An official of the Princeton Review claimed in an article in *Education Week*:

> We're in business to make money. . . . What's nice about our business is that we can make money while helping kids.[44]

Edelman claimed that the group that wins the battle over definitions gains power for itself and silences the voices of others. The business community won the war over definition of what constitutes effective schools, thereby empowering its own members—testing companies, textbook publishers—while effectively silencing the voices of educators and students.

Profits from Curriculum Policies   As we described in Chapter Five, the largest corporations involved with textbook publishing have been enriched by government policy on what schools should teach and how they should teach it. The business sector involves itself in education policy in order to generate profits through the sales of books and materials. Harold McGraw III serves simultaneously as CEO of McGraw-Hill, chair of the Education Task Force of the Business Roundtable, and as a member of President Bush's kitchen cabinet. During 2000, states began to mandate phonics-first programs to teach reading. As politicians debated similar policies at the national level, the profits of McGraw-Hill—which sells most of those products—increased by 28 percent in six months. Its income approached $900 million in a year of high-stakes policy making.[45] The passage of the No Child Left Behind legislation caused Mr. McGraw to comment:

> It's a great day for education. . . . We have an unprecedented opportunity to bring meaningful improvements in education.[46]

Profits from Privatization Policies: The Education Industry   With the crash of Internet investments and uncertainties of the technology corporations, investors turned their attention to schools as new profit centers and investment opportunities. Entrepreneurs, following the lead of Chris Whittle of Channel One, declared that schools can be run efficiently by the private sector and still turn significant profits. Investment management firms embraced this view about future prospects of Education Management Organizations (EMOs). Lehman Brothers investment firm asserted:

> [W]e've taken over the health systems; we've taken over the prison system; our next big target is the education system. We will privatize it and make a lot of money.[47]

The reform of Chicago Public Schools, promoted by several associations of large corporations in the city, aimed in part for fiscal flexibility and enabled district officials to outsource and privatize many school functions. This not only shifted the balance of power from educators to corporate leaders, but also purchased political power and loyalty from those entities that received outsourcing contracts.

Among corporations that seek profits from managing schools Edison Schools, Inc. was, as of 2000, the industry leader and favorite of investment houses. Edison planned to take over public schools as whole entities, enter into partnerships with public schools, especially charter schools, and provide specific services such as transportation, food, accounting, as well as programs for handicapped students.

Have predictions about profits come true? Most for-profit EMOs are privately held and thus exempt from rules of disclosure. Of those for which information is available, only five of the 21 EMOs made a profit in 2000, and the profitable ones were small, regional operations. Edison Schools, Inc. and Nobel are publicly held, but obtaining accurate information about the performance of EMOs—even such basic information as the number of schools the corporations deal with at any one time—presents difficulties. Getting reliable information about the schools' finances, operations, and achievement outcomes nears impossibility.

Edison's own reports to investors present a rosy view, not shared widely among scholars. Until 2002, investment analysts retained their enthusiasm for Edison, supporting Edison's account that negative reports in the press and a constant barrage of criticism were the causes of its poor performance. Edison and its investment allies staked optimism not on actual profits generated, but on the fact that its yearly losses were decreasing. Edison stocks had opened for public trading in 1999 at $18, rose to a high of $30 in 2000, and then sank to less than one dollar in 2002. The Security and Exchange Commission investigated Edison and found it to be out of compliance with a variety of disclosure and accounting regulations.

Up to that time, most investment houses accepted Edison's claim that profits would come once the company expanded and obtained enough new contracts, eventually leading to economies of scale. Edison's political connections were grounds for optimism. In Edison's campaign to take over schools in New York City, it had the support of Mayor Rudy Giuliani.

Governor Tom Ridge and later Governor Mark Schweiker, had political connections with Edison officials and acted as a driving force in gaining contracts to run the Philadelphia schools. Edison and its vocal and persistent political allies ignored the evidence that many existing Edison contracts were being cancelled at the same moment that New York and Philadelphia were signing on.

Even at Edison's nadir, some investment analysts retained their faith. After the SEC ruling, Merrill-Lynch offered Edison a generous line of credit ($35 million) and a positive endorsement of its stock. Gerald Bracey suggested that this support followed some motivation other than rational investment. A Merrill-Lynch spokesperson blamed the media for Edison's declining stock price:

> We have never seen a company attract so much negative publicity, especially when the value position is such a noble one.[48]

But a business writer in Philadelphia responded to the rhetorical question, "would you still recommend Edison stock?":

> Not unless your approach to investing allows you to put political ideology ahead of fundamentals.[49]

Edison fought off bankruptcy when an angel investor stepped in to supply capital. Edelman would love the irony. The for-profit education industry professes belief in the free market and scorns the bureaucratic inefficiency of government-run public school systems. However, there is little that is free about the education market. Like Edison, most EMOs are highly subsidized by private donors, foundations, and venture capitalists. Lending institutions have been both generous and forgiving. EMOs use these grants and loans to acquire property and set up their business operations. Alex Molnar reported that the billionaire founder of Gap stores provided $25 million to Edison when it entered the California market. This would have been a tax-deductible contribution and another diversion of wealth from the tax base.

Despite its continued losses and absence of returns to investors, Edison was nevertheless extremely profitable to the entrepreneurs as individuals. Insiders took large first cuts of revenue in the form of salaries, management fees, and loans to themselves. They also were able to sell their own shares before the price went down, reaping considerable profit. The corporate insiders of Edison made millions of dollars. Whittle had proceeds of over $15,000,000 since the company started publicly trading in November 1999. Paul Allen, who co-founded Microsoft and backed Edison through his Vulcan Ventures Company, collected proceeds of $22,500,000.[50]

Bracey reported the particulars of Edison's balance sheet, quoting one of the few Wall Street analysts who doubted:

The loss per student has fallen from $3,927 in 1996 . . . to $389 in 1999–2000. . . . Since its inception, the project has lost $1.36 for every $1.00 it has made. . . . Although the company shows no profit, Whittle personally is doing quite well. His base salary for 1998–99 was $296,636. . . . Whittle has also received more than $1 million from Edison for "professional services" and a loan of $5.6 million which he could use to buy 1.45 million shares of the company at $1.50 a share, tax free.[51]

A primary goal for the corporate sector is to privatize public institutions to reduce public expenditures and also to transfer greater wealth into private hands. Edison is a special case of the pursuit of private wealth by manipulating education policy. In 2001 and 2002 the scandals of large corporations, investment houses, and accountancy firms tarnished the corporate halo. Perhaps the lesson to be learned is that political spectacle wraps corporate special interest in the costume of free enterprise, and the "genius of capitalism."[52] We have also learned that the bottom line is never as solid as it seems, either in profitability of corporations or in the achievement test scores of schools.

How does the corporate community achieve its goals? What are the mechanisms it employs? Consider the following strategies.

Proclaim a Crisis
We have cited numerous instances to argue that the achievement crisis has been constructed and has been sustained despite evidence to the contrary. In this chapter we add that the construction was intentional and aimed to undermine public institutions and divert resources in other directions. Edelman stated that the rhetoric of crisis leads the public to accommodate to privations and to reallocation of power. The appearance of crisis had to be sustained so that the public would not resist privatization, commercialization, and a decline in values other than efficiency and productivity.

Gerald Bracey found that all of the articles written about private investment in schools began with the premise that schools were in crisis. He quoted a newsletter of the Education Industry investment specialists:

From an investment perspective this crisis has created an enormous opportunity and powerful momentum for those companies with solutions to our educational problems.[53]

Anyone who challenges the official view that schools are in achievement crisis (and only choice or accountability policies will save them) is branded an enemy. Anyone who questions the feasibility or inequities of the proposed political agenda are labeled "educrats" or "apologists for the education establishment." Educators—teachers, administrators, university professors, and education researchers—are painted as villains. They provoke the ire of some supporters of the business agenda and frequently become the targets of public criticism. They are usually accused of supporting the status quo or of not being responsive to the public will. The following quotation of the Heritage Foundation condemned the Regional Education Laboratories and the U.S. Office of Educational Research and Innovation.

> In light of OERI's potential to contribute significantly to the quality of the nation's education, however, a review of its activities is especially disappointing. Its work is fragmented and apparently vulnerable to politicization and manipulation. This is especially true for OERI's regional education laboratories. . . . A review of lab Internet sites turns up few details on free-market ideas or initiatives such as school choice, even though some recent studies on school choice programs do demonstrate their successes and appeal to inner-city parents. On the other hand, the labs have been active promoters of fads. Rather than note proven methods of success to boost students' academic achievement, they emphasize such measures as making students "feel positive" about the classroom and school environment, "situational learning," "better academic self-concept," and "developmentally appropriate" teaching.[54]

In an article in the *Washington Post*, Secretary of Education Rod Paige attacked critics of the high-stakes testing (typically educational researchers):

> Anyone who opposes annual testing of children is an apologist for a broken system of education that dismisses certain children and classes of children as unteachable. The time has come for an end to the excuses, for the sake of the system and the children trapped inside. Both the system and the children need reform. . . . The centerpiece of the president's No Child Left Behind plan is a system of high standards, annual testing against those standards of every child, and a system of accountability that makes schools responsible for results. . . . Those who say this will result in a system in which teachers simply teach to the test don't understand the plan. . . . The opponents of testing would have us cling to the status quo, and I have yet to hear an argument in favor of that.[55]

In the political spectacle, actors construct allies and enemies. The above statement casts anyone with a view contrary to the dominant policy (and even those with evidence to back it up) as enemies and dopes.

Repeat a Consistent Message
Language of the business sector exhibits an interestingly univocal character. In contrast to the many complex and often contradictory viewpoints among education researchers and practitioners, the business view is relatively straightforward and simple. Even though their business interests and areas of expertise vary significantly, when they address education reform, they speak with a single voice. Edelman discussed how this kind of discourse enhances political control and credibility. By choosing from "a circumscribed set of banal texts," speakers are not only able to maintain support of those who already ascribe to some part of their claims but also

can gain a level of social acceptance from those who may, with more information, reject their argument. The business sector speaks with a uniform voice through such organizations as the National Association of Manufacturers, National Alliance for Business, and the Business Roundtable. The Business Roundtable described itself as:

> an association of chief executive officers of leading U.S. corporations with a combined workforce of more than 10 million employees in the United States. The chief executives are committed to advocating public policies that foster vigorous economic growth; a dynamic global economy; and a well-trained and productive U.S. workforce essential for future competitiveness.[56]

The power of the message comes from the way the Roundtable organizes itself. Within the international organization are national organizations, and within that, state and local affiliates. To be a member, a corporation must agree to send only its top executives to board meetings and to support only those local policies that fit the international agenda for schools. In the U.S., membership in the Roundtable is limited to the top 200 or so corporations. It engages in major advertising campaigns to convince the public to support national reforms. It has enormous resources to hire writers, lobby policy makers, and sponsor conferences. To get the agenda out, the Roundtable constructs and distributes reports and briefing papers and, of course, has tight connections with state and federal legislators.[57]

The Roundtable proposed a nine-point policy agenda for K–12 education improvement, entitled "the Essential Components of a Successful Education System." Among the essential components are decentralization, teacher autonomy, and professional development. However, the Roundtable took the opposite point of view in its support of President Bush's No Child Left Behind legislation, which imposed a highly centralized curriculum built around common academic standards—leaving little room for teacher autonomy. Although the legislation declared the importance of professional development for teachers, no funds were allocated for it. In 2001 the Roundtable's Web site called for support of the Bush legislation. The site featured a clock ticking. The face of the clock read, "The clock is ticking for our kids. We need education reform."[58]

The Roundtable put muscle behind its rhetoric in favor of high standards and high stakes tests. An official expressed this warning to policy makers:

> We will support the use of relevant information on student achievement in hiring decisions. We will take a state's commitment to achieving high academic standards into consideration in business location decisions. We will encourage business to direct their education-related philanthropy toward initiatives that will make a lasting difference in school performance.[59]

Although the Roundtable purports to speak for the entire private sector, its composition reveals a decided slant toward the interests of the largest corporations. Asked to comment on AIMS, Arizona small businessmen recognized that the high levels of math achievement that the state policy demanded were quite beyond or irrelevant to new hires of small businesses. One even admitted that he could not have passed the AIMS test in math. That view was countered soon after when the newspaper granted space to a representative of the local Business Roundtable who denied the truth of the local business point of view, reasserted the existence of a crisis in public education, and claimed once again the urgency that every student master advanced math, for the good of the new economy.

Be Willing to Say Anything Before the presidential debates of 2000, the *Washington Post* printed a full-page ad purchased by the Campaign for America's Children claiming that ". . . 90% of American children are stuck in a failing system." Such a claim defies credulity, but one of the Campaign's officials was William Bennett, who is among a group of neo-conservatives who are willing and inclined to say anything and quote any fallacious data to make an ideological point. In a commentary on international comparisons of achievement he stated:

> In America today, the longer you stay in school, the dumber you get in relation to your peers in other industrialized nations.[60]

Bracey quoted Milton Friedman's explanation for why public referenda on vouchers have so far failed to garner the support of voters.

> In each case, a dedicated group of citizens makes a well-thought through proposal. It initially garners widespread public support. The educational establishment—administrators and teachers' unions—then launches an attack that is notable for its mendacity but is backed by much larger financial resources than the proponents can command and succeeds in killing the proposals.[61]

Friedman's claim that voucher critics were well funded was demonstrably false. Bracey stated that in California the advocates for vouchers outspent by two to one the anti-voucher side. Few progressive causes have more than a fraction of the financial support of the conservative foundations when it comes to covering costs and contributing to candidates for office and elected officials.

The willingness to say anything extends to complaints about research and researchers who fail, as Paige said, "to understand the plan." The Education Leadership Council, the right-wing think tank that Lisa Graham Keegan put together, blamed education research for showing that high-stakes tests and mandatory grade retention do not raise achievement or make schools better.

Many researchers are funded by groups of liberal-leaning foundations that have not warmed to reform. Many, too, are based at colleges of education and are loath to venture outside their personal experiences and training. . . .[62]

Keegan's words show as well that no miss-statement is too outrageous when one is in the midst of a political project.

Insure Access to Politicians Through Campaign Contributions
It helps to remember that the Business Roundtable was organized originally to lobby all branches of government for policies that favor large corporations. Campaign contributions buy access to officials. Edison and other Whittle enterprises are known for spending large sums on lobbying and campaign contributions. In 1999, Primedia, an umbrella organization of which Edison was a part, had the largest budget for lobbying of any education entity.[63]

But the question of access is not so simple as "money is power." Boundaries between the government and large corporations are often breached, as corporate leaders are brought into the government and corporations employ officials once they leave office. As we described in Chapter Five, federal policies for high stakes testing and instruction in reading followed a complex trail of connections with vast sums of money at stake. Stephen Metcalf wrote that the families of George W. Bush and Harold McGraw III have close personal ties going back three generations. While he was governor of Texas, Bush made policies favorable to McGraw-Hill by encouraging districts to adopt its packaged programs. He gave an award to McGraw for his contributions to literacy. McGraw in turn gave an award to Rodney Paige, who was then superintendent in Houston and later became Secretary of Education. The Houston network extended to Reid Lyon and Barbara Foorman, whom Bush often called on for advice on education policy. During the presidential campaign, Wall Street analysts labeled McGraw-Hill a "Bush stock," predicting—accurately, as it turned out—that the company would likely reap profits if Bush won the election. Bush appointed Harold McGraw III to his transition team, and McGraw visited the White House on Bush's first day there (Kurt Landgraf of ETS was also a first-day visitor). In his first appeal to Congress, Bush used the now-familiar language when he declared that schools can correct the achievement deficit if they adopt science-based reading programs such as those sold by McGraw-Hill. Metcalf identified other connections as well. Edward Rust, a member of the board of directors of McGraw-Hill, also served on Bush's transition team. John Negroponte was appointed to the United Nations as ambassador after serving McGraw-Hill as executive vice president for global markets.[64]

The flow of wealth and people between private and public sectors nurtures political spectacle. The more porous the boundaries among sectors, the more elite groups can merge and conduct public affairs in private. A university scholar turns education entrepreneur. The director of a private foundation gives a scholar several million dollars to establish policy centers that will support its political agenda. Publishers with agendas subsidize scholars who write books and articles that promote the donor's point of view. A director of a conservative foundation in one decade enters government in the next, where she can write legislation and regulations and provide counsel to public officials. A cabinet member in one presidential administration becomes a corporate partner or lobbyist in the next. Government departments share public relations firms with research institutes and the corporations that stand to benefit.[65] Foundations and think tanks morph, split, combine, and collaborate to fund projects. Ordinary people can barely keep track of the acronyms, let alone the patterns of influence and career movements. Many lines of influence and financing criss-cross and obscure from public view the negotiation and allocation of values. Freedom of information acts and "sunshine laws" can only accomplish so much when negotiation over the tangible values of policies takes place on private phone lines and dedicated Intranet sites with password privileges. The public gets little help from investigative journalists in untangling these networks.[66] But tracking the patterns of a few individuals in education policy proves to be instructive.

Consider Diane Ravitch, noted historian and advocate for neo-conservative values. She accepted on behalf of her university employers somewhere in the neighborhood of $2 million to speak and write about the issues important to the conservative Olin Foundation, according to the watchdog group, Media Transparency. The same source lists Chester Finn, Assistant Secretary of Education in the Reagan administration, as receiving over $1 million to conduct policy research and outreach to promote neo-conservative ideas. Paul Peterson received a lucrative award from a right-wing think tank for his research supporting vouchers. The political scientist John Chubb received $400,000 from the Bradley and Olin foundations to support his research on privatizing schools. Benno Schmidt left a scholarly career to become Chief Executive Officer at Edison Schools, Inc. for a $300,000 yearly salary, plus stock, plus fees. Robert Sweet left a leadership post with the Moral Majority to become Director of the Right to Read Foundation. From there he became a consultant with the National Institute for Child Health and Development (that figured so prominently in Chapter Five) and from there to the staff of U.S. Representative Goodling, where he wrote the Reading Excellence Act and advised legislators in both houses about the only right way to teach reading and do research. Then it was on to a paid staff position in the Executive Branch where he wrote regulations for the legislation that he was instrumental in passing.

Once Secretary of Education under Reagan (a position for which he was vetted by the Heritage Foundation) and then–Drug Czar for George H.W. Bush, William Bennett subsequently occupied a distinguished chair at the Heritage Foundation, writing books and making frequent appearances on television talk shows to promote the values of neo-conservative groups and privatization initiatives. His books and articles describe the decline of American culture and prescribe a set of virtues that Americans must adopt to halt that decline. The group that Bennett founded, Empower America, issues white papers to influence legislators on tax reduction and deregulation policies. Among the legislation targeted by Empower America was a bill to extend the tax exemption that Internet commerce enjoys. However, an important direct beneficiary of the exemption is the company that Bennett founded, K-12. This Internet company sells online achievement tests to parents who want to know how their children are progressing academically, and recommends materials parents can buy to correct any deficits that are discovered in their basic academic skills and cultural knowledge. Michael Milken, once imprisoned for fraudulent dealings of junk bonds, provided start-up capital for Bennett's company.[67]

Lamar Alexander served as the U.S. Secretary of Education for President George H.W. Bush; prior to that he served two terms as governor of Tennessee and as the president of the University of Tennessee. During his years as governor his wealth increased from $151,000 to $1.5 million.[68] During his time as Secretary of Education, Alexander forwarded the "break-the-mold" school reform agenda. He was also pivotal in the creation of the New American Schools Development Corporation that was designed to direct corporate funds into school reform efforts. In addition, Alexander was an early contributor to Whittle Communications, a television network based on selling advertising directly to children by giving schools free TV and satellite equipment in exchange for guarantees that children will watch commercials on a daily basis. Lamar Alexander spent much of the mid-1990s trying without success to capture the 1996 Republican presidential nomination. However, since his time as Secretary, he remained an ally to the corporate leaders involved in education reform and a strong advocate for market-driven solutions such as private-school vouchers and charter schools. His family gained great wealth in the private childcare industry, and he aligned himself to the corporate elite in his support of for-profit schools such as Edison. Later, Alexander joined the ranks of those who sought personal wealth from public education by investing in Edison Schools, Inc. and sold out early before its stock fell. In 2002, he won the

Senate seat from Tennessee and jumped the seniority list to become chairman of the committee that oversees education policy.

Dennis Doyle's name comes up frequently in conversations about reforms that benefit corporate America: SCANS, Workplace 2000, Goals 2000. He figured prominently in the development of Arizona standards and testing policies. His consulting company provided facilitators for each of the teams that developed content standards (see Chapter Two). Later he was part of a think tank that gave positive ratings to Arizona Standards (all the other evaluations of Arizona standards were negative). Doyle played recurrent roles in major policy conferences. Roslyn Mickelson noted that Doyle played a leading role in the IBM reform in Charlotte, North Carolina while at the same time working for the Hudson Institute's Modern Red School House and serving on the board of RJR Foundation.[69]

Doyle's role continued into 2002, when he claimed with satisfaction that the provision of No Child Left Behind act would "pole-ax" public schools. The legislation required that every state and school made "adequate yearly progress" on state tests. Good as this may sound, the statistical standards for achieving this progress were set so high, two-thirds of American schools would fall below that fallacious standard, thus giving the appearance of mass failure in the system. Students in those that fail become eligible for vouchers, which is what Doyle and other neo-conservative activists wanted to achieve.[70]

The John M. Olin Foundation, formed in 1953 by John M. Olin, "inventor, industrialist, conservationist, and philanthropist," financed many conservative efforts including Charles Murray's book, *The Bell Curve*. Olin gave John E. Chubb and Terry M. Moe four grants totaling $110,000 to write *Politics, Markets and America's Schools*.[71] The recipient organization for the grants was the Wisconsin Policy Research Institute, a conservative think tank, and the Brookings Institution. Paul E. Peterson, a researcher from Harvard who promotes school choice, received five grants from Olin from 1994–2000 totaling $850,200. Diane Ravitch was awarded 17 grants from Olin totaling $2,100,650, funneled through Columbia University and New York University. William Bennett was awarded nine grants from Olin for a total of $950,000 while he worked for the Hudson Institute, Heritage Foundation, and Empower America, all conservative think tanks that promote school choice and free market policies in education. Through Vanderbilt University, Hudson Institute, George Washington University, and the Manhattan Institute for Policy Research, Chester Finn collected ten grants from Olin totaling $961,600. The Smith Richardson Foundation funded Ravitch and Finn with $49,500 and $85,000 respectively. The Lynde and Harry Bradley Foundation funded Bennett $75,000 through Empower America.

John Walton of the Wal-Mart fortune contributed over $50 million to CEO America to promote legislation for publicly funded vouchers for private and religious schools. In 1998 Walton and Ted Forstman, a Wall Street venture capitalist, gave another $100 million to found Children's Scholarship Fund, a close affiliate of CEO America. Walton sat on the board of New American Schools, an affiliate of The Modern Red Schoolhouse, a design for schools by the Hudson Institute. Walton also financed Education Alternatives Inc./TesseracT, a for-profit school management company, and once owned close to 250,000 shares of its stock.

Much of the conservative policy work comes from a network of think tanks which produce dozens of studies that promote high stakes testing and free market approaches. Because all these "studies" point to the same conclusions, the public believes them and accords them the privilege of objective science. But by looking closer at these supposedly independent studies, one can see that their conclusions are rarely supported by solid evidence and that those conclusions rarely depart from the ideological presumptions of their source.

Few people are aware of the interconnectedness of the think tanks and their board members, fellows and staff. Funded originally by the ultra conservative Scaife and Coors foundations as well as Paul Weyrich, Heritage is the biggest conservative think tank in the US. It has connections to dozens of smaller organizations across the country that do research and policy writing to influence government. It also counts among its members some of the nation's richest people. Heritage lists the following individuals as policy experts: Bruno Manno, Diane Ravitch, John Chubb, Paul Peterson, and William Bennett. The Hudson Institute is a smaller think tank that spun off from Heritage and promotes similar ideology and research that promotes it. Bruno Manno, William Bennett, Denis Doyle, Chester Finn, and Lamar Alexander helped with Modern Red Schoolhouse Design (MRSh), Hudson's plan for schools for the twenty-first century. The Core Knowledge Foundation (founded by E. D. Hirsch), Arthur Andersen Accounting, and the Manhattan Institute joined the MRSh Design Team. Chester Finn and Diane Ravitch are directors of the Thomas B. Fordham Foundation, the education arm of the Manhattan Institute. It took over the work of the Educational Excellence Network founded by Finn and Ravitch in the 1981. Bruno Manno sits on its Board of Trustees. The Educational Excellence Network works with Hudson, the Education Policy Institute, Goals 2000, and Heritage Foundation's Center for Education Reform. The Koret Task Force is made up of Hoover fellows Eric Hanushek, Terry Moe, Paul Petersen, John Chubb, Chester Finn, E.D. Hirsch, Diane Ravitch, and Herbert Walberg.

Think tanks exist that favor progressive education also, but the funding available to those organizations is only about 10 percent of the conservative think tanks. For example, Designs for Change and Fairtest operate from progressive agendas, but in each case they rely on small donations and low overhead. Nor do they enjoy the web of interconnections with government, foundations, and corporations. Most progressive scholars would be shocked to receive grants and sizable advances for writing books or to have a publisher ready to disseminate them.

A former participant in the complex web of foundations and think tanks, David Brock wrote that during the 1970s:

> major American corporations . . . teamed up with the Wall Street venture capital class to coordinate their political activities. . . . [They] targeted donations in the millions to conservative political action committees . . . promoted right-wing ideology through a network of think tanks and issue lobbies and publications advocating free-market capitalism, deregulation, and lower corporate taxes.[72]

Their actions converged with others interested in "anti-union, anti-leftist, and pro moral traditionalism." Brock quoted a member of this network who spoke about its agenda:

> to "fund intellectual refuges for the nonegalitarian scholars and writers. . . . They must be given grants, grants, and more grants in exchange for books, books, and more books."[73]

Brock took on his former employer and benefactor, the Heritage Foundation, stating that by the 1980s Heritage had grown to an annual income of $18 million and "lavished six-figure fellowships" on people like William Bennett.

> Heritage is a tax-exempt foundation, requiring that it not engage in activities or lobbying benefiting a political party. However, the organization functioned as a de facto arm of the GOP, churning out slick position papers, called Heritage Backgrounders, marketed on Capitol Hill by a specially designated congressional relations shop. The authors of the papers were nominally independent researchers, but were . . . expected to behave as loyal members of the conservative movement "team." Essentially the papers backed up an already fixed ideological viewpoint dictated directly by a tier of Heritage executives . . . and indirectly by the outside foundations that held Heritage's purse strings. . . . Though I had no advanced degrees, I assumed the grandiose title of John M. Olin Fellow in Congressional Studies.[74]

Brock listed parts of the infrastructure created by this confluence of individuals and organizations. Special journals became or were created to serve as ready-made outlets for the research done by writers subsidized by the group: *Policy Review, Commentary, National Interest, American Spectator*. Publishing houses were acquired to produce and market books by the same individuals: Basic Books, Free Press, and Regnery. Legal action groups were funded to pursue the group's agenda: Landmark Legal Foundation, Institute for Justice, Southeastern Legal Foundation. Public relations firms such as Newton and Associates were made available to organize book tours for authors and train them to adhere to a particular message and style. Eric Alterman added that the Bradley Foundation constructed an organization to distribute conservative books and supported more than 400 books in 14 years.[75]

Is there a vast right-wing conspiracy bent on destroying public schools? Living in the political spectacle, it is easy to get carried away. Still, even the most skeptical reader cannot ignore the amount of money spent on behalf of separate, stratified school systems and on the infrastructure of think tanks, subsidized plutocrats, and public relations work on behalf of those causes.

Corporate Work in the Political Spectacle

There are thousands of businesspeople who provide invaluable services to public schools. They do it out of the best, most altruistic, and civic-minded motives.[76] They understand that education has intrinsic worth and human proportions and—most important—is an enterprise distinct from business. This chapter is not about those people.

This chapter instead considers the biggest organizations of the biggest corporations, which attempt to speak for the whole private sector and to reshape public schools toward a narrow vision. They attempt to influence education policy to serve private, special interests and act politically through invisible networks of relationships and in more straightforward ways by doling out money and jobs to sympathetic politicians. They do it with little regard for the roles that schools are meant to serve in a democratic society or for the good of the community as a whole. And because this book is about the political spectacle we show how this special part of the private sector pursues its self-interest largely out of public view, attempting to exert disproportionate economic and political power over policy makers toward their own goals and interests. The political spectacle hides the attempts of the largest corporations to merge with government. Onstage, it professes political neutrality and a motivation to do the best for everyone. Roslyn Mickelson wrote:

> By focusing the public's gaze upon schools, corporate leaders deflect attention from their own contributions to domestic and international economic and social problems.[77]

The corporate sector trades on cultural metaphors of schools and teachers as factories and factory workers (and often not very good ones). It tosses out all—save one—of the purposes that public schools have historically served. To help young people have full, rounded lives, to ask questions, to grow in literacy in the broadest sense, and to prepare themselves for family, civic, and (yes) economic life—these are the educational goals that groups like the Business Roundtable reject. Instead they want to narrow school goals and constrict the range of vision about educational and political life, so that all schools can do is fit students comfortably into existing slots in the labor market.

Notes

1. The source of this vignette is the dissertation research of Barbara Gereboff, who studied Arizona and California teacher education reform policy. This passage is a minor paraphrase of actual conversation at the Arizona summit and a weaving together of the words of three speakers. Gereboff found that the prevailing images about the status of teachers' work coincided with the states' political culture to produce very different policy trajectories and texts. By comparing policies in Arizona and California, she found that industrial metaphors pervaded Arizona's policies whereas professional and humanistic metaphors characterized those of California (Gereboff, 1999).
2. Edelman (1985), p. 97.
3. Edelman (1985), p. 2.
4. Edelman (1985), p. 6.
5. Lakoff and Johnson (1980), p. 5.
6. Lakoff and Johnson (1980), p. 3.
7. Lakoff and Johnson (1980), p. 26.
8. Lakoff and Johnson (1980), p. 35.
9. Lakoff (1996), p. 4. Lakoff considers that all members of a culture operate from some variant of core political metaphors, such as "the nation as family," or "the government as stern father," or "the government as nurturing parent." These core metaphors divide conservatives from political liberals in such a way that seeming contradictions such as pro-life and pro-death penalty convictions can fit plausibly under the unconscious metaphor of "government as strict parent."
10. Callahan (1962).
11. The passion to increase the efficiency of teachers also informed the first education research studies. E.L. Thorndike, the father of educational measurement, teamed up with efficiency experts to test the efficacy of various high school courses. He found that studying Greek did not lead to better achievement in other courses. Because few students studied Greek, classes were small and hence inefficient. Researchers' recommendations led to policy decisions about whether to offer courses with small enrollments. The study of Greek and other specialized studies did not fit the business model of efficiency.
12. Callahan (1962), p. 97.
13. It was once thought that administrators ought to protect women's health and happiness by preventing them from work outside the home, for example, see Apple (1986), Gitlin and Labaree (1996), and Roman and Apple (1990).
14. Valenzuela (1999), p. 61. Also see Ladson-Billings (1994).
15. Borman and Castenell (1993).
16. Martin (1991).
17. House (1998).
18. Levin (1993).
19. Levin (1998).
20. House (1998).
21. In this section we are engaging in interpretive synthesis of several sources but rely most heavily on Barry Clark's text, *Political Economy* (1998).
22. Clark (1998).
23. Coalition for Education Reform, (no date).
24. Gross and MacLaury (2000), p. 1.
25. Gross and MacLaury (2000), p. 1.
26. philipmorris.com, access date, June 28, 2001.
27. *Washington Post* (2001). Supreme Court Strikes Down Tobacco Ad Ban.
28. Metcalf (2002).

29. Business Roundtable website, www.bcer.org.
30. The usual justification for corporate tax relief is that the new company will create more jobs. Saltman cites research that shows a net of new jobs is rarely the result of the corporate move, as most new jobs are exported to countries with cheaper labor costs. In any case the competition is a zero sum game for the communities, but always a sure bet for corporations. Saltman describes corporate welfare as an upward flight of wealth from poorer to richer individuals (Saltman, 2000).
31. Carson, Huelskamp et al. (1992).
32. Ibid. (1992).
33. Quoted in National Education Association (2001).
34. See, for example, Shipps (1997).
35. http://www.ibm.com/ibm/ibmgives/grant/education/programs/reinventing/
36. Quoted by Mickelson (1999).
37. Mickelson (1999), p. 489.
38. Mickelson (1999).
39. In spite of the power of the business elite, the case of Education Village ended by thwarting the agenda of IBM. Through their concerted efforts, members of the public pushed through the provision that a lottery would determine which students were to be admitted. The lottery set aside spots for students in the immediate neighborhood as well as spots for the African-American students who attended under the desegregation order. The remaining spots, about one-third of the schools' enrollment, went to students that IBM had intended to serve exclusively (Mickelson, 1999).
40. Molnar (1996), p. 21.
41. Molnar (1996).
42. Kurt Landgraf (2001).
43. The potential costs of this provision of the policy have not been calculated. However, psychometric analyses of the different definitions of proficiency among the states and analyses of the test themselves suggest that about half of U.S. schools will qualify for this service, simply because of artifacts in the tests themselves.
44. *Education Week* (2002), pp. 19–20.
45. Garan (2002).
46. Quoted in BusinessWire.com, (1/23/01).
47. Quoted in Chomsky (2000) and by Bracey (2001c), pp. 6–7.
48. Bracey (2002b).
49. Bracey (2002b).
50. Other insider stock sales follow:
    Benno Schmidt, Chairman of the board—$403,075
    Jeffrey Leeds, Director—$2,063,300
    Kathleen Mary Hamel, Executive Vice President—$1,194,680
    Christopher Cerf, Chief Operating Officer—$879,925
    John E. Chubb, Executive Vice President, Chief Education Officer—$1,136,678
    Manuel Rivera Officer, Chief Development Officer—$416,062
    Deborah McGriff, Vice President—$852,184
    Tonya Hinch, Executive Vice President—$606,600. See, for example, Thomson Financial Network: http://biz.yahoo.com/t/58/2228.html
    http://biz.yahoo.com/t/e/edsn.html
    http://biz.yahoo.com/t/90/6372.html
    http://biz.yahoo.com/t/97/6372.html
    http://biz.yahoo.com/t/32/6373.html
    http://biz.yahoo.com/t/28/6373.html.
51. Bracey (2002a). http://www.educationnews.org/edison_schools_inc.html.
52. Treasury Secretary Paul O'Neil attributed the Enron failure to the genius of capitalism.
53. Bracey (2001c), p. 193.
54. Heritage Foundation (1998).
55. Paige (2001), p. B7.
56. Business Roundtable: http://www.brtable.org/press.cfm/564.
57. Also see Borman and Castenell (1993).
58. Business Roundtable: http://www.brtable.org/press.cfm/564.

59. Augustine (1999): http://www.bizjournals.com/sanfrancisco/stories/1999/09/20/ editorial4.html.
60. Bracey (2001c), pp. 4–5.
61. Bracey (2001c), p. 72.
62. Bracey (2002a), p. 5, quoting the *Atlanta Constitution.*
63. Center for Responsive Politics (2002). http://www.opensecrets.org/pubs/lobby00/topind 12asp.
64. Metcalf (2002).
65. See Chapter Five for the story of how a public relations firm crafted the summary that led to the enrichment of a publisher. Also recall from the Prologue that a song was written to praise Reading First, by the recipients of government grants for television production Schemo (2002b).
66. McChesney (1999).
67. People for the American Way (1999): www.pfaw.org/issues/education.
68. People for the American Way (1999). Also see Bracey (2002a).
69. Mickleson (1999), p. 498.
70. Bracey (2002d).
71. Chubb and Moe (1990).
72. Brock (2002), p. 71.
73. Brock (2002) p. 72.
74. Brock (2002), pp. 72–73.
75. Alterman (1999) referred to this as part of a war of ideas. But the authors were required to stay on a particular message and style so as to make it possible for the public to adopt what previously had been unpopular ideas, such as school segregation and eugenics.
76. Mickelson (1999).
77. Mickelson (1999), p. 477.

CHAPTER 7

Finale¹

Having eyes, see ye not? And having ears, hear ye not?
And do ye not remember?
Mark VIII, 18

At the beginning of the book we asked whether schools constructed in the political spectacle are the schools we want—schools that enhance the best in children and in society. To guide the reader to answer that question we provided a set of theoretical ideas that frame schools within education policy and education policy within a perverse, irrational, and anti-democratic form of politics. We brought together a mass of concrete details that tie those ideas to the hard ground of experience of real people in real times and places and institutional contexts. We have made the case that all of the elements of political spectacle are present in the current political culture, with significant consequences on policy, hence on schools themselves. In this final chapter we synthesize this evidence and analysis into ten lessons we hope to pass on to the reader. We then ask whether education policy, as the field traditionally defines it, can do any good at all in the current political climate.

Ten Lessons

I. Participation in the American Political Process Is Low— Low Relative to Other Historical Eras and Low Compared to Other Democratic Nations

A democratic republic cannot survive without active political participation. But, in the most recent presidential election, only about half of the people eligible to vote had registered, and of those registered, less than half cast ballots. This represents a substantial decrease from voting rates in the 1960s when 63 percent of those eligible to vote actually cast ballots for president. In other democracies, voting rates exceed 75 percent of those eligible. Compared to voting rates in presidential elections, the percentage of Americans voting in local and state elections is still lower, suggesting that even in the conditions in which government is closest to their lives, most people do not participate in elections. Worse, these low voting rates represent an upper limit to participation in other kinds of political actions, such as attending local debates, supporting candidates, soliciting signatures on petitions, and the like. Opinion polls show that politics fail to engage much interest. Edelman wrote that elections served as a kind of ritual that obscured the absence of real participation in democratic deliberation. Political spectacle works best when democracy is only formal and not genuine. As Carl Boggs wrote in *The End of Politics*,

> The erosion of civic values [can be traced to depoliticalization]. Vital elements of the political enterprise—participation, community, and governance—have been distorted or obliterated . . . creating a mockery of the Aristotelian ideal of *homo politicus*.[2]

Although voting is low on the average, not everyone avoids politics. Boggs wrote that in 1996, the richest 20 percent of Americans cast 75 percent of the ballots. What is more, the richest one percent of Americans made 80 percent of contributions to political campaigns.

The evidence suggests that education now prepares a small, select political class. Members of this class possess tacit knowledge about how the system works and a network of family and friends to interpret it and recognize how it can serve their own interests. Schools further equip this class with formal knowledge of politics, history and economics. Schools teach them in separate classes and schools so that these students acquire formal knowledge denied to others. Meanwhile, education prepares those others—a separate, larger class—to be spectators, cynical about having any power to decide their fates by political means. The political spectacle alienates these people from political action and disengages them from authentic participation. And finally, schools prepare a third class without any political capacity and experience, formally disenfranchised because they have immigrated or are imprisoned.

In a climate of high-stakes testing and regimented schools, civics and science are the first subjects to be sacrificed in favor of repetitive drilling on the skills that the tests emphasize. As we have shown throughout the book, classes like physics and civics get deleted only in schools for disadvantaged students, thus exacerbating the disproportion of cognitive and civic capacity among rich and poor people. In the political spectacle, people backstage have little incentive to prepare ordinary people for active citizenship.

II. Economic Resources of Americans Are More Stratified Than Any Time Since the 1920s, and the Trend Is Toward Even Larger Disparities Between Rich and Poor

The richest one percent of Americans possesses more than half of the nation's wealth. The poorest 80 percent possess only six percent. The differential in wealth between the rich and poor has grown steadily, with a spectacular rise in the number of millionaires during the Reagan administration. A report by the United Nations in 2002 found that the gap has worsened and that the poorest 20 percent of Americans make only one-quarter of the nation's median annual income. In Japan, the poorest 20 percent make one-half the Japanese annual income. A Congressional Budget Office report found that the poorest 20 percent of Americans were worse off in 1997 than they were in 1979 (in income, corrected for inflation and taxes). During the same period the number of extremely rich Americans rose precipitously, and the annual incomes of the top one percent were increased by nearly a half million dollars.[3] The top one percent paid five percent less of their income in taxes in 1997 than in 1979.

Political conservatives accuse liberals of engaging in "class warfare" just because they repeat these simple but obvious facts. Conservatives maintain that America is still the land of opportunity in which anyone can rise above their circumstances, especially in a free market economy. The ideal may be true—for a few—but tangible evidence points to the contrary. Christopher Lasch wrote that the elites "have a common stake in suppressing the politics of class."[4]

Those same conservatives who suppress talk about class also reject programs such as increasing minimum wage—a step that experts say would reduce some of the disparities between rich and poor. The Center on Budget Priorities wrote that Bush's tax-cut legislation increases these disparities. Do we engage in class warfare by reporting these facts? Is the word worse than the deed? At least we are not acting to create them.

Robert Reich wrote that the degree of economic stratification threatens the social compact shared by Americans. That implicit compact involves three promises: that "everyone should have an opportunity to develop his or her talents through publicly supported education"; that "hard-working people should be paid enough to support themselves and their families and stay out of poverty" and social insurance is available in emergencies; that "when companies do well their employees do too"—in other words, insuring a secure workforce through corporate responsibility and public institutions. Disparities of wealth have had the effect of segregating the rich from the rest of society so that they have fewer opportunities to develop empathy and sense of community.[5]

Can a republic survive such deep divisions between the rich and the poor? Even Adam Smith thought otherwise.

III. Disparities in Family and Neighborhood Wealth Mirror Disparities in the Schools That Children Attend. Wealthier Children are Concentrated in Some Schools and Separated from Poorer Children

Disparities in wealth mirror disparities in the populations of schools. Wealthier children are concentrated in some schools and separated from poorer children, who are isolated in poor schools. Race and ethnicity mirror differences in families' financial resources. Public financial support for schools mirrors the wealth of the families who send their children there. Even where both rich and poor attend the same school, they are isolated from each other in separate tracks and programs.

Enormous differences exist in money allocated to schools in more advantaged and less advantaged neighborhoods.[6] For example, over ten thousand dollars separates the annual per pupil expenditures of typical schools in New York City from schools in nearby Long Island. To exacerbate the official budget disparities, richer schools receive substantially more in private donations. As Jean Anyon pointed out in her historical analysis of Newark schools, such disparities are often the consequence of state laws that support public schools by property taxes rather than by income or sales taxes.[7] Thus differences among districts in relative value of their property translates into disparities in school resources. Even within a single district, disparities among schools are created and tolerated despite legislation and court rulings to correct them. Jonathon Kozol's book *Savage Inequalities* depicted these disparities in graphic and heart-wrenching terms, and we do not need to repeat them here. By whatever means, policies and institutions solidify the relationship between the poverty and race of the children within a school and the level at which that school is funded.

Do disparities in funding matter? Some researchers say yes and others say no. Their answers often depend on how they define and measure school achievement. Their answers often depend on their initial assumptions and worldviews. Their answers often depend—sadly, from our point of view—on their political ideologies and those of their funding agents. In any case, research can't tell the whole story. Nor is research even necessary. The disparities in financial support of schools for the poor and the rich smack you between the eyes. Neo-conservatives and the corporate interests claim that money does not matter. Perhaps money alone does not improve schools or erase disparities, but money can buy up-to-date textbooks, libraries, science laboratories, computers, certified teachers, experienced teachers, health and guidance services, smaller class size, safe playgrounds.

When people say that money doesn't matter, ask them about the resources available at the schools their children attend.

Court cases and state policies have tried to correct financial inequities among schools. But no matter how well intended, most of them fail. Though court orders mandate redistribution, legislatures fail to fund remedies to redress disparities. Instead of complying, states and districts defy court orders or file a never-ending series of appeals. In Texas, this process went on for a decade, as it did in Arizona. In New Jersey over twenty years of legal and legislative conflict separated the judgment in the Abbot case from the governor's agreement to abide by it. While lawyers argued and filed motions, urban schools languished.

Financial disparities among schools reflect the race of children who attend them. Gary Orfield wrote that the chance of an African-American student attending a school with white students was lower in 1999 than in 1971.[8] As we showed in Chapter Four, mandates for desegregation and financial equity often suffer from watered down and vacuous responses, which follow the interests of the few while cloaking policies in the rhetoric of justice. Arguments for "liberty" and "school choice" also cloak backstage practices that culminate in the segregation of students and stratification of educational opportunities, as we showed in Chapter Three. These consequences turn fairness on its head. We quote George Orwell's *1984*:

> . . . if leisure and security were enjoyed by all alike, the great mass of human beings who are normally stupified by poverty would become literate and would learn to think for themselves, and when they had done this, they would sooner or later realize that the privileged minority had no function, and they would sweep it away. In the long run, a hierarchical society was only possible on a basis of poverty and ignorance.[9]

IV. Achievement Tests Measure the Relative Wealth of the People Who Attend a School. No Test Yet Devised Has Escaped the Pattern of Inverse Correlation Between a School's Average Test Scores and the Percentage of Its Student Body Who Receive Free Lunch

If tests measure neighborhood wealth, then, on the average, the highest scoring schools are located in richer neighborhoods with better educated and culturally endowed families—regardless of some underlying degree of school effectiveness. This is a statistical and psychometric pattern, not a deterministic one. Of course there are exceptions, like the school in a poor neighborhood with high test scores. These exceptions occur at a rate consistent with statistical expectations.

If tests measure the wealth of students who go there, then rich and high-scoring schools will claim superiority on false grounds. We observed this in Boulder (Chapter Three), when the already sorted and tracked charter and focus schools claimed superiority because their test scores were higher than the children sorted and left behind. More importantly, schools populated by economically disadvantaged students will be tagged as failures, no matter how truly effective they are. Achievement tests measure selection, not treatment.

Since socioeconomic advantage is relatively stable, achievement test results rarely fluctuate, even when new programs are introduced. When scores go up precipitously the best explanations for the increase are 1) a change in school population, 2) a program of coaching and training students on materials that emulate the items of the high-stakes test, also known as "teaching to the test," and 3) a pattern of exempting and excluding from testing those students likely to score low.

If a writer notes the relationship between socioeconomic advantage and achievement test scores she is likely to be accused of racism, of engaging in class warfare, of making excuses for the failures of schools.[10] None of these accusations is true, but they function to disparage the writer and deflect attention from genuine disparities between schools for the rich and schools for the poor. Class differences matter in understanding the configuration of educational opportunities and test results. Score differentials are not the way they are because of the "soft bigotry of low expectations," as President George W. Bush once said. They result, instead, from biased tests, from financial and other kinds of neglect—Anyon called it grand larceny—and a failure of empathy.

Much was made that the No Child Left Behind legislation would force states to disaggregate achievement test data so that the public could judge whether a particular school was closing the gap between white and non-white students. The theory assumed that schools could be made accountable for closing the achievement gap and would do so to avoid government penalties. In light of the stable relationship between test scores and degree of wealth, however, one can see the emptiness of this goal. If all it took to improve the achievement of children of poverty and color was to become aware of the gap, then the gap would have been closed long ago. Policies such as this, no matter how well intended, amount to mere gestures. They focus attention on outputs of a system, and not on what it takes in resources and good teaching to make a genuine difference.

There is no achievement crisis, we repeat, except in schools attended by children of poverty and color. Gerald Bracey examined the international achievement comparisons of 2001 and the claim that schools were in crisis. The U.S. schools ranked at midpoint in the distribution of 28 nations. Secretary of Education Rodney Paige reacted to these average scores with dismay. Bracey showed that—if you consider only the scores of white students—the U.S. ranks among the top four. But if you consider only the scores that Hispanic students made, the U.S. rank falls to the bottom of the ranking.[11]

Declaring that no general crisis exists in public schools should not imply that we are apologists for public schools. There is much that we feel needs to be improved. Our point is that the sounding of alarms about all public schools is more political gesture than tangible reality, except where children of poverty and color are concentrated. Can the corporate community and public generate comparable alarm in the face of "A Nation of Disadvantaged at Risk"?

V. High-Stakes Testing Policies Produce Symbolic Benefit to the Public and Tangible Benefits to Producers of Tests and Curriculum Packages. High-Stakes Testing Policies Produce Vicious Burdens on Students of Poverty and Color, and the Schools That Serve Them

Because assessment policies belong to the political spectacle, one must distinguish between apparent effects and real effects. By demonstrating what appears to benefit education, politicians can claim victory for their leadership. But real effects are hard to find, and states themselves rarely even look for them. As we demonstrated in Chapter Two, independent research has never shown that high-stakes testing leads to better achievement. Apparent effects are inflationary, illusory. But they serve the purpose of enhancing the political and professional careers of those who champion them.

Evidence mounts about the consequences of high-stakes testing Audrey Amrein and David Berliner's study typifies most of the research that shows a lack of impact on the levels of achievement in public schools. However, the burdens and costs are painfully obvious to anyone paying attention to school budgets and allocations of resources. High-stakes testing is the darling of many policy makers, but things have not gone smoothly for testing policies in the most of the states.

In Arizona, Massachusetts, Ohio, Virginia, and Wisconsin, grass roots resistance to high stakes tests has forced states to delay, revise, or retreat from their assessment policies. Delays or changes have occurred for other reasons in Alabama, Alaska, California, Delaware, and Maryland. As in Arizona, political events trigger changes in assessment policy. New regimes or old regimes that confront political problems fire their test publishers and hire new ones, change the content of tests, fiddle with the cutoff scores that define students' success and failure, delay the impositions of consequences. Most states experience wave after wave of changes that leave educators in constant policy flux and citizens grasping for the meaning of meaningless numbers.

As of 2001, at least 19 states had experienced major errors in their testing programs. Yet because of the limited numbers of test contractors, some firms that failed in one state later bid successfully for contracts in other states. Limited time and money preclude the possibility that the tests can be constructed in such ways that their results are valid. The professional associations with interests in proper testing practices have standards but no way to enforce them or even reveal malpractice.

Can adverse impacts, even perverse, long-term effects of assessment policies be justified, offset by the greater good? Defenders sometimes claim that negative effects ought to be weighed against the renewed legitimacy that public schools have purchased by becoming more accountable. They say that low scores draw attention to schools that serve the poor. Or they deny negative effects altogether. In any case, what degree of proof would change their minds? As we know, the political spectacle deals in ambiguous words, code words, and phrases. Again quoting Orwell, the essence of language in the political spectacle is:

> To know and not to know, to be conscious of complete truthfulness while telling carefully constructed lies, to hold simultaneously two opinions which cancel each other out, knowing them to be contradictory and believing in both of them, to use logic against logic, to repudiate morality while laying claim to it, to believe that democracy was impossible and that the Party was the guardian of democracy, to forget, whatever it was necessary to forget, then to draw it back into memory again at the moment when it was needed, and then promptly to forget it again.[12]

Could it be that modern assessment policy is as much a profit center as it is a means to improve schools? Testing corporations have won tangible benefits behind the scenes and beyond public scrutiny. One of the first people whom President Bush met after his election was Kurt Landgraf, CEO of Educational Testing Services and its profit-making subsidiary. Landgraf must have run into the president's old friend Harold McGraw III, the owner of one of the largest publishing textbook and testing corporations, who also met the president that day.

VI. High-Stakes Accountability Policies Are the Means: Privatization Is the End

This is a statement that evidence can neither prove or disprove. Yet it makes sense. Having been led to expect so much from assessment policy, and later noticing that so little comes of it, the public may further decrease its trust in education. Perhaps the public would then be more apt to support vouchers. Maybe that was the point.

From *A Nation at Risk* to the present day, invoking a crisis in schools is only a pretext for transferring control from the public to the private sector and—a paradox, certainly—from local to federal government. As Edelman wrote, invoking a crisis creates anxiety in the public and compliance to privations and risk that the state wants on some other grounds. Invoking a crisis in school achievement also serves as pretext for the voucher campaign.

Horace Mann envisioned a system of schools financed by state taxes and available to all, indeed, providing equal education to all. He believed that providing equal education for all children, irrespective of family origin and wealth, promotes the common good. Democratic participation by citizens in the goals and operations of schools would promote fairness. In the political spectacle, however, democratic participation is an illusion.

In spite of Mann's ideals, elite families avoided the public schools in favor of selective private schools for their children. Irish immigrants withheld their children from public schools because of a profound Protestant bias. White southerners pressed the state to provide schools for their children that would exclude former slaves. When the Supreme Court struck down that possibility, they sent their children to private academies for whites only.

Contrary to what choice advocates say, therefore, public schools have never been monopolies, let alone "socialist" schools or government schools, or whatever incendiary labels they might deploy. School choice was always available, at least to some families.

In Chapter Three, we described how elite parents in Boulder took advantage of opportunities provided by Colorado choice policies to tip the scales in their favor. They professed public interests in public while pursuing private interests in private. They silenced opposition, practiced the discourse of derision, and made a mockery of democratic deliberation. They conducted business in private and capitalized on connections and media savvy. They thoroughly cowed the district officials (who ought to have taken responsibility for re-balancing cultural and financial capital) to get what they wanted for their own children—and only for their own children.

Absent political spectacle, could choice policies have transformed public schools so thoroughly in Boulder, in Arizona, or New Zealand? Political spectacle diminishes democracy. Weakened democracy nourishes political spectacle. In the political spectacle, even the words "choice" or "market" fog the mind. Most people eat the thin gruel of words while the few operate backstage to obtain more tangible feasts for themselves.

VII. Corporate Interests Dominate Education Policy

The very largest corporations, represented by the Business Roundtable, speak with a common voice on a common agenda. They say that governments should force schools to raise academic standards and impose penalties and rewards to motivate educators to fix the problems that achievement tests reveal. They say that these policies will raise achievement, more or less by fiat, without any additional funding (which is already, they say, more than ample). They say that improvement in educational productivity improves economic growth and competitiveness. They say that schools must act like businesses by adopting the management tools that work so well in industry. They say that school administrators must act like Chief Executive Officers and bear that title, irrespective of their abilities as educators.

These assertions may be sincere, but they are not the whole story. Corporations also have a special agenda that operates behind the rhetoric. Corporations seek efficiency in the public sector—attaining the goals with the least tax dollars, which leads them to push for school vouchers and away from expensive policies such as reduction of class size. Corporations seek to avoid taxes. Yet United States corporations are among the least taxed of any in the industrial world. Half of the 88 largest corporations paid less than the corporate rate of 35 percent, and 17 percent (including Enron) paid no taxes at all in the year 2000. Nearly 1300 corporations with assets exceeding $250 million reported no income and thus paid no taxes. Corporations seek to reduce their labor costs by transferring to the public sector what they might ordinarily spend to train and upgrade employees. Corporations seek to improve efficiency by influencing government to remove regulations on the way they do business, even if regulations are meant to protect the safety of workers, the health of the environment, and the certification of teachers.

Human capital theory expresses the view of corporations that a better-educated public creates a more productive economy. However, there are good reasons to believe that economic growth has other causes and may be the cause of, not the consequence of, educational productivity. In other words, the existence of good jobs motivates more students to stay in school and work harder to prepare for them. If the latter is true, current reforms have little chance to succeed. Even if it did succeed (attain an academic success rate of 75 percent—the Roundtable goal), neither the schools themselves nor the labor economy could absorb all these successful students. Good jobs are not available even for the numbers now well qualified; that is, according to standards that existed before government reforms. In fact, schools operate on the assumption that many students fail no matter what. Even now most urban school systems set their budgets according to the assumption that half the entering freshmen will not last until their senior year. If all those who entered did stay on (that is, if the Roundtable policy happened to work and no child was indeed left behind), they would have no desks to sit in, no classrooms, no teachers, and no good jobs.

Roundtable rhetoric proclaims that schools must raise achievement to prepare students for the future jobs in technology. However, most economists concur that the greatest job growth takes place in low skill and temporary occupations—jobs without security, health benefits, or career prospects. High-tech jobs are not expected to grow to absorb the graduates of the newly reformed schools. Because of globalization—capital travels faster than labor—corporations have incentives to move their operations abroad, where the labor costs are cheaper. Meanwhile, those with U.S. jobs have no unions and no collective consciousness. They lack the security to speak out against the management excesses and unfairness. What's more, they lack the leisure to participate in politics, a necessity for democracy to be sustained, as Thomas Jefferson said.

Some observers argue that corporations push high-stakes accountability because these policies crystallize the existing division of students into a class of literate and skilled knowledge workers and managers versus a class of barely literate workers ready to assume low-wage occupations. Even if not so insidious, the Roundtable agenda constricts the functions of schools to their narrowest and meanest.

The private sector insists on high-stakes testing, but we now know high-stakes testing drives out goals and purposes of schooling other than the narrowest version of basic skills in the key areas of math, reading, and writing, which the private sector believes are relevant for the work force. Music, art, physical education, civic education, humanities, broad perspectives on literacy, including critical literacy: all these goals are displaced, particularly in schools for the poor. Recall that Thomas Jefferson said the sole purpose of education in a democratic republic was the training of youth to preserve their republic and protect themselves from tyranny. Political capacity, civic virtue—these are educational purposes one seldom hears about any more. In *Thoughts on Government,* John Adams wrote: "Laws for the liberal education of youth, especially for the lower classes of people, are so extremely wise and useful that to a humane and generous mind, no expense for this purpose would be thought extravagant."

The largest corporations and their neo-liberal allies recommend the unfettered free market as the best way to organize, not just the economy, but also the rest of society. This perspective has dominated the discourse since the Reagan administration. Even Presidents Carter and Clinton cleaved to the power of free enterprise and smaller government as keys to economic growth and prosperity—as if there were no competing theories of political economy, and no values other than the unfettered pursuit of wealth. In most discussions, invoking the free market closes off alternative views.[13] Yet, invoking the free market acts as a symbol that hides actions by the largest corporations to skew the free market in their favor. They push for government action to impose regulations on their competitors and remove regulations from themselves. They obscure information (on which a free market is predicated) to position themselves as performing better than they are, through accounting tricks and the like. The free market may be wonderful in many ways, but it is not virtuous beyond the health of society. Other nations manage effective mixing of market economies with broader social goals. Decrying "big government" has become a reflexive reaction that fails to grasp that institutions of all kinds are needed to protect the public from the excesses of laissez-faire capitalism.

The largest corporations dominate education policy in the same way they influence government policies of all kinds—to advance their own special interests. They provide funds to politicians through campaign contributions, and speaking and consultant fees. They pay candidates of both parties. They pay local and national candidates. Contributions open doors for the lobbyists who represent corporations, which enjoy disproportionate access relative to the politicians' own constituents. So shrinks the arena for democratic participation for ordinary people. As Christopher Lasch put it, "When money talks, every body else is compelled to listen."[14]

Corporations seek influence over education policy through their personal relationships with presidents and governors. Executive officers of the largest corporations funded and had major roles in influencing nearly every major government conference on education. We showed in the previous chapter how interconnected are government officials and corporate leaders. Christopher Lasch referred to this pattern of interconnections as the "merger of the elites" and argued that it threatened democracy. At the very least it tilts policy away from the values and needs of ordinary people, and even more so, people of poverty and color.

Businessmen rule. Corporations support public institutions begrudgingly. They proudly avoid taxes and lobby against regulations that otherwise protect the public interest and obstruct private enrichment. They criticize the socialized state—until the times when they want concessions in the wake of, for example, bankruptcy or disaster or military misadventures. Yet they can't seem to avoid scandals, bubbles, excesses—junk bonds, savings and loan crash, Enron, and so on. More often than not they fail to concern themselves with their workers, whose wages interfere with the price of stocks. They threaten, if the government doesn't change policies to advantage them, to move their operations to other countries where labor is cheaper and where taxes are lower.

Fascism, said Mussolini, represented the consolidation of corporate power and the power of the state. In the political spectacle, corporations profess free market but practice corporatism, the attempted merger of government and business.

Advertising and other forms of commercialism have intruded on American schools in unprecedented means and degrees; further evidence that corporations dominate education policy. Corporations push for policies that open up new profit centers. Several avenues have opened for them, but the most far-reaching and odious is commercialization of schools. In his book, *Giving Schools the Business* and his annual reports, Alex Molnar keeps track of the degree to which corporations tap into public schools as a direct source of profits. Corporations offer contracts for advertising their products. Those schools that accept them are, for the most part, schools short on money. For an impoverished school faced with tough decisions about what programs to cut, accepting a partnership with a corporation or a contract for advertising and exclusive product marketing makes some sense. In contrast, schools with other sources of wealth such as private fundraising and a rich property tax base need not make such a choice. In Chapter Six, we provided evidence for the plastering of schools with advertising, the outrageous curriculum packages that corporations push onto those schools. To enter into contracts and partnerships with corporations almost always requires costs and risks for a school—costs and risks that remain unexamined at the outset. In exchange for contributions from a corporation like Pizza Hut (for the Book-it program), like General Mills (for the Gushers "science" lessons), like Colgate-Palmolive Company (Dental Health Classroom Program), schools lose instructional time. The corporations gain brand recognition and brand loyalty. Their profit motives are obscured by the rhetoric of philanthropy. Partnerships between corporations and schools are rarely among co-equals in power and respect.

It is but a brief stretch from such evidence to conclude with Molnar and others that corporations are seeking, through these arrangements, new customers and new markets of children, captive in schools—new sources of private wealth.

Our explorations convince us that corporations export consultants, executives, and modes of thinking and practice to public schools. The analogy between business and schools is fallacious. Standards, benchmarks, diagnosis and measurement, raw material, middle management, consumers, quality control, accountability—all these ideas and practices that may work for businesses and industry—produce distortion when applied to schools.

Why should the public fawn on corporate leaders as the saviors of public schools? In the current era of piratical capitalism and corporate scandals, an attitude of skepticism seems more appropriate. When we hear Enron, do we think of Edison, Knowledge Universe, K–12, and the Modern Red Schoolhouse? Should we?

VIII. Federal Government Control Over Public School Goals, Instruction, Assessment, and Management Is Greater Now Than Ever Before in American History

Control over public schools has migrated from home to school to district to state to the federal government. The control by the federal government over school goals, instructional processes, methods of assessment and management is greater now than ever before in American history.

During the second half of the twentieth century many states gradually usurped authority over school districts through legislation on accountability, testing, goals, teacher certification, and spending. As well, the

Federal government began to assume authority through the Civil Rights Act and legislation mandating inclusion of handicapped children and supplemental education for disadvantaged students (Title I of the Elementary and Secondary Education Act, or ESEA). However, there was no national curriculum, as there is in many other nations. With Goals 2000, the Reading Excellence Act, and the No Child Left Behind, the history of school governance changed.

In theory, Goals 2000 represented a national commitment to high and common standards that public schools everywhere should put at the top of their priorities. The Federal legislation focuses on a narrow perspective of achievement in a few core subjects as a means of preparing students for places in the new economy. Legislative intent served to displace all the other purposes for which public schools have been organized: civic preparation, education in liberal arts and humanities, and human development and communitarian goals. Further, tests of the national standards followed standards, along with rewards and punishments linked to schools' compliance.

In the end, the parties compromised on mandated testing of all children in grades three through eight, every year, on reading and math tests developed and administered by each state (subject to federal approval) and linked statistically across the states. States must publish separate scores for demographic groups so that the gap in achievement between rich and poor, white and nonwhite, can be targeted (as if the mere knowing of the discrepancy was sufficient to solve it). The federal government provides grants to states and districts that show improvement on their percentage of students attaining the standard called "proficient" (even though the states vary greatly in how they define that concept). The federal government will penalize districts whose performance targets are not reached. It requires that all teachers be "highly qualified." Under the Reading First provision, it authorized $900 million to districts to help them adopt "scientific-researched based" reading programs (a coded word for phonics) and more money for "Early Reading First," to fund similar programs for preschoolers. The bill was signed into law in January 2002. Almost immediately, in his budget, President Bush failed to fund the provisions of the law fully and instead allocated money for income tax credits for parents to use for private schools. The money that was authorized in the federal budget, though a massive $50 billion, is inadequate to finance the school improvements imposed by the law, once the states pay for testing and reading programs. Policy researchers estimated that only nine states already had assessment programs that matched what the federal government had just mandated.[15]

The capture of authority over schools by the Federal government took place largely out of sight. Although the congressional debates were public, people would have to watch days of C-Span and even then, they would have encountered discourse that was skewed and symbolic. The commit-tees were stacked from the outset with members already favorable to na-tional testing and basic skills teaching. The staff fed lines to the legislators and made sure that only those who were known advocates of those per-spectives got to testify. Anyone stating alternative research or experience was excluded and deprecated. Furthermore, precious few of the public could have known—even if they shared the perspectives underlying the legislation—that the bills fundamentally altered the authority structure of public schools that had existed since the advent of public schools.

Should people be concerned? When the federal government and its allies in the corporate world possess so much control over public schools, there is little left for parents and the public to participate in the decisions that affect children. Democracy requires that each citizen possess equal power to partic-ipate in discussions of policies that concern them, as Thomas Jefferson said.

IX. Education Policy Suffers Because Mass Media Are Concentrated in the Hands of a Few Corporations That Pursue Profits

Both Democrats and Republicans supported legislation that removed restric-tions on media corporations. As far as the public knew, those laws were meant to increase competition, but had the opposite effect. Now both print and elec-tronic media operate as semi-monopolies that can eliminate competition and control the flow of information to the public. The music, television, radio, and newspaper industries are owned by a half-dozen conglomerates with enormous wealth and political power. The political process that resulted in media conglomeration was conducted out of public awareness. When media did reveal aspects of the Telecommunications Act of 1996, they emphasized congressional worries about indecency. What they did not cover was who stood to gain and lose by the provisions of the act. Likewise, government ac-tion in 1999 ensured that the Internet lost its essence of democracy and free-dom (what its authors originally intended it to be) in favor of commercial advertising and corporations' control of entry portals.

Why is this evidence so important in understanding political spectacle? The most powerful media interests set advertising costs including the costs of political campaign advertising. High advertising costs make it necessary for politicians to seek large campaign contributions, thus skewing discourse and obligation toward elites and corporations. Successful politicians then intercede on behalf of big media to resist regulations—regulations that might require that the corporations provide free airtime for all politicians, including those from minority parties.

Big media pursue profits over the public interests, attending to what sells papers and attracts viewers. Thus they focus less and less time and space on hard news, especially world news, and more on the lives of celebrities (including corporate moguls), scandals, sports, instructions on how the public should arrange their lives, as well as grisly crimes and disasters, both natural and man-made. Instead of in-depth discussion of national issues, with enough context and background for people to understand them, they provide the public with short bursts of contentious debates among opinion-makers who move from network to network. Contemporary media concentrate on the ever changing, up-to-the-minute crisis, meat for spectacle. To the vast corporations that control the media, anything that is unprofitable gets cut; as a result, public television and radio—their independence and public funding already reduced—have short futures.

Thus corporate media control information, reducing access of ordinary people to hard news and international perspectives. During the "war on terrorism" (two loaded words characteristic of political spectacle) of 2001–2002, the Pentagon denied reporters access to battlefields, spoon-fed them reports that neglected civilian casualties, and satisfied their hunger for video by supplying file footage of Gulf War battles. Although it pales in comparison with the war, education reform also earns only surface platitudes from the media. During the push for the No Child Left Behind legislation, television focused lenses on the President reading books to school children but neglected to report the vested interests of textbook and test publishers (which are themselves siblings in the family of media conglomerates).

The public can no longer count on investigative reporting, let alone critical investigative reporting about education policy, to reveal the interconnections of schools, government, and corporations. Reporters and editors shy away from reporting on problematic issues of their corporate owners, as McChesney showed. America still enjoys freedom of the press, but now journalists censor themselves. Media critics and journalists outside the mainstream must rely on the Internet to diffuse any contrary message.

Calling the media liberal in bias is nothing but old news—a neo-conservative canard. The essence of contemporary media is corporate and commercial. Corporations aim to offend no one, to take the middle ground on all political issues in order to increase market share and to avoid annoying big advertisers and owners. Consider the coincidence of events in February, 2002. The FCC removed the regulation that restrained the media giants from acquiring individual stations. Ten days later ABC proposed to replace the news program, *Nightline*, with *the David Letterman Show*. The owner of ABC, Disney, failed to inform the head of its own news division. Disney executives wanted viewers to wake up to the same channel they had been watching when they went to bed. They believed this was a way to improve corporate profitability. An executive sneered at any "sentimental" decision to preserve news at the expense of profits.

What has this to do with education policy? Democratic participation depends on solid information. But media follow their own conventions, which usually means entertaining features and dramatic "crises." There is so much advertising and mindless entertainment that we forget that there is something that we might be doing about schools.

X. Politicized Research Bodies Ill for Education Policy

In political contexts, research functions politically. Define class size as ratio of pupils to teachers in a classroom, and researchers show that smaller classes lead to higher achievement. Define class size as the ratio of pupils to professionals in a school, and researchers show the opposite, though each study may be methodologically competent within its own sphere of assumptions. It is a fact of life in the social sciences that different studies yield alternative outcomes. In the political spectacle the selection of definitions, measures, and methods form patterns with political interests.

Policy research enters the political arena in several ways. First, a study often functions more as a symbol than as a source of scientific knowledge. Just to quote a study makes a political actor appear rational and reasonable as if he or she looked to science for policy answers. For this purpose, a technically bad study is just as good as a technically competent one. Lisa Graham Keegan could assert that research had shown vouchers to be effective and fair. The fact that the voucher studies might have been less than technically fine, and in fact were the subject of substantive and technical controversy, did not have to come into the conversation. President George W. Bush and his Secretary of Education Rodney Paige could answer any criticism about the possible effects of the Reading Excellence Act by drawing the questioner's attention to the studies commissioned by the Texas Education Agency, not withstanding that agencies and researchers with obvious interest and investment in the outcome had conducted the studies. President Bush was able to claim that "we know" how to teach kids to read because of the Texas studies, even though the evidence of those studies loses credibility the closer one examines them.

Research has been co-opted. Government, rather than professional researchers, controls what research receives funding and what research is considered valid. Now we researchers are discovering what teachers and teacher educators must feel when their professional standards and definitions are hijacked from them.

Think tanks and political foundations fund research studies. But unlike scientists, they don't do so to find the truth, one way or the other. They purchase results compatible with their interests. They create a market for research and researchers and then control it. Most education policy researchers have little expectation for having their work supported or for getting rich as a result of it. They usually write books "on spec" with hope that they will be published. Rarely do books meant for professional audiences (trade books) make money. However, the most well-endowed foundations—usually conservative ones—sponsor their own publishing houses, provide up-front contracts to likeminded scholars or would-be scholars so that they will receive money while their work is progressing, ensure publication and wide-spread dissemination and marketing in addition to opportunities for paid speaking engagements, with the authors then receiving the usual book royalties later. The public is led to believe that the work is pure science; nor are they aware of the cushy relationship of researchers to foundations and think tanks. The profession of education researchers—which has the most to lose or gain at the loss of authority that the government take-over portents—makes no protest.

The evidence in this book strongly suggests that political interests shape policy far more than does research, and furthermore that political interests shape research itself. The body of evidence—from outside the network of think tanks—is clear about the negative effects of requiring students to repeat their grades if they fail a test. The vast majority of studies conclude that grade retention fails to increase students' achievement and increases the chances of those students dropping out. Moreover, the sad history of failed policies of mandatory retention is well recorded. As recently as the 1980s, New York City mandated grade retention for failing students but soon had to retract the policy because of its unanticipated negative consequences.

Nevertheless, the current popularity among politicians for policies to end social promotion renders them blind to research and experience. Scholars who served in the last three presidential administrations developed selective amnesia. They both "knew" and did not know, in Orwell's terms, that retention does more academic harm than good. The fervor of their leaders to end social promotion trumped their scholarly knowledge, a blinding that also explains their lack of acknowledgement of research and experience on the negative effects of high-stakes testing and vouchers.

Yet another example of selective information-gathering and faulty memory is the case of research on teaching children to read. Politicians were already convinced about the "one correct method" and failed to deliberate with researchers and practitioners on the other side of the debate. State and federal governments sponsored research and development that slanted the argument toward one side and excluded, condemned, and chastised scholars and research on the other side. Politics and economic interests aside, any fair reading of the evidence leads to the conclusion that neither side prevails. In such a situation (we are also thinking of the controversies on the efficacy of mammography) where the research is equivocal, policies should hedge their bets and support neither or both sides. But politics are never aside, so that the side of the reading debate with the most power won a great victory. So great was that victory that the winning side now has the power and will to suppress further research that might threaten it, and moreover, to define what research is valid and worthwhile.

Even though some researchers attempt to stay out of the political process, they contribute to the politicization of their work by insisting that their own studies are definitive and that researchers with contrary evidence are simply wrong. This kind of discourse sets up a dialectic that hardens into fixed perspectives. Research becomes politicized when the will to certainty intersects the will to power. Researchers aspire to positive knowledge—conclusive and even exclusive. Any researcher has ambitions that her study will provide a definitive answer to a question. But social science never achieves certainty. Too often, then, when studies on a topic conflict, the discourse turns ugly. Rather than admitting that one's own study falls short of certainty, researchers resort to crude name-calling. One researcher declares, "My study is objective and her study is biased." Or, "His study used outmoded or flawed methodology and is therefore worthless."

Such talk takes what ought to be a rational dialogue among colleagues and turns it into dialectic in which only one of the researchers and one of the studies can be true and correct and competent. Such talk prohibits a discussion in which experts might dig into the guts of a study to figure out how—by using method A—finding 1 was inevitable and finding 2 was impossible. Or, how the selection of sample X rather than sample Y prevents one from generalizing to a different population. Or, how the context in which a study took place makes it difficult to apply to alternative contexts. These are the ordinary analyses that methodologists pursue, yet in a policy context, a researcher risks her authority and status and usefulness to policy makers if she admits any such contingent or less-than definitive conclusions. Instead the different methods and conclusions of the two studies becomes an arena for competition, a winner-take-all battle over whose "science" triumphs (and wins prizes). Thus, politics gobble up science and turns it into politics.

Political opponents find such conflicts familiar. After all, the winner in a political contest gets to—often exclusively—allocate values. Inconclusive knowledge is something that politicians cannot use. A winning party needs a "winning" science.

This feeds into the conventions of mass media, which love to stage conflicts. A reporter gets wind of a new study and calls the author for a quotation. Then he or she calls a researcher with an alternative point of view and sets the stage for a debate among experts that is largely free of the substance of the study itself. For example, when the question of class size comes up, a reporter may call Jeremy Finn who will claim that reducing class size improves achievement. Then the reporter calls Hanushek who says the opposite. The difference between their positions is a straightforward one—alternative definition of class size, but the reporter rarely digs that out. What the public reads is a stand-off.

Differences among studies on any topic are a fact of life in social sciences. But in a political context, when studies differ, each side throws projectiles at each other and maintains the truth and applicability of its own conclusion. Policy makers choose up sides and throw their political weight behind one or the other, often declaring that their favorite researcher's science is better than the opposition's. This is not the only way to meld policy with research that fails to reach a consensus. The Precautionary Principle is followed in Europe in matters of environmental policy. Until science settles on a single conclusion, policy makers choose a course that they believe results in the least risk. If U.S. policy on reading had followed the precautionary principle, given that the research is a wash, it would have encouraged and funded a variety of approaches. Instead, it declared that one side had the best science and threw its authority behind a single approach.

Orwell wrote in *1984* that freedom is the freedom to say that two plus two does not equal five. But when dealing with policy on a grand scale, research evidence functions primarily as a symbol and tool of political dominion, hiding, of course, behind the name of "science."

What do these lessons portend?

The Fate of American Schools

> *Wake up to what our schools really are: drill centers for the habits*
> *that corporate society demands . . . to turn them into servants.*
> John Taylor Gatt, "Against School," *Harpers*

The No Child Left Behind Act centralized and standardized federal control over what schools must strive for, what schools must teach, how they must teach it, how the consequences of schools should be judged, and the mechanisms for enforcing them to comply and conform. This law imposed extensive, detailed regulations that matched its intent and heavy penalties on those states and schools that failed to comply. Administrators of the law were appointed especially for the consistencies of their philosophies with the law and their zeal to enforce it. Discretion is limited to those schools that can afford it.

Only about three states had, as of 2002, testing programs in place that matched the federal requirements for testing every student in grades three through eight on reading and math. The rest were required to develop tests that would calibrate with the National Assessment of Educational Progress. Most states had to adopt reading programs to confirm to requirements of Reading First, the federal program that mandates phonics-first as the method of teaching reading. These mandates, mostly unfunded, consume money that states might otherwise have spent on other things more likely to improve schools, such as upgrading teachers' competence and compensation, decreasing class size, or providing all-day kindergarten.

The penalties for failure to improve students' academic proficiency are severe and biased toward privatization. The system for determining which schools failed was rigged to make most schools (up to 80 percent by some calculations) appear to fail, simply because of artifacts in tests themselves; that is, because of statistical artifacts rather than some underlying degree of effectiveness. Students in "failing" schools become eligible for vouchers to be spent by parents at other schools and for after-school programs and the like, run by private, parochial, and for-profit schools.

The specificity of the program, the systemic quality of the law and its implementation, and the severity of its penalties mean that schools will find it hard to wiggle out of high-stakes testing and a rigorous, traditional, standardized curriculum focused on the most basic academic skills of reading and arithmetic.

If even some of the research on the effects of state policies is true, then we can expect some of the following consequences of Federal policies. Privitization policies produce more stratified and segregated schools without any of the supposed benefits of competition on neighborhood public schools. High-stakes assessment policies narrow the curriculum, knock out whole subjects such as science, art, and social studies, restrict instruction to the most standardized and restricted kinds, de-skill and de-professionalize teachers, absorb vast amount of instructional time and energies in preparing for, and taking, mandated tests, and inflate test scores in such a way that adequate information is distorted. Using test results to determine grade promotion and graduation increases the proportion of students who drop out of school rather than graduate. Phonics-first reading programs yield some positive effects, but only on the simple reading skills that make up part of reading, and not for all students, and not on any broader kind of literacy. We regard these policy effects as official, authoritatively allocated, damage. These conditions intersect and, we believe, will yield alternative fates to three kinds of schools.

The first category of schools (Category A) consists of public schools that command resources sufficient to shield themselves from the worst depredations of federal policy. Category B consists of non-public schools that profit from Federal and state privitization policies and administrative regulations. Category C schools consist of the remainder of public schools.

Category A schools exist in places with adequate financial bases, usually depending on property taxes that advantage themselves and disadvantage urban schools. Even when state funds are less than adequate, wealthy parents make up with private donations what the state fails to fund. The costs of unfunded mandates make up a smaller (compared to schools in category B) percentage of funds available, so that schools can still purchase supplementary materials, maintain libraries, and provide nearly the same kinds of educational opportunities to students attending them. Students come to school with greater levels of literacy and social experiences and require that fewer dollars be spent on special programs, such as programs for English language learners or programs for the economically disadvantaged. In particular, the special education population is likely to be a few percentage points lower, and it generally takes 2.5 times more money to educate a special needs child than a regular education child. Parents with fiscal capital overcome many of the effects of birth defects and handicapping events that affect their children during their pre-school years. Parents with cultural capital ward off the worst of the effects of high-stakes testing, and effectively resist government mandates of which they disapprove. These schools take advantage of correlation between social class and achievement test scores, and bask in the glow—however false—that high scores provide. This impression of effectiveness insulates schools from the worst of government mandates. They have latitude to follow (if they choose) more progressive forms of education and broader kinds of educational goals. The positive climate of these schools attracts a more competent and stable population of teachers.

Schools in Category B are populated by students whose parents took advantage of privitization policies to leave public schools behind. Private schools, parochial schools, home schools, virtual schools, and schools that operate for profit pursue their own visions of curriculum, their own visions of school organization, free from federal mandates and regulations.

Schools in Category C are likely to suffer the worse depredations of federal policies. Compared to schools in Category A, these schools are less likely to receive adequate funding, even before federal policies make things worse. As a result of federal and state testing policies they must devote a larger percentage of the funds they have available to copy tests and materials that prepare students to take them. Because their students score low anyway—because of the bias built into our society and our achievement tests—they are forced to spend more time in test preparation and more resources on remediation for those who fail.

Negative effects of high-stakes testing policies fall most heavily on students of poverty and color. Since achievement tests discriminate against these children, average scores of their schools will be lower. As a consequence, the states put most pressure on those schools to raise scores. Those schools then devote more time teaching to the test. They neglect broader content. They spend their limited funds on test preparation materials, software, consultants who hold pep rallies, Saturday and after-school "academies," and so on, even when their available text books are decades out of date and their library shelves empty. Jean Anyon observed about schools in

Newark that reforms followed each other like tides. Just as teachers were beginning to understand and implement one new mandated policy, a new one would come in and take its place. Books would finally arrive for the now-defunct program just in time that the new reform demanded new texts. Teachers felt overwhelmed, off-balance, incapable of learning about each program, bereft of training and support.

For those left behind in "C" schools an accountability system based on test scores will almost always punish disadvantaged schools and pupils, regardless of mitigating circumstances or the quality of the teachers. What this means is that children in these schools will suffer the mindless repetition of the dumbed-down curriculum and the curriculum based almost entirely of teaching to the test. George Madaus discovered some time ago that children of color and poverty were much more likely to get impoverished curricula and continuous preparation for tests.[16] Linda McNeil and Angela Venezuela showed this condition has worsened. The National Research Council confirmed this from evidence from Chicago Public Schools. Teachers and principals in poor neighborhoods—the ones under the most external pressure to raise scores—are the ones first relieved of their positions. Or, if they are good, they can find a less demoralized school climate in the suburbs. In Texas, principals lost their tenure rights, so that school boards can fire and replace them if they fail to lift their school's scores. Schools in Category C are more likely to be targets of policies that require states to take over their operations and replace their superintendents and boards of education. But there is little evidence that shows these changes in governance have much effect on the quality of schools. What they do accomplish is to impose a chaotic climate of constant change.

Schools in Category C are so short of money that they must comply with federal regulations that specify the kinds of curricula that they can offer. This means that a large proportion of their funds will be consumed by purchasing massive curriculum packages like Open Court, and that little money is left over to supplement this narrow vision of schooling. However, the positive results of programs such as these are far from guaranteed. In programs such as Open Court, teachers must follow scripts religiously, and teachers with richer perspectives on teaching have little incentive to stay in these schools and, given teacher shortages, positive incentives to move to schools in the other categories.

Schools in Category C are strapped for funds, and federal money for Title I programs are granted contingent on a school's compliance with mandates for testing and reading instruction. These are the schools most likely to enter into performance agreements with corporations to advertise and promote the purchase of potato chips, candy, and soft drinks. These schools have few choices.

In theory, of course, families whose children attend schools in Category C have choices. They can spend their vouchers elsewhere. In practice, however, it is the private schools that have the choice of students, given current and foreseeable markets. Schools in Category C will not wither away under the forces of market competition, but they will continue to suffer from the neglect of the state.

Families whose children attend schools in Category A and Category B resemble each other in what Richard Rorty called "the succession of the successful" from public institutions. Anyon's history of Newark public schools demonstrates the centripetal course that advantaged parents followed—away from commons and commoners. Industrial leaders moved their families from the core to the periphery of the city, later from the periphery to the suburbs. The fathers commuted by trolley, later by car, from their homes to their factories, passing within sight of the increasingly congested and poor neighborhoods. Wives and children of the industrialists lost visual access to the neighborhoods and schools they had left behind. Later still, the industrialists moved the factories themselves away from the city. They lost, therefore, even the chance to see the conditions they created and abandoned.

No matter how much political conservatives dress up school choice in the language of equity and liberty and free market, the sad truth is that not every parent will have choices, will make choices, or will make informed choices. Not every parent will make choices that further the common good or insure that the best educational choices will be available to all. The fate of American schools is in the hands of people with the most cultural and political capital. And they are using their capital in ways that further separate, segregate, and differentiate opportunities. Wealth and cultural capital will diverge even more, following its entropic course.

What happens when advantaged families abandon urban public schools? Those who leave often grow detached and distant, no longer making even visual contact. They see no reason to support less advantaged schools, no longer feel the connections that bind people together, for better or worse. They even invent justifications for why the poor deserve less than what their own children get from schools.

A more separated, segregated, unfairly supported system—one more calculated to provide a rich education to the rich and a poor education for the poor—could not be created if someone now set out to design one. A judge in New York told the truth about American willingness to tolerate the differences that only a blind person could miss. A lower court had declared that New York's methods for funding schools violated the constitutional guarantee of equal funding. It ruled that some schools were so poorly funded that they could not provide an effective education toward state standards. The appellate court in July, 2002 overturned that ruling, holding that the state had fulfilled its duty to "provide sound basic education" if students had enough education to qualify for jobs as fast food cooks and messengers. Speaking for the majority, the judge reasoned, "Society needs workers in all levels of jobs, the majority of which may be low-level." An eighth grade education is about right, reasoned the justices, to enable people to serve on juries and stay off welfare.[17]

Because private schools are able to avoid scrutiny, as they have already avoided it in Milwaukee and Florida, the whole breaking up will all happen off-stage. Meanwhile, even if existing and new voucher schools meet the demand of some parents to enroll their children there, some children will remain in neighborhood schools. These schools are likely to exist in a more impoverished condition. Are we willing to tolerate the conditions these children are likely to face, the conditions that we would not tolerate for our own children?

Perhaps the cruelest irony is that siphoning public money from public schools to reimburse parents for private school tuition purports to help poor and minority children. Voucher advocates make a good case that poor children should not be trapped in poorly performing schools in their neighborhood. But their argument is merely a pretext for public funding of religious and private schools for their own children (as we observed in Boulder) and having a private school education paid for from the public treasury. A more honest appeal would be to demand that all children receive a quality education, the same as what they would want for their own. A familiar neo-conservative and religious conservative doctrine holds that right-thinking parents must protect their children from the sin and degradation of the community, even as the Lord will divide the sheep from the goats.

The End of Policy

> *Reports of the death of reality [suggest] that everyone is a spectator . . .*
> *that there is no real suffering in the world.*
> Susan Sontag, *Regarding the Pain of Others*

The lessons recounted above seem shockingly pessimistic. If you believe any or all of them, what might you do? It is tempting to sit back and say to yourself, "It's all politics, all politicians are the same, it was ever true, the poor will always be with us." But cynicism and defeatism are part of, and exacerbate, the political spectacle. It is important to be clear-eyed and wide-awake about how the real allocation of values occurs largely out of sight of the public and benefits the few while burdening the many.

Certainly, cynicism and defeatism are natural responses when there are such tight interconnections among neo-conservatives, religious conservatives, neo-liberals and their foundations, designated researchers and authors, all backed by massive funds of the largest corporations to whom politicians of both parties are indebted—all more or less working in the same direction. Their actions could not have been so effective in the clear light of day. Political spectacle obscures them in nearly impenetrable fog. Neither honest journalists nor policy researchers are able to clear away that fog.

The strong interconnections of these groups, against the backdrop of structural inequalities in the society, make normal policy work close to impossible for anyone hoping for more progressive policies. Gone are the days when scholars could study an issue, make a report to policy makers, and have any expectations that things might change for the better. Now we are lucky enough to get a hearing and in that hearing not be chastised and denigrated for suggesting any reform—no matter how clear the evidence of its efficacy—that departs in the least from the dominant political agenda.

Lorrie Shepard reminded us of those somewhat good-old-days. We did research on kindergarten readiness, and policy and practice changed for the better as a result of our work: fewer readiness tests, fewer kindergarten retention, some better understanding of the predictability that a child retained in grade grows into the adolescent who drops out of school. That view of policy seems quaint.

The No Child Left Behind legislation closed off possibilities for scholars and others to speak truth—or at least evidence—to policy makers and make schools better. And by better we mean schools that provide more nearly equal opportunities to everyone, schools that offer science, art, literature, schools that help students become broadly literate, well-rounded adults, not only able to feed the labor pool but to develop good lives and participate politically for themselves and their communities. Our reading of the current legislation leads us to believe that it pushes schools away from that ideal. We are out of step with what Rodney Paige called "the plan."

So if you want to make things better, don't bother calling the governor or briefing your senator or doing a study—all worthy activities—expecting that the state will change policy toward bilingual education or whole language or conceptual math or racially integrated schools without tracks. Don't expect to halt the centripetal force toward privatization. Those things aren't part of the plan.

In the political world after September 11, 2001, the approval rating of President Bush rose precipitously. Much was made of the need to support our commander in chief. You heard this: Now is not the time to criticize policy, while there's a war on (in spite of the inability of anyone to define the war as a war or to say how the nation would know that it had ended). Yet the Bush administration missed few chances to use the war as a pretext to advance proposals unrelated to the war; for example, repeal of the capital gains tax, confirmation of controversial judicial appointments, passing the economic stimulus package, privatizing social security. Less than a week after the terrorist strike on the World Trade Center, President Bush urged Congress to finalize his proposal for high stakes national testing. His tortured argument linked high academic achievement to economic growth and economic growth to national defense.

What is the possibility of change? Education policy is so thoroughly entrenched in a network of related government officials, corporate leaders, researchers, publishers, and their allies that democratic participation by ordinary people is all but impossible. Indeed, it is only with difficulty that one can think of American democracy at all. A more appropriate label might be oligarchy: a small group of insiders powerful enough to determine policy. And the processes they use are well hidden. The media have little incentive to report what happens, what alternatives are considered, who may benefit and who bears the risks and costs. Research is little more than a tactic of the regime; researchers provide the results desired by the regime or risk losing future contracts, funds, and access. Even the best, most even-handed and circumspect policy researchers lose credibility when they remain silent while others steal their authority and define what is science. In the political spectacle, "junk science" is whatever research one's political opponent reports.

Imagine any scenario that might culminate in a rationalist, democratic, instrumental reconsideration of the policy to test every school child from third to eighth grade. How much political power would it take to accomplish this feat? Would the process meet with resistance, backstage negotiation, financial, and ideological interests? Who would benefit? How could the public even define and calculate the gains and losses? Would the test and textbook publishers sit as equals around a table with ordinary people—parents with schoolchildren or teachers—and deliberate with them as equals while profits were risked?

We find it hard to imagine such a scenario. Any attempt at, for example, redistributing finances among rich and poor schools—or for that matter, providing high quality, universal kindergarten, delegating responsibilities for schools to local parents and professionals, reducing the ratio of children to teachers, while upholding the qualifications of teachers in those classes, removing advertising and commercials from schools, reinstating goals of civic capacity—would fall under the theatrical spell, the screenplay and cast of characters; relapse into symbols and ambiguous language, and hide material transaction backstage.

Tight interconnections among government and corporations, government and schools, researchers, and media came about under cover of political spectacle and they sustain political spectacle. The passing of the No Child Left Behind Act closed the circle. The exclusive definitions and regulations of these laws and the placement of advocates in the administrative offices that translate and enforce them leave little room for a progressive policy agenda. Proscriptions on the content and methods of research drive out new knowledge that might cast doubt on the dominant themes and prevent prospective researchers from examining issues from a broader perspective. The professional associations of both educational researchers and testing experts have done little to reclaim cultural authority to define standards and nothing to enforce practice. The professional associations in which educators participate are hamstrung. They must fight against persistent charges that they defend the mediocre status quo, that they work only in their self-interest and that they resist policies to privatize schools.

Guerilla Theater

What then must we do?
Luke III, 10

We have offered a pessimistic view of the prospects of changing the shape of education policy and schools. The social structures that tie together economics, labor, and government determine the shape of schooling and render it stable over long periods of time. Political spectacle obscures the undercover work of the few merged elites behind the symbols constructed to distract and distance the rest of us from knowing about the conditions of schooling and participating in policy making.

But there are other ways to look at change besides the structural view offered so far. Instead of simple determinism one can think of change as the complex series of events and interactions that occur in contexts of time and place, that gradually accrete (or not), and may lead to change. Humans take action. Events occur. The causes of change in relation to policy targets occur not in a closed system. Rather, events, and human reactions to the events occur in an unfolding, contingent, and interdependent sequence of big and small happenings within a sociopolitical context. This is a far more optimistic view of society and of education policy.

Stephan J. Gould, paleontologist and philosopher of science, asks us to imagine a tape recording. Rewind the recording to some point in the past, change one event and inquire whether subsequent events would play out in exactly the same way.[18] Gould's thought experiment works in historical research. What would have happened if Suleiman had not paused and then turned back from his assault on Byzantium and hence Eastern Europe? And how does one explain what happened? The thought experiment also works if we consider what made a policy turn out the way it did. Effects of policy programs depend on a certain things occurring or co-occurring along the way—things that can be neither predicted nor controlled. Would things have played out the same in Tennessee if the legislators had not included the teachers in planning STAR, if a different combination of legislators had been elected, if a surplus had not been available in state budget, if around a bargaining table, stake holders had defined class size differently than they did? To answer, one must arrange all these happenings and conditions chronologically and weigh alternative explanations.

History supports the view that series of events can unlock even the most tightly woven net. The condition of politics and the degree of political spectacle have not been constant and inevitable. The 1930s and 1960s were times of strong democracy and relative economic equality. The current era is more like the 1880s and 1920s, with the significant economic inequalities of those eras, which flow into educational inequalities, an increasingly atomized and distanced electorate, and politics that seem like theatrical entertainment.

As we wrote in the first chapter and repeat here, the political spectacle represents the cultural intersection of governance, the economy, and media at a given time. During strong democratic eras (such as the 1930s and 1960s), citizens vote more often, most citizens participate in organizations—parties, unions, business associations —that compete for policy values (with government acting as referee among competing groups). There is a powerful sense of the common good. The public has the best chance of influencing policy formation and government generally. Ordinary citizens enjoy individual rights and freedoms, including the right to vote in elections. Public institutions exist to provide checks on the power of markets or religion. The language of politics is the language of concrete phenomena. Citizens bid for honest allocation of values and costs, and officials operate more often in the open than backstage. Citizens have more access to information about how values get allocated and more chances to contest unfair or irrational actions by government.

Transitions between times of weak and strong democracy often take place when social inequities are at their worst, exacerbated by the excesses of political and business elites. Consider the state of American politics in 1900. McKinley's administration looked very similar to today's oligarchic merger of corporate power with government power, exploitation of labor and the environment, and policies that work for the special rather than the common good. Free market ideologies provided a screen for corporatism, construction of great individual fortunes, and impoverishment and diminished security for ordinary people. Based on social structural explanations, one would have predicted a stable future—more of the same. A chance event brought Theodore Roosevelt to the presidency. And although he was far from a paragon of progressive virtue, at least he committed his administration to renewal of labor rights and the preservation of the natural environment. He contested the dominance of the corporate moguls by challenging monopolistic practices, trusts, and combinations. A chance event set these changes in motion, but they could not have been sustained without a public prepared for them.

America has seen such salient changes in the hours when structural stability seemed impregnable. Then, something happens to provoke other things to alter the social landscape. Consider the time of the McCarthy hearings in the 1950s. One witness's laughing denunciation of the Senator broke his stranglehold on rhetoric and action. America has seen such salient changes in the hours when structure seemed to have strangled political agency. What might that mean for education policy?

The world according to Gould—the world where events result from complex, contingent, sometimes unpredictable progressions of events—is also the world of the Tipping Point theory. Malcolm Gladwell's popular rendering of social epidemics proposes that significant changes can happen—not gradually but "at one dramatic moment" as a result of contagion, often from a small, marginal, and seemingly insignificant progression.[19]

In education policy the connections between corporations and government, power and money, class and education now seem tight and deterministic and obscured in the political spectacle. Perhaps we should look to the more open systems described by Gould and Gladwell. That is, we should devote our intentions and efforts away from the grand, systemic change from the top.

Gladwell wrote that social epidemics start with small causes and depend on people with gifts to engage in particular kinds of action. They depend on Connectors, socially charismatic people at the center of large networks of people, who can bring people together from different walks of life and spread the word about the new thing. Social epidemics depend on Mavens, individuals with the message, who have a rich store of facts and can recognize trends and possible points where an entry can be made. They package and pass along specialized information they collect. Mavens also know the technologies for getting out the message, can channel relevant information and sort out relevant information from the millions of noisy bits—almost like a portal and hyperlinks on the Internet. Salesmen are those who persuade people to join in and adopt the new thing. They must provide energy, enthusiasm, and optimism; point out the concrete benefits of the new thing.

But the object of the planned contagion must have "stickiness." By that Gladwell means substance, concrete effects, not just abstract concepts. To have stickiness requires an agent who continuously examines the thing in action to see how to revise it for the better. He uses *Sesame Street* as an example of an intentional contagion with all these elements. With few precedents and little predictability, children's educational television was developed, tested in concrete experience, refined, and eventually made major changes in children's programming. To illustrate further the power of small causes that make sudden, significant effects, Gladwell cites the experience of New York City, in which officials made a substantial impact on the crime rate by seemingly small changes, such as fixing broken windows and cleaning up graffiti, prosecuting people who defaced subway facilities or jumped turnstiles to beat the fares. These actions had little to do with broad structural changes like addressing poverty or racism.

Taking this theory and these examples, what if the "thing" that you want to effect has to do with education; say, ending the deleterious effects of high-stakes testing on students of poverty and color. What would you do? If you sit back and wait for a change in regimes, you stand to lose an entire generation of children who drop out of school rather than confront the same exit test for the nth time.

What is the cumulative effect when more words—printed in trade books like this one—merely add to the political spectacle? Here are three answers.

Clarity is the Antidote to Political Spectacle

The political spectacle thrives in the dark, nurtured on secrets backstage. From the point of view of the audience, the only light is the spot light that the director controls. Dissenters must do everything they can to shed light on the details of everyday life as students and teachers experience it. To counter the political spectacle, one must understand the particulars of everyday life both for the schools and for the hidden corners where policy is made. Maxine Greene called for "wide-awakeness."[20]

Art is the Antidote to Political Spectacle

In the late stages of his career, Murray Edelman wrote the book *Art and Politics*. In it he argued that art sometimes serves the political spectacle by supplying banal, repetitive, propagandistic images that deaden critical response on the part of the public. Yet art also awakens perceptions and sensibilities that political language and ritual have put to sleep. Art transforms experience and helps people look at the world—and the condition of public schools—in new ways and to question the pat answers that politicians dole out. Art is thus provocative and potentially subversive. Seamus Heaney wrote that art functions to make people aware of the depredations of society yet also has "the paradoxical effect of raising spirits and creating hope":

> Activists have different priorities than artists do, but they, too, are forced to acknowledge the prevalence of the atrocious while maintaining faith in the possibility of the desired.[21]

Art gives people fresh ways to look at the events of everyday life and a new way to consider the conditions of politics and schools.

Political Actions Is the Antidote to Political Spectacle

Political spectacle swims in language and symbolism. The corrective for political spectacle is direct action. By supporting the kinds of programs and candidates that support democracy and community, one combats political spectacle and its deleterious effects on public schools. Some of these are: alternative political parties, living wage programs, attainable housing, reform of corporate welfare and campaign finance, micro-financing, micro-radio and -television, voter registration and voter rights, and free political advertising. Thus, direct political action toward promoting a more robust democracy and social well-being eventually undergirds education policy, whereas, endless discussions and papers about education policy have little effect on the conditions of democratic society, and hence, make little impact on schools. What might?

The Praxis Project

Scholars might change the ratio of their words to their direct actions. They might assist and support projects that might potentially lead to changes from the margins. They might become or recruit Connectors, Mavens, and Sales persons to create social epidemics and then help to sustain them against the opposition they will certainly attract. They might look for points at which separate projects overlap, so that volunteerism can be moved to the political level. They might help to diffuse communications technology so that these groups could keep in touch and recognize a common trajectory and purpose. They might function as friendly critics or formative evaluators to improve the stickiness and substance of these projects. Since it is impossible to know for sure where the tipping point might be, a large fleet of different projects might be launched.

Progressive scholars and others must challenge the ambiguities and distortions of the political spectacle whenever they encounter them—challenge them by pointing out their specious referents and substituting more credible referents, the concrete particulars of everyday life. They might act as investigative journalists to uncover and reveal the backstage allocation of values that the political spectacle conceals. Gerald Bracey, Michelle Fine, Alex Molnar, and David Berliner cannot be cloned, but they can be emulated. They might become the mavens for creating what Apple called "heretical alliances"—tactical joint operations between organizations that ordinarily propose divergent goals and tend to avoid, even loath each other. Apple cited as an example the temporary alliance of Ralph Nader with Phyllis Schafly to oppose Channel One.[22]

Understanding that improving schools is complex, expensive, and tied into improving social life generally, we can poke holes in the slogans that politicians spout in lieu of authentic reforms. Understanding that reforming schools with top-down mandates causes more harm than good, we can support local changes that come about by building local capacity and will. Understanding that dictatorial mandates from the courts and governments rarely result in real improvements, we must engage in local democracy—persuading people that it is in their best interests to work toward the good of all children in all schools.

The Literacy Restoration Project
High-stakes testing deprives students of science, social studies, and the arts; excessively absorbs instructional time, reduces instruction to repetitious, test-like work sheets and test preparation. Standardized, highly scripted programs like Open Court deny students opportunities to read real books, write, think, solve problems, and ask critical questions. The pro-phonics perspective requires that all students master the narrowest little skills first— *before* they get books. Credible evidence shows that experiencing books is the cause of children's comprehension of books. Neglecting this evidence, programs like Open Court become total institutions. They deprive teachers of the responsibility to choose materials and methods suited for their own students. Those programs absorb so much of the school day and so much of the school budget that little of either is left over.

Many teachers feel angry and guilty because, by following state and federal mandates, they deprive children of opportunities to become literate through reading and writing. Some teachers now provide those opportunities voluntarily, outside of school time. What if concerned professors and community members joined teachers in various private enterprises to restore literacy to children's lives, through book clubs, literacy circles, poetry readings, theater programs, school gardens, affiliates of Habitat for Humanity, or science clubs? The possibilities are many, but they are outside the policy arena. They become political when the separate groups form a network of participants in communication with each other.

If teachers seem unlikely to do this work, there exists an army of people in any city that are trained and certified as teachers, but have retired or left schools for other occupations. If even a portion of this group retains the passion for working with students (in less bureaucratic contexts, perhaps), someone could recruit and organize them for after-school teaching projects.

The Test Resistance Project
David Berliner once addressed a public meeting to discuss dissatisfactions with the AIMS test. The meeting took place in upscale Scottsdale and he told them the best way to get rid of the tests was for upscale parents to keep

their kids home on test days and to draw as much media attention as they could. Eugene Garcia, as Dean at University of California-Berkeley, recommended that Hispanic families refuse to participate in state tests. Local and state resistance groups operate in many states, in many forms, and with various motivations. So far they have no network, although FAIRTEST, a private organization, provides a communication framework that could link the groups together and provide formidable political opposition to the factory model of schooling whose logical end is high-stakes testing. Professors can contribute by writing briefs and linking the organization to the best evidence and resources available.

The Alternative Accountability Project
The public has a reasonable right to ask that schools demonstrate their effectiveness. That said, we know that mandated tests fail to provide valid information and produce adverse effects on the curriculum. Is this a paradox? Some say that the progressive education movement and later the whole language movement failed to "stick" because they did not provide alternative ways to demonstrate the qualities of their programs. Perhaps experts concerned about traditional tests might work with progressive teachers to devise credible ways to demonstrate the progress they see in classes. In her presidential address to the American Educational Research Association, Lorrie Shepard provided a model for helping teachers construct assessments and use them to advance instruction as well as to display the nature of their classrooms. Teachers could, for a few examples, show videotapes of children reading at different times during their primary years, report the readability index of the books that individual children read, display the writing and publishing projects the children undertook. Teams of teachers, parents, and outside critics could review the evidence and rate or judge it, then make the information public.

Alternative accountability must be local. People close to the action can judge the credibility of the reports themselves. People at a distance only feel comfortable with quantities, hence standardized tests. It would be the responsibility of testing experts and scholars generally to work as friendly critics for local schools and stand behind the efforts.

The Reclamation Project (For Children Left Behind)
Tying promotion and graduation to specific test results fails to raise school achievement but dramatically raises the drop-out rate. The evidence is solid. Students made to repeat their grade are ten times more likely to drop out of school, compared with their equally low-achieving peers. Moreover, those who remain are subject to repetitive instruction, the weakest teachers, and the least interesting curriculum. What can be done to interrupt this trajectory? Professor Henry Levin of Teachers College, Columbia wrote that, to reclaim these children left behind in the wake of policy man-

dates, schools should single them out for special treatment: the most able teachers and the best curriculum, and a rapid re-entry to grade levels appropriate for their age. Levin proposed the model of Accelerated Schools to accomplish this task. Policy scholars who believe this evidence might encourage more jurisdictions to implement such programs, help evaluate them, and document their progress and consequences.

The De-Commercialism Project

Alex Molnar's Commercialism in Education policy center at Arizona State University catalogues instances of schools that enter into contracts and partnerships for commercial products and advertising. His center revealed that over the past decade commercial contracts increased by 248 percent, advertising spaces in schools increased 539 percent, corporate sponsorship of curriculum increased 1875 percent. The Center tracks such statistics and organizes scholars to write op-ed pieces in the media and conduct research that addresses these issues. Consider a next step: to find schools willing to do away with their ads and restructure their finances to do without the corporate contributions. What would happen if money could be found to compensate schools for relinquishing their corporate contributions?

The Parent Power Project

In the poorest parts of the world, Paulo Freire entered into joint projects with members of a community to study their own situations and work out what to do. Perhaps policy professors could write fewer scholarly articles and work with parents in Freirian deliberative research. Perhaps they could enable parents to enhance their own capacities for civic life and critical literacy, as well as their children's capacities to live a good life. And Universities—which profess to have a service mission—should value these activities by its professors as much as they do publications in journals.

The Street Level Policy Project

Michael Lipsky wrote that in bureaucracies, the real policies are those that the street-level bureaucrats act out with their clients. That is, the U.S. Congress might pass legislation that requires phonics first for every student, but teachers can transform the policy by providing a kind of education very different than that defined in the legislation. Peter Hall wrote that every policy is transformed as it passes from policy makers to administrators to teachers. If this is true, teachers and parents might initiate creative adaptations and modifications of curriculum and instruction for their children, behind classroom doors to make school opportunities better. There are already plenty of examples of Arizona teachers, for example, that defy the ban on bilingual education recently enacted by the state. They see from their own experience that few immigrant students can master English in the requisite one year of immersion; so they close their doors and do what they believe is best, with the blessings of the parents.

Professors and others who want to encourage creative adaptation toward better practice might help teachers to frame their practices in the rhetoric of the policy. For example, we know of a teacher-educator who declares for phonics but smuggles a much richer curriculum under the screen. Such actions become political to the extent that they are known in like-minded communities, united in common purpose.

The Anti-Roundtable Project

The Business Roundtable has had the biggest effect on the shape of education policy. Over time and continents, it has spoken on behalf of the special interests of the largest corporations. Behind the rhetoric of higher standards hide the vested interests of the largest corporations and their friends.

However, there are so many caring and generous people from the business world who already understand and appreciate education as an institution fundamentally different from corporations and factories. We know of many dissenters from the Roundtable ideology: successful corporate leaders, small business people, and entrepreneurs who apprehend the multiple purposes of public schools. We can celebrate these people, recruit them to present an alternative vision.

The Women Project

We believe that women in corporations as well as women active in volunteer organizations represent a wealth of competence and probably see the social world less like factories or military organizations (and more like social or moral communities). Perhaps they might be sensitive, for example, to demonstrations of the savage inequalities that exist in their cities. Organizations such as the League of Women Voters and American Association of University Women might be convinced of the necessity to change policies one school at a time. Some parent organizations in well-off schools might be convinced to distribute some of the funds they raise for their children's schools to the broader public good.

The Communitarian Project

The dominance of the business model and human capital theory has reduced the purposes of education to a single goal: preparation of students for the labor market. Abandoned are goals of democratic and civic participation. Developing the communitarian project means assisting local schools to make room, if necessary outside of school hours, for students to pursue goals of caring and self-government as well as volunteer projects in their neighborhoods.

The Small-Is-Beautiful Project

Sufficient evidence and experience support the claim that small classes work better, that small schools work better, and that school bureaucracies work better when streamlined.

Smaller classes are what advantaged people want for their own children. Smaller classes provide teachers opportunities to understand each child, to accommodate to each student's needs, to read more of each student's writing—just for a start. Michelle Fine and her colleagues have shown the virtues of small schools, particularly middle and high schools. They reduce alienation that students feel from the impersonal giants that comprehensive schools have become. They recommend breaking existing large schools into autonomous schools of no more than 500 and provide opportunities for educators, students, parents, and the community to work together to develop ambitious standards, curriculum, and structure and to participate jointly in assessing the progress of the venture. In both small classes and small schools, there are more opportunities to develop caring communities.

Large bureaucracies alienate their clients, develop interests and agendas within different departments and spend too much energy in competition with each other. The answer is not, as the neo-liberals would say, injecting of market discipline. Rather, with the help of evaluators and organization specialists, administrators might determine—with the help of their staff— how to serve their functions in a more efficient and effective manner.

None of these projects are likely to be successful inevitably. Teachers need to gain expertise about how to take advantage of lower numbers of students. Policy makers involved in class size reduction have to keep an eye on the consequent changes in supply of teachers and how good teachers get allocated to richer and poorer schools. School staffs have to learn how even small systems can become impersonal in the wrong hands and to resist the tracking and stratification that may occur in "schools-within-schools."

The Arts Project
The arts counter political spectacle by transforming experience and waking up perceptions and emotions of the public. Art makes the public look differently (or for the first time) at the conditions of everyday life and public schools. There is probably not a more graphic and awakening image of schooling than the factory model presented in the film *The Wall*, based on the album by Pink Floyd. No one can forget the hideous footage of children moved along a conveyer belt and dropped into the meat grinder.

The film has not yet been made that follows students through the mind-numbing days in a school under the influence of high-stakes testing. The photo montage has yet to be published that places side-by-side pictures of palatial schools and the savaged schools nearby, with voiceover interviews with the policy makers who turn their backs on the inequality. Opportunities are infinite for artistic renderings of public schools in the political spectacle.

The Union Democracy Project
We observe that professional associations for teachers and other professionals adopted the rhetoric and the goals of the corporate and

government combine. They participate in the oligarchy or at least rarely raise principled objections to it. Perhaps these associations have grown so large and structured that they no longer address the issues closest to teachers' work. Perhaps that is the reason that members quit or become passive. What if the professionals worked toward better advocacy for children and for public recognition that schools have broader educational purposes than just preparing children for the work force? Democracy is a practice; we can get better at it in the arenas of professional associations. Carl Boggs wrote:

> As people join oppositional movements they typically begin to assert their claims for justice, equality, and democracy. . . . Collective action becomes politicized as it takes the form of direct action, momentary uprisings, parallel power in counterinstitutions, organizing coaltions, alliances, and parties—all linked to pedagogical activities.[23]

The Saul Alinsky Project

Alinsky provides a model of community activism at local levels where ordinary people can band together and build neighborhood centers for health, welfare, and other local needs. Schools could be part of the community centers, so that, for example, parents could participate in literacy activities for both their children and themselves. School staff could recognize medical problems and send children down the hall to receive treatment. Community center staff could work as a clearinghouse to refer people to agencies and services that are meant to assist them. The center makes sure that parents have a voice in setting up educational programs best suited to their children. Such centers also provide avenues for political activism and change.

The Good Data Project

Although policy researchers are actors in the political spectacle and policy research functions politically, we believe that research can generate useful knowledge. It is possible to perform a political analysis of a study just as it is possible to critique its methodological elements. For example, the political analyst might ask who benefits and loses from the study and its outcomes, whether the researcher was independent or bound to a political or economic agenda, how the study was reviewed and disseminated, whether the evidence was open to scrutiny of scholars and the public. Such a political analysis should not displace scholarly review. Indeed, peer review is needed now more than ever, and is under attack from neo-conservatives because it shows the weaknesses of many studies sponsored by think tanks. Political analysis and scholarly analysis instead ought to complement each other.

To regain their credibility and self-respect, researchers must look to new standards of practice that encompass the political nature of policy research. For example, the profession needs to develop and fund an independent panel to assess policy studies and judge the political element of each study. No study is free of perspective; yet the panel might publicize the political as well as the technical elements. For example, the panel might address the question of who and what interests a study benefits and risks, who commissioned and funded the study, whether the researcher is known for studies of a particular slant, whether the researcher has vested (financial and ideological) interests in the outcome of the study, whether the design examined a limited or fuller range of issues and employed multiple perspectives, whether the study went through the process of scholarly review, whether the data were public, where the study was presented, and whether the study was interpreted with integrity.

Such a panel would restore the cultural authority of policy researchers and invigorate the profession. In addition, participating in the good data project probably means that researchers will have to work independently, without government funds for the most part, or solicit funding from the small cast of progressive donors. Just as important as traditional researchers are investigative journalists that can bring to light local arrangements and reveal the conditions of school life in the political spectacle.

Anxiety, Despair, Hope, and Political Action

There is reason for hope. A political culture that has been constructed can be deconstructed and reconstructed. Although democratic participation is now quiescent, American institutions still exist in potentiality, waiting to be revived and reclaimed: the Constitution, Bill of Rights, elections and electoral rights, courts for airing and redressing grievances, regulatory laws still on the books, public interest policy and law centers, the Internet to provide divergent views, labor and stockholder rights. These institutions can be used to promote social policies that expose and unlock the merged elites.

The political spectacle lulls ordinary people to indifference, to political passivity, to cynicism. Meanwhile the few rich and powerful—of both political parties—further empower and enrich themselves at the expense of the rest. Political spectacle provides the symbols and the rhetoric and makes rational analysis that might uncover it all but impossible. In the contemporary cultural climate, education policy makers and critics stand little chance to repair the inevitable failures that current programs are bound to produce. To counter the political spectacle requires ingenuity, courage, and energy. And we can expect at best small, local changes at the margins, by persuading people to do better and finding the resources they need to do better, and to act toward all students in ways that we and our own children would like to be treated. This is a moral, an intellectual, a political project aimed to restore and preserve the public, the civic, the democratic, and the communitarian foundations of American society, against the privatized, the individualistic, and the separatist tendencies in our culture.

The ethicist Randy Cohen reminds us that virtue is relational and social:

> The idea of civic life is generous, encouraging you to see yourself as living among other people, and to identify yourself as one of those others, with common purposes and problems. The marketplace is where interests clash. . . . Privatization is a world of antagonists at worst, of autonomous, isolated figures at best. But in an age where all of our lives are interconnected—in our economy, our infrastructure, even our health—this notion of the lone cowboy is a fantasy. Civic life . . . is a public park, paid for by all of us and enjoyed by all of us. Its ethical necessities demand that we act in ways that make other people's well-being a part of its use. Private life—where right-wing ethics prevail—is a walled pool in your backyard. You need consider no one else, you need compassion for no one else.[24]

Political spectacle can be best understood as a condition of political life, for a period of time until the next era of reform comes about, in which deprivations for the many are effectively hidden behind a stage curtain and costumed in rhetoric; a period when democracy and rationality and sense of community are suspended; in which we surrender to the most cynical of slogans, as this last vignette shows.

NO CHILD LEFT BEHIND (AND OTHER FABLES)

"No Child Left Behind." That's what President George W. Bush calls his education policy. He appropriated the phrase from Marion Wright-Edelman, and if you look at her work, you know she means it—that she has the details of real children's lives when she says it. Bush has other uses for that phrase: to conjure images of Bush as compassionate, Bush as democratic and inclusive, Bush as advocate of high achievement and accountability, Bush as practitioner of tough love.

"No Child Left Behind." The phrase scans well in headlines. It rolls readily from the lips. It captures the discourse of political rivals. Who could be against it? The phrase (along with the other lines—No Child Should be Trapped in a Failing School, All Children Should be Held Accountable to the Same Standards, The Soft Bigotry of Low Expectations, All Children Must Read by Fourth Grade, Rote Works) provide cover stories for policy makers to make it look like they care.

"No Child Left Behind." The Devil, it is often said, resides in the details and contends for territory there with God. Even the most empty and cynical political gestures, when translated into concrete programs, reverberate down the food chain from President or Senator to Education Secretary through the bureaucrats with their fat books of new regulations, to schools, to classrooms and children. Long past the time that the politicians stop noticing, unanticipated and perverse side-effects, market irrationalities, externalities, opportunity costs, unintended outcomes run in tandem with the effects that policy makers originally had in mind—and usually outrun them. In short, stuff happens, and when it happens to poor children, it's usually bad stuff.

What Governor Bush did for Texas students, he promised to do for the nation's children. He used the purported success of the Texas Assessment and Accountability System (TAAS) as part of his campaign for President. The theory behind TAAS is that the threat of flunking motivates teachers to teach harder and students to study harder. Only threats and high expectations and greater effort stand in the way of academic excellence and economic prosperity. That's the theory.

Details. Pesky details. Did TAAS work? To raise their TAAS scores schools, especially those with large proportions of disadvantaged students, transformed themselves into test preparation academies—just like little factories. Teachers drill their students over and over on work sheets that look just like the TAAS items. Day after day, the same stuff. No more social studies. Say good-bye to art and adios to languages. Science? Get real. Music stands no chance. Even recess gets cancelled. No more writing, except for practicing the pat, four-paragraph, six-trait essay. A whole industry has grown up in Texas to sell materials and training for teachers in order to get TAAS scores up. Soon this industry will expand its product and profits across the map. To a neighborhood near you, perhaps.

Details. Here are the details if you want to look at them. TAAS scores rose by a small amount (at best, but the research is in dispute), but the drop-out rate soared. Under the TAAS policy, somewhere between 75,000 and 100,000 (depending on the method of analysis) were lost to Texas schools every year. The effects do not fall equally upon the rich and the poor, the just and unjust or the white and nonwhite. Nearly half of the Black and Latino students are left behind by TAAS. But where do they go? Not to the moon, although they might as well have been blasted out of the atmosphere for all the concern expressed about them by policy makers.

Or perhaps the policies that Bush supports are good and true according to a particular definition of "child." No child—the elect of God, the select of Darwin—will be left behind. But . . .

If, just for a moment, as he takes his bow, we can stop applauding the star of the show, we might hear the sounds of tens of thousands of something—less-than-children, a tribe of Caliban beneath the gaze of the gods, departing the backstage door toward an alien fate.

Notes

1. This chapter takes the form of an essay. Material cited in previous chapters will not be cited again here.
2. Boggs (2000), p. 37.
3. ABC News (2002).
4. Lasch (1995), p. 114.
5. Reich (2002), p. 13.
6. Darling-Hammond (2001) wrote that the wealthiest 10 percent of school districts spend 10 times more than the poorest 10 percent, and spending ratios of 3 to 1 are common within states. She wrote that students of color lack access to well-qualified teachers, for these reasons: noncompetitive salaries, dismal working conditions, dysfunctional personnel practices in urban districts, lack of recruitment incentives, over-reliance on alternative certificate and emergency certificate career patterns, inadequate support for new teachers.
7. Anyon (1997).
8. Orfield and Eaton (1996).
9. Orwell (1949), p. 168.
10. In *The Bell Curve*, Hernstein and Murray purported to show the deterministic relationships between intelligence and race as justification for neglect of schools of color as well as for separation. The reader should judge which claim is racist.
11. Bracey (2002b) challenged the validity of assertions about the low ranking of U.S. public schools.
12. Orwell (1949), p. 31.
13. The Illinois Business Roundtable challenged the National Professional Teaching Board to prove the superiority of teachers with its professional license. The only "bottom-line" proof they found acceptable was differences on achievement test scores. The Roundtable has the virtue of consistency, if nothing else. But it overlooked many tangible details (the relationship of schools' test scores to wealth in the neighborhood and the content of the NPTB standards, which are much broader than any standardized test can measure). Requiring that every educational program can only be proved by achievement test differences guarantees that all programs must aim for the bottom, for the minimum standard.
14. Lasch (1995) p. 22.
15. Olson (2002b) enumerated the number of states not prepared for NCLB.
16. Madaus et al. (1992), Madaus and Clark (1998).
17. Campaign for Fiscal Equity (2002); Herbert (2002).
18. Gould (1989).
19. Gladwell (2000), p. 19.
20. Greene (1995).
21. Heaney (2001), p. WK 13.
22. Apple (2001).
23. Boggs (2000), p. 102.
24. Cohen (2002), p. 23.

Bibliography

ABC News (2002). Income Gap Growing, ABCNews.com. http://abcsource.starwave.com/sections/us/DailyNews/incmes000118.html.

Adams, M.J. (2001). Alphabetic Anxiety and Explicit Systematic Phonics Instruction: A Cognitive Perspective. In Neuman, S. and Dickinson, D. *Handbook of Research on Early Literacy* (pp. 66–80). New York: Guilford Press.

Alterman, E. (1999). The "Right" Books and Big Ideas. The Nation.com. http://past.thenation.com/issue/991122.1122alterman.shtml.

Altheide, D. L. and R. P. Snow (1991). *Media Worlds in the Postjournalism Era.* New York: Aldine De Gruyter.

American Educational Research Association (1999). *The Standards for Educational and Psychological Testing.* Washington, D.C.: American Psychological Association.

Amrein, A. and D. Berliner (2002). High-Stakes, Uncertainty, and Student Learning. Education Policy Analysis Archives. http://epaa.asu.edu.

Anyon, J. (1997). *Ghetto Schooling : A Political Economy of School Reform.* New York: Teachers College Press.

Apple, M. (1982). *Education and Power.* Boston: Routledge & Kegan Paul Ltd.

Apple, M. (2001). *Educating the "Right" Way.* New York: Routledge.

Apple, M. W. (1986). Are Teachers Losing Control of their Skills and Curriculum? *Journal of Curriculum Studies* 18(2), 177–184.

Apple, M. W. (1988). *Teachers and Texts: A Political Economy of Class and Gender Relations in Education.* New York: Routledge & Kegan Paul.

(1996). Arizona Chief Puts Name and Face Front and Center. *Education Week, 20.*

Arizona Student Assessment Program: Assessment Development Process/Technical Report. Riverside Publishing Company (no date).

Ash, T. G. (2000). A Reality Show That's Riveting the World. (2000, November 8). *New York Times.* Editorial Desk.

Augustine, N. R. (1999). Building a Common Agenda Improving U.S. Education. *San Francisco Business Times.* http://www.bizjournals.com/sanfrancisco/stories/1999/09/20/editorial4.html

Bacon, D. (2000). The Money in Testing (September, 2000). *Z Magazine,* 40–44.

Ball, S. J. (1994). *Education Reform: A Critical and Post-Structural Approach.* Philadelphia: Open University Press.

Barker, J. (1999). McCain Touts National Test for School Voucher Program. *Arizona Republic,* (June 15) A5.

Blackmon, M. (1991) Schools in Decline. Boulder Daily Camera: 1B (1991, December 15).

270 · Bibliography

Bennett, W. (2001). A Cure for the Illiteracy Epidemic. *Wall Street Journal*, A24. (2001, April 24).

Berliner, D. C. and B. B. Biddle (1995). *The Manufactured Crisis: Myths, Fraud, and the Attack on America's Public Schools*. Reading, MA: Addison-Wesley.

Boggs, C. (2000). *The End of Politics*. New York: Guilford Press.

Boorstin, D. J. (1987). *The Image: A Guide to Pseudo-events in America*. Chicago: University of Chicago Press.

Borman, K., L. Castenell, et al. (1993). Business Involvement in School Reform: The Rise of the Business Roundtable. *The New Politics of Race and Gender* (pp. 69–83). C. Marshall (ed.). London: Falmer Press.

Bourdieu, P. and J. C. Passeron (1977). *Reproduction in Education, Society, and Culture*. Beverly Hills, CA: Sage Publications.

Bracey, G. W. (2001a). The 11th Bracey Report on the Condition of Public Education, Phi Delta Kappa. Online. http://www.pdkintl.org/kappan/k0110bra.htm.

Bracey, G. W. (2001b). Test Scores in the Long Run: Not Important. Education Disinformation Detection and Reporting Agency. Unpublished paper.

Bracey, G. W. (2001c). *War Against America's Public Schools*. Boston, Allyn & Bacon.

Bracey, G. W. (2002a). Edison Schools, Inc. EducationNews.org. http://www.educationnews.org/edison_schools_inc.htm (2002, February 12)

Bracey, G. W. (2002b). Edison Schools Inc: Chris Wittle's Grand Illumination Dims. (Unpublished paper).

Bracey, G. W. (2002c). International Comparisons: An Excuse to Avoid Meaningful Educational Reform. *Education Week*. (2002, January 23) 30, 32.

Bracey, G. W. (2002d). Poison Pill Bill. http://www.america-tomorrow.com/bracey/EDDRA/EDDRA25.htm.

Bracey, G. W. (2002e). The Rotten Apple Awards. http://www.america-tomorrow.com/bracey/EDDRA/EDDRA27.htm.

Brock, D. (2002). *Blinded by the Right: The Conscience of an Ex-conservative*. New York: Crown Publishers.

Bruner, R. D. (1995). Harold D. Lasswell. *Encyclopedia of Democracy, Vol III* (pp. 723–725). S. M. Lipset. Washington, D.C.: Congressional Quarterly Press.

Burns, M. S., P. Griffin, et al. (1999). *Starting Out Right: A Guide to Promoting Children's Reading Success*. Washington, D.C.: National Academy Press.

Bushweller, K. (2001). Delay High-Stakes Graduation Exam, Alaska Board Says. *Education Week* (2001, January 10): 25.

Business Coalition for Education Reform (no date). National Partners, Business Coalition for Education Reform. 2002. http://www.bcer.org/partners_new/index.html.

Business Roundtable (2001). The Business Roundtable Urges House and Senate to Act on Education Reform; Says, "Clock is Ticking." Business Roundtable. http://www.brtable.org/press.cfm/564.

Callahan, R. E. (1962). *Education and the Cult of Efficiency*. Chicago: University of Chicago Press.

Camara, W. J. and A. E. Schmidt (1999). Group Differences in Standardized Testing and Social Stratification (pp. 1–18). New York: College Entrance Examination Board.

Camilli, G., S. Vargas, et al. (May 8, 2003). *Teaching Children to Read:* The fragile link between science and federal education policy. *Education Policy Analysis Archives, 11*(15), http:epaa.asu.edu/epaa/v11n15/.

Camilli, G. and L. A. Shepard (1994). *Methods for Identifying Biased Test Items*. Thousand Oaks, CA: Sage.

Carson, C. C., R. M. Huelskamp, et al. (1992). Perspectives on Education in America: Sandia National Laboratories. *Journal of Education Research*(May/June), 259–310.

Center on Budget and Policy Priorities (2001). Pathbreaking CBO Study Shows Dramatic Increases in Both 1980s and 1990s in Income Gaps Between the Very Wealthy and Other Americans. Center on the Budget. http://www.centeronbudget.org/5-31-01tax-pr.htm

Center for Responsive Politics (2002). Influence.INC: Lobbyists Spending in Washington (2000 Edition). Center for Responsive Politics. http://www.opensecrets.org/pubs/ lobby 00/topind12.asp.

(2002). C.F.E. Versus State of New York. Campaign for Fiscal Equity (2002, June 25). http://www.cfequity.org/ns-nysl.htm.

Chall, J. S. (1995). *Learning to Read: The Great Debate*. Fort Worth: Harcourt Brace College Publishers.

Chenoweth, K. (2002). Phonics Debate Linked to Nature of Educational Research. *Washington Times* (2002, March 28), GZ05.

Chomsky, N. (2000). *Chomsky on MisEducation.* New York: Rowan and Littlefield.

Chubb, J. E. and T. M. Moe (1990). *Politics, Markets, and America's Schools.* Washington, D. C.: The Brookings Institute.

Clark, B. (1998). *Political Economy.* Westport, CN: Praeger.

Cobb, C. and G. V. Glass (2000). Ethnic Segregation in Arizona Charter Schools, Education Policy Analysis Archives. http://epaa.asu.edu/epaa/v7n1/10/28/99.

Cohen, R. (2002). The Politics of Ethics. *The Nation* (April 8), 21–23.

Coleman, J. S. and T. Hoffer (1982). *High School Achievement: Public, Catholic, and Private Schools Compared.* New York: Basic Books.

Cronbach, L. J. (1979). *Toward Reform of Program Evaluation.* San Francisco: Jossey-Bass.

Cronbach, L. J. (1982). *Designing Evaluations of Educational and Social Programs.* San Francisco, CA.: Jossey-Bass.

Darling-Hammond, L. (2001). Apartheid in American Education: How Opportunity is Rationed to Children of Color in the United States. *Racial Profiling and Punishment in U.S. Public Schools* (pp. 39–44). T. Johnson, J. E. Boyden and W. J. Pittz (eds.). Oakland: Applied Research Project.

Davis, B. (2001). Phonics Maven Is at Center of Bush's Education Plan. *Wall Street Journal* (2001, April 23), A24.

Dewey, J. (1902). *The School and Society.* Chicago: University of Chicago Press.

Eaton, S. E. and E. Crutcher (1996). Magnets, Media, and Mirages: Prince George's County "Miracle" Cure. *Dismantling Desegregation* (pp. 265–290). G. Orfield and S. E. Eaton eds. New York: New Press.

Edelman, M. (1985). *The Symbolic Uses of Politics.* Urbana, Illinois: University of Illinois Press.

Edelman, M. (1988). *Constructing the Political Spectacle.* Chicago, IL: University of Chicago Press.

Edelman, M. (1995). *From Art to Politics.* Chicago: University of Chicago Press.

Edelsky, C. (1996). *With Literacy and Justice for All.* London: Taylor and Francis.

Ehri, L. C., S. Nunes, et al. (2001). Systematic phonics instruction helps students learn to read: Evidence from the National Reading Panel's meta-analysis. *Review of Educational Research, 71* (3), 393–447.

Ericson, R. V., P. M. Baranek, et al. (1989). *Negotiating Control: A Study of News Sources.* Toronto: University of Toronto Press.

Fetler, M. (1994). Where Have All the Teachers Gone?, Education Policy Analysis Archives. http://olam.ed.asu.edu/epaa/v5n2.html.

Finn, J. D. and C. M. Achilles (1999). Tennessee's Class Size Study: Findings, Implications, Misconceptions. *Educational Evaluation and Policy Analysis,* 21(2), 97–110.

Fleck, T. (2001). Days of Paige: Did Bush Pick a Master Educator or an Overpaid Front Man (2001) (January 11). *Houston Press.* (January 11).

Flesch, R. F. (1986). *Why Johnny Can't Read: And What You Can Do About It.* New York: HarperCollins.

Foorman, B. F., J. M. Fletcher, et al. (2000). Misrepresentation of Research by Other Researchers. *Educational Researcher,* 29(6), 27–37.

Foorman, B. F., D. Francis, et al. (1998). The Role of Instruction in Learning to Read: Preventing Reading Failure in At-risk children. *Journal of Educational Psychology* 90, 37–58.

Friedman, M. (1962). *Capitalism and Freedom.* Chicago: University of Chicago Press.

Gabler, N. (1998). *Life: The Movie.* New York: Vintage Books Division of Random House.

Garan, E. M. (2001). Beyond the Smoke and Mirrors: A Critique of the National Reading Panel Report on Phonics. *Phi Delta Kappa,* 83(March), 500–506.

Garan, E. M. (2002). *Resisting Reading Mandates.* Portsmouth, N. H.: Heineman.

Gelberg, D. (1997). *The "Business" of Reforming American Schools.* Albany: State University of New York Press.

Gereboff, B. (1999). Professionals or Bureaucrats: Cultural Imperatives in Teacher Certification Policies. *Educational Leadership and Policy Studies* (pp. 88–108). Tempe: Arizona State University.

Gitlin, A. and D. F. Labaree (1996). Historical Notes on the Barriers to Professionalism of American Teachers: The Influence of Market and Patriarchy. *Teachers' Professional Lives.* I. F. Goodson and A. Hargreaves (eds.). London: Falmer Press.

Gladwell, M. (2000). *The Tipping Point.* Boston, Little, Brown and Company.

Glass, G. V. (1976). Primary, Secondary, and Meta-analysis of Research. *Educational Researcher*, 5, 3–8.

Glass, G. V. (1978). Matthew Arnold and Minimum Compentency. *Educational Forum*, 42(2), 139–144.

Goffman, Erving (1959). *The Presentation of Self in Everyday Life.* Garden City, NY: Doubleday, Anchor Books.

Gould, S. J. (1989). *Wonderful Life.* New York: W. W. Norton.

Graue, M. E. and S. Smith (1996). Parents and Mathematics Education Reform: Voicing the Authority of Assessment. *Urban Education*, 30(4), 395–421.

Greene, Maxine (1995). Releasing the Imagination. San Francisco: Jossey-Bass.

Greider, W. (1992). *Who Will Tell the People: The Betrayal of American Democracy.* New York: Simon and Schuster.

Grissom, J. B. and L. A. Shepard (1989). Repeating and Dropping Out of School. *Flunking Grades: Research and Policies on Retention* (p. 34–63). L. A. Shepard and M. L. Smith (eds.). Philadelphia: Falmer Press.

Gross, P. W. and B. K. MacLaury (2000). *Measuring What Matters: Using Assessment and Accountability to Improve Student Learning.* Committee for Economic Development Research and Policy Committee. New York, National Alliance of Business.

Haney, W. (2000). Myth of the Texas Miracle in Education. Education Policy Analysis Archives. http://epaa.aso.edu/epaa/v8n41.

Hanuschek, E. A. (1994). Money Might Matter Somewhere: A Response to Hedges, Laine, and Greenwald. *Educational Researcher*, 23(4), 5–8.

Hayek, F. A. (1944). *The Road to Serfdom.* Chicago: University of Chicago Press.

Heaney, S. (2001). Poetry's Power Against Intolerance. *New York Times* (August 26), WK 13.

Heinecke, W. F. (1997). Desegregation as the Transformation of Intentions: A Case Study. *Educational Policy Studies.* Tempe, AZ, Arizona State University.

Henriques, D. B. and J. Steinberg (2001). Right Answer, Wrong Score: Test Flaws Take Toll. *New York Times* (May 20) 1, 22.

Herbert, B. (2002). The Bare Minimum. *New York Times.* (June 27): A27.

Herbst, S. (1993). *Beyond Numbered Voices.* Chicago: University of Chicago Press.

Heritage Foundation (1998). Why Congress Should Overhaul the Federal Regional Education Laboratories.

Herrnstein, R. and C. Murray (1994). *The Bell Curve: Intelligence and Class Structure in American Life.* New York: The Free Press.

Heubert, J. P. (2000). High Stakes Testing and Civil Rights: Standards of Appropriate Test Use and a Strategy for Enforcing Them. http://www.harvard.edu/groups/civilrights/conferences/testing98/drafts/heubert2.html.

Heubert, J. P. and R. M. Hauser (1998). *High Stakes: Testing for Tracking, Promotion, and Graduation.* Washington, D.C.: National Academy Press.

Hilgartner, Stephen (2000). *Science on Stage: Expert Advice as Public Drama.* Stanford, CA: Stanford University Press.

Hill, Steven (2002). *Fixing Elections: The Failure of America's Winner Take All Politics.* New York: Routledge.

House, E. R. (1993). *Professional Evaluation.* Newbury Park, CA: Sage.

House, E. R. (1998). *Schools for Sale.* New York: Teachers College Press.

House, E. R., G. V. Glass, et al. (1978). No Simple Answers: Critique of the Follow Through Evaluation. *Harvard Educational Review*, 48(2), 128–160.

House, E. R., R. Linn, et al. (1982). Reports on New York City's Promotional Gates program. New York, Office of Program Evaluation, New York City Schools.

Howe, K. R. and M. Eisenhart (2000). A Study of Boulder Valley School District's Open Enrollment System. Boulder, CO, University of Colorado.

James, C. (2000). An Apocalyptic Attitude Gripped the TV Commentators, Not Their Viewers. *New York Times* (December 17), 48.

Jennings, M. M. (1997). None of the Above: New Approach to Student Testing is Wrong. *Arizona Republic* (January 12) H 1–2.

Judis, J. B. (2000). *The Paradox of American Democracy: Elites, Special Interests, and the Betrayal of Public Trust.* New York: Pantheon Books.

Kakutani, M. (2000). Polarization of National Dialogue Mirrors Extremists of Left and Right. *New York Times* (November 26) A 29.

Kantor, H. and R. Lowe (1995). Class, Race, and the Emergence of Federal Education Policy from the New Deal to the Great Society. *Educational Researcher*, 24(3), 4–11.

Keegan, L. G. and J. Root (1996). Why We Formed the Education Leaders Council. *Education Week* (February 21) 39.

Kingdon, J. W. (1995). *Agendas, Alternatives, and Public Policies*. New York: Harper-Collins.

Knorr-Cetina, K. D. (1981). *The Manufacture of Knowledge*. Cambridge, U. K.: Cambridge University Press.

Koretz, D., R. L. Linn, et al. (1991). *The Effects of High-stakes Testing on Achievement: Preliminary Findings about Generalizations Across Tests*. American Educational Research Association: Chicago.

Kossan, P. (2000). Keegan Asks Advice, Not "Food Fights." *Arizona Republic* (November 28) B1.

Kozol, J. (1991). *Savage Inequalities*. New York: Harper-Collins.

Krashen, S. (1993). *The Power of Reading*. Westport CT: Heinemann.

Krashen, S. (1999). *Three Arguments Against Whole Language and Why They Are Wrong*. Westport, CT: Heinemann.

Labaree, D. F. (1992). Power, Knowledge, and the Rationalization of Teaching: A Genealogy of the Movement to Professionalize Teaching. *Harvard Educational Review*, 62(2), 123–154.

Labaree, D. F. (1997). *How to Succeed in School* Without Really Trying*. New Haven: Yale University Press.

Ladson-Billings, G. (1994). *The Dream-Keepers: Successful Teachers of African American Children*. San Francisco: Jossey-Bass.

Lakoff, G. (1996). *Moral Politics: What Conservatives Know that Liberals Don't*. Chicago: University of Chicago Press.

Lakoff, G. and M. Johnson (1980). *Metaphors We Live By*. Chicago: University of Chicago Press.

Landgraf, K. (2001). ETS: President Bush's Education Agenda Holds Promise for American Education, http://www.ets.org/news/01/012501.html.

Lang, S. S. (2000). As Graduation Standards Get Tougher High School Dropout Rate Rises, Economists Find (references study by Dean R. Lillard), Cornell University News Service. http://www.news.cornell.edu/releases/00/.html.

Lasch, C. (1995). *Revolt of the Elites and the Betrayal of Democracy*. New York: W. W. Norton Company.

Lasswell, H. D. (1965). World Revolution of Our Time: A Framework for Basic Political Research. *World Revolutionary Elites*. H. D. Lasswell and D. Lerner (eds.). Cambridge, MA: M. I. T. Press.

Lauder, H. and D. Hughes (1999). *Trading in Futures: Why Markets in Education Don't Work*. Philadelphia: Open University Press.

Levin, H. (1998). High Stakes Testing and Economic Productivity. Cambridge, Civil Rights Project, Harvard University. http://www.law.harvard.edu/groups/civilrights/conferences/testing98/drafts/levin.html.

Levin, H. M. (1993). *Education and Jobs: A Proactive View*. Seventh Annual International Research-Practice Conference on Education and Work, Toronto, Ontario Institute for Studies of Education.

Lewis, C. (2000). Media Money. *Columbia Journalism Review* (September–October) 20–27.

Linn, R. L., M. E. Graue, et al. (1990). Comparing State and District Test Results to National Norms: The Validity that Everyone Is Above Average. *Educational Measurement: Issues and Practices* 9(3), 5–14.

Lugg, C. A. (1996). *For God and Country: Conservatism and American School Policy*. New York: Peter Lang.

Lugg, C. A. (In Press). Education Policy in a Media-driven Age: The Rise of PRolicy. *Journal of School Leadership*.

Lyon, R. (no date). In Celebration of Science in the Study of Reading Development, Reading Difficulties, and Reading Instruction: The NICHD Perspective. Bethesda, MD, National Institute for Child Health and Development.

Madaus, G. and M. Clarke (1998). The Adverse Impact of High Stakes Testing on Minority Students: Evidence from 100 Years of Test Data, Harvard Civil Rights Project. http://www.law.harvard.edu/ civilrights/conferences/testing98/drafts/madaus_clarke.html

Madaus, G. W., M. M. West, et al. (1992). The Influence of Testing on Teaching Math and Science in Grades 4–12: Executive Summary. Chestnut Hill, MA: Center for the Study of Testing, Evaluation, and Educational Policy, Boston College.

Marshall, C., D. Mitchell, et al. (1989). *Culture and Educational Policy in the American States*. New York: Falmer.

Martin, L. (1991). What Work Requires of Schools: A SCANS Report for America 2000. Washington, D.C.: United States Department of Labor.

McChesney, R. W. (1999). *Rich Media, Poor Democracy: Communication Politics in Dubious Times.* New York: The New Press.

McDonnell, L. and R. Elmore (1987). Getting the Job Done: Alternative Policy Instruments. *Educational Evaluation and Policy Analysis*, 9(2), 133–152.

McDonnell, L. M. (1994). Assessment Policy as Persuasion and Regulation. *American Journal of Education*, 102, 394–420.

McDonnell, L. M. (1997). The Politics of State Testing: Implementing New Student Assessments. Los Angeles: Center for the Study of Evaluation, University of California.

McNeil, L. and A. Valenzuela (1999). The Harmful Impact of the TAAS System on Testing in Texas: Beneath the Accountability Rhetoric. Harvard Civil Rights Project. http://www.law.harvard.edu/civilrights/conferences/testing 98/.

McNeil, L. M. (2000). *Contradictions of School Reform.* New York: Routledge.

McQuillan, J. (1998). *The Literacy Crisis: False Claims and Real Solutions.* Portsmouth, NH: Heineman.

Mead, G. H. (1934). *Mind, Self, and Society.* Chicago: University of Chicago Press.

Mehrens, W. A. (1998). *Consequences of Assessment: What is the Evidence?* American Educational Research Association: San Diego CA.

Metcalf, S. (2002). Reading Between the Lines. TheNation.com. http://www.thenation.com/doc.mhtml?i=20020128&c=1&s—Metcalf

Mickelson, R. (1999). International Business Machinations: A Case Study of Corporate Involvement in Local Educational Reform. *Teachers College Record*, 100(3), 476–512.

Miller, J. (1991). Report Questioning "Crisis" in Education Triggers Uproar. *Education Week* (October 9), 1, 32.

Miller-Kahn, Linda (2000). Parents, Power, and Policy. Boulder, CO: Unpublished paper.

Molnar, A. (1996). *Giving Kids the Business: The Commercialization of America's Schools.* Boulder, CO: Westview Press.

Molnar, A. (2000). Colonizing Our Future: The Commercial Transformation of America's Schools. *Social Education*, 47(November/December), 428–438.

Moore, D. R. and S. Davenport (1990). School Choice: The New and Improved Sorting Machine. *Choice in Education: Potential and Problems* (pp. 187–223). W. L. Boyd and H. J. Walberg (eds.). Berkeley, CA, McCutchan Publishing Company.

Mosteller, F., R. J. Light, et al. (1996). Sustained Inquiry in Education: Lessons Learned from Skill Grouping and Class Size. *Harvard Educational Review*, 66, 797–842.

Murphy, M. (1996). Symington Moves to Right Seeking Votes. *Arizona Republic* (May 5), 1, 13.

National Commission on Excellence in Education (1983). A Nation at Risk: The Imperative for Educational Reform. Washington, D.C.: United States Department of Education.

National Education Association (2001). The Conservative Network. http://www.nea.org/publiced/paycheck.html.

National Institute for Child Health and Human Development (2000a). Report of the National Reading Panel: Teaching Children to Read: An Evidence-Based Assessment of the Scientific Research Literature on Reading and its Implications for Reading Instruction: Reports of the Subgroups. Washington, D.C., U.S. Government Printing Office, NIH Publication.

National Institute for Child Health and Human Development (2000b). Report of the National Reading Panel: Teaching Children to Read: An Evidence-Based Assessment of the Scientific Research Literature on Reading and its Implications for Reading Instruction (Summary). Washington D.C.: U.S. Government Printing Office, NIH Publication.

Noble, A. J. and M. L. Smith (1994). Old and New Beliefs about Measurement-Driven Reform. *Educational Policy*, 8(2), 111–136.

Noddings, N. (1984). *Caring: A Feminine Approach to Ethics and Moral Education.* Berkeley: University of California Press.

Nye, B., L. V. Hedges, et al. (1999). The Long-Term Effects of Class Size: A Five-Year Follow-Up of the Tennessee Class Size Experiment. *Educational Evaluation and Policy Analysis*, 21(2), 127–142.

Oakes, J., K. H. Quartz, et al. (2000). *Becoming Good American Schools.* San Francisco: Jossey-Bass.

Olson, L. (2001a). States Adjust High-Stakes Testing Plans. *Education Week* (January 24), 1, 18.

Olson, L. (2001b). Study Questions Reliability of Single-Year Test-Score Gains. *Education Week* (May 23), 9.

Olson, L. (2002a). A "Proficient" Score Depends on Geography. *Education Week* (February 20) 1, 14–15.

Olson, L. (2002b). Testing Systems in Most States Not ESEA-Ready. *Education Week* (January 9), 1, 26–28.

Orfield, G. and S. E. Eaton (1996). *Dismantling Desegregation: The Quiet Reversal of Brown v. Board of Education*. New York: The New Press.

Orwell, G. (1949). *1984*. New York: Harcourt-Brace (Penguin Edition).

Paige, R. (2001). Why We Must Have Testing. *Washington Post* (2001, May 13), B07.

Paterson, F. R. A. (2000). The Politics of Phonics. *Journal of Curriculum and Supervision*, 15(3), 179–211.

People for the American Way (1999). Privatization of Public Education, People for the American Way Foundation. www.pfaw.org/issues/education.

Pearson, P. D. and L. De Stefano (1993). An Evaluation of the 1992 NAEP Proficiency Levels, Report One: A Commentary on the Process. *Setting Performance Standards for Student Achievement: Background Studies*. R. Linn, R. Glaser and G. Bohrnstedt (eds.). Washington, D.C., National Academy of Education.

Peterson, P. and J. P. Greene (1996). School Choice in Milwaukee. *Public Interest* (Fall), 38–56.

Porter, T. M. (1995). *Trust in Numbers: The Pursuit of Objectivity in Science and Public Life*. Princeton, NJ: Princeton University Press.

(2001). Quality Counts. *Education Week*, 20, January 11, 2001.

Reich, R. B. (2002). *I'll Be Short: Essentials for a Decent Working Society*. Boston: Beacon Press.

Rich, F. (2000a). May the Best Man Lose. *New York Times* (November 8), A31.

Rich, F. (2000b). No Business Like Show Business. *New York Times* (September 23), A31.

Ritter, G. W. and R. F. Boruch (1999). The Political and Institutional Origins of a Randomized Controlled Trial on Elementary School Class Size: Tennessee's Project STAR. *Educational Evaluation and Policy Analysis*, 21(2), 111–125.

Roman, L. G. and M. W. Apple (1990). Is Naturalism a Move Away from Positivism? *Qualitative Inquiry in Education* (pp. 38–73). E. Eisner and A. Peshkin (eds.). New York: Teachers College Press.

Rothstein, R. (2000). Lessons: Polls Only Confuse Education Policy. *New York Times*, B 15.

Rumberger, R. W. (1995). Dropping Out of Middle School: A Multi-Level Analysis of Students and Schools. *American Educational Research Journal*, 32, 582–625.

Sacks, P. (1999). *Standardized Minds*. New York: Harper Collins.

Saltman, K. J. (2000). *Collateral Damage: Corporatizing Public Schools—A Threat to Democracy*. Lanham, MD: Rowan and Littlefield.

Schemo, D. J. (2002a). Education Bill Urges New Emphasis on Phonics. *New York Times* (January 9).

Schemo, D. J. (2002b). "No Child Left Behind" Is a Hit Song to Bush Team. *New York Times* (June 23), YNE16.

Schemo, D. J. (2002c). Now, the Pressure Begins for Bush's Reading Expert. *New York Times* (January 19), A 12.

Schiller, L. (1999). *Perfect Murder, Perfect Town*. New York: Harper Collins.

Schneider, A. L. and H. Ingram (1997). *Policy Design for Democracy*. Lawrence, Kansas: University of Kansas Press.

Shannon, P., J. Edmondson, et al. (2002). *Expressions of Power and Ideology in the National Reading Panel*. Annual Meeting, American Educational Research Association, New Orleans.

Shavelson, R. J. and L. Towne (2002). *Scientific Research in Education*. Washington, D.C.: National Academy Press.

Shepard, L. A. (1991). Inflated Test Score Gains: Is the Problem Old Norms or Teaching to the Test? *Educational Measurement: Issues and Practices*, 9(3), 15–22.

Shipps, D. (1997). The Invisible Hand: Big Business and Chicago School Reform. *Teachers College Record*, 99(1), 73–116.

Simon, H. (1982). *Models of Bounded Rationality*. Cambridge, MA: MIT Press.

Skrla, L. (2001). Accountability, equity, and complexity. *Education Researcher*, 30 (4), p. 15–21.

Slavin, R. E. (1987). Ability Grouping: A Best-Evidence Synthesis. *Review of Educational Research*, 57, 293–336.

Smith, M. L., G. V. Glass, et al. (1980). *Benefits of Psychotherapy*. Baltimore: Johns Hopkins University Press.

Smith, M. L., W. Heinecke, et al. (1999). Assessment Policy and Political Spectacle. *Teachers College Record*, 101(2), 157–191.

Smith, S. (1995a). It's a Fact: Our Public Schools Aren't Working. *Boulder Daily Camera* (June 3), 3B.

Smith, S. (1995b). Why the Schools Must Change. *Boulder Daily Camera* (November 4), 4C.

(2000). The Soft-Money Conventions. *New York Times.* Editorial Desk. August 6, 2000.

Stake, R. E. (1986). *Quieting Reform.* Urbana, IL: University of Illinois Press.

Steinberg, J. (2001). Ideas & Trends; Grilling the Little Ones: Online Testing for Kids. *New York Times* (January 21), WK 4.

Steinberg, J. and D. B. Henriques (2001). When a Test Fails the Schools, Careers and Reputations Suffer. *New York Times* (May 21), A1, A10.

Stone, D. (1997). *Policy Paradox: The Art of Political Decision Making.* New York: Norton.

Stotsky, S. (1998). Analysis of the Texas Reading Tests, Grade 4, 8, and 10, 1995–1998, Education-News.org. http://www.educationnews.org/analysis_of_the_texas_reading_te.htm.

Sudetic, C. (2001). Reading, Writing, and Revenue. *Mother Jones* (May/June), 83–95.

(2001). Supreme Court Strikes Down State Tobacco Ad Ban. *Washington Post.* June 28, 2001.

Taylor, B. (1992). District Under Seige. Boulder Daily Camera: GE 3A (1992, March 22).

Taylor, D. (1998). *Beginning to Read and the Spin Doctors of Science.* Urbana, IL: National Council of Teachers of English.

(2002). Test-Preparation Firms May Stand to Benefit from ESEA Changes. *Education Week*, 19–20. January 23, 2002.

ThomsonFN.com (2001). Insider Trades, Thomson Financial Network.

Traub, J. (2002). The Test Mess. *New York Times* (April 7), 46.

Valenzuela, A. (1999). *Subtractive Schooling: U.S.-Mexican Youth and the Politics of Caring.* Albany: State University of New York: Albany Press.

Wallace, M. (1994). *The Contribution of Mass Media to the Education Policy Process.* Annual Meeting of the American Educational Research Association, New Orleans.

Weiss, C. (1998). *Evaluation.* Upper Saddle River, NJ: Prentice-Hall.

Wells, A. S. and I. Serna (1996). The Politics of Culture: Understanding Local Political Resistance to Detracking in Racially Mixed Schools. *Harvard Educational Review*, 66(1), 93–118.

Yatkin, J. (2000). Minority View (NRP Study). Sandy, OR: Oregon Trail School District.

Index